The Rise of Megacities

Challenges, Opportunities and Unique Characteristics

The Rise of Megacities

Challenges, Opportunities and Unique Characteristics

editors

Jerzy Kleer
Polish Academy of Sciences, Poland

Katarzyna Anna Nawrot
Poznań University of Economics and Business, Poland

World Scientific

NEW JERSEY • LONDON • SINGAPORE • BEIJING • SHANGHAI • HONG KONG • TAIPEI • CHENNAI • TOKYO

Published by

World Scientific Publishing Europe Ltd.
57 Shelton Street, Covent Garden, London WC2H 9HE
Head office: 5 Toh Tuck Link, Singapore 596224
USA office: 27 Warren Street, Suite 401-402, Hackensack, NJ 07601

Library of Congress Cataloging-in-Publication Data
Names: Kleer, Jerzy, editor. | Anna Nawrot, Katarzyna, editor.
Title: The rise of megacities : challenges, opportunities and unique characteristics / edited by Jerzy Kleer (Polish Academy of Sciences, Poland), Katarzyna Anna Nawrot (Poznań University of Economics and Business, Poland).
Description: New Jersey : World Scientific, [2017]
Identifiers: LCCN 2017030403 | ISBN 9781786344267 (hc : alk. paper)
Subjects: LCSH: Urbanization. | Cities and towns.
Classification: LCC HT361 .R57 2017 | DDC 307.76--dc23
LC record available at https://lccn.loc.gov/2017030403

British Library Cataloguing-in-Publication Data
A catalogue record for this book is available from the British Library.

For any available supplementary material, please visit
http://www.worldscientific.com/worldscibooks/10.1142/Q0125#t=suppl

Desk Editors: Suraj Kumar/Jennifer Brough/Shi Ying Koe

Typeset by Stallion Press
Email: enquiries@stallionpress.com

FOREWORD

Edward L. Glaeser

Fred and Eleanor Glimp Professor of Economics
at the Harvard University

Much of humanity now lives in megacities that would have seemed unimaginably large to almost all of our ancestors. Until the start of the 19th century, humanity's largest cities never grew much beyond one million inhabitants. Two centuries later, the globe contains more than twenty agglomerations with more than ten million inhabitants, and many more such megacities lie in humanity's future. The introductory essay of this fascinating volume estimates that over 700 million people will live in megacities by 2030. To understand the future of our urban planet, we must grapple with the nature and causes of these super-sized metropolises.

Until the mid-19th century, the world's largest cities were invariably the capitals of large empires. Rome may have been the world's first million-person city around 50 B.C., when Rome's power enabled vast flows of grain from Spain and Egypt to feed its urbanites. Successive capitals of China — Chang'an, Kaifeng and later Beijing — all may have been the world's largest city in their day. Abbasid Baghdad and Tokugawa Edo also owed their growth to political power. Even the growth of Victorian London, for all its commerce and industry, reflected in part its place as the nerve center of the greatest empire the world have ever seen.

Many of today's megacities, including Beijing, Cairo, Delhi, Karachi, Mexico City and Moscow, are capitals of nations so populous that they are almost imperial. Their growth reflects, in part, the advantages of proximity to the corridors of power. Oligarchs and slum-dwellers alike can gain from being close to national leaders. Delhi's strong metro system and its political independence are advantages enjoyed by India's capital, but not by other large Indian cities, like Mumbai. Greater Tokyo, the world's largest megacity, passed the ten million person mark in the years after World War I, when it became the capital of Japan's large Asian empire.

But there are other megacities that are commercial, rather than imperial, following the model of New York, rather than Rome or London. Shanghai, Mumbai, Sao Paolo, Kolkata and Osaka are all cities whose strength lies in trade rather than taxes. All of these places grew great due to their ports, and they have long been conduits across continents. When an Indian farmer came to Kolkata in the 1860s or Mumbai in the 1960s, they were leaving a world of geographic isolation and entering into a city that was part of a global trading network.

Why have megacities emerged over in such numbers over the past 50 years? In most cases, rural migrants have been pulled by economic opportunity. The financial success of Japanese industrialists in Tokyo and Osaka provided wages that were extraordinarily high relative to rural earnings. Agglomeration economies can become hyper-charged in vast agglomerations, and workers follow productivity.

But there were also agglomeration economies in 19th century cities, and yet those cities remained far smaller. Europe urbanized before Asia or Latin America, yet today it remains a continent made of mid-sized agglomerations, not megacities. The most natural explanation for urban dispersal in Europe is the interplay between transportation costs and urban size.

When transportation costs are high, as they were in Europe or the U.S. in 1850, then cities naturally spread themselves throughout the rural hinterland. Food was expensive to ship to far away urban areas, and urban manufactured goods were costly to ship to far flung farms. Those costs explain why Cyrus McCormick moved from Virginia to Chicago to sell his mechanical reapers to the multitude of midwestern farmers. Christaller's Central Place Theory aptly describes traditional German cities and towns that were dispersed throughout the farmland, providing services to the local agrarians who were tied to the land.

In the 21st century, the costs of moving food and manufactured goods are low. The companies of Sao Paulo and Shenzhen sell to a global marketplace, and they can easily import food from far away. Consequently, the centrifugal push to be close to farmland has disappeared and newer urban systems naturally produce greater concentrations of population.

Better transportation within the city has also abetted the growth of megacities. Much megacity growth occurs in slums on the urban fringe. If poorer workers still walked to work, as they did in 19th century Europe, they could never get to jobs in the urban core. Jitneys and metro systems now enable the residents of vast metropolitan areas to make their way across town, although it remains true that many megacity commutes exceed an hour.

Urban growth was also historically checked by the demons that come with density, such as crime, congestion, contagious disease and high housing costs. Plague both deterred farmers from coming to teeming tenements, and also directly reduced urban populations. The 19th century cities, such as Paris and New York, invested enormously in water and sewerage, which radically reduced mortality rates.

Medical breakthroughs, including penicillin and pasteurization, now make it possible to survive the plagues that persist in poor world megacities that have not invested in expensive health-related infrastructure. The increased pull of megacities reflects both the economic benefits of concentration, increasing unchecked by any need to be near the land, and reductions in the disamenities of urban life, especially fewer urban deaths from disease.

Lower transportation costs have also reversed the historic relationship between agricultural prosperity and urban growth. Throughout most of history, cities only grew when agriculture also flourished. Urbanites could only survive when they could be fed and when an abundance of farm wealth pushed up the prices paid for urban manufactured goods. In 1960, there was a strong positive correlation between agricultural productivity and urbanization across countries, which is exactly what we should expect in a closed economy (Glaeser, 2014).

Yet as Matsuyama (1992) taught us, the connection between industrialization and agricultural productivity is reversed in an open economy. In an open economy, countries that are bad in agriculture specialize in industry. Consequently, we should expect globalization to lead countries that have weak agricultural endowments to stop farming.

America only became a majority urban country in 1920, when its per capita income was over $7,500 in modern dollars, largely because it needed that agricultural wealth to feed large cities and generate demand for urban manufactured goods. Today, we see megacities emerging in places like Pakistan that have far lower income levels, partially because the residents of Karachi do not need to sell to local farmers and they can import food from abroad. Glaeser (2014) shows that the relationship between agricultural productivity and urbanization is much weaker in small open economies than in large closed economies. I also show that the link between agricultural productivity and urbanization has fallen dramatically over the last fifty years, partially because the world's trade linkages have become stronger. Today, the link between agricultural productivity and urbanization is effectively zero in the world's smaller, more open economies.

In our medieval past, poverty and warfare brought people back to the land, trying to desperately avoid starvation. Today, cities offer a better chance for survival amidst deprivation, because they are where foreign aid flows most freely and where failed states maintain the last semblance of law and order. Megacities can become places of relative safety in war-torn countries like the Democratic Republic of the Congo.

For all the downsides of megacity density, most urbanites prefer their locations to the alternative of rural poverty. The residents of urban India, for example, say that they are much happier than rural Indians. Even when megacity growth has been fueled more by rural chaos more than urban success, cities can offer hope. Yet as this book reminds us, we should never sugarcoat the megacity experience. Crime, contagious disease and congestion come when density is unchecked by effective public policy.

While today's megacities have their antecedents in ancient Rome and Kaifeng, there are crucial differences between today's vast metropolises and anything in our urban past. Most obviously, today's megacities are much bigger. Just as importantly, they must deal with all of the downsides of density, with neither wealth nor political competence.

The great imperial cities of the past were poor by modern standards. Per capita incomes in Rome were perhaps about $1,000 per capita in modern dollars, and the same was probably true in Abbasid Baghdad or ancient China. Yet these imperial cities were remarkably well-governed for their time, precisely because only a relatively well-governed state could become a durable empire.

Julius Caesar did not have access to Singapore-style electronic road pricing, but he could ban wheeled vehicles from Rome's streets for the first ten hours of every day. There is little chance that the government of the Congo could achieve a similar feat. The fire-fighting efforts of ancient Chinese cities display administrative ability that seems far beyond today's poorest megacities.

A second primary difference between today's megacities and the cities of the past is that the growth of many developing world megacities seems to be driven by fertility rather than migration. Historically, urban death rates were higher than fertility rates, and so cities always needed to import citizens to growth. The work of Jedwab *et al.* (2017) finds that the robust fertility rates in developing world megacities explain much of their growth.

Migration-led growth requires cities to be attractive to rural–urban migrants. Fertility-led growth just requires high enough birth rates and people who are not able to go back to their farms. Consequently, fertility-led growth allows cities to grow, despite massive failures in urban governance.

A third difference between the past and the present is that the upside of urbanization is much greater today. Across the world's poorer countries, urbanization in 1960 was a strong predictor of subsequent national economic success (Glaeser, 2014). Megacities in Africa offer a chance to leap to middle-income status by trading with the rest of the world. Just as importantly, cities have long been conduits of knowledge, and megacities offer the possibility for technology to flow across continents, as seen in the rapid rise of cities like Shenzhen and Bangalore.

Even more hopefully, cities can occasionally turn into wellsprings of democracy and better government. Dictatorships are more likely to fall in more urbanized countries (Wallace, 2014), partially because cities enable the coordination that is needed for revolutions and coups. Perhaps urbanization can even lead to durable civic organizations that discipline the governments that follow dictatorships.

The promises and pitfalls of megacities growth make this book particularly timely. These cities are growing, and it is a fool's errand to try to stop their growth. The wise fight is to try to make them more livable. Most of this work will be done by the residents of those cities themselves, but outside scholars can also play a role.

For example, it is easy to think that these cities just need more infrastructure: better roads and water mains. They do need those things, but the benefits of these investments can easily be wasted unless infrastructure is paired with better institutions. Without congestion pricing, new roads quickly become overcrowded. Without regulation, the urban poor often choose not to pay for connections to water and sewer systems. The last mile problem then stops the infrastructure from serving its purpose.

We must better understand how institutions and infrastructure come together to provide better urban health. We must learn how to manage public and private land in megacities. We must teach donors how to spend their money more wisely.

The fight to improve the functioning of developing world megacities is one of the great vocations of the 21st century. When these cities flourish, the lives of their residents improve and they can lift up entire nations. I am glad that the writers and editors of this volume have chosen to join in the fight.

References

Glaeser, E.L. (2014). A world of cities: the causes and consequences of urbanization in poorer countries. *Journal of the European Economic Association*, 12(5), 1154–1199.

Jedwab, R., L. Christiaensen, and M. Gindelsky. (2017). Demography, urbanization and development: Rural push, urban pull and… urban push? *Journal of Urban Economics*, 98, 6–16.

Matsuyama, K. (1992). Agricultural productivity, comparative advantage, and economic growth. *Journal of Economic Theory*, 58(2), 317–334.

Wallace, J. (2014). *Cities and Stability: Urbanization, Redistribution, and Regime Survival in China*. Oxford University Press.

ABOUT THE EDITORS

Jerzy Kleer is a Professor at the Institute of Economic Studies, Polish Academy of Sciences and a Deputy Head of the Committee of Future Studies "Poland 2000 Plus", Polish Academy of Sciences. His research interests include the history of economic thought, the issue of cooperatives and the public sector, developing countries and development economics, problems of socialist economies and their transformation, and the world economy at large. In the course of his career he has participated in conferences and seminars on all continents and lectured across Europe, including at the Faculty of Social Sciences, University of Kuopio, Finland (1980s and 1990s); Ost-West Kollege, Koln (1983–1997); Europaische Akademie, West Berlin (1985–1995); University of Munster, Germany; University of Giessen, Germany. He has provided consultancy in the field of economic and social problems of less developed countries and socialist economies to institutions including the United Nations University, Tokyo, Japan (1983–1987), Arbeitsgemeinschaft fur Genossenschaftliche Institute Sozial und Politik, International Social Association, Seville (2004–2008), and the European Commission (2005–2007) among others. Professor Kleer has authored over 350 scientific publications, including over 30 books and around 900 popular-science publications. His academic achievements have earned him numerous awards, including from the International Cooperative Alliance for contributions to the theory of cooperatives (Geneva–Nuremberg, 1988) and from the International Kondratieff Foundation for contributions to the social sciences (Moscow, 2010).

Katarzyna A. Nawrot is an Assistant Professor at the Poznań University of Economics and Business and a member of the Committee for Future Studies "Poland 2000 Plus", Polish Academy of Sciences. Previously she was a research fellow at the Graduate Institute of International and Development Studies in Geneva (2011–2012) and J.F. Kennedy School of Government at Harvard University (2013–2014). Her research interests include developing countries, development and cultural economics, development studies, international economics, the history of economic thought and the world economy at large. Katarzyna also explores the challenges to global development. She has led or participated in several research projects for the National Science Centre in Poland, European Commission, and other international institutions and recently finalised a project on the economic potential and developmental possibilities of developing countries in Africa. Her academic achievements earned her numerous awards, including one for outstanding young scholars from Poland's Minister of Science and Higher Education in 2012. Recently she has been nominated to the European Young Leaders (EYL40), Class of 2017. Katarzyna has lectured at universities in Europe, Asia, and Africa; carried out field research and volunteering in developing countries and emerging economies, and has advised and provided consultancy for national and local governments, the European Commission and other public and private institutions in Europe and worldwide. She has published numerous articles and books on issues relating to development, governance, integration, and regional cooperation.

LIST OF CONTRIBUTORS

Malwina Bakalarska Assistant Professor, Institute of Mediterranean and Oriental Cultures, Polish Academy of Sciences, Poland.

James Donald Mason Fellow, Kennedy School of Government; Harvard South Africa Fellow at the Center for African Studies, Harvard University, USA.

Bogdan Góralczyk Professor, Center for Europe, University of Warsaw, Poland.

Calestous Juma Professor of the Practice of International Development, Kennedy School of Government, Harvard University, USA, Twitter @ Calestous.

Wojciech Kazanecki Team of Young Researchers, Committee of Future Studies "Poland 2000 Plus", Polish Academy of Sciences, Poland.

Jerzy Kleer Professor, Institute of Economic Studies, Polish Academy of Sciences; Deputy Head of the Committee of Future Studies "Poland 2000 Plus", Polish Academy of Sciences, Poland.

Piotr Korcelli Professor, Institute of Geography and Spatial Planning, Polish Academy of Sciences, Poland.

Ewa Korcelli-Olejniczak Associate Professor, Institute of Geography and Spatial Planning, Polish Academy of Sciences, Poland.

Tadeusz Markowski Professor, Faculty of Management, University Lodz; Institute of Geography and Spatial Planning, Polish Academy of Sciences, Poland.

Adnan Morshed Associate Professor, School of Architecture and Planning, The Catholic University of America, Washington DC, USA.

Katarzyna A. Nawrot Assistant Professor, Department of International Economics, Poznań University of Economics and Business; Committee of Future Studies "Poland 2000 Plus", Polish Academy of Sciences, Poland.

Jessen Page Professor, University of Applied Sciences & Arts of Western Switzerland (HES-SO), Switzerland.

Agata Penconek Assistant Professor, Faculty of Chemical and Process Engineering, Warsaw University of Technology, Poland.

Konrad Prandecki Institute of Agricultural and Food Economics, National Research Institute; Committee of Future Studies "Poland 2000 Plus", Polish Academy of Sciences, Poland.

Gaurang Rami Professor, Department of Economics, Veer Narmad South Gujarat University, India.

Sylwia Śmietanko Team of Young Researchers, Committee of Future Studies "Poland 2000 Plus", Polish Academy of Sciences, Poland.

Bohdan Szklarski Professor, American Studies Center, University of Warsaw, Poland.

Piotr Szyja PhD candidate, Institute of Political Sciences, Polish Academy of Sciences; American Studies Center, University of Warsaw, Poland.

Maria Szyszkowska Professor, University of Warsaw; Committee of Future Studies "Poland 2000 Plus", Polish Academy of Sciences, Poland.

Yogesh N. Vansiya Assistant Professor, Department of Economics, Veer Narmad South Gujarat University, India.

Feng Wenmeng Associate Research Fellow, Research Department of Social Development, Development Research Center of the State Council (DRC), China.

Zygmunt Ziobrowski Professor, Institute of Urban Development, Cracow, Poland.

Urszula Żuławska Professor, Faculty of Management, Social Academy of Sciences, Warsaw, Poland.

Elżbieta Żuławska-Sobczyk Master, Architect, Center for Latin American Studies, University of Warsaw, Poland.

ACKNOWLEDGEMENTS

The editors would like to express their gratitude to all the authors for their contributions. We would also like to thank Iwona Leydon and Daniel Sax for translation and proofreading of some parts of this volume. We are very grateful to Professor Kerry Brown for encouraging us to publish the book and introducing us to World Scientific. Finally, we want to thank World Scientific for publishing this volume and the people that have been steering this manuscript into the publication stage, especially Jane Sayers for many discussions and immense support in crafting this book and Mary Simpson for her valuable assistance through the publication process.

CONTENTS

INTRODUCTION

Jerzy Kleer and Katarzyna A. Nawrot

Surging population numbers and the resulting emergence of megacities represent a new phenomenon of the 21st century, occurring on a rapidly growing scale. It brings both numerous challenges and opportunities to the economic development of nations and world development at large, ones which have yet to be fully explored.

Megacities, that is, cities which encompass over 10 million inhabitants — and which may in some cases contribute more than one-third of the domestic product of the countries where they are situated — are becoming unique entities in their own right, challenging the developmental policies, governance, and cohesion of states. Their distinct character very much depends on the region where they are located, the advancement of the economies they are part of, and the role they play as an agglomeration. The differing speeds of their expansion and differing maturity of the urbanization processes they are part of mean that they face different challenges in their development and governance, ranging from the economy, labour market, housing, urban infrastructure, and connectivity, to their energy supply, security, the scope of poverty, environment, society, and public sphere, etc. On the other hand, the surge in population numbers in the megacities will also bring certain new opportunities for fostering innovation and also improving education and public services — especially in

Africa and Asia, where such objectives might be easier to achieve with greater concentration. The scale of intensification in the challenges, opportunities, or even threats related to the emergence and rise of megacities here depends on the conditions in which these agglomerations have been formed or are forming, especially in terms of the dividing line that runs, with a certain simplification, between the developed and developing worlds. Crucial importance should be attributed here to governments and the determination they show in understanding particular threats arising from the rise of megacities and finding the ways to mitigate them and in exploiting the chances resulting from the unprecedented demographic potential. Nevertheless, various megacities, be they mature ones — like Tokyo, the North American megacities, or the European cases — or emerging ones, can provide lessons for governance in numerous countries where they are currently growing, shedding light on the issues they may face in the future and thus offering a chance to alleviate or leapfrog them. Accordingly, the complexity of megacities requires a broader approach in order to comprehensively grasp examples of best practices in governance as employed by countries in different regions and at different levels of economic development.

This volume thus takes a multidisciplinary and interdisciplinary approach to the subject of megacities, gathering together insights from scholars, researchers, and practitioners on the growing megacity phenomenon. It examines both the major new challenges that the expansion of megacities brings for development at large and the opportunities they might create for the public good. As such, the book fits into a broader discussion on the ongoing transformation of the world economy, in which megacities are becoming important players. Consequently, the views presented in the book vary from conceptual deliberations on the phenomenon, highlighting its complexity, to examinations of certain challenges megacities pose to societies, the environment, the economy and different levels of government, to analyses identifying particular opportunities and proposing certain solutions, and to case studies highlighting lessons learned and best practices. This comprehensive approach, it is hoped, will help provide a more global perspective on megacities, taking into account both the similarities and the differences between megacities around the world.

The book is structured in four interconnected parts. The first part serves as an introductory and conceptual background, highlighting *The Complexity of and Challenges in the Emergence of Megacities*. It opens with an empirical analysis by Jerzy Kleer and Katarzyna A. Nawrot on the demographic changes in the world economy, especially as pertains to urban growth and the rise of megacities, while setting the background for an introduction to an integral theory of megacities. That is followed by a theoretical study by Jerzy Kleer on the degradation of the public sphere in megacities, and by a conceptual and theoretical discussion of the developmental processes in metropolises and megacities offered by Piotr Korcelli and Ewa Korcelli-Olejniczak. The issues undertaken further range from the problems of governance and challenges faced by public authorities of megacities, explored by Tadeusz Markowski, and different patterns of megacities' development, presented by Zygmunt Ziobrowski. The section further examines the challenges and threats the emergence of megacities brings for economies, the environment, and societies in a detailed analysis by Konrad Prandecki, Wojciech Kazanecki, and Sylawia Śmietanko and then continues with the topic of air pollution in megacities and its consequences for human health, considered by Agata Penconek, followed by a philosophical discussion on the impact of megacities on human nature by Maria Szyszkowska. The different aspects tackled in this section of the volume are interconnected and are observed — *albeit* to differing degrees — irrespective of the regional or national context, and thus highlight crucial aspects in the development of megacities.

The second part of the volume aims to confront certain *Opportunities in the Development of Megacities* from various regional, national, and multidisciplinary perspectives. Feng Wenmeng presents the Chinese perspective with its distinctive characteristics of urbanization in one of the fastest and largest emerging market economies, indeed the one with the largest number of existing and projected megacities. The Indian context is further examined by Gaurang Rami and Yogesh Vansiya. This is followed by an African perspective presented by Katarzyna A. Nawrot, Calestous Juma, and James Donald, arguing that despite the rising challenges that emerging megacities in developing countries face, they have a chance to alleviate them by repositioning a megacity towards innovation ecosystem. Jessen Page, in turn, investigates the issue of energy in megacities and the possibilities for the successful transition of a megacity towards a Smart City. What future lies ahead for megacities in Europe is discussed lastly in this part by Jerzy Kleer and Katarzyna A. Nawrot.

The third part of the volume serves as a diverse set of selected megacity *Case Studies*. They examine Tokyo — the biggest megacity to date, with depopulation problems faced by Japan, and Delhi — a rapidly growing megacity in one of the most populous developing countries, presented in comparative analysis by Katarzyna A. Nawrot; Shanghai as an example of a megacity with Chinese characteristics and the world's first megalopolis, explored by Bogdan Górlaczyk; Mexico City analyzed from the perspective of sustainable development by Urszula Żuławska and Elżbieta Żuławska-Sobczyk; Dhaka — a fast-growing South Asian megacity examined by Adnan Morshed; Lagos, serving as a case from Africa, presented by Malwina Bakalarska, and New York as an American example and a city of progress, argued by Bohdan Szklarski and Piotr Szyja. The cross-country analysis aims to grasp the various challenges faced by megacities in countries of differing levels of development and urbanization, while referring to the problems and issues undertaken in the first two parts of the volume, thus providing implications and lessons learned for the best practices in megacities development and governance.

The fourth part of the book — the *Epilogue* by Jerzy Kleer and Katarzyna A. Nawrot — gives the final conclusions to the volume.

This book originated from the Committee of Future Studies "Poland 2000 Plus", Polish Academy of Sciences. While undertaking the project "Global Threats as Barriers to Development" in collaboration with Poland's National Security Bureau and under the patronage of the President of the Republic of Poland, the Committee recognized the developmental problems of the largest cities as being among the most important and therefore deserving of separate attention. The Committee thus concluded that in the context of global threats and challenges, special attention needs to be paid to the dynamic development of urban areas, especially the problems that are engendered by the rise of "megacities" in the world economy. Consequently, the Committee has devoted a great deal of attention to the problem of megacities, followed by a conference in November 2014 and the first edited volume entitled *Megamiasta przyszłości — Szansa czy zagrożenie rozwoju* [Megacities of the future: Chances or threats to development] published in Polish in 2015. The importance and dynamics of the megacity phenomenon encouraged the researchers from the Committee to reach out to a growing community of researchers working on megacity issues, and the present volume represents the ultimate result, including some original, revised contributions from the above Polish volume, supplemented by contributions of international experts in the field, for which the editors would like to express their gratitude.

All in all, the contributions in the book touch upon many of the problems that humanity faces in the future, given that continued urbanization is a foregone conclusion. Urban centres continue to attract people in search of work and better living conditions, and the largest cities are also growing dynamically through their own natural population growth, especially in developing countries. Cities are becoming global cities, and through their development of their surrounding regions they are also giving rise to megaregions, which will form a global network of megaregions.

The ongoing rise of megacities leaves us without a doubt that they, as well as their connectivity and networks of interdependencies, will play a growing role in the contemporary world economy. Thus, the phenomenon requires in-depth studies of multidisciplinary and interdisciplinary character, attempting to capture its complexity while yielding better understanding of the challenges and opportunities they might bring for the world community. It is to this more in-depth understanding that the various chapters of this volume aim to contribute.

Jerzy Kleer and Katarzyna A. Nawrot
Warsaw, March 2017

Part I

The Complexity of and Challenges in the Emergence of Megacities

1

THE RISE OF MEGACITIES — AN EMPIRICAL OVERVIEW OF THE DEMOGRAPHIC CHANGES IN THE WORLD ECONOMY AND AN INTRODUCTION TO AN INTEGRAL THEORY OF MEGACITIES

Jerzy Kleer and Katarzyna A. Nawrot

1.1. Introduction

The goal of this preliminary chapter is to set out an empirical analysis of the demographic changes in the world economy, especially as pertains to urban growth and the rise of megacities, while setting the background for an introduction to the theory of megacities. We set the stage for these considerations by first examining the evolution and characteristics of the demographic transformations of the world economy since 1950, as well as projections through 2100. This is followed by an empirical analysis of the rise of megacities, undertaken from different perspectives. On that basis, we next make an attempt to identify models of how various megacities arose, trying to categorize them in groups with certain characteristics. We then discuss the underlying forces driving the rise of megacities, including the major factors behind rapid population growth in such agglomerations.

The chapter ends with some theoretical considerations, in an attempt to lay the groundwork for positing an integral theory of megacities, as a growing phenomenon expected to continue — bringing both challenges and opportunities — in the 21st century.

1.2. Demographic Changes in the World Economy

To understand the rise of megacities in the contemporary world economy, the unique characteristics of this process, as well as the opportunities and challenges that follow it, it is important to analyze the demographic changes occurring at the global level. Since 1950, the world population has increased dramatically, from 2.5 billion to 7.3 billion as of mid-2015, making for an almost three-fold rise. According to the median variant of UN predictions, the world population is expected to reach 11.2 billion by 2100, which will mean an increase of an additional 3.9 billion from 2015, or an overall surge of 8.7 billion as compared to 1950 (UNDESA, 2015).

The biggest increase in population from 1950 to 2015 was observed in Asia, estimated to account for around 62% of the total world population growth over the period. This surge of approx. 3 billion people in Asia alone mainly came in China and India, which saw their populations more than double and triple to reach 1.4 billion and 1.3 billion, respectively. The two countries remain the most populous in the world, together accounting for a cumulative share of 36.6% of the world population. During the same period of 1950–2015, the population increased by 957.3 million in Africa, 465.5 million in Latin America and Caribbean, 189.4 million in Europe, 186.2 million in North America, and 26.7 million in Oceania. As a result, significant changes have ensued in the structure of the world population: as of 2015, 59.8% of the world population lived in Asia (4.4 billion), followed by 16.1% in Africa (1.2 billion), and 10% in Europe (738.4 million). Latin America and the Caribbean accounted for 8.6% (634.4 million), North America 4.9% (357.8 million), and Oceania 0.5% (39.3 million). Europe's share had decreased by more than half, from 21.7% in 1950, while Africa's share rose by 7%, from 9.1% in 1950. UN projections further show that the greatest increase in the world population in the 21st century will occur in Africa, with a surge of around 3.2 billion expected

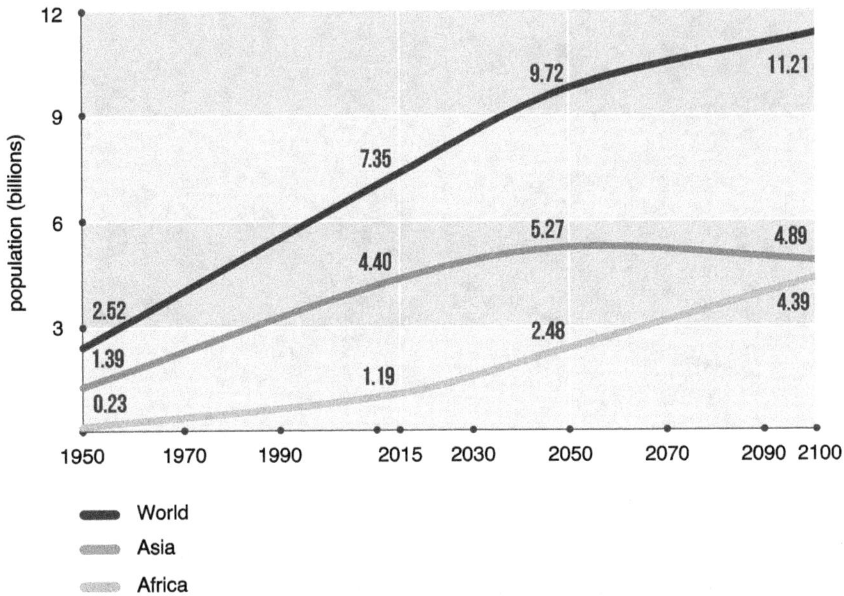

Fig. 1.1. Population of the world, Asia and Africa, 1950–2100

Explanations: 1950–2015 — estimates; 2015–2100 medium-variant projection.
Source: Authors' own elaboration on data from UNDESA (2014), UNDESA (2015).

between 2015 and 2100.[1] This means that by the end of the century, 39.1% of the world population will be living in Africa and 43.6% in Asia (Fig. 1.1). For Asia, this will mean a decrease, from an around 60% share today. Europe's share of the world population is expected to decline to less than 6%, and Northern America's is to remain around 5%. Also, Latin America and the Caribbean's share is projected to fall by 2.2–6.4%, and Oceania's share will slightly rise to around 0.6% over the same period (UNDESA, 2015).

One of the main characteristics of the ongoing demographic changes has been the process of urbanization, occurring irrespective of the region analyzed. The share of the urban population has been constantly growing, but only in the first decade of the 21st century has it reached the share of

[1]For more discussion regarding population growth in Africa see Rynarzewski *et al.* (2017: 91–94).

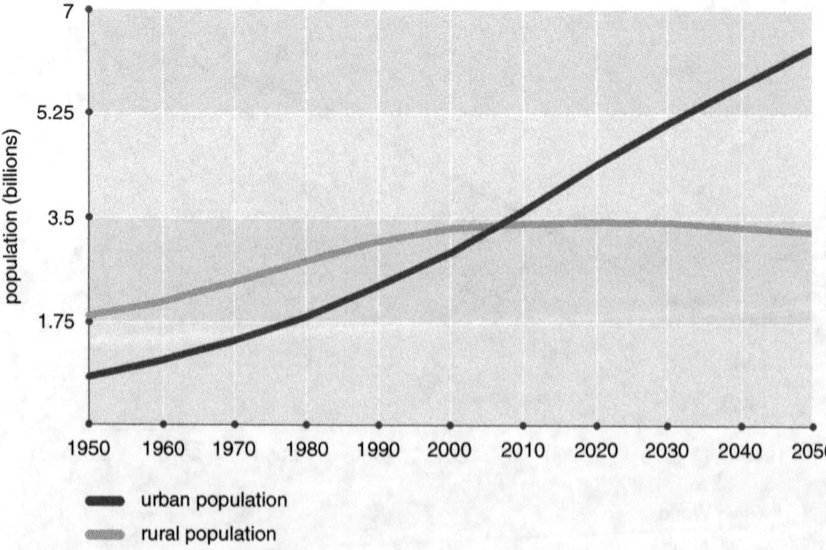

Fig. 1.2. Urban vs. rural population of the world, 1950–2050

Source: Authors' own elaboration on data from UNDESA (2014).

the rural population, being estimated at around 54% (Fig. 1.2). Thus, almost 2/3 of the world population rise in 1950–2015 was concentrated in urban areas. Also, future population growth is likewise expected to be focused predominantly in urban areas, mostly in developing countries, including those least developed. Thus, we can also expect negative externalities associated with urban agglomerations, including further expansion of slums with the attendant consequences (Nawrot, 2014: 108; Nawrot, 2015: 308).

Both the level and the rate of urbanization vary by region and country. High income countries are the most urbanized, while the fastest rate of urbanization is recorded in countries at a low level of development, which results from numerous factors including high fertility rates, falling mortality, and above all migrations from rural to urban areas. Regionally, the highest level of urbanization is recorded in North America (82%), Latin America and the Caribbean (80%), and Europe (74%). Africa remains the least urbanized, with 40% of its population living in urban areas. In Asia, the share is gradually approaching a balance between rural and urban inhabitants, the latter accounting for 48% in 2015. On the other hand, the rate of urbanization was the highest in Africa, followed by Asia and also Latin America and the Caribbean. The population in urban areas of Africa increased almost fifteen-fold, rising from 32 million in 1950 to 471.6 million in 2015. In Asia, an almost nine-fold increase was observed — from 244.6 million to 2.113 billion, whereas Latin America and the Caribbean saw a more than seven-fold rise — from 69.3 million to 502.8 million. This means that the largest numerical increase in population numbers living in urban areas occurred in Asia. The changes took a much lower pace in both Europe and North America, following their already high levels of urbanization in the 1950s (UNDESA, 2014).

The predictions indicate that urbanization will continue worldwide (Fig. 1.2), while still varying by region and by country. However, the overall rate of urbanization will continue to decline, with the expected level of urbanization to reach 66% in 2050. The highest rate of urbanization is projected to occur in Africa, with its population living in urban areas to reach 50% around 2040 and 80% by the end of the century. From the perspective of the analysis of megacities, two conclusions can be drawn from these projections: first, they entail a rising number of cities, including megacities, and second, they mean rising population numbers in existing megacities. Each of these two aspects will be further examined.

1.3. Demographic Rise of Megacities

In order to properly examine the demographic rise of megacities (defined here as urban agglomerations with over 10 million inhabitants), it is crucial to draw a broader picture of development of cities of different sizes. If we assume 1990 as a basis of the analysis, we can observe that the number of cities in the world with above 300,000 inhabitants increased from 976 to 1,729 over the last 25 years. This process is not expected to slow down in the years to come, and by 2030 the figure is expected to rise to 2,225. The strongest growth was observed in the category of megacities, with their number rising almost three-fold, from 10 megacities in 1990 to 29 in 2015. The number of large cities in the next category — between 5 million and 10 million — doubled during this time, with the number of

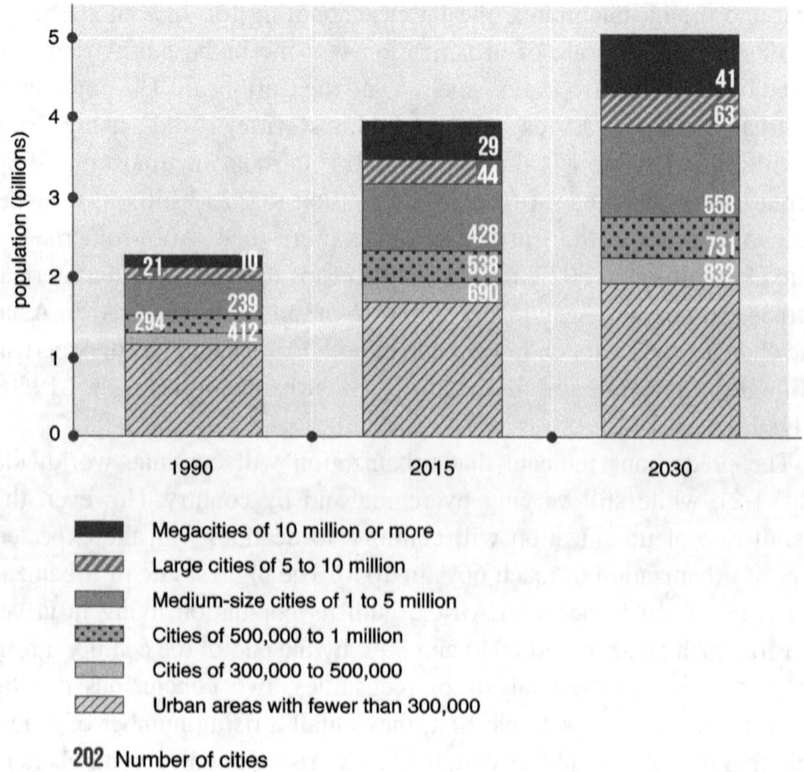

Fig. 1.3. Global urban population growth, highlighted by different population categories of cities, in 1990, 2015, 2030

Source: Compiled by the authors based on UNDESA (2014).

still smaller cities developing at a slower pace (Fig. 1.3). These figures illustrate that the most significant changes pertained to the largest urban agglomerations. Projections indicate that the process of growth in the number of cities will continue, *albeit* more slowly. The rate will be still high for megacities, a category which by 2030 is expected to number 41. Moreover, the number of smaller towns — between 300,000 and 500,000 inhabitants — is projected to grow at a faster rate (Fig. 1.3).

The analysis of cities based on their population size gives us a different overview of the ongoing demographic changes in urban areas. The most

Table 1.1. Urban population in cities of different population categories in 1990, 2015, 2030 (in million)

Categories of urban settlement	1990	2015	2030
Megacities (10 million or more)	152.7	471.3	729.9
Large cities of 5–10 million	157.0	306.9	433.9
Medium-size cities of 1–5 million	459.5	847.2	1127.9
Cities of 500,000 to 1 million	202.1	371.0	509.4
Cities of 300,000 to 500,000	157.4	261.8	318.9
Urban areas with fewer than 300,000	1156.4	1699.2	1938.1
Together	2285.0	3957.3	5058.2

Source: Compiled by the authors based on UNDESA (2014).

significant rise in population was observed in megacities (Table 1.1), where the population increased more than three-fold from 152.7 million to 471.3 million between 1990 and 2015 and is projected to rise to 729.9 by 2030. The lowest rate of population increase is observed in cities of small size, with up to 300,000 inhabitants, where in the years 1990–2015 the population rose from 1.156 billion to 1.699 billion, and will increase by a further 239 million by 2030. However, most of the urban population is expected to live in cities of this category. Thus, the process of change in the population of cities depending on their size shows a quite clear upward trend in the largest cities, primarily megacities, together with a certain deceleration of growth in the smallest towns — between 300,000 and 500,000 residents (see Table 1.1).

Thus, according to existing forecasts, there is every indication that cities will account for around 66–76% of the world's population, or more than 6.3–7.3 billion people, in 2050. Regardless of the exact size of that population, one thing is certain: megacities will become home to more and more of humanity. Already in 2010, megacities accounted for more than 5% of the world's population, with their number standing at just 23. Even if we assume that the number of megacities will not exceed 50 in 2050 and the average population of each megacity will not exceed 20 million inhabitants, this still means approx. 10% of the global population will be living in megacities by that time.

If we look more closely at the above-presented demographic changes in world cities, it is interesting to observe that in 1950 there were two megacities — New York–Newark and Tokyo–Yokohama, then with 12.3 and 11.3 million inhabitants respectively (Table 1.2). In the ranking of the largest cities they were followed by London (8.4 million), Osaka (7 million), Paris (6.3 million), and Moscow (5.4 million). The list of the largest urban agglomerations (the top 30) then also included four Latin American cities — Buenos Aires (5.1 million), Mexico City (3.4 million), Rio de Janeiro (3.1 million), San Paulo (2.3 million); one African city — Cairo (2.5 million); five Asian cities — Kolkata (4.5 million), Shanghai (4.3 million), Mumbai (2.9 million), Tianjin (2.5 million), and Shenyang (2.2 million); four cities in the US — Los Angeles (4 million), Philadelphia (3.1 million), Detroit (2.8 million), and San Francisco (1.9 million), and eight in Europe, including Berlin (3.3 million), St. Petersburg (2.9 million), Manchester (2.4 million), Birmingham (2.2 million), Rome (1.9. million), Milan (1.9 million), Barcelona (1.8 million), and Madrid (1.7 million). This clearly shows how urbanization was then mostly concentrated in Europe.

Osaka joined the group of megacities in the 1960s, with a population of 10.6 million, followed by Mexico City and San Paolo in the late 1970s. In 1990, five additional megacities were recorded — Mumbai, Kolkata, Los Angeles, Seoul, and Buenos Aires. At the beginning of the 21st century they were further joined by Delhi, Shanghai, Cairo, Rio de Janeiro, Dhaka, Beijing, Karachi, and Moscow. There were then 17 megacities altogether (as Seoul fell out of the ranking) with a cumulative population of 255.1 million (see Table 1.2).

According to UNDESA (2014), there were 29 megacities in 2015, ranging from Bangalore (10.1 million) and London (10.3 million) to Shanghai (23.7 million), Delhi (25.7 million), and Tokyo (38 million) — the latter remaining the biggest megacity uninterruptedly since 1954. By 2030, the group of megacities is set to increase by another 12 agglomerations including Chennai (then with 13.9 million), Lahore (13 million), Hyderabad (12.8 million), Lima (12.2 million), Bogota (12 million), Johannesburg (11.6 million), Bangkok (11.5 million), Dar es Salaam (10.8 million), Ahmadabad (10.5 million), Luanda (10.4 million), Ho Chi Minh City (10.2 million), and Chengdu (10.1 million).

Table 1.2. The demographic trajectories in 1950–2030 of world's cities by population (population in thousands)

Urban agglomeration	1950	1960	1970	1980	1990	2000	2010	2015	2020	2030
Tokyo	**11,275**	**16,679**	**23,298**	**28,549**	**32,530**	**34,450**	**36,834**	**38,001**	**38,323**	**37,190**
Delhi	1,369	2,283	**3,531**	**5,558**	**9,726**	**15,732**	**21,935**	**25,703**	**29,348**	**36,060**
Shanghai	**4,301**	**6,820**	**6,036**	**5,966**	**7,823**	**13,959**	**19,980**	**23,741**	**27,137**	**30,751**
São Paulo	**2,334**	**3,970**	**7,620**	**12,089**	**14,776**	**17,014**	**19,660**	**21,066**	**22,119**	**23,444**
Mumbai (Bombay)	**2,857**	**4,060**	**5,811**	**8,658**	**12,436**	**16,367**	**19,422**	**21,043**	**22,838**	**27,797**
Ciudad de México (Mexico City)	**3,365**	**5,479**	**8,831**	**13,028**	**15,642**	**18,457**	**20,132**	**20,999**	**21,868**	**23,865**
Beijing	1,671	**3,900**	**4,426**	**5,366**	**6,788**	**10,162**	**16,190**	**20,384**	**24,201**	**27,706**
Kinki M.M.A. (Osaka)	**7,005**	**10,615**	**15,272**	**17,028**	**18,389**	**18,660**	**19,492**	**20,238**	**20,523**	**19,976**
Al-Qahirah (Cairo)	**2,494**	**3,680**	**5,585**	**7,349**	**9,892**	**13,626**	**16,899**	**18,772**	**20,568**	**24,502**
New York–Newark	**12,338**	**14,164**	**16,191**	**15,601**	**16,086**	**17,813**	**18,365**	**18,593**	**18,793**	**19,885**
Dhaka	336	508	1,374	3,266	**6,621**	**10,285**	**14,731**	**17,598**	**20,989**	**27,374**
Karachi	1,055	1,853	3,119	**5,048**	**7,147**	**10,032**	**14,081**	**16,618**	**19,230**	**24,838**
Buenos Aires	**5,098**	**6,598**	**8,105**	**9,422**	**10,513**	**12,407**	**14,246**	**15,180**	**15,894**	**16,956**
Kolkata (Calcutta)	**4,513**	**5,652**	**6,926**	**9,030**	**10,890**	**13,058**	**14,283**	**14,865**	**15,726**	**19,092**
Istanbul	967	1,453	2,772	4,397	**6,552**	**8,744**	**12,703**	**14,164**	**15,099**	**16,694**
Chongqing	1,567	2,275	2,237	2,961	4,011	**7,863**	**11,244**	**13,332**	**15,233**	**17,380**
Lagos	325	762	1,414	2,572	4,764	**7,281**	**10,781**	**13,123**	**16,168**	**24,239**
Manila	1,544	2,274	**3,534**	**5,955**	**7,973**	**9,962**	**11,891**	**12,946**	**13,942**	**16,756**
Rio de Janeiro	**3,026**	**4,493**	**6,791**	**8,784**	**9,697**	**11,307**	**12,374**	**12,902**	**13,326**	**14,174**
Guangzhou, Guangdong	1,049	1,272	1,542	1,870	3,072	**7,330**	**9,620**	**12,458**	**15,174**	**17,574**

(Continued)

Table 1.2. (*Continued*)

Urban agglomeration	1950	1960	1970	1980	1990	2000	2010	2015	2020	2030
Los Angeles–Long Beach–Santa Ana	**4,046**	**6,530**	**8,378**	**9,512**	**10,883**	**11,798**	**12,160**	**12,310**	**12,454**	**13,257**
Moskva (Moscow)	**5,356**	**6,170**	**7,106**	**8,136**	**8,987**	**10,005**	**11,461**	**12,166**	**12,474**	12,200
Kinshasa	202	443	1,070	2,053	3,683	6,140	**9,382**	**11,587**	**14,118**	**19,996**
Tianjin	**2,467**	**2,935**	**3,318**	3,750	4,558	6,670	**9,451**	**11,210**	**12,816**	**14,655**
Paris	**6,283**	**7,411**	**8,208**	**8,669**	**9,330**	**9,737**	**10,460**	**10,843**	**11,271**	11,803
Shenzhen	3	8	22	58	875	6,550	**10,223**	**10,749**	**11,287**	**12,673**
Jakarta	1,452	**2,679**	**3,915**	**5,984**	**8,175**	**8,390**	**9,630**	**10,323**	**11,298**	**13,812**
London	**8,361**	**8,196**	**7,509**	**7,660**	**8,054**	**8,613**	**9,699**	**10,313**	**10,849**	11,467
Bangalore	746	1,166	1,615	2,812	4,036	5,567	8,275	**10,087**	**11,837**	**14,762**
Lima	1,066	1,756	2,980	**4,438**	**5,837**	**7,294**	8,955	**9,897**	10,756	**12,221**
Chennai (Madras)	1,491	1,915	3,057	4,203	**5,338**	6,353	8,523	9,890	**11,241**	**13,921**
Seoul	1,021	2,361	**5,312**	**8,258**	**10,518**	**9,878**	**9,796**	9,774	9,818	9,960
Bogotá	630	1,269	2,383	3,525	4,740	6,356	8,506	9,765	10,696	11,966
Chukyo M.M.A. (Nagoya)	**2,237**	**4,297**	**6,603**	**7,777**	**8,407**	**8,740**	**9,165**	9,406	9,491	9,304
Johannesburg	1,653	2,137	2,764	3,202	3,709	5,605	7,992	9,399	10,361	11,573
Krung Thep (Bangkok)	1,360	2,151	3,110	**4,723**	**5,888**	6,360	8,213	9,270	10,137	11,528
Hyderabad	1,096	1,241	1,748	2,487	4,193	5,445	7,578	8,944	10,279	**12,774**
Chicago	**4,999**	**6,183**	**7,106**	**7,216**	**7,374**	**8,315**	8,616	8,745	8,871	9,493
Lahore	836	1,264	1,964	2,882	3,970	5,452	7,487	8,741	10,054	**13,033**
Tehran	1,041	1,873	3,290	**5,079**	**6,365**	**7,128**	8,059	8,432	8,909	9,990
Wuhan	1,069	1,653	2,039	2,516	3,417	6,638	7,515	7,906	8,364	9,442

Chengdu	646	1,580	1,750	2,150	2,955	4,222	6,234	7,556	8,766	10,104
Ahmadabad	855	1,181	1,695	2,484	3,255	4,427	6,210	7,343	8,452	10,527
Hong Kong	1,682	**2,621**	**3,472**	**4,623**	**5,766**	6,835	7,050	7,314	7,550	7,885
Thành Pho Ho Chí Minh (Ho Chi Minh City)	1,213	1,400	1,970	2,716	3,038	4,389	6,189	7,298	8,309	10,200
Shenyang	**2,148**	**2,699**	3,156	3,418	3,651	4,562	5,676	6,315	6,932	7,911
Madrid	**1,700**	2,392	**3,521**	4,253	4,414	5,014	5,787	6,199	6,476	6,707
Philadelphia	**3,128**	**3,930**	**4,396**	**4,540**	4,725	5,156	5,449	5,585	5,709	6,158
Kitakyushu–Fukuoka M.M.A.	1,403	**2,681**	**4,072**	**4,726**	5,269	5,421	5,556	5,510	5,447	5,355
Luanda	138	219	459	771	1,390	2,591	4,508	5,506	6,837	10,429
Barcelona	**1,809**	**2,468**	**3,482**	3,837	4,101	4,355	4,934	5,258	5,478	5,685
Dar es Salaam	84	162	357	855	1,474	2,272	3,870	5,116	6,727	10,760
Sankt Peterburg (Saint Petersburg)	**2,903**	**3,398**	**3,980**	**4,645**	4,989	4,719	4,872	4,993	5,020	4,955
Roma (Rome)	**1,884**	**2,456**	3,135	3,390	3,450	3,385	3,592	3,718	3,796	3,842
Detroit	**2,769**	**3,548**	**3,966**	3,807	3,703	3,899	3,730	3,639	3,606	3,886
Berlin	**3,338**	**3,260**	3,206	3,056	3,422	3,384	3,475	3,563	3,626	3,658
San Francisco-Oakland	**1,855**	2,200	2,529	2,656	2,961	3,230	3,283	3,300	3,336	3,615
Milano (Milan)	**1,883**	2,395	3,017	3,168	3,063	2,985	3,056	3,099	3,124	3,162
Manchester	**2,422**	**2,427**	2,396	2,343	2,282	2,345	2,538	2,646	2,758	2,968
Birmingham (West Midlands)	**2,229**	2,338	2,370	2,357	2,301	2,280	2,429	2,515	2,610	2,808

Explanations: Values in bold mark the status of being among the world's 30 largest cities in the given year; values shaded grey mark the status of megacity in the given year; the table is structured according to the population size of the cities in 2015.

Source: Authors' own elaboration on data from UNDESA (2014).

These facts concerning the rise of megacities since 1950 allow us to identify a few important trends, namely: (i) an increasing pace at which new megacities are emerging; (ii) the changing dynamic of their development depending on the region and level of development of the countries involved; and therefore (iii) a significant shift in their geographical location. Certain regularities can be identified from the ongoing demographic transformation.

First, in the 1950s and 1960s, megacities were concentrated in Europe, the US, and Japan. In terms of location, they all existed in developed countries. This was subsequently followed by the rise of South American megacities in the 1970s and 1980s — all in developing countries. This latter trend has since largely continued, as gradually through the 1990s the Asian megacities of East Asia and the Indian subcontinent started to expand. Since the 1990s, a dense network of cities with 1–5 million inhabitants has been developing, in some cases evolving into megacities, mainly in Asia, a consequence of rates of urban growth. It was not until 1990 that another megacity situated in a developed country emerged — Los Angeles, followed again by Paris in 2010. Although it remains unclear which economies will be considered "developed" in 2030, if we assume today's classification, by that date there will be six megacities in developed countries: Tokyo, Osaka, New York, Los Angeles, Paris, and London (compare Fig. 1.4). Presently there are megacities located on all the continents. Projections show that by 2030 they will be mainly concentrated in Asia; however, we are observing a rising trend in this regard in Africa, as a result of rapid urbanization on the continent. Despite the predicted slowdown in the development of world cities by 2030, the dynamics are expected to remain focused in Africa, and it is the rise of African cities that will drive the dynamics of world urbanization.

1.4. Models of Megacities' Emergence

Population is obviously a crucial criterion underpinning the megacity phenomenon, yet it is not the only one. Equally important, or perhaps even more important, is the economic criterion — in particular how megacities relate to the economic level of the states in which they function. Megacities located in developed countries with high income, in developing countries of middle income, or in least developed countries of low income all differ,

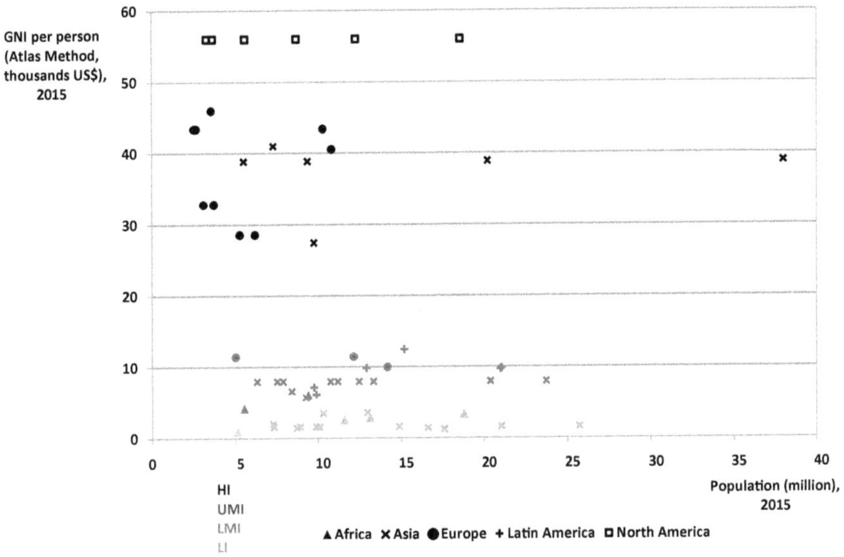

Fig. 1.4. Cities and megacities vs. GNI per person, 2015

Explanations: 60 biggest cities in the world as for 1950 were included in the analysis; HI — high income countries; UMI — upper-middle income countries; LMI — lower-middle income countries; LI — low income countries.

Source: Authors' own elaboration on data from UNDESA (2014), World Bank (2016).

and do so in at least two fundamental respects: not only in terms of wealth, but also in terms of the time and pace of their emergence. The rise of such megacities as New York, Tokyo, or London was a relatively long and evolutionary process that required the presence of the right environs, public sphere, institutional and legal order, not to mention such fields as housing, adequate health care, and so on. Other megacities, which mostly emerged much more recently, have followed quite different trajectories, with problems that have escalated at different paces and have been, or are being, resolved differently.

Analysis of the changes in the population in megacities and their rate of growth, presented in Figs. 1.5 and 1.6, illustrates certain regularities and allows us to posit three fundamental models for the emergence of megacities:

- Model 1: "Evolution" megacities — a model characterized by evolution and planning;

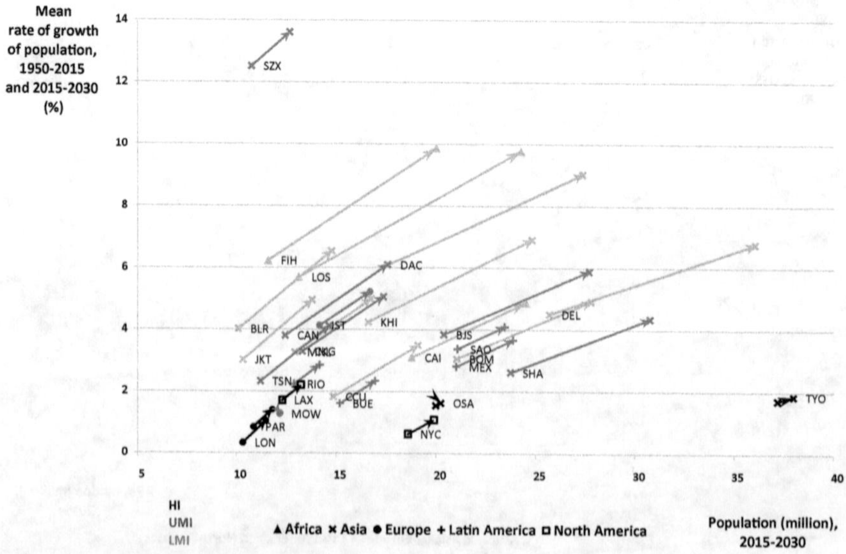

Fig. 1.5. Megacities in 2015

Explanations: The world's 29 megacities as of 2015 were included in the analysis; HI — high income countries; UMI — upper-middle income countries; LMI — lower-middle income countries; the starting point of each vector represents the population in 2015 and mean rate of growth of population in 1950–2015 whereas the end point marks the population in 2030; the slope of the vector depicts the mean rate of growth of population in 2015–2030.

Source: Authors' own elaboration and calculations on data from UNDESA (2014).

- Model 2: "Emerging" megacities — a model characterized by fast growth and mainly planning;
- Model 3: "Galloping" megacities — a model characterized by very fast, chaotic growth and the rapid escalation of numerous negative externalities.

Megacities following the first of these three models have chiefly been characterized not only by evolutionary development but also by bottom-up growth over a long period of time. More importantly, their evolutionary changes began before the second phase of globalization, more specifically in the last years of the 19th century and the first half of the 20th century. Three major characteristics of this "evolution" model are plain to see. The first of these was gradual growth in population numbers, practically as a derivative of economic expansion. Examples include New York and Tokyo, where the mean rate of population growth

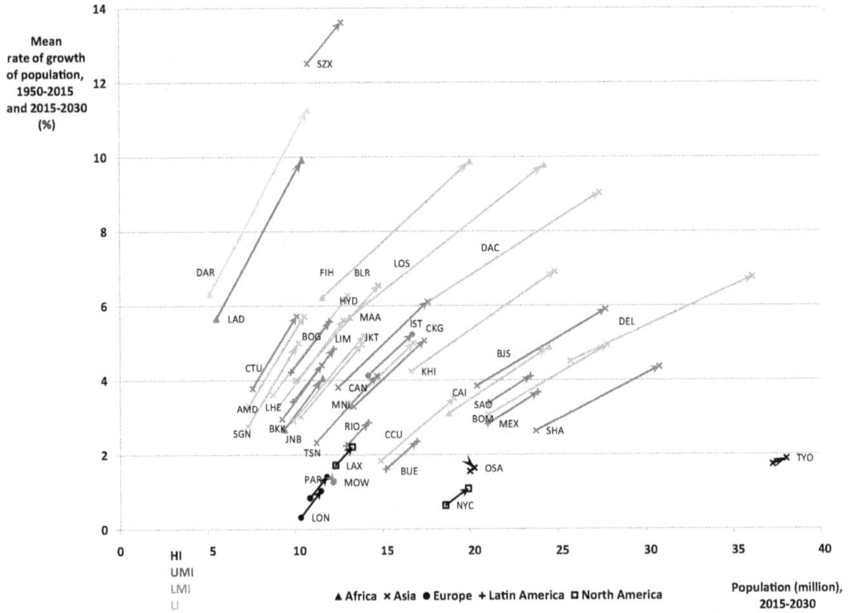

Fig. 1.6. Megacities in 2030

Explanations: 41 megacities in the world projected for 2030 were included in the analysis; HI — high income countries; UMI — upper-middle income countries; LMI — lower-middle income countries; LI — low income countries; the starting point of each vector represents the population in 2015 and mean rate of growth of population in 1950–2015 whereas the end point marks the population in 2030; the slope of the vector depicts the mean rate of growth of population in 2015–2030.
Source: Authors' own elaboration and calculations on data from UNDESA (2014).

over the years 1950–2015 did not exceed 2% — see Fig. 1.5. The second was the gradual shaping of their urban environs, leading to relatively harmonious and regular urban development, not only gradual but to some extent also planned. The third characteristic was the gradual shaping not only of the spatial order but also the institutional and legal order, which emerged as these cities continued to expand. Overpopulation, if any, could be "exported" to colonies and dependent territories of the colonial powers, at least in Europe's case. Although the rapid development of those major agglomerations was not free from various negative externalities and pathologies, it was possible at that time to eliminate those to a greater or lesser degree, or at least to alleviate their impact.

Besides, New York and Tokyo, other cities to a certain extent and with their own particular characteristics followed this same evolutionary pattern of megacity rise, including Osaka, Los Angeles, and the European cities of London, Paris, and Moscow.

Moscow, Russia's only megacity, seems to be a special case in that as it expanded under the socialist model of a centrally-planned economy. Since the breakup of the Soviet Union and the introduction of the market economy, its model also remains controlled by the state, as does the influx of people to urban areas. It is difficult to predict the future development of the socio-economic model in place in Russia, but it is not likely to be similar to the one prevalent in the economies of the Euro-Atlantic rim. More probably, Russia will continue to follow a hybrid model, combining also Chinese characteristics and that of the other Asian countries.

The second trajectory, which we will refer to as the "emerging" megacities model, largely involves a phase of fast population growth (around 2–4% mean rate of growth in 1950–2015) plus dynamic economic growth and development of the countries they are located in. Megacities in this group are mainly situated in emerging markets — to a large extent China, but also Brazil, India, Indonesia, Philippines, and Mexico. All these countries are also ranked as newly industrialized economies, which has significantly influenced the character of urbanization and pattern of such megacities' emergence. Obviously, this differs depending on the given urban agglomeration and country, and consequently has its own characteristics, as will be presented in more detailed case studies of particular megacities in third part of this volume.

However, in the second model we need to emphasize distinctiveness of the Chinese megacities, characterized by two unique features. First of all, the emergence of such urban giants was a top-down process, because the introduction of the market economy in China, which started in the late 1980s, has taken place under the strict control of the state leadership and the power wielded by the Communist Party. Although the private sector is taking shape, at a rather fast pace at that, it still remains state-controlled. Second, the influx of people to major agglomerations, such as Shanghai and Beijing, is a controlled process and all new arrivals are required to obtain residence permits — under the *Hukou* System. Despite that, there still are, of course, underprivileged inhabitants who are not official residents and, by the same token, cannot avail themselves of certain state-provided benefits. Although there are certain symptoms suggesting that the authorities will be trying to resolve this problem, it remains doubtful to what extent they will permit uncontrolled migrations of people from rural areas to cities, at least in the near future. There are, however, plans to still relocate millions of people from rural areas to cities in the coming years, as the largest potential in expanding internal demand in China is considered through urbanization, identified by the state as main contributors to economic growth in the coming decade (Keqiang, 2012; Nawrot, 2012: 18; Changsheng and Jianwu, 2014: 38; World Bank and DRC, 2014). Thus, we can conclude that this special category pertaining chiefly to China can be essentially attributed to fast or very fast growth and planning. A unique example of this is the city of Shenzhen (SZX), the most dynamically emerging city in the 20th century — see Figs. 1.5 and 1.6. Shenzhen grew from a village of 3,000 people in 1950, to 58,000 in 1980, reaching 6.55 million in 2000 and attaining megacity status by 2010 (see Table 1.2). Although the mean rate of population growth in 1950–2015 exceeded 12%, the process was still managed and planned by the authorities.

The rise of megacities following the third, "galloping" model, in turn, has looked completely different. The most distinguishing characteristic is that such megacities' emergence has coincided with the second phase of globalization and remains strongly linked to the population-explosion megatrend. The market economy spread rapidly to the new states that emerged in the aftermath of the collapse of the colonial system, and megacities emerged extremely quickly in that group of countries. Thus, major locations of such huge agglomerations of galloping character are developing countries — mainly lower-middle income countries and low income countries of Africa and South Asia — see Fig. 1.6. It is particularly evident for the projected rise of cities and megacities by 2030 — for example, the cases of Dar es Salaam (DAR), Luanda (LAD), Kinshasa (FIH), and Lagos (LOS), among others. Their explosive growth has been underpinned by the population's shift away from agriculture and the aforementioned demographic upsurge. Such occurrences have taken a particularly negative toll on the environment and urban planning, leading to chaotic urbanization lagging far behind population growth, economic growth, and development of their countries, the absence of an institutional and legal order, or respect for such order (to the extent that it exists). At the same time, it is practically impossible for the excess population to be "exported" anywhere, yet demand for labour in practice remains very insufficient, and it is even harder to create an adequate infrastructure for relatively decent standards of living. There are, it appears, no reasons to believe that the coming two decades will bring any possibilities for the creation of both a sufficient number of jobs and relevant improvements in infrastructure, soft and hard, in megacities of this third group. Thus, we can assume that numerous factors will emerge that will foster growing social tensions, which may lead to numerous protests or rebellions.

It is difficult to forecast the evolution of these three models, especially the third and partly also the second. This is because turning the megacities in those groups into relatively well-functioning entities will be extremely difficult, requiring not only determination on the part of the authorities but above all time, resources, and a vision of future development. The situation is further complicated by what is perhaps the most difficult factor, namely the ongoing transition from one stage of civilization to another. Megacities that belong to the second and third model are largely, though not all, on the borderline between the industrial stage of civilization and post-industrial civilization (a knowledge-based society).

We need to strongly emphasise that the models and trajectories identified here represent just a first attempt at categorizing such urban agglomerations in the relevant respects. They surely require further research and in-depth analysis of certain characteristics, before a more precise evaluation and typology can be posited.

1.5. Causes of the Accelerated Rise of Megacities

1.5.1. Underlying driving forces of the rise of megacities

Before we move the discussion towards the theory of megacities, we find it important to examine the sources of the accelerated rise of megacities and their urban population growth over the last decades.

It can be stated that it was not until the late 1980s that megacities began to experience their ongoing rapid expansion, and as such they represent a relatively new phenomenon. Thus, we make an attempt to identify the forces which have driven their emergence and further expansion. We essentially associate them with three different processes that are universal in their nature, namely:

- the ongoing human population explosion,
- globalization as a process involving the spread of the market economy,
- the information revolution, as a foretoken of an imminent transition from one stage of civilization to another, namely from the industrial civilization towards the civilization of knowledge.

Although the general nature and manifestations of these processes are widely known, we will begin this analysis by examining each of them in turn and elaborating on some of their distinctive aspects.

Firstly, the rapid expansion of the human population can be attributed to the emergence of industrial civilization. Back at the beginning of the 18th century, the world's population stood at 603.2 million people. That figure more than doubled by the middle of the next century, reaching 1.263 billion, then continued to rise throughout the following 100 years, reaching 2.5 billion in 1950 (HYDE, 2017) — a four-fold increase over the course of 2 centuries. At least until 2010, the sources of that unprecedented surge lay in the impact of industrial civilization, which transformed working conditions and facilitated growth in production of both food products and other essential commodities, including above all housing, especially in cities. We should stress, however, that at this point industrial civilization has spread beyond its Euro-Atlantic cradle and has come to cover other areas worldwide.

The second important component of those changes has been globalization, or more specifically the second phase thereof, which began in the 1970s with the emergence of conditions for institutions based on free-market rules. Although such rules continue to differ on the global scale, the fundamental principles upon which they are based, especially private ownership, remain dominant. Such change has been facilitated by a number of important yet quite diverse processes in individual groups of countries. Three types of such factors deserve brief mention here. The first, historically perhaps the most important one (definitely the first to occur), was the shift away from the model of the welfare state in the most developed capitalist countries. An initial step towards that process came with the abandonment of the gold standard in the United States, which served as the first stimulus for globalization and paved the way for the next step, namely wide-ranging deregulation in the United States and the United Kingdom in connection with the policies of President Ronald Regan and Prime Minister Margaret Thatcher. Such reforms allowed the market economy to expand significantly on the basis of the private sector. The next of those factors was de-colonization, leading to the emergence of numerous new countries, which started to adopt the market economy with varying intensity. Such processes were influenced by internal and, above all, external circumstances. De-colonization itself also seems crucial in the development of cities and megacities, as the process gave rise to a need for centres of administrations in those emergent countries. It led to the centralization of power and inflows of people to the newly established capitals.

Finally, the last process was the fall of socialism as a model of development that stood in opposition to capitalism, wherein the economy was centrally planned, or based on directives from the state. Former socialist republics experienced and embraced the rapid spread of the market economy, as the most important mechanism underlying and regulating economic activity.

This current (second) phase of globalization can be seen as defined by three main distinguishing characteristics. The most fundamental of these has involved the adoption of the neoliberal model of economics as the basis for economic behaviour and thus forms of activity. In neoliberalism, the market is regarded as the only and the most effective way of allocating factors of production. Such processes led to the opening up of economies, which was expected to result in the most efficient harnessing of factors of production. Finally, the global market and relatively open economies created conditions conducive to the emergence of international corporations operating on a global scale. All national economies were pulled into the orbit of the global market to a greater or lesser degree. To what extent that process has actually precipitated the adoption of uniform rules-of-the-game across the global market is another issue, one that will be partially addressed below.

The third fundamental process underlying the rise of megacities and shaping their characteristics has been the information revolution, exerting a fundamental impact on their economic and, perhaps especially, political and social development. This will be considered in greater depth below, but here we should place special emphasis on one consequence that is crucially important from a certain perspective, namely the shortening of time and space. Considering globalization in tandem with the information revolution — the approach we are taking in this study — therefore offers an especially powerful way to shed light on some of the distinctive characteristics of megacities.

1.5.2. Causes of accelerated urban population growth in megacities

Furthermore, it is crucial to explore the major factors that underlie the rapid population growth experienced by such agglomerations as megacities. The most fundamental of these population-conducive factors consists in ongoing economic processes altering the forms of economic activity. In more developed economies, these changes have involved, for several decades, a shift away from industry towards the service sector. In less developed countries, however, this has involved an accelerated transition to the industrial stage of civilization coupled with growth in the service sector. A high concentration of both industry and services, especially modern and advanced services, is typical of cities, not only in old urban agglomerations but also in the newly emerging ones. This accelerated transition stems from numerous and varied causes, including economic, political, educational, and above all infrastructural ones. In urban centres, transportation and communication are easier and probably also less expensive. The information revolution has admittedly brought about fundamental changes in this respect, both in specific countries and on a global scale, but it has done very little to change the significance of location, especially for the enormous service sector, which is linked to the financial sector, especially its decision-making centres.

Equally important is the concentration of political power in cities, at both central and regional level, as well as political parties. Being in close proximity to the political authorities is significant for various forms of activity, offering opportunities to exert influence and forge a system of links to the expanding administrative apparatus. This likewise pertains to educational and cultural centres, as well as non-government organizations, affording them greater opportunities to take joint action and exert pressure on local governments.

The growing importance of urban agglomerations, especially those of considerable size, is observed also from the perspective of education possibilities and its advancement. This is linked with the predominance of the service sector in cities, which, in turn, encourages the advancement of education at all levels in urban agglomerations. Modern services, especially in the ever-more powerful sector of finance, require specialist knowledge, which can be offered by higher education establishments, and those are fundamentally linked to major agglomerations.

Perhaps the single most important factor behind surging urban population numbers in megacities is the pursuit of gainful employment. From this perspective, agriculture is undergoing a certain marginalization, turning into an increasingly industrialized and modernized sector that is ever-more efficient and requires ever-more qualified workers. Another additional factor is the belief — not necessarily a well-founded one — that cities offer, at least potentially, significantly better standards of living by providing access to better, higher-income jobs. Whether this notion indeed reflects the reality is debatable: average pay levels in cities are higher than in rural areas or in the agriculture sector, but only some of those who migrate to cities may benefit from that fact.

The problem is a lot more complex, as the supply of labour greatly exceeds demand, not only in less developed countries but also in developed ones. Many available reports and numerous detailed studies indicate that the gap between labour supply and labour demand is indeed vast (see, for instance, the papers gathered in Strzelecki *et al.*, 2014). Cities are characterized by the concentration of enormous labour resources that are not being harnessed at all or not being harnessed on par with their qualifications. That is one of the most serious problems facing the modern world: according to very cautious estimates, nearly one-third of all labour resources are in a very unfavourable situation, that is, with little chance of finding relatively gainful employment (Kleer, 2014). Such a situation is visible in cities, especially in big cities, and in particular in megacities.

The last factor that should be described here is health care. Surging population numbers, especially in cities, are linked to medical advances, which play a huge role that is indeed difficult to overestimate. Major health care centres have always been located in cities, significantly encouraging growth in the urban population, as access to such centres is theoretically easier and faster in urban agglomerations. Initially, it pertained only to selected, more affluent social groups. Over time, however, they have continued to spread to embrace other groups as well, though not necessarily on a universal basis. We should also add here that the old vision of health care as one of the public goods available free of charge, especially in welfare states, still lingers in the social awareness.

Let us now pause here and attempt to sum up, in a nutshell, what it is that drives the growth of population in megacities and acts as such a draw: first of all, the prospect of finding satisfactory employment, since megacities have become major centres of economic activity; secondly, education centres, which offer knowledge and opportunities for learning a profession that meets modern-day requirements; thirdly, possibilities related to such aspects as medical advances, gradual improvement in financial and housing conditions, job security, and perhaps security at large. Fourthly the ease of movement should be mentioned here, both thanks to the development of transportation infrastructure in the aftermath of globalization and because of the opening up of national economies and major migration flows, with a significant share of people on the move ultimately settling in large cities and megacities. Finally, the instruments of the information revolution facilitate greater visibility of the virtues and vices of such cities, and despite all the inconveniences and shortcomings of life there, all those arriving in megacities hold out hope that luck will ultimately prove to go their way. A number of the factors described here mesh together intricately into a certain interrelated whole.

1.6. Introduction into an Integral Theory of Megacities

Megacities were initially defined as urban areas with more than 4 million inhabitants (Dogan and Kasarda, 1988), then 8 million (Gilbert, 1996), and finally more than 10 million (UNDESA, 2008), with the latter figure currently being the generally accepted population criterion. While we cannot say that this view is universal, as some scholars for instance apply the term "megacity" to all urban agglomerations with a population of more than 5 million (Kraas *et al.*, 2014), the increasingly prevalent criterion — and the one applied in this volume — is nevertheless 10 million.

As megacities did not really emerge until the turn of the 20th and 21st centuries, when the urban population started to soar and major agglomerations started to expand at a disproportionately rapid pace, we can state that they represent a new phenomenon in the contemporary world economy. As such there is not yet really any overall theory referring to megacities inclusively, comprehensively able to explain the dynamics and character of their rise, the functions they play and might play in the future, as well as the advantages and negative externalities which follow from their emergence. Such an integral theory has yet to be developed for a number of reasons, many of which have also had a profound impact on research related to urban areas in general; several of these are as follows:

(1) With the advancement of science — especially after the onset of the industrial revolution, the formation of industrial civilization and expansion of Enlightenment thought — such research was initiated, but it was mainly (though not exclusively) concentrated on local and municipal government.
(2) Cities were usually an integral part of the larger state in which they were located (although there were also numerous city-states, for instance in the area of today's Italy), and as such they were viewed as an important factor in the cohesion of the state, due to the location of the seat of state power or its representative.
(3) Urban development was for centuries rather slow, and numerous wars and clashes on the European continent actively contributed to the repeated conquest and often destruction of urban centres.
(4) The true expansion of cities as a major phenomenon in its own right has occurred virtually only since the mid-20th century, and only then giving a serious impetus to the development of scientific inquiry dealing with different aspects of urban agglomerations.

As the phenomenon of megacities can be studied from the perspective of numerous disciplines, the existing literature has discussed it from many different perspectives, often not easily comparable. While it is understandable in this regard that any new phenomenon, especially one so complex, tends to be described, in the early stages at least, from whatever angle possible and to whatever extent it can be assimilated into an insulated manner or homogeneous approach. The problem has become more complex as the development of agglomerations has taken on a certain momentum (which in the case of megacities happened in the second half of the 20th century), as a result of which they have gained greater prominence in the world economy and are therefore of growing importance as uniform constructs and objects of research.

Based on an analysis of the existing literature and our own empirical research, we can conclude that the disciplines, sub-disciplines, or theoretical constructs that already have or could be applied to the study of megacities include (though are not exclusively limited to) the following:

- architecture and urban studies,
- demography,
- development economics,
- geography and economic geography,
- political science,
- public health and health services,
- public policy and administration,
- sociology,
- theories of economic systems,
- theories of networks,
- urban anthropology,
- urban economics.

In Table 1.3, we elaborate on some of these particular disciplines, noting the relevant sub-disciplines and approaches that may be usefully applied to the study of megacities.

We believe that there is no discipline able, on its own, to comprehensively and adequately explain megacities, their emergence, characteristics, and externalities resulting from their continued rise. Rather, multidisciplinary and indeed interdisciplinary approaches need to be applied. Such a broad, interdisciplinary approach to megacities studies, although not yet fully applied or shaped, can already be embraced in a specific mixture of

Table 1.3. Overview of disciplines and sub-disciplines for the study of megacities

Discipline	Stream and context
Anthropology	Urban anthropology
Architecture and urban studies	Architecture, city infrastructure, urban planning
Demography	Population of megacities trends and policies, migration, fertility and mortality, family and household studies
Development economics	Economic growth, development, urbanization, urban poverty
Geography Economic geography	Urban studies, space, spatial planning, environment, resources
Policy and administration	Public policy and administration
Political science	International relations, governance issues, urban governance, political power in urban agglomerations, political power of urban agglomerations
Public health and health services	Health, sanitation, disease control, public services
Sociology	Race and ethnic relations, ethnic tension, social structures, social interactions, mafia and gang violence, urban sociology and community relations, social behaviour in the urban context, social policy
Urban economics	Urbanization, economic efficiency of agglomeration

the disciplines identified in Table 1.3, related to one other to a greater or lesser extent.

1.7. Conclusions

What overall picture emerges from this introductory chapter? Firstly, empirical analysis of the demographic changes in the world economy, conducted from different perspectives, underscores the ongoing high level of urbanization. The highest population growth from 1950 to the beginning of 21st century was recorded in Asia, largely going hand-in-hand with a growing scale of urbanization there. However, by the end of the 21st century, 39% of the population is expected to live in Africa with more than 80% in urban areas. This means that the future dynamics of the world urbanization will be driven mainly by African cities, where urbanization processes are projected to speed up after 2020. Furthermore, our analysis has shown that — of all the categories of cities in terms of their size — it is the largest cities, especially megacities that have evolved and will continue to develop the most. The geographical concentration of urbanization and thus the location of cities and megacities has so far shifted from Europe towards developing countries, mainly to Asia, and is expected to further expand in Africa. The distinctive characteristics of different megacities, contingent on their region and countries and thus on the economic level of the states they emerged or are emerging in, led us to categorize them into three models of "evolutionary," "emerging," and "galloping" trajectories, depending on the timing and pace of their development.

The observed rise of megacities, as well as their connectivity and networks of interdependencies, show the significant role they play in the contemporary world economy and in the development of the modern-day world. Thus, as we have stressed, the phenomenon requires in-depth studies of multidisciplinary and interdisciplinary character, for gleaning a better understanding of megacities and consequently for complex policy implications. This conclusion has become widely recognized in the field, and it is indeed a fundamental assumption for many of the contributions to this volume.

References

Changsheng, C.H. and H. Jianwu (2014). A 10-year outlook. Falling growth potential and a new start of economic success. In Liu Shijin *et al.* (Eds.) *China's Next Decade: Rebuilding Economic Momentum & Balance*. Hong Kong: CLSA Books.

Dogan, M. and J.D. Kasarda (Eds.) (1988). *The Metropolis Era. Vol. I: A World of Giant Cities*. Newbury Park, CA: Sage.

Gilbert, A. (Ed.) (1996). *The Mega-city in Latin America*. Tokyo: United Nations University Press.

HYDE (2017). The History Database of the Global Environment (HYDE). Summary of historical population data. Retrieved from http://themasites.pbl.nl/tridion/en/themasites/hyde/basicdrivingfactors/population/index-2.html [access: 08.03.2017].

Keqiang, L. (2012). The greatest potential in expanding domestic demand is urbanization, *People's Daily* (Feb. 16, 2012).

Kleer, J. (2014). Marnotrastwo zasobów jako przejaw kryzysu systemowego. In J. Kleer (Ed.). *Czy kryzys światowych zasobów?* Warszawa: Komitet Prognoz "Polska 2000 Plus" przy Prezydium PAN.

Kraas, F., S. Aggarwal, M. Coy and G. Mertins (Eds.) (2014). *Megacities. Our Global Urban Future*. London: Springer.

Nawrot, K.A. (2012). 中国正处在十字路口中国, 2012 年09-10月刊总第28期, 环球亚洲杂志, 14-19 (EU-China Summit: China at a crossroads. Global Asia Magazine. No 28, November–December 2012, 14–19).

Nawrot, K.A. (2014). *Kraje rozwijające we współczesnej gospodarce światowej. Przyczynek do ekonomii rozwoju*. Warszawa: Wydawnictwo Naukowe Scholar.

Nawrot, K.A. (2015). Analiza porównawcza azjatyckich megamiast na przykładzie Tokio i Delhi. In J. Kleer, and Z. Strzelecki (Eds.). *Megamiasta Przyszłości. Szansa Czy Zagrożenie Rozwoju*. Warszawa: Komitet Prognoz "Polska 2000 Plus" przy Prezydium PAN, 299–311.

Rynarzewski, T., K.A. Nawrot, K. Zajączkowski and E. Cieślik (2017). *Potencjał gospodarczy i możliwości rozwojowe Afryki. Polska perspektywa*. Warszawa: Polskie Wydawnictwo Ekonomiczne.

Strzelecki, Z., E. Kryńska and J. Witkowski (Eds.) (2014). *Kryzys jakości życia*. Warszawa: Komitet Prognoz "Polska 2000 Plus" przy Prezydium PAN.

UNDESA (2008). United Nations, Department of Economic and Social Affairs, Population Division. *World Population Prospects: The 2007 Revision*. New York.

UNDESA (2014). United Nations, Department of Economic and Social Affairs, Population Division. *World Urbanization Prospects: The 2014 Revision*, CD-ROM Edition. New York.

UNDESA (2015). United Nations, Department of Economic and Social Affairs, Population Division. *World Population Prospects: The 2015 Revision*, Volume I: Comprehensive Tables. New York.

World Bank and DRC (2014). World Bank and the Development Research Center of the State Council, P.R. China. 2014. *Urban China: Towards Efficient, Inclusive and Sustainable Urbanization*. Washington DC: World Bank.

World Bank (2016). World Bank Database. Retrieved from http://worldbank.org [access: 15.03.2016].

Xian, Z. (2014). Urbanization. Quality more important than speed. In Liu Shijin *et al.* (Eds.), *China's Next Decade: Rebuilding Economic Momentum & Balance*. Hong Kong: CLSA Books.

2

MEGACITIES: DEVASTATION OF THE PUBLIC SPHERE

Jerzy Kleer

2.1. Introduction

The chapter analyzes the phenomenon of the devastation of the public sphere — understood as the system of interrelated links between society and the institutional/legal order, including its national-level and local institutions — specifically as it occurs in the world's largest urban centres (megacities). One of the central tenets is that as various countries have been drawn into the global-economy system at different times, with dissimilar economic levels and differing, sometimes even conflicting cultures, the continuity of their public spheres have become disrupted in various ways and their systems of values violated. Nowhere is this better evident than in megacities, where such degradation of the public sphere can only be expected to deepen in the foreseeable future.

We set the stage for these considerations by first examining the nature of the public sphere (particularly as it impacts upon major urban agglomerations), next by discussing the power of megacities and studying the evolving relationship between "central" (state) and "local" (city) authority. We then analyze the disruptions and pathologies resulting from the devastation of the public sphere in megacities, depicting them as existing an interrelated four-way configuration, namely: corruption, organized crime, the distinctive nature of the modern labour market, and problems related to the social (public) infrastructure. Overall, we posit that these components of the degradation of the public sphere are turning into a new regularity in the ongoing transition from the industrial to the knowledge-based stage of civilization. In closing, we briefly analyze the potential for the concept of global public goods to offer some means of resolution for the increasing degradation of the public sphere, particularly in megacities.

2.2. What is the Public Sphere?

The notion of the "public sphere" is a particularly crucial one for megacities, in that such high concentrations of people require the formulation of rules and regulations that govern the spatial functioning of such densely populated areas.

In general terms, the "public sphere" is here understood as a system of interrelated links between society and the institutional/legal order, together with its central and local institutions; it manifests itself in interactions between the state and society, between employers and employees, and between the organizational units of the state. As such, the public sphere has many dimensions and is shaped by various forces and mechanisms that change under the influence of economic expansion, demographic change, technological advancements, and culture. A particular influence is also exerted by spatial organization, sanctioned by the institutional and legal order put in place by the state or its institutions.

Roughly speaking, we can distinguish two systems that impact the shape and nature of the public sphere. One of them results from the controlling powers of the state, the other from mutual interactions between private entities that operate in a certain area. The two systems are strongly interrelated, enabling them to complement one another, and also to check and modify one other. We can posit, therefore, that the public sphere undergoes change, at varying speed, under the influence of numerous internal and external factors. Such a general assertion is theoretical but also universal and timeless: it makes no mention of the particular nature of this order, or the mutual relations between the system created by the state and the system shaped by private entities. In some periods, the public order may be influenced to a greater degree by the state's institutions vested with executive powers, in others by forces not directly linked to the state.

However, when one of these two sides wields dominant influence over the public order, this usually creates a certain disequilibrium that over time leads to degradation, be it greater or lesser in scale. At the theoretical level, we are unable to pinpoint such points of equilibrium, not to mention disequilibrium, because the pace of modern-day change is extremely rapid across all fields yet differs in each case.

At the general theoretical level, it is possible to identify four processes that have had a decisive impact on change in the public sphere. The most important of these was globalization, in tandem with the dissemination of the market economy based on the neoliberal model of economics, which demanded as much freedom for private entities as possible while striving to keep the state's regulatory functions to a minimum. This was the driving force for the opening up of borders and the free movement of factors of productions, goods, and services. The second was the information revolution, which created a network of relations that enveloped the world, reducing the constraints of time and space and altering the traditional understanding thereof, allowing people to learn more about "others," both as entities and as individuals. The third of these processes was the completion of de-colonization, which led to the emergence of numerous new states and the establishment of an institutional and legal order in these countries. The fourth and final was the collapse of socialism. In the countries affected, the public sphere had to be reorganized essentially "from scratch."

We mention these processes here chiefly in order to highlight the fact that they changed along different timeframes and wrought various consequences, both positive and negative. Irrespective of the nature of those changes, their simultaneous occurrence has inevitably led to the significant degradation of the public sphere, to a greater or lesser degree. There are a wide diversity of factors affecting mass and public interactions, which we will list here not so much in order of significance as in terms of their persistence. The first of these is the cultural system, which wields the greatest and, more importantly, the longest-lasting influence over mass and public interactions. The second is linked to the bonds that are created in the course of constant day-to-day professional activities and other forms of both social and political activity. The third characteristic of social interactions results from mutual relations between the state and society that take place via state institutions, chiefly ones linked to the public sector. These interactions do not function in isolation, but of course exert various forms of mutual influence, which impacts on the nature of the public sphere, sometimes bringing positive change, sometimes leading to its degradation. Moreover, note that the interactions in the public sphere that bear particular significance are those that follow from the cultural system: this is because culture wields both direct and indirect influence over other interactions, namely those related to working conditions and state institutions, or more broadly public institutions.

In order to understand the impact of culture on other manifestations and characteristics of social interactions, one must be fully aware of what components make up the cultural system and why changes within it are long-term phenomena. Without going into detail here, we will cite only the most important, formative components of the cultural systems. These are: language, tradition, religion, history, and attitudes to the state (Kleer, 2013). Combinations of these components vary by country, regardless of the fact that some of them are or may be convergent or very similar in specific states. What distinguishes individual communities most from one other pertains on the one hand to tradition and history and on the other to the relationship or mutual relations with the state. Relations between the state and society revolve around the extent to which the state is regarded as an overriding value, the degree of trust in the state, the extent to which members of society accept the state's general modernization goals, the nature of attitudes towards common goods, and acceptance of the state's policy towards various social groups in the context of equal rights, obligations, tolerance, as well as citizens of foreign countries and international organizations.

All these components of the cultural system, taken together, demonstrate why culture changes at a much slower pace than the other elements that form the public sphere and why it often represents an important element of its degradation. However, as we will address below, that is not to say that this is the only cause behind such disruption.

2.3. What Underlies the Power of Megacities?

As we have already noted in this volume, although population remains the most important criterion defining a megacity, other factors are also important for how dominant a given urban agglomeration is. The most important of these is economic potential, which may differ in individual cases yet is always of decisive importance. This chiefly means financial power, created in the modern-day world by financial institutions, ranging from stock markets, banks, and various financial consortiums to the headquarters of major corporations, especially international ones. From this perspective, megacities are places where important economic and financial decisions are made, impacting on economic processes stretching well beyond the city's borders, not only in its home country but across many economies, sectors, and branches, spread all across the globe. That, in turn, means that megacities remain very strongly "plugged into" the global economy. To put it yet another way, megacities are nexuses where decisions about the allocation of capital get made to a large or even decisive degree. At the same time, such decisions take account not so much of the situation or needs of the specific region, or the interests of the people employed by such corporations, as the interests of the organizations themselves, with profit-seeking always or almost always being the foremost criterion. As such, corporations may opt to relocate their business activities out of their country of origin, to economies in other cultural zones, in search of higher profits.

Megacities also serve as hubs of innovation, as sources of new organizational solutions, and as powerhouses of creativity on the part of individuals and institutions, all components that have a decisive impact on modern-day development. This is because they are home to numerous R&D facilities belonging to commercial organizations and institutions, collaborating with such centres of knowledge as colleges and universities, which are generally concentrated in major urban agglomerations. Such centres attract the most talented and the most creative individuals, offering potential career opportunities in business, science, and politics.

As a rule, megacities are major education centres characterized by the presence of numerous schools and universities, ensuring a higher calibre of education and, more importantly, creating better opportunities for later employment, either *in situ* or with organizations and enterprises elsewhere, as a diploma from a reputable university offers numerous privileges.

The phenomenon of megacities' power of attraction might best be explained psychologically rather than economically, in terms of migrants thinking along the lines of gaining possible opportunities. There is a perception that it is easier to make contacts in megacities, to meet someone who will more quickly recognize the value of the skills and ideas that young people have and help them get a better start in life.

Obviously, megacities have more advantages of this sort than we can fully list here. However, we should note one especially important aspect, namely their political clout. This influence is sometimes wielded indirectly, because important political decisions are made not in New York but in Washington, not in Shanghai but in Beijing. However, the influence of megacities on political decisions is still quite considerable, chiefly thanks to their economic power.

2.4. Central vs. Local Power

The problem of central vs. local power is an extraordinarily complex one, meriting special treatment here for at least several reasons. The population and GDP of a single megacity are, in many cases, equal to those of an average-sized country. Moreover, as we have noted, megacities are often home to numerous institutions that have influence stretching far beyond the borders of the given state. At the same time, relations between a specific megacity and the central government of the country to which it belongs have been further complicated by the persistent nature of certain measures by which states function and by certain conditions in which megacities exist as urban agglomerations.

We should start with the perhaps seemingly trivial statement that every city in any country is, of course, subject to the power of the central authorities of that country. In this sense, megacities, according to their traditional division, wield merely "local" authority and their powers result from the model in place in a given state. Although such powers may be greater or smaller in scope in particular cases, we should bear in mind that the model of the modern state was born in the mid-18th century, whereas megacities, at least in their fundamental mass, are a product of the latter half of the 20th century. Under this model, central state authorities are vested with a broad set of powers, which may be partially devolved to the local or regional authorities in a way that stems from the particularly balance of forces existing between them. Megacities, as a new phenomenon in this respect, have not been sufficiently addressed either in theory or in practice. Although such issues have been raised in some preliminary analyses (e.g. Barber, 2013), demanding that greater powers need to be delegated to city-level officials, such publications nevertheless resemble press commentaries more than scientific studies. As such, the problems remain essentially unresolved.

Without presenting a detailed analysis, here I would like to point out several issues that lie on the borderline between economics and politics. A state as a sovereign entity has the power to enter international agreements, whereas cities have traditionally been deprived of such powers. In most countries, the situation has not changed. Yet, in the modern-day world, major agglomerations are nevertheless forced to reach various international understandings, chiefly of an economic nature. This is done through the decision-making centres of major multinational corporations and financial institutions that engage in dealings with various states, which often translates into differences between the interests of multinational corporations or financial institutions and the interests of specific countries.[1]

Conflicts that arise in this field are less acute yet a lot more persistent, manifesting themselves in the reregistration of businesses to tax havens, the relocation of entire facilities to countries where production costs are lower, or in social approval for numerous "counterfeit" products. The list runs much longer, but all these phenomena are significant violations of the idea of state sovereignty. The activity of megacities is also part of this context.

Moreover, this problem seems even more complicated if we look at it from the global perspective. Modern-day globalization strives for the emergence of a global market governed by uniform rules respected by all of its participants. For that reason, such rules are, or should be, uniform. Specific countries, however, are highly diverse, not only in terms of their population numbers, economic development, social and political models, as well as the length of their existence as sovereign states but above all in terms of culture.

[1] One example being the sanctions imposed against Russia by the EU and the United States after the annexation of the Crimea.

One may of course complain that the state, as such, is an obsolete institution, yet it would be premature to consign the notion to the dustbin of history, since national identities are linked to the existence of states and to the attendant cultural systems, neither of which might be eliminated in any forecastable timeframe. Instead, we can identify the fundamental problems the modern state will need to resolve. After establishing this context, we should look at the possible relations that may develop between states as sovereign entities and megacities as major agglomerations.

Security should be regarded as an issue of fundamental importance in the modern era, and it has indeed been one of the priorities of the modern state since its inception. More importantly, the scope of the field has expanded continuously, both for political and above all economic and social reasons, which have also been the driving force behind the emergence of a new social structure. These same factors have simultaneously provoked constant and rapid movements of people from one place to another, and more importantly, the emergence of new, previously unknown types of labour. If we take into account all the changes that the modern state has undergone, we can observe not only the transition from the agrarian to industrial stages of civilization but also the beginnings of a knowledge-based society. Although the state has changed, the threats have not shrunk in scale or type, but have instead been continually on the rise. Security institutions have also changed and consolidated their power, but such alterations have progressed at a much slower pace than the emerging threats. When the level of threats to security changed more rapidly, so, too, did the institutions that safeguard security manage to respond, *albeit* with a certain delay; but the emergence of globalization, the opening up of national economies, and the widespread free movement of goods, services, and people have put security institutions at a disadvantage. States, and especially their major agglomerations (particularly megacities), have become multicultural and witnessed the emergence of threats linked to the coexistence of people who come from a variety of cultures and therefore subscribe to different values and have different world outlooks that cannot be mutually reconciled in a short period of time. Cultural changes take place a lot more slowly than economic or political changes. In this context, we can indeed talk of a clash of cultures and even civilizations, as described by Huntington (1996). Manifestations of this conflict, whether in the form described by Huntington or otherwise, are chiefly visible in urban agglomerations, in particular in megacities.

Consequently, a problem arises over the extent to which general state solutions in the sphere of public order, especially security, are adequately applicable to the functioning of megacities. Although most threats are universal in their nature, their intensity varies greatly within specific states, with the greatest dangers occurring in large urban centres.

Consequently, the following theoretical and practical question presents itself: Might the modern-day state end up devolving a large portion of its powers to megacities? There is, as yet, no good theoretical or practical answer to this question, for two quite different reasons. Devolving a greater scope of powers to major urban agglomerations may prompt their authorities, now or in the future, to seek to assume an ever-growing scope of power, not only in the field of security, thus prompting a profound modification or disruption of the existing institutional and legal order on the scale of the state. That, in turn, may mean more autonomy, if not formal or actual separation, from the state's jurisdiction and authority. Such tendencies can be observed in almost all major agglomerations, but one question seems fundamentally important yet also extremely difficult to answer: How much authority can be devolved to megacities without violating the cohesion of the state? The central authorities want to retain as much such power as possible, which hinders such agglomerations. As things now stand, conflicts between these decision-making centres are growing in number.

Another equally important problem, perhaps even more important, is posed by efforts to ensure relative stability on the scale of the state (stability not just in economic terms). The absence of such stability causes numerous problems in many fields of human activity, in the aftermath of numerous and very rapid changes exerting a significant impact on living conditions in society. This is further augmented by the greater visibility of political, economic, and social processes in today's world. Modern electronic technologies render problems related to living conditions and people's quality of life easily comparable, both within a specific country and on the international scale. One of the reasons behind this is the tendency to put economic growth on a pedestal as the main criterion of success in both quantitative and qualitative terms. Quantitative growth does not translate automatically into qualitative growth, as has been already proved in a sufficient number of cases.

In this context, the public sphere takes on special significance. This is chiefly, but not exclusively, because of demographic changes, understood in two ways: on the one hand, it is a result of the aforementioned rapid population growth, especially over the past half-century, while on the other, it is due to the even more rapid growth in urban population numbers, especially in major agglomerations. The problems posed by efforts to ensure relatively good living conditions for urban inhabitants are trapped in a certain institutional and legal vacuum. There are, as yet, no good solutions. Would it be sensible, both economically and socially, to devolve greater powers in shaping the public sphere to megacities? That we do not know for sure. Certain megacities have managed to resolve some of these problems to a certain degree, while others have failed. More importantly, however, all of them have witnessed the emergence of new, previously unknown problems or problems that did not exist on such a scale in the past. Examples of numerous positive solutions can be found in New York, London, and Tokyo, but even so, problems related to the public sphere are difficult to resolve, because they are present practically everywhere and are subject to such rapid and far-reaching change. Such change, however, is not the same everywhere, but instead varies in intensity, and without going into great detail we can state merely what can be empirically verified: that the most extensive and profound change takes place in megacities. This provides a broader context for the fundamental dilemma between the central authorities and the local authorities. Should the central authorities devolve a large share of their powers to the local authorities in areas experiencing the most profound, intensive, and rapid change? If the central government decides to take this step, we may witness the ever-more-autonomous status (or even secession) of existing megacities as well as other agglomerations that have yet to exceed 10 million inhabitants, which may indirectly undercut state cohesion.

Indeed, this poses an especially grave problem: over the past several decades, major agglomerations have rapidly expanded their numerous international links, not only economic, financial, and technological ones but also those related to scientific research and to major human migrations, both legal and illegal. Migrations, especially when they occur on a large scale, are invariably provoked by persecution on political, racial, or religious grounds, and as a rule, people decide to move from one place to another in search of better living conditions. Usually, the destinations of such migrations are major agglomerations, which, as previously mentioned, offer the best chances of finding better conditions of living, at least in the eyes of migrants.

2.5. Sources of the Degradation of the Public Sphere

The above discussion has now brought us to the pivotal problem of this chapter, namely the disruption of the public sphere in general, with special emphasis on such degradation in megacities. Let us first note that the degradation of the public sphere has two fundamental components, both of which have existed for decades, despite having different sources and functioning in different conditions. From a certain perspective, they are both well-known phenomena: one of them consists in the consequences of the dissemination of the market economy based on the neoliberal model of economics, while the other consists in social interactions that are rooted in fear, partly for psychological and partly for financial reasons. These two components are on the one hand responsible for the distinctive nature of the public sphere in today's world, and on the other they remain sources of its degradation.

In the long history of the dispute between supporters and opponents of the free market, a crucial juncture came with the dismantling of the welfare state, a model that had been dominant in developed capitalist states; this began for various reasons in the early 1970s. Together with the fall of socialism, rapid globalization, and the opening up of national markets, that process favoured the free market in the version proposed by the Chicago school of economics. Importantly, this model came to be presented as universal, applicable as a certain theoretical concept not only to economic processes but also to other social sciences (Becker, 1990). As such, the model was treated as a general-solution "toolbox" that was not built upon any particular values. That was, and still is, the fundamental shortcoming of this model, because certain values must lay at the foundation of any such model. That has entailed certain consequences, which will be discussed later in this analysis. For now, let us note that the adoption of this model as a universal concept, without heed for existing conditions, has had far-reaching consequences, which in the first place has imposed a focus on quantitative values, with individualism being put on a pedestal as an instrument of evaluation. That, in turn, has led to the marginalization of collaborative activities and goals.

Yet, the public sphere, as we understand it in this chapter and as we have defined it above, precisely consists in interactions between individuals and entities that function and act together for the sake of mutual benefits that are not necessarily measurable in quantitative terms and do not have a strictly pecuniary value. It represents, or should represent, the emergence and pursuit of certain common goals based on certain clear, *albeit* not necessarily uniform, values (Kleer, 2014). As such, the aforementioned reliance on individualism and the prioritization of quantity (over quality) has been at odds with and has wrought fundamental changes to the existing public sphere, namely its considerable degradation.

The market economy and individualism push for, or even require, the ever-greater accumulation of goods, wealth, capital, as well as certain imitative behaviour. Such a mechanism leads to far-reaching individualism along with the imitative adoption of existing institutional solutions, goods, and behaviours. People's pursuit of what they would like to have but do not, including what others do not yet have, drives not only the expansion of the market but also the transition to a market-focused society, in which people would like to be able to buy whatever they want and have the necessary resources to do so (Sandel, 2012). That, in turn, means that the market and market rules are devoid of any values and eliminate morality.

As a result of this type of market mechanism functioning both in specific countries and on a global scale, conditions were created for the emergence of a global elite, whose members could communicate and engage in business deals with one another despite their differing economic and political interests, thus creating a system of networks bonding together the wealthy. This, too, has contributed to the degradation of the public sphere at both national and international level, although that is in a sense another issue. We can only add that this system of links is, and will always be, an obstacle to the emergence of a relatively harmonious public sphere at the two aforementioned levels.

Since all this has affected countries that were drawn into the global-economy system at different times, with dissimilar economic levels and differing, sometimes even conflicting cultures, as the continuity of their public spheres has become disrupted and their systems of values violated, this has naturally led to the emergence of a range of numerous pathologies. These are phenomena that affect other spheres, too, but nowhere are they as powerful or intense, taken together, as they are in megacities. These disruptions and pathologies can be constructively construed as existing in an interrelated four-way configuration of factors, namely: corruption, organized crime, the nature of the modern labour market, and problems related to the social (public) infrastructure. In what follows, we will examine each of the four vertices of this configuration in turn, in order to lay out a broader context for discussing a certain more general phenomenon that has not yet been sufficiently articulated (at least not always and definitely not everywhere).

But first, let us posit a certain hypothesis which, in the present author's view, aptly describes the modern-day reality, at least with respect to megacities: coupled with changes in the fundamental means of production (as capital comes to be replaced by knowledge), surging urban population numbers, and especially the emergence of megacities, the aforementioned components of the degradation of the public sphere are turning into a new regularity in the ongoing transition from the industrial to the knowledge-based stage of civilization. Such a process is universal and existing theoretical concepts or even practical solutions in place in the modern state are unable to tackle this issue. This is further compounded by another factor, namely the simultaneous coexistence of many stages of civilization (agrarian, agrarian–industrial, and industrial civilization as well as the beginnings of a knowledge-based civilization), which even overlap with one another, posing additional difficulties in resolving these problems.

Various aspects of the above four-way configuration have been described on many occasions, but here they will be examined in terms of their impact on the disruption of the public sphere at country-specific and global level. On the one hand, all these components have become very tightly intertwined. On the other, megacities have caused them to acquire new, previously unknown dimensions through their mass scale and impact on other forms of activity in both the private and the public sector, which have become very closely interwoven, indeed on an unprecedented scale. More importantly, any reverting to the old order is out of the question (West, 2012).

2.5.1. Corruption

In the modern-day world, corruption is based not so much and not only on the shortcomings of individual human beings as on the distinguishing features of the era. We will now seek to bring into sharper focus three processes characteristic of present-day development and the conditions in which the world's community functions.

The first of these is the international nature of activity on a global scale, where sovereign states nevertheless remain dominant. One of the manifestations of this is that the institutional and legal order of every state, despite numerous modifications, is not well adjusted to the existing area (territory) and the preferences that prevail there. More importantly, this order, despite the influence of external forces, is characterized by a significant degree of continuity. Yet, on the other hand, the pace of changes taking place in various spheres is so rapid and the interests of individual countries are so divergent that they may not be taken into account, at least not to a sufficient degree. Consequently, entities that operate in the global market may respond to this by opting not to heed rules and prohibitions, or to respect them only to an insufficient degree, in order to gain the relevant benefits. This may be done, at least partially, by corrupting representatives of public administration and individual politicians. This is made all the more easier by the fact that pay levels in this group are significantly below the salaries of top executives at major corporations or even middle-level management. In the modern era, as we have already noted, income is one of the most important criteria of prestige and this is why corruption has emerged on an enormous scale. Of course, one may argue over in which kinds of countries the administrative apparatus and politicians are especially susceptible to corruption, but that would require a separate analysis. Available studies show that there is practically no country in the modern-day world that is wholly corruption-free, although we can probably say that the political system, level of economic development, and type of culture are largely interdependent factors in this context.

2.5.2. Organized crime

Like corruption, various forms of organized crime and mafia groups similarly occur at the level of an individual state but also have a more general global nature. And again, although such phenomena are present everywhere, they are especially well-organized and function particularly effectively in major agglomerations, especially in megacities.

Mafia activity may vary, but there are several phenomena that are new, at least in terms of their scale, being a product of the contemporary world and of what sociological literature refers to as post-modern society. Firstly, the consequences of the information revolution have been coupled with the rapid advancement of a certain moral and lifestyle revolution that has largely challenged the existing prohibitions against narcotics, prostitution, illegal immigration, smuggled goods, and counterfeit products, holding instead that these are not only profitable but also to some degree acceptable forms of activity among certain rather large social groups (not necessarily those with the lowest income levels). In some countries, they even might enjoy informal permission, if not from the state authorities then from certain groups of politicians and representatives of public administration. Secondly, organized criminal groups are strongly interlinked and therefore often permeate one another, at least in terms of the pursuit of certain goals related to illicit business activity. For that matter, organized crime often serves the interests of the world of business, sometimes domestically, sometimes internationally. In certain cases, it may even be used to address specific political problems.

Irrespective of the scale of such activity in individual countries or in specific megacities, this phenomenon invariably leads to the degradation of the public sphere. Such negative phenomena tend to grow in scale as income differentials widen. Social groups with the highest income levels often resort to the services of criminal groups to advance the interests of specific individuals or the organizations they represent.

Such organizations certainly also existed before the globalization era, for example, in the period of prohibition in the United States. Although the repeal of prohibition did nothing to eradicate mafia organizations and organized criminal groups, the scale of the phenomenon was indeed much smaller then, as compared to the modern-day world. Nowadays such phenomena can be observed both in developed and in developing countries, with megacities being major centres of such organizations, at least in terms of the scope of their activity.

Overall, we can doubt whether it is possible for this problem to be resolved in the context of specific states, because this is a phenomenon of an international nature that, whilst degrading the public sphere in specific countries, prevents the establishment of a certain harmonious order on a global scale.

2.5.3. The distinctive nature of the modern labour market

In one sense, issues related to the labour market that contribute to the degradation of the public sphere, especially in major agglomerations (megacities), are simple to consider, yet in another sense they are extremely complex. The task is a simple one in that it is not difficult to list numerous and highly diverse groups of individuals whose employment status is insufficiently secure, who are constantly in search of employment, who can only find employment well below their qualifications, or who live on welfare or remain permanently excluded, forced to live in slums. The larger the agglomeration, the broader the scope of such phenomena, as is especially but not exclusively visible in megacities following the path of the third model of megacities rise described in the previous chapter (characterized by rapid and chaotic development in developing countries).

Yet, while listing the components making up the complex nature of today's labour market is relatively simple, this will still not fully capture the particular distinctiveness of the labour market — even if we highlight the emergence of the "precariat" (Standing, 2014) as a new social group that consists of young, educated, and often highly qualified potential workers employed under what are sometimes called "junk contracts," or short-term agreements that offer little job security. Rather, we can attempt to sum up the distinctive essence of today's labour market in a few points. Firstly, we need to note what might be referred to as the greater visibility of unemployment, chiefly in major cities (megacities), where job seekers are usually young and well-educated people; megacities are also particularly characterized by the presence of sizeable slums, concentrations of people without jobs, apartments, and public support. Secondly, a growing problem in megacities is that labour supply exceeds demand and this gap continues to widen, not only in crisis periods but also in times of prosperity, chiefly because the information revolution and technological advancements continue to eliminate jobs, both in the service sector and in industry. In this context, we should stress that neither the scholarly research community nor the public authorities properly anticipated the consequences of the growing importance of the service sector in the economy, specifically from the perspective of employment. Thirdly and perhaps most importantly, there are various forms of unrest or rebellions that may take place in major agglomerations for political, social, and cultural reasons. Megacity inhabitants, especially young people whose start in life has not been very successful, are usually more susceptible to various populist movements, no matter what their particular political leanings may be.

All this contributes very powerfully to the devastation of the public sphere. This is partly because there once used to be institutions and mechanisms that in the past mitigated emerging unemployment or even exclusion, but globalization coincided in time with a population explosion and the collapse of the welfare state. The introduction of the neoliberal model of economics led to the wide-ranging commercialization of public services, which in the past had worked as a kind of safety-valve alleviating tensions related to unemployment, housing, and social assistance for the excluded or those in need. The confluence of all these processes at one and the same time has led to the devastation of the public sphere on a previously unknown scale and, more importantly, to the emergence of new threats.

All these aspects are especially visible in megacities, which have been expanding rapidly without reasonable urban planning efforts or funding for social assistance, not to mention health care, education, and other services that were in the past left to the discretion of the local authorities, supported by the central government. More importantly, as yet, no reasonable vision has been proposed for the potential resolution of such problems, at least over the course of the next several decades. Without attempting to rank the all individual components of the degradation of the public sphere in any more comprehensive way, we can conclude that the modern labour market in the broad sense is the most destructive factor for the public sphere, both through the squandering of labour resources (both well-educated workers and those less educated or uneducated) and through the creation of a potentially explosive element.

2.5.4. Problems related to the social (public) infrastructure

A developed, well-operating social infrastructure is especially sorely needed in major urban agglomerations, especially megacities. This means not only infrastructure related to the labour market but above all the infrastructure that ensures the relatively correct functioning of the whole of the urban sphere. This first and foremost means security, good and efficient transportation, sufficient housing (especially public housing), a good energy network, such public services as education, health care, social assistance, rational urban planning, and the proper climate-related architecture, in addition to many other elements. From this perspective, it is impossible to treat all megacities in any uniform way, given the diversity of infrastructural problems they face and the varying degree to which those problems are being resolved. Nonetheless, degradation of the public sphere occurs in every megacity, despite varying in strength and intensity.

2.6. Several General Conclusions

So, can the degradation of the public sphere be mitigated or countered? If so, then how? To attempt to answer those questions in very general terms, let us start by reiterating that megacities pose a challenge:

- to the states in which they are located,
- to their own native population and incoming migrants,
- often to the external world, to which they are directly linked.

The differing challenges in this array can or must be resolved differently depending on country-specific factors, on the economic and political model in place in a given country, and on the degree of their universality (to what extent they apply to a only a single country, a larger group of countries, or even the whole of the world).

If we consider this problem in the context of the sovereign state, these challenges raise issues of two different sorts. The first pertains to the area of social infrastructure, which largely remains at the discretion of the local governments and is linked to the powers vested in them by the central authorities, that is, the extent of de-centralization and devolved authority on the one hand, and the efficiency and determination shown by the local authorities on the other. The second hinges on the dominant economic and political model and cultural system.

Megacities are "producers" of modern innovation in the broadest sense, whilst being simultaneously characterized by the most advanced degradation of the old order (here meaning both the institutional and legal order and traditional bureaucracy together with various attendant pathologies, mentioned earlier in this analysis). New measures and solutions, not necessarily revolutionary ones, may be developed by local governments on condition that the central government devolves some of its powers to them. These may, or in fact should, pertain to areas or problems that do not occur in other regions of the country, or do so only a very small scale. That is one of the most sensitive issues, in that they may be perceived as detracting not only from the formal powers of the central authorities but above all from their prestige. Nonetheless, this process will necessarily continue as megacities continue to grow in strength.

The largest challenges that megacities face are posed by their native residents *vis-à-vis* incoming migrants. Such challenges will continue to cumulate as a result of the deficit of various public services and goods, which may lead to various forms of unrest and rebellions, especially as there are more and more people who can be described as "others," "outsiders," outgroup members: migrants that hail from elsewhere and adhere to different cultural systems. In any city of millions upon millions inhabitants, such phenomena are nothing unusual, at least not in the modern era. At the same time, there is nothing to indicate that such processes might be resolved in the foreseeable future (say, the next two decades), for a number of important reasons — here, we will name three of them that are especially conducive to conflict. The first is the aforementioned modern labour market, chiefly as a result of enormous transformations related to the transition from one stage of civilization to another and, by the same token, the process of adjustment, which is extremely difficult both to job seekers and to economic entities. Another is the constant influx of migrants from other regions in the same country as well as legal and illegal immigrants from other countries, a process that exacerbates the situation yet is difficult to stop. It hinders any reasonable planning in the creation of jobs, because the future is largely unpredictable, both from the perspective of the public administration bodies and in terms of the behaviour of economic entities, which may, given open markets, opt to transfer their business to locations they see as more attractive.

The second issue is a result of the dominant economic model, which has led to the commercialization of most public goods. If we assume that households can somehow manage to cope under conditions of full or relatively full employment, today's situation in the labour market is in many cases dramatic. At the same time, institutional solutions under the neoliberal model provide no possibility of satisfying even to a minimum degree the demand for these public goods and services, especially in such agglomerations as megacities. This is one of the most serious flash points and sources of social unrest, especially in major agglomerations, where numerous conflicts can arise between communities rooted in various cultures.

The third major challenge posed by the expansion of megacities is the degradation of the environment, both the environment in which the urban community functions and its external expansion. Since the demand for land, needed by expanding urban agglomerations, is growing constantly, more and more land is simply being "taken in" without enough attention being paid to the environmental consequences thereof, which impact significantly on the living conditions of the inhabitants of such areas. It is difficult to predict all the long-term consequences of this process, but there is no doubt that they are and will remain negative.

These final considerations have taken account of the most important country-specific problems, but have so far omitted international relations. Yet, as we have noted, megacities do have numerous ever-expanding external links, chiefly via financial institutions and economic entities that operate in the global market. On the one hand, this situation brings certain, sometimes numerous benefits. On the other, it also hinders attempts at reforming the functioning of megacities. As we have mentioned repeatedly, this process is hampered by the dominant model in the global market as well as by the interests and ambitions of certain global powers. As such, we can conclude that is every indication that degradation of the public sphere, at the megacity level, national level, and on the global scale, will continue to deepen.

2.7. Conclusions and Prospects

We will not, however, finish this chapter on such a pessimistic note. Although the degradation of the public sphere will indeed continue to intensify under the influence of the neoliberal model of economics, which is now dominant on a global scale and will probably remain so for a period that is difficult to determine, there is a certain theoretical and partially also functional concept that stands a certain chance of mitigating these negative consequences, which we will now briefly examine.

But first, before we present it, let us note that none of the existing general economic, political, or social concepts provides relevant instruments, be they theoretical or practical, for the resolution of the existing difficulties. This is because the world is too diverse for any single concept to be able to suffice for this purpose.

For over a decade and a half, attempts have been made to explore the notion of *global public goods* and promote the concept as a remedy for the extant problems (Kaul *et al.*, 1999; Ott, 2002; Kaul, 2003; Kleer, 2006; Stiglitz, 2006; and many others). In this framework, some such goods are seen as having certain special characteristics that entail certain partial solutions of a global reach, others are regional in their reach, still others pertain to only several countries that face problems of a similar kind. However, here we can list five common characteristics of global public goods that underlie their potential effectiveness in the resolution of most of the problems that have accumulated — including ones that have yet to arise in the course of further development.

The first characteristic is the voluntary nature of understandings reached between at least two countries striving to resolve a specific problem. In most cases, such arrangements should be open: other states that can see benefits from such joint action should be free to join in, as long as they respect the established rules. This approach is in turn related to the second principle, namely compromise-seeking, which means the possibility of negotiating the form of common measures to be taken, the domain they should pertain to, the timeframe of such a mutual understanding (which is especially important in certain situations), as well as its scope and methods of funding. In order to be effective and efficient, every public good requires specific outlays. Since various states that differ in their economic potential and amount of resources are free to join such understandings, the issue of how specific projects should be financed invariably poses a difficult problem to resolve. The third principle pertains to trust between the parties to such common understandings. Such trust is generally important, in that specific solutions can benefit all partners, but here it also takes on even greater significance, because not all states are equally strong and they function amidst differing conditions. Hence, this principle should ensure that no state will take advantage of its less powerful, less efficient, or less affluent partners. The fourth principle is the adoption of partial solutions, at least at the initial stage. This is extremely important, as the actual results of efforts to resolve partial problems may demonstrate the effectiveness of further cooperation. If partial solutions prove effective, the partners may agree to expand them to cover other areas. The fifth and final characteristic involves not only the taking of common action but also the "production of common goods," which brings benefits to each country individually. When this happens, it brings into focus the fundamental principle behind the emergence of a real public good.

Whether such a theoretical concept is realistic will be determined by the practical solutions applied. Some of them have worked well in practice. Indeed, there are many, though maybe not enough, examples of such solutions, which have nonetheless not always been evaluated in the same way (although that represents a separate issue to address).

Today, it is difficult to say to what extent this theoretical concept will ultimately triumph, given the prevalent character of avarice and greed for profit. But we should expect that at some point in the future, perhaps not too distant, perhaps quite distant, the devastation of the public sphere will grow so problematic that the world, certainly individual counties, and especially megacities, will conclude that it is time to make attempts to remedy the situation. Perhaps then, the theoretical concept of global public goods will be tested through greater application in practice.

References

Barber, B.R. (2013). *If Mayors Ruled the World: Dysfunctional Nations, Rising Cities*. New Haven & London: Yale University Press.

Becker, G.S. (1990). *The Economic Approach to Human Behavior*. Chicago: Chicago University Press.

Huntington, S.P. (1996). *The Clash of Civilizations and the Remaking of World Order*. New York: Touchstone.

Kaul, I. (2003). *Providing Public Goods: Managing Globalization*. Executive Summary. New York: Oxford.

Kaul, I., I. Grunberg and M.A. Stern (1999). *Global Public Goods*. New York: Oxford University Press.

Kleer, J. (2006). *Globalizacja a państwo narodowe i usługi publiczne*. Warszawa: Komitet Prognoz "Polska 2000 Plus" przy Prezydium PAN.

Kleer, J. (2013). *Kulturowe uwarunkowania modernizacji. Droga do spójności społeczno-ekonomicznej*. Warszawa: PWN.

Kleer, J. (2014). Instytucjonalizacja przestrzeni publicznej poprzez dobra publiczne. *Gospodarka Narodowa*, 5, 29–52.

Ott, A.F. (2002). *The Public Sector in the Global Economy: From the Driver's Seat to the Back Seat*. Cheltenham: Edward Elgar.

Sandel, M. (2012). *What Many Can't Buy: The Moral Limits of Markets*. New York: Farrar, Straus and Giroux.

Standing, G. (2014). *The Precariat: The New Dangerous Class*. London: Bloomsbury.

Stiglitz, J.E. (2006). Global public goods and global finance: Does global governance ensure that the global public interest is served? In J.P. Touffut (Ed.). *Advancing Public Goods*. Paris, 149–164.

West, S. (2012). The decline of the welfare state. Can the European Union harmonize pension policy? *Colgate Academic Review*, 5(8), 47–57.

3

FROM METROPOLIS TO MEGACITY

Piotr Korcelli and Ewa Korcelli-Olejniczak

3.1. Introduction

The notion of *megacity*, which is generally defined by referring to sheer population size of an urban centre (an urban agglomeration), may be more closely interpreted when confronted with the traditional, well-established notion of *metropolis*. This seems to be in particular so since, while the two concepts are frequently used interchangeably (Hall and Pain, 2006), they may also be perceived as mutually contrasting.

Most of the large cites today aspire to the rank of a metropolitan centre. The definitions of a metropolitan centre, however, as applied in international comparative urban studies, comprise several other criteria aside from population number, which are regarded as the notion's essential components. They relate both to specific characteristics of the built environment, such as the presence of unique urban design forms, advanced technical infrastructure, and high quality of public space, as well as to the performed metropolitan functions (Knox and Taylor, 1995). The latter, in addition to highly specialized economic activities with long range of influence in the domain of finance, include corporate control and high-tech industries, as well as important political and symbolic functions. At the same time, the notion of contemporary metropolis is associated with centre of culture, research and education, innovations, international transport, and tourism (ESPON, 2004). All this forms the basis for the growing interaction among metropolitan centres and the emergence of inter-metropolitan networks (Florida, 2002).

Other prominent features of the modern metropolis pertain to its administrative regime and social structure, by emphasizing the importance of local governance, the share and the role of the middle class, and the functioning of the civil society. Metropolitan cities are normally characterized by high social diversity and social mobility as well as high tolerance level which, together with the available resources of talent and advanced technology, sustain creativity, hence providing such centres with competitive advantage in their economic interactions on national and international urban systems scale.

Metropolitan cities tend to be strongly integrated with their close hinterland — the suburban and peri-urban zones — constitutive parts of *metropolitan areas.*[1] For the sake of empirical analyses, it is usually the metropolitan area, delineated according to spatial extent of metropolitan labour and housing markets that is identified with the notion of metropolis. According to some views, one can speak of metropolitan areas *per se* when not solely the central city, but the outlying zones (i.e. the metropolitan ring) as well perform metropolitan functions by providing locations to important institutions and high ranking, specialized economic activities.

Since most of the criteria used in order to identify metropolises among larger sets of urban centres are of qualitative nature, this category tends to become inflated, so as to include cities varying largely in size and range of influence. This is especially true in the case of policy-oriented studies and documents, which refer, among others, to metropolitan centres of the European, national and regional rank. Effectively, one deals with a hierarchical pattern of cities of metropolitan and semi-metropolitan character.

---

[1]The shaping of metropolitan areas is conceptualized as a model of city development stages (Berg van den *et al.*, 1982), or, city life cycles (Hall and Hay, 1980), consisting of successive phases of: spatial concentration (or, urbanization), de-concentration (suburbanization), dispersion (des-urbanization) and, finally, spatial re-concentration (re-urbanization). Economic mechanism of this transition in given in Alonso's (1964) Urban Land Use Theory.

The very apex of such a hierarchy is occupied by *world cities* (Friedmann, 1986), or *global cities* (Sassen, 1991)[2] selected on the basis of limited sets of attributes only — mainly the ranking and spatial range of economic functions. Among such urban centres one finds, along with North American and European metropolises, also the so-called peripheral cities, the large urban agglomerations of Asia, Latin America, and, more recently, Africa. According to these classifications based on population numbers, cities in the latter group account already for the majority, and will undoubtedly achieve full dominance in near future. Their accelerated growth during the last several decades is closely related to the expansion of economic corporate activities of transnational scale and the emergence of global financial markets.

In line with global standards, one can observe a tendency to diversification of large urban centres along with the advancing globalization phenomena, and, at the same time, to a blurring of some of the traditional dividing lines between them. In this chapter, questions are raised concerning factors that contribute to these seemingly contradictory developments. The section below presents a review and evaluation of selected future urbanization scenarios for Europe, with links to those concepts that point to discontinuities in observed "metropolization" trends. Section 3 is focused on functional and physical evolution of the rapidly expanding megacities in developing countries, with the scope of change illustrated by referring to several representative cases. The final section offers a discussion on universal and place-specific traits in the evolution of large cities, and on the global dimension of their interdependence.

3.2. Metropolitan Development Trends and Scenarios for Europe

The global market dynamics, together with the transition towards information processing economy and the prevailing neoliberal policies are often held responsible for the acceleration of the metropolization processes in Europe (Hall, 1993).[3] The national capital cities (and in larger

---

[2] Differences between the two concepts are explained in Derudder *et al.* (2012).

[3] In case of Europe, it is not more than 10–12 million inhabitants within metropolitan area boundaries (ESPON, 2007). In this context, the following opinion by Hall (1990: 181),

countries, the major regional centres) in particular function as the poles of attraction for specialized economic activities and qualified labour resources. The metropolization phenomena are actually promoted by political factors at both city and national levels, with an aim to strengthen the international competitiveness of large urban centres, and of the countries in which these cities are situated (Kunzmann, 2008).

Under a high urbanization level and slow changes in overall population,[4] the problem of a city size becomes overshadowed by issues related to spatial structure, including the utilization of urban (especially of suburban and peri-urban) space. In numerous, future-oriented studies, these questions, as well as relations between cities of various functional types and size categories are traced against the possible impact of, and interaction between, exogenous factors in the area of technology, economy, demography, the natural environment, and public policy. An illustrative analysis of the significance of such factors and their spatial outcomes is provided in the form of future development scenarios with a mid-21st century perspective, elaborated in the EU 6th Framework Programme Project entitled *Peri-urban land-use relationships,* which is referring to the work of IPCC — The International Panel on Global Climate Change, an organisation of the UN Environmental Programme (Nilsson *et al.*, 2013; Korcelli *et al.*, 2012).[5]

In the A1 — *Hyper-tech* scenario, the development of new technologies combined with a decrease of energy expense lead to a contraction of transport cost and an increase in spatial population mobility. They anticipate a rapid diffusion of innovations, related to an expansion of the ICT sector, as well as the overall economic growth spurred by noticeable progress in international collaboration. According to this scenario, the

---

referring to de-industrialization, and the so-called *regional shift* — de-concentration of economic functions towards medium-to-large cities may be of interest: "these trends seem to spell a new and deep threat to the traditional great city that owed its rise to the manufacturing and port activities of what Patrick Geddes and Lewis Mumford called the Paleotechnic era."

[4]Numerous cities in Europe experience a decrease of population size, and the problem of *shrinking cities* is frequently discussed in urban studies literature.

[5]The emerging patterns of social and economic segmentation in large North American cities have been generalized by Soja (2000) in his concept of *postmetropolis.*

metropolization of space accelerates. Labour markets in large urban centres become extended owing to the decreasing friction of space, even if some of daily commuting to work becomes replaced by tele-working. Suburban and peri-urban zones expand further, forming dispersed, spatially discontinuous settlement patterns. At the same time, because of population outflow, some inner-city districts witness a progressing deterioration of the urban fabric, including a degradation of technical infrastructure. Notable changes affect rural areas that experience continuing population losses. Owing to a growing productivity, a part of agricultural land is turned into green open spaces, such as natural reserves and landscape parks. On the national, as well as international level, a concentration of highly specialized functions in a limited number of first-order metropolitan areas brings a relative decline in importance of regional centres and smaller towns.

The A2 Scenario of *Extreme water* presents a future in which technological progress is slower, and economic development weaker, while strongly differentiated in space. The intensification of global warming with vacillations of water balance constitutes the main exogenous factor of change. In countries and regions with efficient systems of public administration and planning (Randstad, Holland, or the region of London) proactive adaptation strategies are applied which mitigate the impact of natural disasters upon economic activity and human settlement. In other areas, ecosystems instability may impair economic and social functions (in sectors such as transportation or tourism) that are of vital importance to some cities and regions, and can lead to disintegration of settlement systems. As a result, there is an increase of socio-economic polarization in space. These problems are aggravated by the rapidly growing number of immigrants — the "environmental refugees" both from within, and outside Europe.

According to the B1 Scenario of *Carbon-Control World,* rapid technological progress, and collaborative approaches creating conditions for gradual convergence of GDP *per capita* at international level are focused upon a rational utilization of natural resources, the already depleted oil and gas reserves in particular. New resource efficient technologies are developed and instruments introduced (including taxation) aiming to control energy consumption and pollution. This leads to a high total energy and transportation cost. Public transport infrastructure is extended and its use promoted. Under such conditions, production and distribution become re-oriented towards local markets, while territorial expansion of metropolitan areas is halted as the effect of changing locational preferences of companies and households. There is a return to compact urban forms and a clustering of settlement in peri-urban zones. This does not, however, prevent a continuing depopulation of peripherally situated rural regions and an economic decline of smaller urban places.

The B2 scenario of *Social Fragmentation* presents a pattern of socio-economic polarization of urbanized space which stems from advancing population ageing what generates immigration and, effectively, changes in ethnic composition of the city inhabitants. A major consequence of these trends is a decline in mutual trust and cooperative attitudes on a civic, as well as a national and international scale. Conflicting interests arise in relation to the position and interests of various ethnic communities, as well as with regard to the directions and volume of intergenerational financial transfers. Growing social disintegration finds a reflection in the intensification of spatial divides. Large cities, their inner districts in particular, are being inhabited increasingly by recent immigrants (their concentration in metropolitan centres is one of the general international migration rules). Conversely, the native population occupies the suburban zones, as well as "green enclaves" situated in more distant, peri-urban areas. With large urban centres suffering from aggravating social and economic crisis, the medium-sized and smaller towns experience a renaissance, by attracting residents as well as both routine and more specialized production and service functions. There are growing spatial disparities in socio-economic development on intra- and interregional as well as international level.

The above scenarios can be interpreted as four alternative solutions out of the theoretically unlimited number. These are not equally probable directions of urban change. Scenario A1 is the nearest to the presently observed, on-going metropolization tendencies in Europe. Conversely, Scenario B1, a rather utopian sustainable development path, implies a trend turnaround, and a return to more traditional settlement forms of compact cities and nested, hierarchical urban networks. In the two other scenarios, that is, A2 and B2, the vulnerability of contemporary patterns of human settlement to negative external forces is underlined, however, within long-term perspective.

The latter of the two scenarios is of particular interest in the context of the present chapter, as it implies a growing interdependence between processes and phenomena that affect large urban centres at the global level. Demographic change, especially population ageing, and its long-term consequences relating to shrinking labour resources and immigration pressure, are well recognized issues both in scientific and policy focused debate in Europe, and the need to design complex adaptation strategies is often articulated (Kotowska, 2014). Such strategies, however, can hardly prevent the anticipated transformation of socio-spatial structure of large European cities, since the observed demographic change is paralleled and reinforced by globalization-induced economic change. Delocalization of manufacturing production to countries with low labour cost, combined with increasing immigration volume, are reflected by a growing segmentation of labour markets and an intensifying social polarization of urban space. Such trends lead to the emergence of the *dual city* (Kempen, 1994), in which new socio-economic disparities are superimposed upon their earlier patterns. Therefore, certain traditional boundary lines between the "old" metropolitan cities of the developed countries and the "new" megacities tend to become less distinct than before.[6]

3.3. Peripheral Megacities — Patterns and Factors of Change

In confrontation with contemporary metropolitan centres of Europe or North America, the megacities of the South tend to display contrasts with regard to such typological criteria as quality of urban space, social structure and community development, or city-hinterland relations. They experience a rapidly growing importance in the field of specialized economic activities that are normally allocated to the category of metropolitan functions. This tendency is clearly reflected in the gradual extension of the so-called global city networks (Taylor *et al.*, 2012), which are delimited

---

[6] For a more extensive discussion on alternative scenarios and their implications see Korcelli-Olejniczak and Korcelli (2015).

on the basis of office locations of transnational corporations performing advanced services such as offering expertise in advertising, law, financial services, business accountancy, and management consultancy. At the same time, along with the emergence and development of the so-called new industrialized countries, one can observe a growing differentiation among the megacities in question, with some of them "graduating," that is, becoming internationally recognized as major, global metropolises.

Insofar as the rate and patterns of change are concerned, there are some general directions related to the overall development level of the respective countries or their aggregates, as well as tendencies specific to individual cities and regions. For example, Mumbai (Bombay), India's main economic centre, has witnessed de-industrialization, similar to the one experienced by European metropolises; its famous textile industry shrunk dramatically during the 1980s and the 1990s, mainly as an effect of relocation to smaller urban places. This became a source of a deep socio-economic crisis in the city. More recently, the new economy has been growing based on financial and other services, as well as information technology. It has brought about an increase in the number of relatively highly paid jobs, hence, generating the development of new upper-middle class which constitutes only a tiny share of the city's estimated 12 million inhabitants (Nijman, 2012).

While Mumbai is often listed among global cities, Accra, the capital of Ghana can be characterized as a "globalizing city in transformation" (Grant, 2012). Although only a very small part of activities carried on there is directly encompassed in the global economic circuit. There are, however, notable spillover effects, in the form of flows and development impulses, from the formal to informal sector of economy. The inflow of foreign direct investments, together with those linked with remittance funds, is accompanied by growing social polarization of the rapidly expanding urbanized area, with enclaves of modern residences, offices, and services situated in the vicinity of the spreading slum districts.

In the case of Jakarta, the rapid growth of the city and the urban agglomeration during the last decades has been closely tied with the development of export-oriented manufacturing activities, branches such as apparel, and electronic industries. The relatively stable employment provided by this sector, even at low-income level, may be interpreted as a factor restricting social polarization in the Indonesian capital (Parnreiter, 1999). Concurrently, the burgeoning state administration, together with the growth of related services are held responsible for notable increments in the size of middle-income groups, and for modernization of some parts of Jakarta's urban space.

A different development stage is exemplified by the case of Mexico City — a classic representative of megacities of global significance. Its dominant position at the national level has to some extent diminished since the late 1980s, owing to the emergence of the industrialized zone along the northern border with the United States, as well as the development of major tourist and recreational centres in the south. Mexico City's economic profile markedly changed, with an increase of the service sector, including notable strengthening of the role of economic control functions (Parnreiter, 2012) at the expense of manufacturing, which had earlier been favoured by import-oriented policies of the state. This change has been conducive to growing social polarization. Due to problems arising from the sheer size of the urban agglomeration and a high concentration of population and work places within a bounded territory that features difficult environmental conditions, Mexico City has witnessed net migratory outflow which is targeted mainly at smaller urban centres in the surrounding region (Aguilar, 1999; Aguilar and Lopez-Guerrero, 2014).

As the examples above indicate, all the differences among the cities, notwithstanding their contemporary development trends, can be traced to global economic integration. Still, initial conditions represent an important factor in this respect. Thus, intensive immigration and explosive growth correspond to a city development phase in which, as in the case of Jakarta, export-oriented manufacturing activities (crude oil prospecting and extracting in Accra) become its leading exogenous function. When globalization processes mark a transition from manufacturing-based to service sector-based model, one of the significant consequences is increasing socio-economic polarization of urban space (Parnreiter, 1999).

The latter point brings us back to the questions raised at the outset of the chapter, as the turn towards service-dominated functional profile is the major trend in the case of large urban centres of developed countries today. So is the socio-economic polarization of urban space. Hence, in terms of dynamics, one can ask with regard to relationships between the notions of metropolis and the megacity, whether it may be relevant to speak of a continuum, which includes both explicit as well as intermediate, or transitional development forms.

Concerning the future, it is important to note that, while in developed countries (in Europe in particular, also in Japan), demographic factors are among those that co-decide about the observed stagnation, or even shrinking of population of numerous urban centres and metropolitan areas, they perform a fundamental role in the dynamic growth of large cities in the developing world. These factors will most probably also determine the continuation and, in some parts of the globe, an acceleration of this trend during the next several decades. Lutz *et al.* (2007), have noted a bifurcation of recent demographic trends on the global level. Whereas in regions, which are characterized by low fertility rates, their further, often even faster than so far, decline is recorded, those regions that feature generally high fertility level experience its slower than earlier anticipated decrease. According to current forecasts, today's population number of Africa will most certainly double, and may even exceed 2 billion before the end of the 21st century.

Insofar, as the growth of urban population numbers depends (in varying over time proportions, see: Ledent, 1982) upon two main components, that is, the natural increase in urban places and rural to urban migration, changes in urbanization level are related to the latter factor. A substantial increase in the share of urban population will continue to be an unquestionable tendency in numerous developing countries during the next several decades. This will reflect both the role of push factors in rural areas, including progressing commercialization of agriculture, as well as growing spatial population mobility in general. As to pull factors, urban to rural migration may in the future be stimulated due to possible intensification of de-localization trends concerning selected service activities in high labour cost countries.

A question should be raised at this point, namely, to what extent will the growing population numbers and increasing urbanization level in developing countries result in further expansion of megacities, both in terms of their size and their numbers, in those world regions. At this point, it is appropriate to refer to the work of Todaro (1979), who proved that, when a major share of total economic activity is accounted for by its informal sector, it is a perception of chances, rather than a real probability of gaining a job that determines individual migration decisions. Certainly, the former factor will continue to point to large urban centres as preferred destinations for labour oriented migration streams. Similar rules pertain to investors who take decisions based on risk minimization, whereas both scale and agglomeration economies can also be achievable in cities of a smaller size. Hence, even though the very large urban centres do offer greater urbanization economies (including technical infrastructure and labour resources), it is mainly processes and preconditions of social nature that have the decisive role in choosing such cities as locations, both in the case of migration and economic investment decisions.

This leads us to the question of limits to growth of contemporary megacities. The problem can be examined by interpreting cities as complex systems (Albeverio *et al.*, 2008), ones that are difficult to control, yet characterized by high, and specific at various spatial scale level of self-organization. According to this approach, a large city (urban agglomeration) ceases to expand once it crosses a size threshold, one that is defined by its internal functional effectiveness, as well as its ability to compete in the domain of less than highly specialized functions (such as less technologically advanced manufacturing activities) with smaller urban centres. Before reaching the target size, the city's spatial structure tends to evolve by assuming a more decentralized, polycentric pattern. Such development sequence is well illustrated by the case of Mexico City mentioned earlier. Following these considerations, the growth limits of today's megacities can be estimated to correspond with the population of 15–20 million inhabitants.

When interpreted in these categories, the future of megacities may be seen through lenses of a positive development scenario, the main driving force of which, however, would have to be long-term economic and social development, a progress taking place at the level of individual countries and world regions. This, in turn, would depend upon a host of external political, environmental, as well as other preconditions. An alternative scenario is one of their continuing rapid, chaotic expansion, to be accompanied by growing internal tensions, and leading towards breakages of basic infrastructure and a decline of functions performed, a consequence of which would be a dwindling number of workplaces, and an initially selective, but in a longer perspective large-scale population outflow. Such a course of events could be initiated at a local or regional level by a massive, city-bound population exodus from rural areas, an effect of natural disasters, and a general deterioration of environmental conditions related to climate change. Once their absorption capacity was exceeded, the megacities could no longer fulfil their complex functions of integrating local economies into global economic circuit. With regard to spatial population flows, their position would change from one of the important destinations to that of mainly origins of migration and refugee movement, on both internal and international scale.

3.4. Discussion and Conclusions

Global interdependence of large city development, which is of multidimensional character, has been studied extensively by focusing on functional network relations (Taylor, 2004; Derudder *et al.*, 2012). This work is devoted to a brief discussion of some of its other aspects, those that pertain to structural properties of urban centres, as well as to their possible future development trajectories.

As noted earlier, whereas in Europe or North America, major cities are perceived as *metropolitan* by referring to qualitative criteria primarily; elsewhere, the large urban centres, whose position on a global scale is recognized, are identified mainly by the population size, and tend to be labelled as *megacities* (Parnreiter, 1999, 2012). Although, in the course of the globalization process and the accompanying development process, the latter cities are acquiring some attributes traditionally attached to the metropolitan status such as those related to urban physical substance and functional profile, the distinction between the two categories, and the two underlying notions is likely to persist, owing at least to a broadly defined cultural factor. This is illustrated by the following quote concerning the future of Accra, which:

> "… may be in a permanent state of *becoming* neither a world city nor a traditional African city but rather a combination and integration of the two in ever more diverse and complex way"
>
> Grant (2012: 461).

The words can refer to large Indian, or East Asian cities, which, while growing and globalizing, still tend to preserve their distinctiveness.

In such circumstances, the *world city* hypothesis may be interpreted as an integrative concept, in the sense that it is no longer possible to discuss relationships between the notions of *metropolis* and *megacity* without referring to this category. In this concept, the role and functions of economic control performed by the city on a regional, national, or supranational scale are emphasized (Derudder *et al.*, 2012). In addition, in the *world city* concept, strong mutual relations between the city's external links and its internal spatial socio-economic situation are accounted for explicitly.

As far as the problem of future change is concerned, one should point to interdependence between its alternative paths, as outlined in the form of development scenario. On the other hand, possible impact of what has been outlined here as a megacity crisis is among relevant questions. In the light of such an internal crisis, especially when it would involve large urban agglomerations in African countries, the probability of the arrival of the *social fragmentation* scenario in Europe would greatly increase. This could actually lead to more serious social, economic and political consequences.

As to other aspects of observed rapid global urbanization trends, it may be appropriate to place them against long-term demographic change. As it is well documented in international statistics (HABITAT, 1996), these countries that witness most rapid increases in the share of urban population tend to experience the fastest decline of the rates of natural population growth. Although fertility decrease on a national scale cannot be attributed directly to the urbanization process, the latter can be perceived as *an agent* of demographic transition, as it is strongly associated with the primary factors which include evolving marital patterns, health and educational status, and family planning programmes (Keyfitz, 1982).

In this dynamic interdependency matrix, an important role may be attributed to large urban population concentrations in developing countries. The living and working conditions that prevail in such urban areas are reflected by specific patterns of migration, age composition, and fertility when compared with other areas, in particular in relatively low levels of population reproduction (Korcelli and Just, 1983). Hence, the increase in the number of megacities and their growing share in the total population may contribute to the acceleration of global demographic changes which, according to some demographic forecasts (Lutz *et al.*, 2004), would lead to the end of world population growth before the end of this century.

References

Aguilar, A.G. (1999). Mexico City's growth and regional dispersion. In A.G. Aguilar and I. Escamilla (Eds.). *Problems of Megacities: Social Inequalities, Environmental Risk and Urban Governance*. Ciudad Mexico: Universidad Nacional Autonoma de Mexico.

Aguilar, A.G. and F. Lopez-Gerrero (2014). Spaces of poverty and social disadvantages in Mexico City. In L. Mierzejewska and J. Parysek (Eds.). *Cities in a Complex World: Problems, Challenges and Prospects*. Poznań: Bogucki.

Albeverio, S., A.D. Giordano and A. Vancheri (Eds.) (2008). *The Dynamics of Complex Urban Systems. An Interdisciplinary Approach*. Heidelberg, New York: Physica-Verlag.

Alonso, W. (1964). *Location and Land Use. Toward a General Theory of Land Rent*. Cambridge, Mass: Harvard University Press.

Berg van den, L., R. Drewett, L.H. Klaassen, A. Rossi and C.H.T. Vijverberg (1982). *Urban Europe: A Study of Growth and Decline*. Oxford: Pergamon Press.

Derudder, B., A. De Vos and F. Witlox (2012). Global city/world city. In B. Derudder, M. Hoyler, P.J. Taylor and F. Witlox (Eds.). *International Handbook of Globalization and World Cities*. Cheltenham, UK & Northampton, Mass., US: Edward Elgar.

ESPON (2004). The role, specific situation and potentials of urban areas as nodes in a polycentric development. Project 1.1.1. Final Report. European Communities, Luxembourg.

ESPON (2007). The study of urban functions. Project 1.4.3. Final Report. European Communities, Luxembourg.

Florida, R. (2002). *The Rise of the Creative Class: And How it is Transforming Work, Leisure, Community and Everyday Life*. New York: Basic Books.

Friedmann, J. (1986). The world city hypothesis. *Development and Change*, 17, 69–83.

Grant, R. (2012). Accra: A globalizing city. In B. Derudder, M. Hoyler, P.J. Taylor and F. Witlox (Eds.). *International Handbook of Globalization and World Cities*. Cheltenham, UK & Northampton, Mass., US: Edward Elgar.

HABITAT (1996). *An Urbanizing World. Global Report on Human Settlements 1996. United Nations Centre for Human Settlements*. Oxford University Press, Oxford.

Hall, P. (1990). Europe after 1992. In *Urban challenges. Report to the Commission on Metropolitan Problems*. Statens offentliga utredningar, Stockholm.

Hall, P. (1993). Forces shaping urban Europe. *Urban Studies*, 30(6), 883–898.

Hall, P. and D. Hay (1980). *Growth Centres in the European Urban System*. London: Heineman Educational Books.

Hall, P. and K. Pain (Eds.) (2006). *The Polycentric Metropolis: Learning from Mega-city Regions in Europe*. London: Earthscan.

Kempen, van E.T. (1994). The dual city, social polarization, social segregation and the life chances. *Urban Studies*, 31(7), 995–1015.

Keyfitz, N. (1982). *Global Prospects for Population Growth and Distribution*. WP-82-36. International Institute for Applied Systems Analysis, Laxenburg, Austria.

Knox, P.L. and P.J. Taylor (Eds.) (1995). *World Cities in a World System*. Cambridge: Cambridge University Press.

Korcelli, P. and P. Just (1983). Metropolitan growth and population development at the national level. *Regional Development Dialogue*, 4(1), 1–27. United Nations Centre for Regional Development, Tokyo.

Korcelli, P., M. Grochowski, E. Kozubek, E. Korcelli-Olejniczak and P. Werner (2012). Development of urban-rural regions: From European to local perspective. Institute of Geography and Spatial Organization, P. Ac. Sc., Warszawa.

Korcelli-Olejniczak, E. and P. Korcelli (2015). On European metropolisation scenarios and the future course of metropolitan development in Poland. *Geographia Polonica*, 88(1), 107–121.

Kotowska, I.E. (2014). Mastering demographic change in Europe. *Nauka*, 4, 21–27.

Kunzmann, K. (2008). Futures of European space 2020. *Journal of Nordregio*, 8(2), 12–21.

Ledent, J. (1982). The factors of urban population growth: net in-migration versus natural increase. *International Regional Science Review*, 7(2), 97–125.

Lutz, W., W.C. Sanderson and S. Scherbov (Eds.) (2004). *The End of World Population Growth in the 21st Century. New Challenges for Human Capital Formation and Sustainable Development*. London and Sterling: Earthscan.

Lutz, W., W.C. Sanderson and S. Scherbov (2007). A world of simultaneous population growth and shrinking unified by accelerating ageing. Popnet, International Institute for Applied Systems Analysis, Laxenburg, Austria, 39, pp. 1–3.

Nijman, J. (2012). Mumbay as a global city: A theoretical essay. In B. Derudder, M. Hoyler, P.J. Taylor and F. Witlox (Eds.). *International Handbook of Globalization and World Cities*. Cheltenham, UK & Northampton, Mass., US: Edward Elgar.

Nilsson, K., S. Pauleit, S. Bell, C. Aalbers and T.S. Nielsen (Eds.) (2013). *Per-urban Futures: Scenarios and Models for Land Use Change in Europe*. Berlin, Heidelberg: Springer Verlag.

Parnreiter, Ch. (1999). Peripheral mega-cities in the globalization: Mexico City, Bombay and Jakarta compared. In A.G. Aguilar and I. Escamilla (Eds.). *Problems of Megacities: Social Inequalities, Risk and Urban Governance*. Universidad Nacional Autonomia de Mexico.

Parnreiter, Ch. (2012). More than an ordinary city: The role of Mexico City in global commodity chains. In B. Derudder, M. Hoyler, P.J. Taylor and F. Witlox (Eds.). *International Handbook of Globalization and World Cities*. Cheltenham, UK & Northampton, Mass., US: Edward Elgar.

Sassen, S. (1991). *The Global City*. Princeton, NJ: Princeton University Press.

Soja, E.W. (2000). *Postmetropolis. Critical Studies of Cities and Regions*. London: Blackwell.

Taylor, P.J. (2004). *World City Network: A Global Urban Analysis*. London: Routledge.

Taylor, P.J., B. Derudder, M. Hoyler and F. Witlox (2012). Advanced producer servicing networks of world cities. In: B. Derudder, M. Hoyler, P.J. Taylor and F. Witlox (Eds.). *International Handbook of Globalization and World Cities*. Cheltenham, UK & Northampton, Mass., US: Edward Elgar.

Todaro, M. (1979). Urbanization in Developing Nations: Trends, Prospects, and Policies. *Working Paper, No. 50*. Center for Policy Studies, The Population Council, New York.

4

GOVERNANCE OF MEGACITIES — SELECTED ASPECTS OF INTERNATIONAL EXPERIENCE

Tadeusz Markowski

4.1. Introduction

Megacities are places of intense economic, social, and spatial restructuring which occurs as a result of impulses and demands of the global economy. Such cities are generating additional economies of scale in the form of — often underestimated — internal demand for new products and services. These benefits help reduce the risk of innovation, accelerate innovativeness of solutions implemented in companies, and, subsequently, allow faster expansion of products on international markets. Large cities, due to accumulated property and capital, become a kind of countries within a country. Analysts of contemporary processes of urbanization distinguish micropolises, metropolises, or even megapolises. This is not just fashionable substitution of traditional names associated with the hierarchy of urban centres, but simply the perception of the fact that modern settlement systems are differently organized and interact with and respond to socio-economic processes of globalization in a different manner.

Modern metropolises are accompanied by a qualitatively new process of urbanization determined by metropolization of space (Markowski and Marszał, 2006; Liszewski, 1999). It reaches far beyond the administrative area of the central city. Apart from positive effects in the form of location of metropolitan (global) functions, as well as the emergence of new centres in places best communicated globally (in international logistics nodes, airport hubs, multimodal railway, and motorway nodes, etc.), there are also many negative effects of spatial and social processes, which managers of metropolitan areas should focus on. Negative effects of metropolization of space occur, among others, in the form of phenomena such as an increasingly amorphous spatial structure, growing social polarization, and exclusion of parts of urban space from processes of participation in the economic system.[1] Despite their growing problems, the largest megacities continue to grow despite proclamations about their impending collapse. It seems that one can hypothesize that megacities are still attractive for the economic development as their space facilitates raising more easily financial capital for public–private ventures to overcome structural and quantitative thresholds in their expansive development than in medium-sized and small cities. Effective governance at the mega-metropolitan scale becomes an important factor in overcoming structural barriers. As a result, areas of megacities constantly release new spaces and resources that allow to obtain permanent external sources for building global competitive advantages due to the involvement of large corporations and innovative companies participating in this process. The chapter signals the greatest challenges of contemporary processes of globalization faced by public authorities of megacities and presents an overview of the most important trends in building new structures of metropolitan governance. In the final part of the chapter, the author draws conclusions and provides recommendations concerning the national metropolitan policy in the context of institutional aspects of governance.

[1]Polish metropolises that is, are — with few exceptions — a largely passive (reactive) recipient of negative effects arising from metropolization of economy and consumer markets. This is accompanied by land speculation and scattered build-up, as well as locating warehouse and production facilities in the metropolitan area in breach of spatial planning rules.

4.2. Challenges and Problems of Contemporary Megacities

Adjustment processes in human urban centres have always taken place, but their contemporary dynamics and scale is incomparably greater. In the period of industrialization, dynamic processes of urbanization made cities absorb local villages and settlements. Thus, territorial expansion into new areas occurred, and new demands were met by an increasingly stronger power centre. One might ask whether it would not be better to simply continue this process. It seems, however, that, if this type of expansion contributed to an increase in the efficiency of metropolitan systems, such a process would certainly be continued. The processes of urbanization of the 20th century led, however, to a permanent structural lack of compatibility between administrative and functional areas of large urban systems. The contradiction between the functional and administrative development, in turn, led to the emergence of a complex political environment in which it is difficult to reach an agreement on matters relating to important, multifaceted, medium- and long-term objectives such as: the economic development and competitiveness, social cohesion, appropriate public finances, and the efficient provision of public services covering the entire urban areas.

Large systems of urban space have always faced many barriers in terms of centralized governance capabilities. The increasing complexity of territorial systems, which is a consequence of the development of civilization, requires constant verification of competence as well as governance structures of metropolitan areas.

In the geographical research, megacities are treated as a special category of metropolitan cities analyzed in the context of macro-regional, continental, and global relations. The result of this research is an attempt to create a new functional typology of cities and to determine their role in hierarchical and supranational territorial settlement systems. In the practice of governance of the development of megacities, features resulting from their positioning in comparison with other entities are not such important indications. The attention of governing bodies focuses more on issues related to the elimination of negative effects of global relations rather than anticipating new problems and tackling their causes. Hence, certain doubts may arise as to the various recommendations presented and developed by different scientific communities and practitioners in relation to the cities that are assigned, in one way or another, metropolitan characteristics.

In each study of megacities, there emerges the problem of adequate definition and criteria for selection of cities to conduct comparisons and formulate relevant recommendations. Unfortunately, such methodologically correct studies do not exist. Moreover, there are no international institutions that would be willing to finance such research. There is a lack of studies, for example, that would analyze the impact of multinational corporations on real decision-making processes of public authorities and the functioning of global cities or megacities. What is their formal and informal impact on decision-making processes? What is their impact on the intensification of financially negative hyper-competition between the cities of the global network? International corporations behave in a diverse manner towards global cities. Their tactics towards, and relationships with, cities have various dimensions of transparency and accountability depending on the country in which a company's headquarters, subsidiaries, or only assembly plants are located.

It seems that the research on processes and problems related to governing large metropolitan areas can be discussed based on several groups of cities. For example, there are certain similarities between megacities of developing countries characterized by high demographic pressure like in Africa, South America, Mexico, China, and India. There are also megacities of emerging economies such as Brazil or Argentina as well as megacities of developed countries with a constant influx of immigrants such as the USA or Japan. One can also distinguish megacities of East Asia (prospering metropolises), such as Hong Kong. There are also megacities of the European Union. Within the EU countries, one should also look for relevant subgroups in order to find similarities and applicable institutional arrangements. The group of megacities of the new EU Member States is definitely characterized by specific phenomena and problems, including a low level of development of social capital, accelerated processes of social and spatial polarization, accelerated urbanization, a low degree of compliance with the law, or excessively complicated legislation, among others. Each group of megacities has its own dominant problems. In developing countries, these include poverty, exclusion, crime, including juvenile delinquency, drug dealing, along with infectious diseases, natural disasters, terrorist threats, etc. Thus, the issues related to spatial planning take a back seat. Management of urban agriculture is an underrated problem in large urban agglomerations. Due to broken traditional links of food supply chain for megacities derived from rural areas, agriculture in megacities becomes a way to provide an integrated solution to many issues such as the fight against social exclusion, education of children and youth, production of organic food and meeting basic food needs, sustainable waste management, temporary use of abandoned construction sites, etc. Integrated urban agriculture in cities and megacities is relevant in the most developed countries, such as the USA or Canada, as well in some economically less developed countries such as Cuba, or in megacities of South America and Latin America.

Studies show that very dynamic changes in spatial structures occur in megacities, along with processes of scattering, concentration, and reallocation of functions (González, 2010). Regardless of the specific relocation phenomena, the process generates high spatial mobility in daily and weekend cycles. These pulsar effects of varying scale and concerning different social groups are particular challenges in the management of transportation systems. Traditional models of traffic movement often do not allow appropriate decision-making. Thus, the role of intelligent (IT-based) traffic management systems increases.

Assuming that contemporary urbanization processes in key countries around the world have changed their cause-and-effect relationships, the basic question arises: What should the institutional, administrative, and organizational structure accompanying these processes look like? New methods of governance must therefore take into account new phenomena such as:

- growing subversive competition of authorities of territorial units adjacent to the megacity (interested solely in their own short-term development and in playing the subversive game to attract investors concurrent with this interest);
- increasing pulsar effects of daily and seasonal functioning of the megacity;

- fragmentation of space, amorphous and dynamic reallocation of functions (sometimes re-urbanization of centres of megacities — the return of the housing function to city centres, which is associated with increasing inefficiency of transportation systems and the growing importance of leisure time as a function of the quality of life);
- deepening the information gap in some areas and decision-making processes of public authorities responsible for large complex spatial systems.

In building institutional structures for the governance of megacities, one must take into account a number of important political, social, and economic determinants, but also the accumulation of decision-making centres in megacities (corporate headquarters, banks, media, public authorities, etc.). The adoption of the determinant in the form of the location of exogenous functions at the global scale should determine the methods and possibilities of governing such cities, as well as functionally and morphologically related operative areas. One cannot consider the processes of governance of megacities in isolation from the morphological characteristics of the metropolitan area (conurbation, polycentric, monocentric, and bipolar system). The question arises: Where are these functions located? Only within administrative boundaries of megacities? Or also beyond these boundaries? Are the local government territorial structures in the metropolitan area strong and autonomous? Is the leading and coordinating role of the central city visible? In this respect, there are no clear rules, administrative arrangements are variable in time and determined by many factors of political (geopolitics, inter-party struggle), economic, and social nature.

The indicated processes radically alter the functional and spatial relationships of a modern metropolis and impose the need for a new institutional approach. They require building de-concentrated governance systems to increase the efficiency of meeting the relevant needs through the inclusion of local communities in this process. This need results, in concepts of participatory or public governance, as well as de-concentration and de-centralization of power.

The concept of public governance or participatory governance, along with new instruments of integrated governance, becomes an important way to effectively eliminate negative external costs of expanding megacities, and thus allows moving the threshold of population growth and spatial development of cities and urban systems. The research shows that effective governance is or can be an instrument for overcoming the general (classical) rule of economies of scale diminishing along with the size of the city (Alonso, 1971; Regulski, 1982). Therefore, another important hypothesis can be put forward, that is, that effective governance of metropolitan areas aimed at overcoming structural barriers becomes an indirect source of external savings and indirect labour productivity growth in companies and corporations operating in megacities. If this hypothesis is correct, we obtain a new factor of location attractiveness in terms of the economic development of metropolitan areas, which will maintain the scale of polarization in the processes of global urbanization.

This creates important questions, namely how can such a participatory governance system can be created and will it translate into an effective system of participation in decision-making and execution processes. Practice shows that increasing participation in decision-making or lobbying for various public expenditures without incurring by the stakeholders (co-decision-makers) the costs of decisions is and will be a frequent source of social conflict, deepened even more by the actions of politicians focused on populist electoral purposes. We should also pay attention to the trends opposed to participatory governance, for example, the need to overcome the growing information barrier (chaos, high costs, low reliability, etc.) can be a stimulant for the centralization of power and administration in megacities or at least a substantial redefinition of the scope of powers and manner of participation in the processes of management and governance. In any case, a significant revolution looms ahead in the sphere of governing megacities. It is an interesting period of search for new organizational and institutional forms in most cities and countries of the world. There are already some general thoughts and suggestions put forward. We are, however, far from reaching any common conclusions. For example, which governing body should it be? How does the traditional system of state organization fit into all that?

The development of information technology will be conducive to the building of a cooperation agreement between units of territorial administration, as their common exploitation may provide tangible benefits for administrative units that co-create it.

Contemporary challenges that large megacities (conurbations, agglomerations, or polycentric agglomeration systems) face include issues such as risk management in various dimensions, including early warning systems, transportation management, energy flow management (and energy conservation), pollution control systems (air, waste, noise, etc.).

The most important instruments in the governance of megacities are systems of spatial planning based on geo-information systems (GIS) in conjunction with systems of satellite observation (Rapid Urbanization and Mega Cities, 2010). They provide the greatest possibilities for coordination of activities undertaken by public authorities operating in the areas of megacities. External diseconomies are eliminated by improving management of large spatial structures, including linear infrastructure systems and informational flows. Such possibilities are offered by information technology, that is, innovation and technological progress. The scale and complexity of problems arouse widespread interest of large IT companies that see a large market for information technology and the so-called smart systems that manage operations related to the provision of services in metropolitan areas. It seems that many solutions in this area will be provided by the market. Despite this fact, we can see the pressure from global firms that lobby to generate demand from public administration for their software products so that the funds invested in programmes for the public sector could provide return on investment as soon as possible. This meeting point between the private sector and the public sector is vulnerable to corruption, and many international companies have already paid fines for unfair action in the public procurement market. Therefore, it seems that regulations in this area should be sought also at the level of international institutions.

4.3. Experience of Selected OECD Countries

The problem of mismatch of administrative structures of metropolitan areas and heavily urbanized regions has become the subject of discussion and analysis of many international organizations such as the OECD, the European Union, or the NAFTA (Danielewicz and Markowski, 2008).

The OECD report on reforms in governance of metropolitan areas lists three main obstacles to their implementation:

- fragmentation of administrative competence, which results in a lack of links between administrative and functional areas;

- financial and fiscal constraints of local authorities in metropolitan areas[2];
- lack of transparent, understandable decision-making processes (who does what and at what level?) (Kamal-Chaoui, 2003: 2).

The authors of the report clearly state that there are no ideal governance models. Each city in the framework of its general "philosophy" needs to develop its own organizational and institutional model that fits its specific situation and national context.

In the OECD countries, we can distinguish several approaches to creating metropolitan authorities. One of the solutions, the most radical, is the amalgamation of municipalities. This concept is based on the belief that stronger metropolitan authorities improve competitiveness of metropolitan areas. Administrative structures created by amalgamation seek to overcome complex difficulties caused by fiscal fragmentation within the metropolis (in some cases, limiting the scope of liability) and limited power at the local level. A further aim is equalizing population growth and the social structure within metropolitan areas. Advocates of this approach argue that this form can reduce duplication of the same activities, create the effects of economies of scale and better conditions for service provision, improve accountability/transparency, allow more equitable distribution of tax revenues, and improve the efficiency of spatial planning (Kamal-Chaoui, 2003: 3).

Most institutions governing metropolitan areas were founded in the 1960s. Bodies governing metropolitan areas differ in their structure and responsibilities. These bodies include:

- a relatively small number of metropolitan state-mandated councils, as well as consolidated cities-countries;
- more numerous government agencies established for a specific purpose, usually responsible for the provision of one or more of services covering

[2] Metropolitan areas need to adapt to de-centralization and fiscal federalism, increase local autonomy while limiting tax differentiation within the metropolitan area, improve access to investment capital, and include the private sector as a partner in investments and a service provider.

the entire metropolitan area, for example, water supply, waste management, traffic service control, and airport or harbour management;
- jurisdictional boundary review commissions;
- voluntary associations or regional councils of governments, regional planning commissions and state-mandated Metropolitan Planning Organizations (MPOs), often but not always, linked to regional councils (Shaffer, 2004: 114). MPOs were created in the early 1970s and are funded by the federal government.

In studies of US institutional structures of metropolitan governance, the authors conclude that the existing, widely created in the 1980s, metropolitan councils are not able to properly manage these areas. Internal destructive mechanisms and multiplication of problems by those organizational structures have led the authors of various diagnostic reports to the conclusion that such councils should be liquidated. Instead, state agencies of development of metropolitan areas should be established and duplication of activities by the departments of public administration co-creating the metropolitan area should be eliminated (Task Force, 2003).

In addition to the amalgamation, there are many opportunities for cooperation between municipalities. One of such forms is voluntary cooperation, which, however, is often very difficult. An alternative to these solutions is the development of more institutionalized forms of cooperation mechanisms, for example, a system of programme contracts. New governance systems, involving a wide spectrum of partners who act as a network, can in the future replace the current hierarchical structures using contractual relationships such as a partnership between the central government and local authorities (including the regional level). For example, France has developed a mechanism called an "agglomeration contract" (contrat d'agglomération).

Governance of agglomerations is based largely on voluntary cooperation of municipalities. Three forms of cooperation can be observed:

- Horizontal relationships between the central city and other municipalities in the region.
- Cross-cutting relations in the form of public–private partnership.
- Vertical relationships between different levels of government (department, region, country, and the EU) (Herrschel and Newman, 2002: 83).

In light of the above-presented considerations, one must agree that it is impossible to provide clear recommendations and state the key principles. Despite this fact, the OECD decided to develop certain principles, mainly for developing countries. These include the following principles of metropolitan governance (OECD, 2000):

- *Principle of coherence*: Means that the method of governance must be clear, transparent, and understandable to the electorate.
- *Principle of competitiveness*: Means that governance must be geared towards boosting the regions competitiveness, and its organizational structures should be formed in a way that encourages efforts to strengthen the competitiveness of regional resources and not competition based on creating political advantages. As urban regions become the main systems of competition in the modern economy, in the context of increasing mobility of capital, the long-term strengthening of competitiveness of the urban region is done by investing in the so-called soft factors, that is, the development of human and social capital, rather than through discretionary tax reductions or subsidies.
- *Principle of coordination*: The need to respect this principle stems from political, social, and administrative high fragmentation occurring in urban areas. Without coordination, it is not possible to create the right basis for strategic planning in the metropolitan area.
- *Principle of fairness and equality*: All agreements and arrangements of institutional and financial structures must be constructed to ensure the highest levels of integrity and equal opportunities for all cities and municipalities, as well as social groups co-creating the metropolitan region.
- *Principle of fiscal correctness*: Means the organization of the financial system which ensures the correct correlation between the costs of governance of the area and the revenues received. As a rule, in large cities of the OECD countries, debt and tax burdens are the highest in central areas. Such a state cannot be maintained if these areas are to regain the ability to compete for investment on global markets.

- *Principle of flexibility*: Flexibility is essential so that institutions can adequately respond to rapid changes resulting from growing urbanization and rapid economic fluctuations caused by global influences.
- *Principle of holism*: The principle of a holistic view of the metropolitan system is based on the perception and analysis of all the consequences of activities of inter-related urban areas and including them in the decision-making system. Holism does not mean uniformity of governance of the metropolitan area and must be linked with the principle of subsidiarity.
- *Principle of specificity*: Means the incentive to create unique organizational and institutional solutions meeting diverse needs of the areas that co-create the metropolitan area while respecting the universal principles of democracy and human rights.
- *Principle of participation*: Is understood as taking into account the interests of different groups and encouraging them to participate in the governance of the area. New information technologies offer new possibilities for interactive communication.
- *Principle of social orientation in the organization of governance structures*: Is orientated towards meeting human needs. This orientation must, therefore, mean a cross-sectoral approach to governance that limits bureaucracy and functional sectoral focus.
- *Principle of subsidiarity*: Understood as meeting the existing needs by the lowest possible organizational level and, at the same time, limiting the overlaps between different organizational levels of local government units.
- *Principle of sustainability*: Means taking into account environmental protection in an integrated triad of economic, social, and environmental goals.

Each of the general principles recommended by the OECD has a different degree of importance for the national metropolitan system and their significance should be analyzed in the national and global context. The most important general principle is the principle of specificity, that is, the adjustment of the organizational structure to fit local circumstances.

Among the more detailed recommendations, the authors of the report propose the following solutions:

- The adoption of such urban structures of public finance that would fit better the new or modified institutional structures and the division of responsibilities between different levels of government.
- Modernization of administrative structures in order to improve the level and quality of services in the metropolitan area, and to evaluate the impact of actions undertaken through the introduction of evaluation systems.
- Replacing hierarchical structures with new flexible forms of horizontal and vertical cooperation (collaborating relations that incorporate several levels of government or similar jurisdictions in the metropolitan area, sometimes in concurrence with the private sector and/or volunteers).
- Implementation of greater transparency and accountability in decision-making processes, improvement of community's access to information and public services, strengthening local democracy through improved voting procedures.
- Developing a better framework for long-term strategic planning, allowing local authorities to take the initiative in the field of economic development strategies, and working in partnership with the business community and job seekers (Kamal-Chaoui, 2003: 3).

4.4. Conclusions and Recommendations

The creation of modern systems of metropolitan governance will require debunking many myths and stereotypes that accompany the views of local authorities co-creating such areas. One of such myths is the idea that the economic development is attracted towards the central city, away from the area located far from the metropolitan area. Therefore, many cities and municipalities fight for the inclusion of their area in the metropolis, hoping that this administrative allocation would be stimulating for their development. Others, in turn, believe that entities located within the administrative boundaries of the metropolitan area will be dominated by its primary power centre which will take over economic benefits and reduce the autonomy of small units. Debunking such stereotypes and myths requires conducting reliable research.

The key problem in the governance of urban metropolitan areas is their proper delimitation. In most cases, we tend to rigidly restrain the boundaries of the metropolitan area and create a particular institutional governance system for the administratively designated area. In practice, it turns out that this approach is inadequate. As indicated by the US experience, such solutions in the long term do not prevent uncontrolled processes of urban expansion beyond the boundaries of a designated metropolitan area. At the same time, the central zone of the governed megacity still experiences many problems, which are exacerbated by decisions taken by the institutions, which should prevent these pathologies (Task Force, 2003). For example, formal and legal repressions aimed at a more effective use of the already urbanized areas lead to urban expansion beyond the designated administrative boundaries of the metropolis. This leads to the conclusions about the need for flexible treatment of boundaries of the metropolitan area.[3] Our knowledge of the causes of contemporary processes of urbanization is unfortunately incomplete. In many cases, processes of urbanization are the result of competing market forces, the side effects of pathological regulatory systems, land speculation, corruption, etc. Governance of the metropolitan area through the impact on the negative effects does not always lead to the expected results. It is therefore necessary, when introducing new institutional and organizational systems, to include the construction of an adequate system for monitoring their effects. Otherwise, after a while, instead of the continuous improvement of institutions and processes of governance of metropolitan areas, we have to deal with chaotic, random, and sometimes

[3]A question may arise: Why should the boundaries of metropolitan areas not be more rigid? This is due to several reasons: firstly, the increasing flexibility of the economy, which requires a flexible response on the part of its environment, secondly, democratic co-governance also requires openness and constant power sharing across artificial borders of authority. The market economy does not recognize artificial borders and it immediately reveals and multiplies all the pathologies caused by administrative decisions in the field of spatial planning. Meanwhile, in the context of Polish concepts of metropolitan area planning, we are on the best (or worst) way to make the boundaries of such areas more rigid.

radical attempts to change the existing institutional arrangements (based on incomplete knowledge, unreliable intuition, or populist ideology), which not only do not improve the system of metropolitan governance, but actually worsen the negative phenomena.

We must realize that systems of governance are based rather on hierarchical governance and are not partner- or network based. The problem associated with reforming local government lies in the mentality of people in the world of politics that seek to restore the permissive system, which legally mandates and permits action, in place of the subsidiary system. The desire of politicians to strengthen administrative procedures instead of governance procedures is also common. Politically attractive "fight against corruption" through its programmes to combat the effects, not the causes of the phenomenon, will be one of the major problems pushing local administration towards bureaucratic mechanisms promoting the formation of pathological administrative structures.

We still need to learn new (integrated) and partnership-based governance, despite the evident need for it and its theoretical usefulness. The institution dedicated to the development of the metropolitan area needs to have the competences to control a network of partner relationships resulting from the identified properties of the system. Currently, these properties are not well known, especially in a situation when the system is defective (lacks certain components and connections, and very often these are only fragments of unclear, very weak connections or there is even complete lack thereof). Varying levels of relations mean the need for a diverse range of intervention on the part of regional and central authorities.

The effectiveness of governance and institutional forms will be determined by historical conflicts and prejudices, the existing forms of urbanization, etc. The organizational structure and governance in polycentric regions will look different from monocentric ones. In this regard, useful lessons can be learnt from German or Swiss examples.

The openness of the system, its transparency and flexibility in terms of changes in the environment need to guide the creation of organizational structures. The newly established organizational structures must primarily ensure high flexibility in terms of change. A rigid system is doomed to failure, as it will come in with an integrated mechanism of self-destruction.

If we assume that it is to be a democratic governance model, based on the concept of co-governance by various stakeholders, we need to build a structure balancing out political and professional factors so that the institutional system could guarantee the renewal of the value system, erasing pathology and bureaucratic accretions, but at the same time retaining the most important features of modern organizational structure, that is, the ability to learn continuously.

Creating a governance system for the metropolitan area cannot be reduced to reforming the existing institutions or establishing new organizations. The new governance system is not just new organizations, but perhaps, to even a greater extent, it is a change of attitudes, values, and culture of performing governance functions. The practice of developed countries shows that the participatory model, integrating many actors, provides better results than the traditional top-down hierarchical control systems.

It is necessary to introduce a new governance culture, which is conducive to building the identity of inhabitants of the metropolitan area and the nearest place of residence. When it comes to changing the governance culture, the following directions of reforming are mentioned most often:

- the introduction of the system of direct elections of councils and mayors;
- developing leadership skills of local political elites;
- modernizing voting procedures;
- encouraging new forms of social participation and the introduction of more transparent decision-making procedures that will involve residents;
- providing citizens with the relevant quantitative and qualitative information;
- application of the principles of partnership in achieving the desired goals and implementation of inter-sectoral programmes in public–public and public–private systems (e.g. sustainable development, regeneration of brownfield sites and areas with social problems, etc.).

The basic instruments of conducting an integrated metropolitan policy and governance of a delimitated area are primarily planning instruments. The special role of such a mechanism is due to the fact that the system of metropolitan planning provides the basis for coordinating the development and governance of the entire area by using techniques and methods characteristic of the New Public Governance.

In order for metropolitan planning to function as an apparatus of public governance, it must meet a number of criteria congruent to the concept of management by co-governance. These criteria include:

- democratic procedures;
- participatory nature;
- willingness to compromise;
- credibility;
- transparency;
- fairness (social and economic);
- effectiveness (understood as efficacy, advantageousness, efficiency);
- openness to change;
- flexibility.

In the process of creating new systems of territorial governance in metropolitan areas, it is necessary to take into account local socio-political systems. Their perception facilitates the creation of the system that uses local forces and directs the energy and action to realize the desired functions of the objective. Implementation of other systems, contrary to the existing system of values, will cause a counter-reaction. Therefore, while implementing new models, it is necessary to recognize good seed processes and respect local socio-cultural conditions.

References

Alonso, W. (1971). The economics of urban size. *Papers of the Regional Science Association*, 26, 71–83.

Danielewicz, J. and T. Markowski (2008). Zarządzanie w obszarze metropolitalnym — podejście instytucjonalne. In T. Stryjakiewicz and T. Czyż (Eds.). *O nowy kształt badań regionalnych w geografii i gospodarce przestrzennej*. Biuletyn KPZK, issue 237, Warszawa, pp. 73–103.

González, R.R. (2010). Metropolitan management and spaces. *The Open Studies Journal*, 3, 28–33.

Herrschel, T. and P. Newman (2002). *Governance of Europe's City Regions*. London-New York: Routledge.

Kamal-Chaoui, L. (2003). *Metropolitan Governance in OECD Countries*.

Liszewski, S. (1999). Ewolucja funkcji regionotwórczych Łodzi. In Zasięg regionu łódzkiego w świetle badań społecznych preferencji przynależności administracyjnej i powiązań społeczno-gospodarczych, *Acta Univ. Lodz. Folia Geographica Socio-Oeconomica*, Wyd. UŁ, Łódź, pp. 41–59.

Markowski, T. and T. Marszał (2006). *Metropolie, obszary metropolitalne, metropolizacja*. Warszawa: KPZK PAN.

OECD (2000). The Reform of Metropolitan Governance. OECD Observer-Policy Brief. Retrieved from www.oecd.org/publication/Pol_brief/ [access: 15.03.2014].

Regulski, J. (1982). *Ekonomika Miasta*. Warszawa: PWN.

Shaffer, S. (2004). *Principles of American Metropolitan Governance*. Coral Springs: Llumina Press.

Task Force (2003). Task Force on Metropolitan Governance, Center of the American Experiment, December 2003.

5

DEVELOPMENT PATTERNS OF MEGACITIES AND THEIR FUTURE

Zygmunt Ziobrowski

5.1. Introduction

It has been postulated that megacities are the phenomenon of the 20th century; however, is it not how ancient Rome, Constantinople, Persepolis, or Baghdad were perceived in the past? Are the contemporary megacities a driving force of the global growth, or rather an urban catastrophe? What are the characteristics of the modern megalopolises? To what extent is their development a result of planning and management or the external forces poorly, if at all, controlled by the local authorities.

Megacities are generally mono-centric, highly urbanized municipal regions with the population of at least 10 million. Their business infrastructure is strongly connected with the global economy; therefore services, business institutions, and airports situated in these metropolitan areas are of a global scale. The characteristic of a megacity is usually a very high rate — nearly 30% of the whole population — of foreigners, as well as inner, poorly controlled, and dynamic growth. The number of megacities comes close to 30 with most of them located in Asia, followed by Americas, Europe, and Africa. In addition, in line with UN standards, certain highly urbanized, typically polycentric regions in Europe such as The Ruhr in Germany, Upper Silesia in Poland, or Randstad in Netherlands might also be considered megacities.

Megacities are areas with the highest density of population (e.g. Hong Kong or Dhaka), usually struggling with many problems, but at the same time extremely powerful to attract people from all social groups, in majority young, career-driven individuals. In Paris, for example, 46% of citizens are people below the age of 35, over 50% of Parisians are single, and 23% are immigrants. Outside Europe and North America, megacities, offering a very attractive job market and various opportunities, drawing masses of the poor who settle on the city outskirts. Generally, society in large agglomerations is divided into classes with hermetic elites and serious differences in the standard of living. Immigrants participation oscillates around 23–45% of the population. The economy of megacities is much more effective as compared to the national average. Measured in GDP *per capita*, it usually stays 20–35% over the national average. The main objective of the selective analysis is identification of the issues occurring in megacities and trying to find possible solutions to them mainly through planning and managing their development.

5.2. Issues of Megacities and Possible Solutions

The major issues in megacities are the environment pollution, inefficient transport, constant lack of housing, and high rate of crime. Millions of people in megalopolises, especially in the southern hemisphere (Kolkata, Lagos, and San Paulo), live in districts completely devoid of basic services, water supply, drainage systems, and electricity, sometimes even police.

According to Living Planet Report from 2002 published by World Wide Fund for Nature [WWF], the global "ecological footprint" increased by 80% between 1961 and 2002 and exceeded the biological potential of Earth by 20%. Megacities play a considerable role in this process. Major challenges for their development are:

- environment protection (urbanization lowers the standard of living and destroys biodiversity);
- fuel consumption (reducing the usage of coal);
- rapid consumption and motorization (China, India).

According to Globalization and World Cities Group (GAW) in Loughborough University in England, global cities fall into two groups: Alpha World Cities and Beta World Cities. The first group includes London, Paris, New York, Tokyo, Chicago, Frankfurt, Hong Kong, Los Angeles, Milan, and Singapore. The second group entails San Francisco, Sydney, Toronto, Zurich, Brussels, Madrid, Mexico City, San Paulo, Moscow, and Seoul. Majority of them, both from Alpha and Beta group, are megacities.

The authorities of many conurbations undertake large, very often spectacular, projects. In Seoul, for example, they removed a jammed motorway from the centre of the city (similarly in San Paulo), introduced integrated public transport, which allows travelling around the entire city for $1 only, reduces the number of cars in the city traffic, and subsequently lowers the exhaust emission. Electric or hybrid cars begin to dominate the transport. In Shanghai, they introduced magnetic train, which develops an operational speed of 430 km/h and a top speed of 500 km/h. In New Delhi, the public rail system has been further developed to such an extent that 60% of all commuters are in the distance of maximum 15 minutes from the nearest stop. In Rio de Janeiro, the artery along the Copacabana beach has been changed into the largest in the world space for pedestrians and cyclists. Depending on the structure of the commuters, facilities aimed at a specific group are being introduced, for example, if the majority of a given group are women, many stops are connected with shopping centres, cultural institutions for young people (i.e. in Tokyo, Singapore, London, and Hong Kong). More and more often, the so-called Bus Rapid Transit (BRT) is being introduced as a relatively cheap and economical means of public transportation, which supports the "heavy" rail transport and, as a result, allows reducing exhaust emission and crowds (Planning and Sustainable Development..., 2006).

Satellite models of the urbanized regions of Paris or London have been applied in the development planning of Tokyo, where, in the 1960s, in the neighbouring areas new service centres: Shinjuku, Shin, and Yokohama were created and connected with the centre of Tokyo via fast rail.

In the planning of those cities, much attention is paid to improving their functionality although the high dynamics of the growth is not conducive. Improvements and revolutionary solutions in public transport are accompanied by structural changes. It is quite common in those cities that new service centres and job market are planned and realized to concentrate in a fair distance (20–30 km) from the historical centre. Much effort and means are being put to either build or restore the green space, which serves not only the recreational purpose and improving the public space but also cooling the densely built areas (San Paulo). The fundamental direction of the development is the informational economy together with the globalization of the production like for example, in case of megacity regions in China, which leave some cities of Europe and North America behind as places of less advanced technology and service. The question is where these advanced business services are going to be located. The answer may be simple — where the flow of information is the strongest. If so, however, it would be worth knowing how the information flows in cities where virtually everything suits the industry of service, where people introduce ideas but cannot gather them in one place. These people define the main direction of economy in the cities, and so one needs to understand how it operates in comparison to London, Paris, New York, or Tokyo (Llewelyn-Davies, 1997). The key factor in effective planning of megacities is the commuting of the population along with principles of sustainable development. The solution to this problem will be feasible by introducing various means of public transport carrying people over long distance. An example here could be a regional underground covering the whole area or the rail service between London and Madrid (within 6.5 h). These solutions may be competitive for the aviation transport, which should be focused more on transcontinental transit anyway (Hall, 2006). The idea has more and more supporters these days. It needs to be noted, though, that new means of transport will be creating new urban forms. Airports, specifically the large ones, draw in various activities. It has happened in Madrid, where the major trade pillar of the city Via Castellana is rapidly developing in the direction of the Barajas airport.

Another issue is the fact that megacities are like magnets, attracting immigrants who do not realize the high cost of living, which, subsequently, leads to the social division and problems with transport and housing (London, Paris). All megacities are subject to globalization, increasing immigration, de-centralization, outflow of people from the city centre to the suburban regions, and rising social inequalities. The differences among the cities, though, can be well observed in the case of

European vs. American megacities. European cities are characterized by a strong crafts tradition and relatively lower mobility resulting predominantly from language and cultural diversity as well as various traditions and identity of the city (Hall and Pain, 2006).

Commonly, four major sectors of metropolitan economy can be distinguished, namely finance and business, global management (centres of big companies), tourism, and cultural and creative trade, that is concentration of key facilities such as hotels, restaurants, museums, art galleries, and mass media. In such cities, activities very often disappear, being replaced by new ones. The pivotal factors here are the ability to compete and great potential for development. The potential is expressed not only in advanced production but also in advanced consumer service.

Influential zones of megacities are the areas of intense flow of people, goods, services, and information. The geometry of this flow and its frequency is subject to constant changes, however, in the points of relatively high and stable frequency of the flow, new centres of activities are being shaped, preventing the degradation of the entire system.

In the case of megacities, it is rather difficult to determine a clear model of their functional structure. They develop too fast, usually chaotically and without clearly specified plans. Nevertheless, efforts such as in the examples mentioned above show the strive systematically to improve the functionality of those complex urbanized areas with the highest rate of activities concentration. Once mono-centric conurbations, they have recently evolved in the direction of polycentrism, which allows even distribution of day-to-day travels. The new dominant polycentric systems begin to develop into something more than only historic centres, into something that forms Megacity Regions.

Nowadays, we deal not only with polycentric metropolitan areas but also with a spectacular phenomenon, which depends on the formation of polycentric regions of the megacities as it is in the case of China, Pearl River Delta between Hong Kong and Guangzhou or Yangtze Delta between Shanghai, Suzhou, Nanjing, and Hangzhou. This particular region has a population of 80 million and is the largest production complex in the world.

Similar phenomena, on a slightly lower scale, can be observed in Europe. In the South-East England, near London a new megacity region with the population of 19 million is being formed. In this area, around 50 different urbanized functioning micro-regions so-called Commuter Fields have been identified, with London being the largest one. However, even the smaller ones are growing much faster than London. Importantly, though, outside the critical zone of 50–60 km from London, the percentage of people living and working in the same place has increased by 75–85%. The same situation can be observed in other megacity regions. Delta Metropolis is being formed in the Netherlands, Centrope in Austria, and neighbouring countries (Slovakia, Hungary, and the Czech Republic), and CRUS cluster in Poland and the Czech Republic. Various European initiatives such as ESDP[1] and later EPSON,[2] PolyMETREX,[3] to mention a few, emphasize the need to create a network of socio-economical potential (of cities and their regions) in the form of polycentric systems (see Fig. 5.1). European polycentrism means cooperation and connections among urbanized areas, competitiveness of the system, functional relations, and connection of peripheral urbanized regions with the major European and world centres, which would include them in the orbit of dynamically developing world economies. In polycentric Europe, only strongly integrated and cooperating regions stand a chance to increase their competitiveness against other regions.

European Union (EU) faces the necessity to verify its cohesion policy, which results from many indications, above all from the need to improve the orchestration of the Lisbon–Gothenburg strategy. Although subsidizing the most vulnerable regions will remain one of the paramount concerns of the EU, more and more measures will be directed to support the development of the largest city centres. Therefore, many countries attempt to increase the potential of such regions by "grouping" them and adding to the potential by creating a "network of cities" (Ziobrowski, 2008).

Delta Metropolis (Fig. 5.2) is an initiative of the Dutch cities situated in the Rhine Delta (Rotterdam, The Hague, Utrecht, and Amsterdam). The population of this region is 5.5 million. The project is based on an intensive cooperation among the authorities of the four cities in the field of transport and communication system, spatial planning, and, most

[1] European Spatial Development Planning.

[2] European Grouping on Territorial Cooperation.

[3] Network of European Metropolitan Regions and Areas.

Fig. 5.1. Megacities in Europe

Source: Author's own elaboration based on 123RF (2017).

importantly, urbanization and protection of the green areas, management of polders and river system, and the development of city harbours.

The other example of European cities network is Oresund Region including the following sub regions: Oslo, Gothenburg, Malmö, and Copenhagen (see Fig. 5.3). It is a place of living and work for about 4 million people where 11 universities educate 150,000 students.

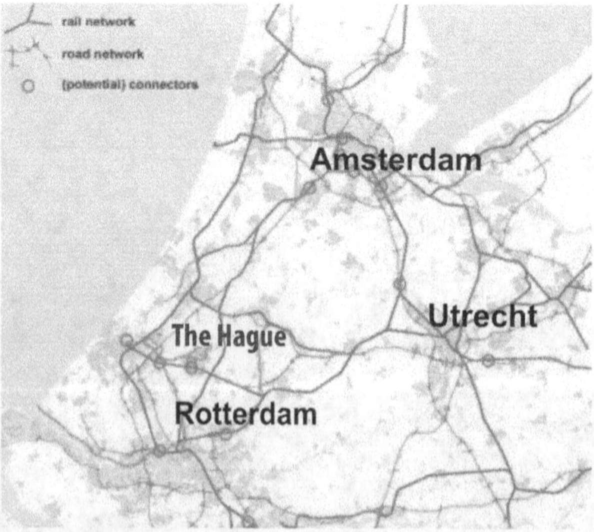

Fig. 5.2. Delta metropolis

Source: Rijksplanologishe Dienst (2017).

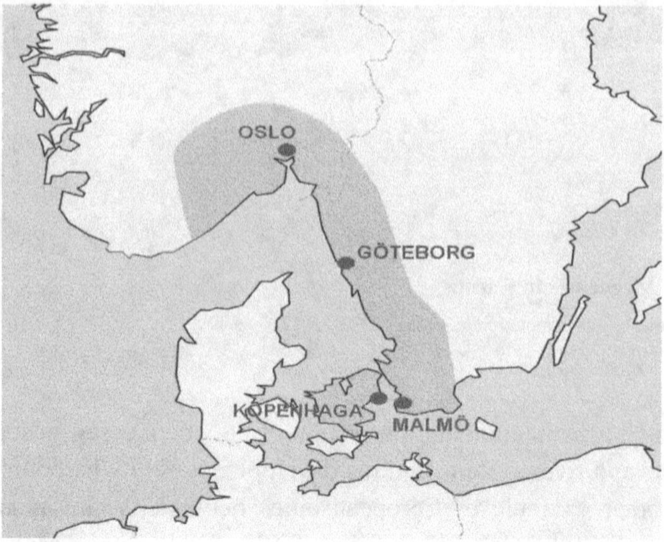

Fig. 5.3. Oresund region

Source: Author's own elaboration.

The region produces 25% of the total GDP of Denmark and Sweden. The main factors of development of the region are biotechnology, as well as medical and high-tech industries. Oresund is the cleanest metropolitan region of the EU. Since 2000, Copenhagen and Malmö are connected by a tunnel and a bridge, shortening the journey between the two cities to half an hour.

Centrope is a polycentric area grouping regions and cities from four Central European countries: Austria, Czech Republic, Slovakia, and Hungary (see Fig. 5.4). Its population is 6.5 million. The shareholders of the Secretariat of the Project — Europaforum Wien agency — Centre for Urban Dialogue and European Policy — are regions and cities located in this area, specifically Vienna, Győr, Bratislava, and Pilsen, but also a few regional development agencies. The main aims, set by the creators of the project in 2003, are job market management outside the borders, economical development achieved through attracting new investments especially within the car cluster, mutual promotion, and development of

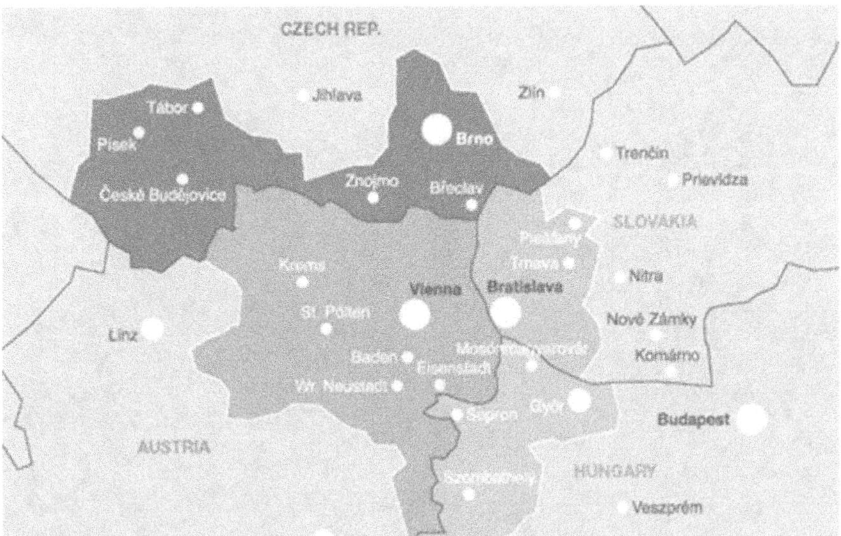

Fig. 5.4. Centrope region

Source: Centrope (2013).

tourism, culture, and education. Secretariat of the project began creating Centrope atlas, which was meant to aid macro-regional development management later on.

The latest concept of the spatial development of Germany is defined by 10 regions of cooperation in the spatial structure of the country. One of the region is located in the east of Germany bordering with Poland and Czech Republic, so-called Saxon Triangle (see Fig. 5.5) grouping together three largest cities of the region: Dresden, Leipzig, and Chemnitz.

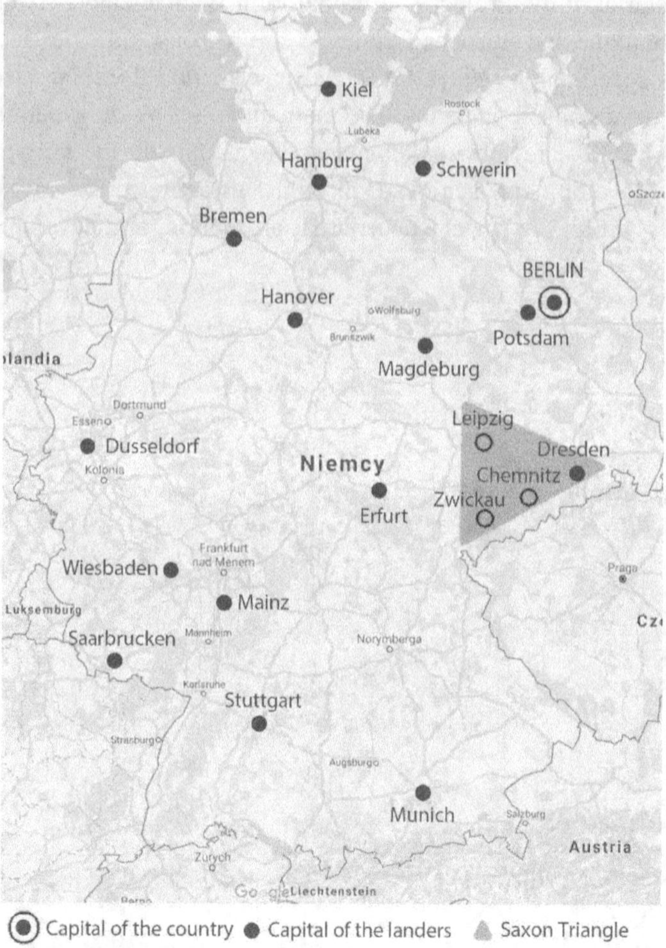

Fig. 5.5. Saxon triangle

Source: Author's own elaboration based on Federal Office for Building and Regional Planning (2004).

An important and large polycentric region in Central Europe might become the area, whose external border is marked by the following cities: Kraków, Częstochowa, Opole, Ostrava, and Bielsko-Biała, and of which the central part is Aglomeracja Górnośląska (Upper Silesia Agglomeration). This polycentric region has been called Cracow-Upper Silesia Cluster (CRUS). Such an intensely urbanized city system may well function as a spatial organization characterized by functional job division, economical and spatial integration, and political cooperation. The main objectives of the CRUS region are increasing the level of competitiveness, which is the answer to the challenges of globalization, strengthening the "network cooperation of the cities," and polycentric development of the EU territory (Fig. 5.6). Moreover, the aim would also be to boost the potential of the large cities, agglomerations, and metropolises which are considered the major "players in the game," having the capability of development diffusion according to their environment.

CRUS cluster conjoins Polish and Czech regions (Fig. 5.6). It has the largest population in this part of Europe — over 7.5 million. The axes of

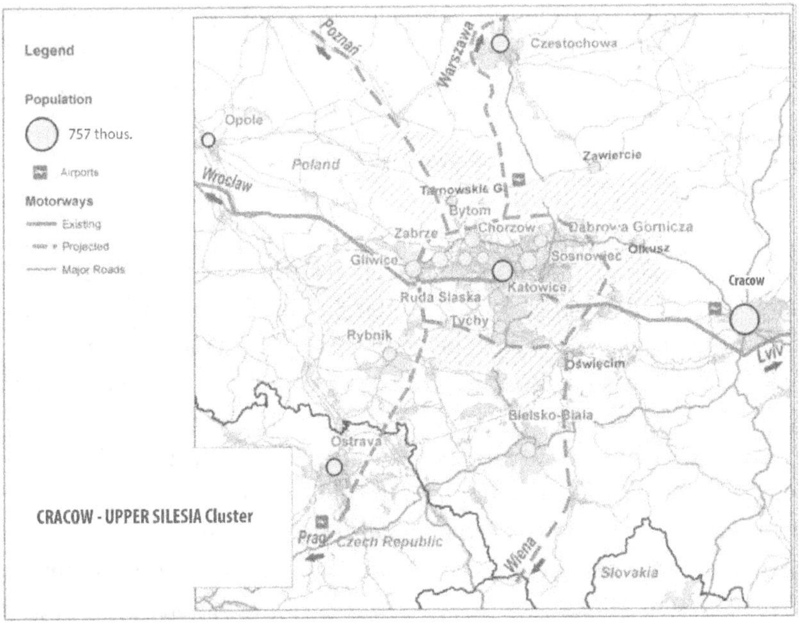

Fig. 5.6. CRUS cluster

Source: Author's own elaboration.

this system are motorways A4 (west–east) and A1 (north–south, still under construction). A characteristic strength of this region is diverse but complementary, dense network of cities, especially in the Upper Silesia Agglomeration, but also in the Rybnik Coalfield District and Ostrava–Karvina industrial basin. Such a city cluster allows providing a certain balance for the other settlement systems in Europe. Therefore, it is necessary to undertake not only actions initiated by the local authorities, but to go beyond the frames of cities, regions, and districts. Increasing the competitiveness in this particular region largely depends on the success of such efforts. For the development of the particular cities and the entire CRUS cluster, cooperation in the following four fields is paramount: transport, economy, human capital, and protection of the environment (Ziobrowski and Jarczewski, 2007).

The increasing worldwide fuel crisis may accelerate the construction of a European fast train network with its axis being Paris–Lille–London and Lille–Brussels–Köln–Amsterdam (PBKAL). This system is meant to cross the Pyrenees and connect with the system of Madrid, and in the southeast below the Alps, it will run the way of Paris–Lyon–Turin. It is also considered to prolong the fast train way from Cologne via Berlin to Warsaw and further to Moscow. This tendency will facilitate the intensification of cooperation among increasing number of cities, cutting in time the distance between them.

The plan of Greater London from 1944, as defined by Patrick Abercrombie, was based on the satellite model. The new cities-satellites-connected with London via fast trains running at high frequency — are 100,000 up to 200,000 Milton Keynes and Northampton (both built in the 1960s) and smaller, about 50,000 Kettering and Corby, all of them well equipped to provide very high standards of service. The old districts such as Thames Gateway or Stratford, 5 km away from, the centre of London, once totally deserted, have now been completely rebuilt with huge service-office-housing complexes of high build intensity including the Olympic Village and sports facilities (New Stratford).

Stockholm was following London through innovative thinking, designing, and building new satellite cities according to the rule of multimodal transport system integration with urban development. Around the train/bus stops and crossroads, a build of high intensity was concentrated.

The General Plan of the Greater Paris from 1965 was based on the same London model. In this case, however, the model was improved by introducing a system of internal motorways in a layout based on radio-centric model. The mentioned General Plan defined multicentric development of this particular mega structure, which apart from Paris included Valle de la Marne, de Tigery, d'Evry, Trappe, and Sergy Pontois. In the last plan from 1994, the multicentric development of the Parisian metropolis was sustained, including two new centres of activities added to the cluster: Val d'Europe and Saclay. Due to this change, even more intense transport connections were planned, which was meant to strengthen the already existing radiocentric system. A new plan, which takes into account new challenges and defines new objectives, is now in progress (Fig. 5.7).

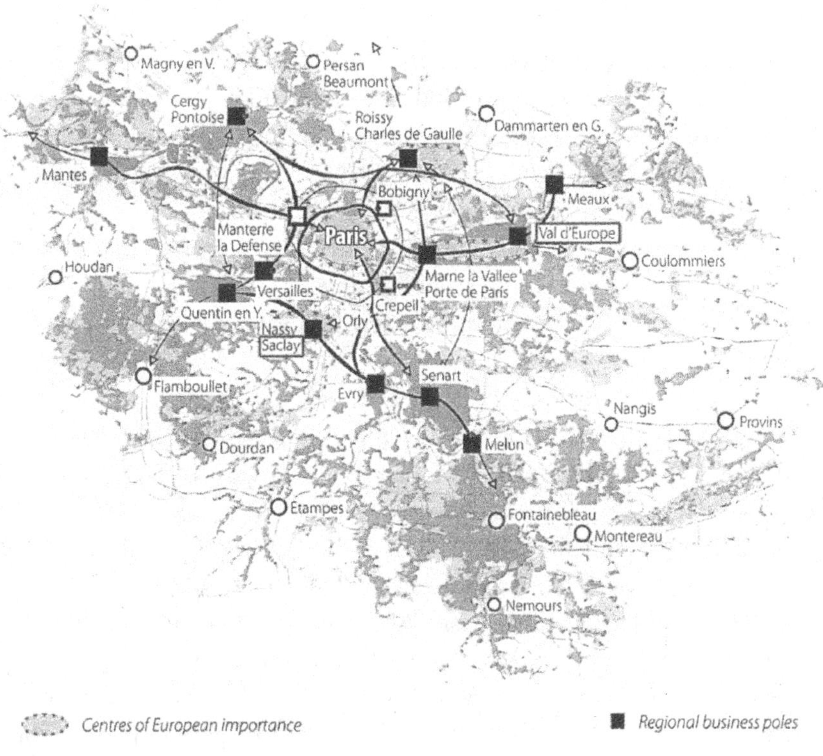

Fig. 5.7. General plan of the Paris region

Source: *Institut d'aménagement et d'urbanisme de la région d'Île-de-France* (2017).

Among the challenges of the plan, there are social and territorial integrity, economic development, and sustaining the international character of the Paris region, at the same time creating new possibilities for the development of the other metropolises such as Lyon, Lille, Marseille, or Toulon. On the agenda, there was also the construction of 53,000 flats per year to satisfy the needs of the existing and future residents, as well as balancing the mobility with development of communication and transport including increased capacity of junctions.

The key directives for the development of Greater Paris are:

- ensuring similar living standard in all cities in the region;
- ensuring conflict — free existence between urbanization and nature;
- building an environmental system conjoined with national and European ecological channels.

The above-mentioned General Plan and the Financial Coordination Plan were among the instruments for realization of the plan alongside with creation of local and regional planning agencies, territorial planning agencies for Paris region, and private–public enterprises and institutions managing the development as well as the real estate.

At present, the rule to maximize access to all destinations is still on the agenda, with preference given to pedestrians, cycling, and public transport. It is meant to deter people from driving cars. The satellite cities, in these terms, are to function as multimodal transport hubs. The same rules were applied in the planning of Greater Madrid in the 1990s.

One of the biggest challenges turned out to be the idea of Urban Renaissance formed in the "Urban Task Force" report in 1999. The idea was directed at the Anglo-Saxon countries to increase density in the rebuilt areas. The right thought, one might consider, posed a few questions though: What density are we considering? What density would comply with the rules of sustainable development? How tall should the buildings be in order to satisfy the needs of the residents rather than investors? The answers may be different depending on the city itself and the urban culture. It is paramount to introduce modern means of public transport and limit the use of cars. The idea has already exceeded Europe. In 1975,

Singapore copied the solutions applied in London and introduced an electronic fee system for accessing the streets. Thanks to this, the traffic decreased by 30%. Applying European solutions, the authorities of the city introduced congestion charge and built the underground system, as well as initiated a high urban density. Underground system has also been built in Rio de Janeiro and San Paulo.

5.3. The Future of Megacities Development

Megacities, although not formally, do function as cities–countries, with population oscillating between 10 million and 30 million (except Tokyo). It is, thus, difficult to register their development in national regulations and planning systems. They function in their own global rhythm. Their number will be constantly rising and their spatial form will continue to evolve in the direction of system with beyond — region or even above — nation spatial scope (Centrope, CRUS cluster). Megacities have powerful development potential. Well-developed business infrastructure, global connection network, and high ability to create and absorb innovations suggest that planning their further development is significant. The question arises, in what direction the development will go and what planning instruments will be adequate to manage this process.

Megacities in the highly developed countries will continue to introduce changes leading to sustainable development. Developing countries, on the other hand, will need improvements in the functioning of those amorphic structures and most certainly a technological breakdown in the field of public transport. It should to be pointed here, that development is never a constant process. For the last few years, one can observe the symptoms of "shrinking" of cities, and the economic crisis lasting since 2008 calls for re-orientating the thought about their future. For the benefit of more effective development management, more attention should be paid to local and regional planning. These are mainly general plans and programmes defining: prognosis of economic development, prognosis of population growth, physical structure of space development models (mono or polycentric, satellite, linear or concentratic), basic categories of utilizing the terrain by dividing it into urbanized terrain, open terrain with highly controlled and limited urbanization, terrain permanently not urbanized, and terrain reserved for the development of infrastructure and transport systems including public transport. Maintaining the division into the basic zones of utilization may stop the chaotic urbanization process and help plan realistic infrastructural and transportation systems and solutions. An inspiration here could be the San Francisco General Development Plan (see Fig. 5.8). Moreover, it might be an idea to put into practice sector development plan for example, of transport and infrastructure systems, or coordinated plans of big urban operations and, finally, commonly used local plans.

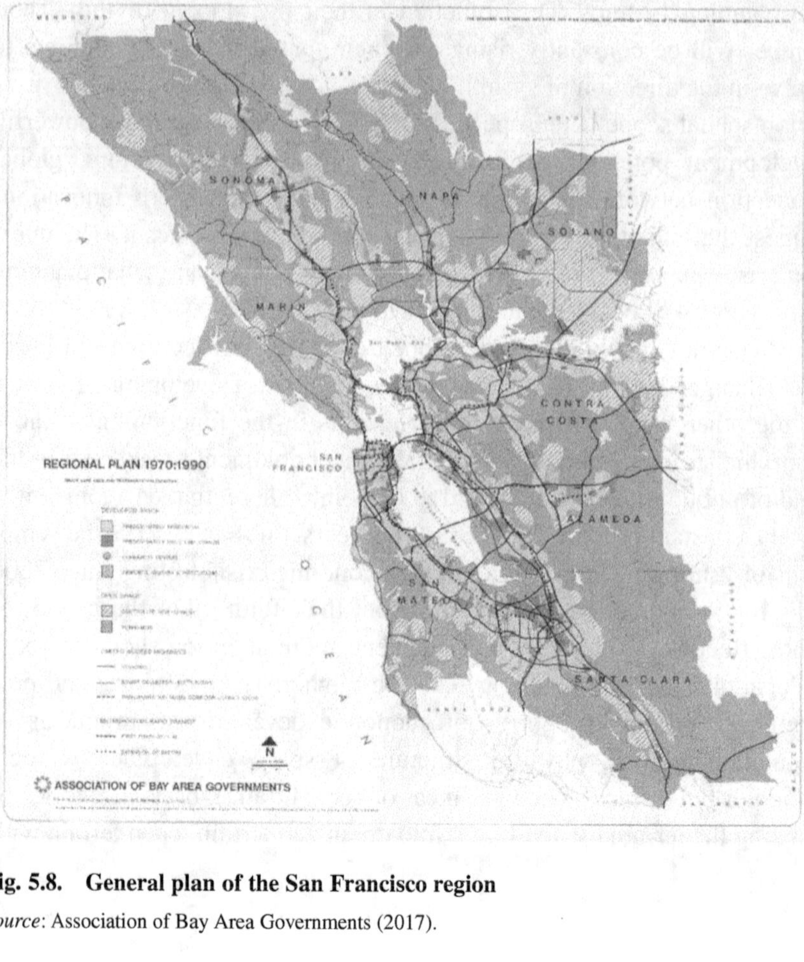

Fig. 5.8. General plan of the San Francisco region

Source: Association of Bay Area Governments (2017).

A general motto for the spatial planning of the development of megacities could be the universal maxim written in the New Athens Charter from 2003. It poses that the concept of a city as a group of small towns or societies connected together corresponds, according to the European Committee, to the vision of a city that is fulfilling the requirements of sustainable development and concern about the environment. A town is understood here as a structural unit that is part of a megacity, having its own identity and cultural climate, clear activity of social connections, and easy access to the basic services. Small towns, being the elements of big cities structure, should not be correlated with low-intensity build-up (Taylor, 2004).

The maxim, however, is not universal enough to be used anywhere else apart from Europe and North America. The future of megacities, whose development so far has been characterized mainly by quantitative changes, may depend largely on the national development policy. If the policy succeeds to concentrate on hampering the process of accumulation of the megacities potential by for example, supporting the growth of the smaller cities, megacities will get the chance to re-orientate their development policy towards qualitative changes. Managing serious changes in such complicated units as megapolises requires more in-depth research in order to identify the development mechanisms (Ziobrowski *et al.*, 2012).

It is expected that global importance of large agglomerations will stimulate the achievement of a high-level productivity and higher levels of ecological balance and, thereby, increase the quality of life there. Megacities are — and will be — a great attraction for both immigrants and tourists. Cities must create a friendly atmosphere for business. They should also provide public administration that is responsible and willing to cooperate in the decision-making process and leading public investments. New, highly effective transport systems and modern, more efficient nature systems will significantly affect the future of the urban structure of megacities.

5.4. Conclusions

Megacities are considered a phenomenon of the 20th century. The question arises whether their development is more the result of planning and management or the external factors. In the planning the development of megacities, much attention is being paid to improving their functionality and life standards as well as applying some revolutionary solutions in the transport system. One of the key factors in the development of megacities is the link between information economy and global production. It is very difficult to define a clear model of the functional structure of megacities because they develop too fast, very often chaotically, and without much planning. Nevertheless, megacities in the highly developed countries will continue to exhibit qualitative changes leading to the sustainable development, whereas those in developing countries will require a technological improvement based on the specificity of their planning system in the field of public transport and standard of living.

References

Association of Bay Area Governments (2017). Retrieved from http://www.abag.ca.gov [access: 16.01.2017].

Centrope (2013). Retrieved from www.centrope.com [access: 02.10.2013].

Europe — basemap (2017), 123RF portal. Retrieved from http://pl.123rf.com/search.php?word=map+europe&srch_lang=pl&imgtype=&Submit=+&t_word=&t_lang=pl&orderby=0&sti=mbsp3z1n2ffrofqg9q|&mediapopup=46701317 [access: 16.01.2017].

Federal Office for Building and Regional Planning (2004). Retrieved from http://www.bbr.bund.de/BBR/EN/Home/home_node.html [access: 16.01.2017].

Hall, P. (2006). *Planning and Sustainable Development of Metropolitan Capital Regions*. Madrid: Direccion General de Urbanismo y Planification Regional, 25–47.

Hall, P. and K. Pain (2006). *The Polycentric Metropolis: Learning from Mega-City Regions in Europe*. London: Earthscan.

Institut d'aménagement et d'urbanisme de la région d'Île-de-France (2017). Retrieved from https://www.iau-idf.fr [access: 16.01.2017].

Llewelyn-Davies (1997). *Four World Cities*. London: Comedia.

Planning and Sustainable Development of Metropolitan Capital Regions, special post conference edition by Direccion General de Urbanismo y Planification Regional. (2006). Madryt.

Rijksplanologishe, D. (2017). Retrieved from www.bbsr.de [access: 16.01.2017].

Taylor, P.J. (2004). *World City Network: A Global Urban Analysis*, London: Routledge. Retrieved from www.eurometrex.org [access: 09.10.2013].

Ziobrowski, Z. (2008). *Polskie aglomeracje jako innowacyjne systemy współpracy*. In T. Marszał (Ed.). *Rola polskich aglomeracji wobec wyzwań strategii lizbońskiej. Studia KPZK PAN* 120, pp. 113–134.

Ziobrowski, Z. and W. Jarczewski (2007). *Kształtowanie Europejskich Centrów Współpracy. Regiony — pismo liderów samorządowych*, numer specjalny.

Ziobrowski, Z., W. Jarczewski and K. Kafka (2012). *Modele zarządzania gospodarką przestrzenną w obszarach metropolitalnych i aglomeracjach. Kompendium*. Kraków: IRM.

6

THREATS AND CHALLENGES POSED BY THE RISE OF MEGACITIES

Konrad Prandecki, Wojciech Kazanecki, and Sylwia Śmietanko

6.1. Introduction

The second industrial revolution brought in its wake a growing population shift from rural to urban areas, and this trend has only continued to grow in strength. The most important manifestation of this increasing urbanization has been the rise of metropolitan areas with populations in excess of 10 million people. Such urban agglomerations, termed "megacities," have risen to become the world's economic centres and cultural hubs, and their role in the modern-day world may be likened to that of the city-states in Ancient Greece or city clusters in medieval Europe. As important as megacities are today, world development scenarios anticipate continuous further growth in their importance, stemming not only from surging population numbers but above all the numerous changes ushered in by globalization. Nonetheless, various ongoing trends and changes in the world may also give rise to a range of threats, challenges, and dangers faced by these megacities of the future, which may significantly affect how their development plays out.

The purpose of this study, therefore, is to attempt to encapsulate and characterize these potential future threats resulting from the rise of megacities. We will do so by performing a critical analysis of the available literature, by applying inductive reasoning and by positing development scenarios. Since sources and studies devoted specifically to the issue of megacities are quite limited in this regard, and so we will in many instances be drawing upon the findings of research into the broader relations between urban and rural areas in general.

The topic is a particularly pertinent one to address, we feel, given that any reliable scenarios for future world development must take account of the potential occurrence of negative phenomena and identify the factors that may lead them to materialize — and, given the great and still-rising importance of megacities, any and all negative phenomena pertaining to them will have a major impact on world development as a whole. Due to the limited space available here, we will present these issues more as a general overview, seeking to depict this problem as a certain whole. Yet, it is of course worth bearing in mind that each megacity functions within its own specific conditions, and that translates into variations in the scale of certain negative phenomena and differing likelihood of their occurrence in each case. At the same time, we acknowledge that this study does not comprehensively exhaust the issue at hand.

Lastly, let us close this introduction by noting one final caveat: the descriptions presented herein are by no means meant to be taken as quantitative evaluations, that is, no attempts are made to determine how likely individual phenomena are or how strongly they might impact on the development of specific megacities.

6.2. Megacities as the Playground for Emerging Threats

Over the past several decades, many threats have taken on global dimensions under the influence of ongoing globalization processes. This has largely stemmed from the increasingly uniform human behaviour manifesting itself across the world, resulting from the previously unknown possibilities for the transmission of information and, by the same token, for the spread of imitative patterns of behaviour.[1] One of the negative consequences of globalization has involved unleashing market forces on a

[1] For more information on trends following from the dissemination of the information revolution and their consequences, see for instance Prandecki *et al.* (2015).

widespread scale, which together with the collapse of the bipolar world model have led to the dominance of greed and egoism in human behaviour (Kleer, 2012). Such phenomena have become prevalent not only at the country-specific or national level but also at the individual level. In consequence, success and prestige have come to be widely identified with wealth. Such trends have also led to the mass commercialization of all possible relations — the most widespread manifestation of this can be found in the tendency to overstate the importance of economic growth (as measured by GDP growth). Such a situation results in growing uncertainty and increased volatility of phenomena — not only as affecting the economic sphere, but also impacting on people's views on moral and religious issues, cultural values, and societal relations.

All these phenomena in a sense set the backdrop for the rapidly growing trend towards urbanization. In 1900, urban dwellers accounted for around 13–14% of the world's population. In 1930, that share rose to 30% (Wawrzyński, 2012). By 2008, over half of the world's population lived in cities (United Nations, 2014). In the modern-day world, the most conspicuous manifestation of urbanization processes lies in the development of megacities. Based on the further extrapolation of this trend and the ongoing social transformations in the world, the rise of megacities is regarded as one of the fundamental megatrends.[2] This follows from the projected rise in population numbers, urbanization scenarios, as well as socio-cultural and economic changes (Prandecki *et al.*, 2013b).

Megacities usually play the role of production, trade, and service centres on a regional scale, sometimes even globally. In this context, we can list such megacities as Delhi, Moscow, London, New York, Beijing, Shanghai, and Tokyo, all of which simultaneously represent major centres of scientific and cultural development. Given their more convenient transport links, especially a well-developed network of flight connections (Wawrzyński, 2012), they are places where ideas are exchanged on an international scale, inventions are designed, and innovations are developed. In the future, this role will continue to grow. Moreover, megacities play a similar role in culture, by creating new trends, fashions, perceptions

[2]More information on megatrends can be found that is, in Naisbitt (1984), Prandecki (2012); Prandecki (2013b); Prandecki *et al.* (2013b).

of the world, and values. Such factors, in particular higher income levels (compared to jobs outside metropolitan areas), lead to increased interest in city life. Greater ease of life in megacities is yet another factor behind their appeal.

Consequently, megacities have grown increasingly independent within their countries of origin, slowly but gradually "breaking away" from their home state.[3] We might even hazard the claim that in the foreseeable future megacities will become separate geopolitical entities, breaking out of the traditional framework of international relations, wherein only sovereign states are recognized as the autonomous entities of international law. In a sense, that will mean a return to the Middle Ages, this time on a global scale. Such cities already include New York, London, Paris, and Shanghai. Moreover, numerous researchers (e.g. Kasarda and Lindsay, 2011; Wawrzyński, 2012) anticipate that the airports of the future will not be mere appendages to cities, situated on the outskirts far away from the centre, but on the contrary, cities will instead be developing around airports as focal points for the movement of people, ideas, and goods (although the primacy of sea transport of goods will not be challenged even in the long term).

Rapidly growing megacities and their ever-increasing importance on a global scale make a certain range of threats more likely to occur. Characterized by a high concentration of people and unprecedented dynamics, megacities are especially susceptible to certain types of crises, social disorganization, and political conflicts, in addition to being affected more deeply by the consequences of natural disasters. All this demands that the analyst take account of a broad range of potential negative scenarios in the development of megacities, including even their possible demise and disintegration. An analysis of the type presented here is intended to serve as a warning: It is aimed at helping to prevent dangerous trends from becoming a reality in the future.

---

[3] One example of the growing role played by major cities can be found in the establishment of a consortium of the 131 largest cities in the United States, initiated by Seattle Mayor Greg Nickels. Its goal is to fight climate change regardless of the lack of interest in such issues on the part of the central authorities in the United States. In 2009, the group consisted of 900 cities with 80 million inhabitants (Inayatullah, 2011).

Three of the fundamental sources of such threats are as follows (Porwit, 2009: 2–3):

- ever-widening differentials between living conditions in rich and poor areas,
- uncontrollable degradation of the environment (both the natural environment and human interactions in the context of cultural and religious relations), leading to insufficiently healthy conditions for the human race,
- manifestations of societal discord, even flagrant violence.

The list of these factors can also be extended to include: Problems with multiculturalism and the impact of the scale of development on governance and political factors (the impact of the state on cities). All these factors may lead to the occurrence of such phenomena as:

- socio-economic exclusion,
- the expansion of zones of poverty (slums, favelas, homelessness, etc.),
- surging crime,
- terrorism,
- transportation problems,
- the uncontrolled and unplanned development of suburbs,
- air pollution,
- limited access to water,
- the occurrence of natural disasters.

All these challenges, to be addressed herein, as well as numerous others not specifically listed in this study, can potentially turn megacities into victims of their own development, even to become causative factors behind the degradation of their whole region. An excellent example of this phenomenon can be found in Detroit in the late 20th century: Although the city never had a population exceeding 10 million inhabitants, and was therefore never technically a "megacity," it was a major population cluster in the United States and its decline as an urban centre has been dramatic.

Most of those dangers have admittedly been widely recognized elsewhere. In many cases, various programs have even been devised with a view to addressing them and mitigating their potential impact. However, we feel that the existing literature fails to provide any comprehensive overview or classification of the risks potentially stemming from the development of megacities. To address this need, in the present study we have divided these potential threats into five fundamental groups: economic threats, social threats, security threats, environmental threats, and infrastructural threats. The mutual connections between these groups and their complexity prevent clear-cut borders from being drawn between them. However, we maintain that this rather general classification makes the consequences of ongoing changes easier to understand and can help raise awareness of the attendant challenges.

6.3. A Proposed Classification of Threats to the World's Megacities

6.3.1. Economic challenges

Most modern-day economic thought relies on a growth-focused theory as the basis for making decisions and carrying out economic reforms. The best-known gauge of growth is the GDP growth indicator, which unfortunately gets wrongly construed as representing a gauge of quality of life (Royo, 2007). Maintaining a high rate of global growth is made possible by rising consumption. The German social theorist Erich Fromm (1976) distinguished two fundamental paradigms for describing people's quality of life, namely the "having" mode and the "being" mode. The former plays a dominant role in the context of those living in major agglomerations: as a result of high population densities and the consequent loss of close social relations with the people around them (neighbours who live on the same street, in the same neighbourhood, and so on), people become anonymous in the hustle and bustle of big cities, and as such behaviour (i.e. ways of "being") is no longer treated as a sign of prestige.[4] Consequently, wealth (i.e. "having") is becoming the simplest way of demonstrating one's status. Cities, particularly megacities, are therefore

[4]Although anonymity has indeed become somewhat superficial, given technological advancements and the information revolution, from the perspective of an individual who has no contact with the controlling authorities (which means a majority of inhabitants), a sense of alienation seems justified.

becoming drivers of consumption on a local, regional, and global scale. Consequently, too much attention is being attached to material goods, with satisfaction and happiness being regarded as contingent on consumption.

The goods accumulated by urban dwellers create the impression that they live better lives. Being employed in a city is widely seen as being advantageous: as involving having an office job in a well-heated building, with lower health risk, and significantly higher salaries than in smaller towns. However, this is to some extent a debatable issue: for example, it is true that the mean household income in the United States is $1,500 higher in big cities compared to smaller towns (Szymańska, 2007), but the costs of living in cities are also higher, which more often than not outweigh the benefits. However, higher income levels are still regarded as a fundamental factor driving the further development of megacities. For that reason, economic issues should be treated as the point of departure when numerous threats of a social nature are being analyzed. Above all, such considerations should focus on the problem of unequal access to wealth.

The world economy continues to develop in spite of the economic crisis of recent years, though economic forecasts are predicting certain shifts in the global balance of power (*cf.* Prandecki *et al.*, 2012, 2013a; Nawrot, 2013, 2014, among others). World Bank estimates indicate that in 2014 developing countries played a dominant role in the economy for the first time since the end of the industrial revolution, generating over 50% of the world's GDP (IMF, 2014). In the international arena, we can observe the emergence of such new powers as Brazil, China, India, Indonesia, and Turkey. Efforts to eliminate global poverty largely place the emphasis on the role of economic transformations (Prandecki *et al.*, 2013b), yet it is rarely noted that such processes lead to widening income differentials in the world as well as within these new powers. That is because income levels rise much faster among the most affluent social groups compared to other strata, especially the poor. A study of income inequality conducted in the OECD (2011) countries in 2013 shows that disproportions grow chiefly as a result of the rapid raise in pay levels among those holding high posts. In 1973, in USA, the CEO-to-worker salary ratio was 22.3. In 2013, that relation had risen to 296 (Davis and Mishel 2014). Furthermore, income levels measured in terms of purchasing power parity among those with average and low incomes did not change in the years 2001–2010 (WEF, 2013). Widening inequalities are likewise visible in China, where this process is very strong and based in part on legal regulations (the *Hukou* System). It has even been remarked that China has built its urban wealth on the backs of its peasants (Treiman, 2012). So far, disparities have been visible not only between urban and rural areas, but also within the same metropolitan area (Shi and Chuliang, 2010). People born in a city end up being paid a lot more for doing the same jobs than migrants (Zhang and Treiman, 2013). Growing disparities lead to reduced satisfaction, social problems, and tensions between various groups in the same city (Jiang *et al.*, 2012). Similar problems are likewise affecting megacities in other developing countries, including Delhi, Dhaka, Karachi, Lagos, and Mexico City.

Generally, it can observed that the expansion of megacities has been more rapid in developing countries (Easterlin *et al.*, 2011), largely due to differences between rural and urban areas in terms of access to goods and their consumption. Inhabitants of rural areas are in a disadvantaged economic situation and therefore are more likely to migrate and more willing to take on the attendant risks. As the economy grows, such differences may narrow, yet the disproportions continue to exist.

However, growing inequality is also visible in highly developed countries, and widening income differentials are a global problem. This is quite poignantly illustrated by a report by Oxfam (2015), written ahead of the World Economic Forum in Davos (WEF), which notes that the wealth owned by the world's eight richest people in 2016 exceeded that of the bottom half of the population (Oxfam, 2017). These groups each own around 1% of the world's wealth (CS, 2014). Moreover, the rich are accumulating wealth much faster than the poor (Kopczuk, 2014; Saez and Zucman, 2014). Credit Suisse's estimates indicate that the number of the richest people whose wealth is equal to that of the bottom half of the population is in fact consistently growing smaller: as recently as in 2010, the number of such individuals stood at 388. What is more, analyses from 2014 demonstrate that the wealth owned by the top 1% rose compared to 2008, while the wealth of the bottom 50% remained at the same level. This means that the richest elite are accumulating wealth also at the expense of the middle class (CS, 2014). Yet, coupled with growing pressure encouraging ever-increasing consumption, this actually causes the demand for goods and services to be satisfied to an ever-smaller degree — a trend Kołodko (1984) has aptly described as the paradox of a lower level of need-satisfaction at a higher consumption level.

The further widening of economic inequalities may lead to tensions and become a flash point for social unrest. Such disparities are growing in intensity in metropolitan areas, where it is easier for crowds of rioters to erupt. What is more, rioters often have a sense of impunity in such places, as the security forces are unable to establish their identity and bring them to face punishment.

A desire to lead an ostensibly easier life (compared to that in rural areas and small towns) prompts many people to leave their home towns and pursue their happiness in large cities, often without realizing how differently social interactions operate there. Such people often fall victim to abuse, crime, and greed. Certain zones of prosperity therefore develop alongside whole zones of poverty (referred to as favelas, slums, etc.), with the latter in many cases expanding at a faster rate than the rest of the given city. The inhabitants of such areas are permanently excluded from access to virtually any of the amenities of modern civilization. They face persistent unemployment, have limited access to new technologies, and earn their living by gathering or by resorting to crime. Differences in standards of living, especially in terms of access to health care, are so wide within cities that the United Nations refers to such zones of poverty as "hidden cities" (UN-HABITAT, 2010). Such problems are especially visible in developing countries, where the share of those willing to abandon their existing lifestyle in search of something ostensibly better is much greater than in the developed countries, whose inhabitants largely already possess sufficient wealth for their survival. Such zones of poverty are characterized not only by worse income conditions but also by poorer standards of living in general, including in terms of access to health care, water, and sanitation. Another challenge is the absence of adequate infrastructure. In wealthier countries, exclusion often results from an inability to financially provide services to such groups, or from their alienation (their own inability to adjust). One of the factors leading to this is the lack of different, positive models of behaviour, demonstrating that one can achieve a lot by working hard.

The great advantage enjoyed by megacities is visible not just in the economic sphere. In addition to unequal access to health care mentioned earlier, one can see differences in education, which in the modern-day world provides a basis for the further development of both individuals and society at large. Generally speaking, megacities are widely believed to offer much greater opportunities to get a better education practically at all levels (*cf.* Knoblauch and Chase, 2015; Midouhas and Platt, 2014, among others). Such differences are especially visible in developing countries, where many members of society have not even completed primary school. China's megacities are the most drastic example of inequality in this respect: under *hukou* regulations, an overwhelming share of children of migrants from rural areas have no access to public education in the city where they reside. Many of them are left excluded, because their parents cannot afford expensive private education. Widening disparities cause persistent divisions in society and prevent its members from identifying with the city.

In the future, social disparities will continue to widen in the aftermath of the information revolution (Prandecki *et al.*, 2015), with one of its manifestations being automatization and the replacement of human labour with robots. As computers and machines that perform tasks without direct human supervision are coming into wider use, forecasts are predicting a downturn in demand for labour (Wierzbicki, 2011). This pertains to almost all professional groups. Indeed, assembly line workers are not the only ones who are being replaced by robots: The same holds true even to a larger degree for office workers and data analysts, whose work is being carried out by computers able to query electronic databases faster than any human being. Professions that require creativity (i.e. designers) or a combination of aesthetic sense and manual labour (gardeners, hairdressers) will remain resistant to these changes in the long term.

Such processes are already visible. The number of workers in the EU countries fell by 8.4 million people over the 5 years of the economic crisis, and this was the main factor driving growing unemployment (Kabaj, 2014). As a result of falling demand, employment may become a luxury good in the long term, which will further exacerbate disparities and social dissatisfaction. In most cultures, employment is increasingly treated not only as a way of accumulating wealth but also as an element of prestige. Being unemployed leads to both limited access to resources and decreased self-esteem, which may consequently lead to depression or even suicide.

The changes being forecast in the labour market will above all affect those living in major cities, where they are abetted by the faster dissemination of new technologies and solutions. Consequently, such processes will further exacerbate social dissatisfaction, thus contributing to a greater risk of economically-rooted social unrest. This entails a growing need for greater financial social assistance in major cities.

Consumerism, which serves as the basis for modern-day economic development, often attempts to promote a shallower sense of happiness, limited to the possession of material goods. Viewed in these terms, life in cities, in particular in megacities, should have an enormous advantage over life in rural areas. Financial motives are a fundamental reason for the popularity of megacities and their rapid development. However, life in such metropolitan areas goes hand-in-hand with many inconveniences, such as overpopulation, environmental pollution, and an excessively fast pace of life. Such phenomena may lead to a sense of anomie (lack of moral guidance from society at large) and alienation (UNDP, 2009), which may affect both individuals and entire social groups. The potential consequences include rebellion, withdrawal, or various ritual demonstrations of being separate.

As this discussion makes clear, the economic threats to the development of megacities (as discussed in this section) should therefore best be viewed as closely linked to and intertwined with the social threats (discussed in the next section), with the two categories together representing the leading internal source of threats to megacity development.

6.3.2. Social threats

Given the significant typological diversity of major cities (stemming from a broad range of geopolitical, historical, cultural, and political factors), any analysis of the social threats inherent in the development of such cities will require an individual approach. When analyzing "overpopulation" as a category, for instance, per-resident housing space figures that are considered utterly unacceptable in the context of New York may be regarded as completely normal in Hong Kong and even luxurious in Dhaka. Therefore, any theoretical considerations of social threats that rely solely on economic indicators and the traditional classification of states into developing vs. developed countries will by no means be exhaustive. One example is Tokyo, a wealthy Japanese city whose inhabitants have very little space *per capita*.

Major cities are developing quickly in developing countries, especially in Asia, South America, and Africa, mainly as a result of internal migrations. Inhabitants of rural areas migrate on a massive scale in search of a better life and settle in cities, which are growing uncontrollably, generating social problems on an enormous scale. It is such rapid urbanization that poses the greatest danger to the harmonious development of the societies in megacities. Migrants form a very heterogeneous group, a fact that exacerbates social inequalities and hinders spatial governance in megacities. One of the most important challenges posed by this process is a very high population density (including overpopulation). Dhaka, the capital of Bangladesh, has an overall population density of 44,000 people per km^2. In the city's slums, however, this ratio reaches the astronomic proportion of as many as 1 million people per km^2, making Dhaka probably the most densely populated city in the world (Machnik, 2013).

Galloping urbanization contributes to the further consolidation of existing social inequalities, unemployment, the grey economy, and surging crime rates. It appears, however, that the greatest challenge is posed by the multiculturalism of megacities and by the related potential for social unrest on racial, religious, and moral grounds. Such issues have not been examined very comprehensively, yet an overview of existing studies indicates that multiculturalism very often leads to a growing sense of being under threat (Arasaratnam, 2013).

Cultural differences may create divisions along various lines, with an individual's place of origin being one of the most fundamental criteria. Individuals born in a specific city usually feel somewhat superior, whatever their actual skills, experience, and qualifications may be. In rapidly developing megacities, this problem does not necessarily play a significant role: most inhabitants are migrants from elsewhere, so there is no clear-cut division between "us" vs. "them." One exception may be China, where discrimination against people of rural origin is actually rooted in legal regulations. Aversion to migrants is equally sorely felt in cities in highly developed countries. One reason for that lies in the structure of such metropolitan areas, which was established a long time ago. Nonetheless, the phenomenon is more visible especially in small towns and localities than in major population clusters, which guarantee a certain degree of anonymity to their residents.

Religious and ethnic differences are even more significant. Such divisions are often interrelated, although issues of nationality often lead to even greater fragmentation of the groups engaged in a conflict. In periods of prosperity, tensions between various social groups do not necessarily lead to the outbreak of significant social conflicts, because people's material needs can be satisfied at a relatively satisfactory level. However, the prospect of growing unemployment or falling income levels (such as pay cuts) and growing uncertainty leads to greater perception of the threat posed by "others" (those who are culturally, ethnically, or religiously different). This prompts greater integration among those who share similar interests, views, religious beliefs, or blood ties.

It is worth stressing that these problems affect all megacities. Although the differences may vary in scale, heterogeneity is a typical phenomenon in such vast urban agglomerations. Such differences are more visible in highly developed countries, where multiculturalism takes on global dimensions, but the problem also exists in metropolitan areas located in developing countries, where it typically encompasses only local ethnic and religious differences. However, the religious and ethnic challenges faced by cities in India or in Pakistan's Karachi may be seen as comparable to those facing New York and London; the only difference lies in their source. In India, they are rooted in religious differences between various groups endemic to the country (and other countries located in that region of the world), further exacerbated by the caste system. No significant religiously based friction should be expected in Karachi, yet tribal differences between various communities from throughout Pakistan, as well as Afghanistan, Iran, and some Arab countries, make the city a vast melting-pot facing problems approaching the same scale as those of the megacities in the Western world.

The escalation of negative trends goes hand in hand with the emergence of a sense of anomie. It results not only in greater integration among various groups but also in the emergence or closer development of cooperation within various subcultures whose members share the same lifestyle and distinguish themselves from others by having their distinctive language and rituals. Such groups also include various organized crime groups.

Megacities exhibit an extraordinary mix of various cultures. This necessitates a search for new policies in urban development and also ways of fostering cooperation among these communities (John, 2013). Nevertheless, cultural differences pose major obstacles to finding common ground for such cooperation. Studies conducted in the United Kingdom (Tip *et al.*, 2012) have shown that the greater the extent to which members of the British majority believe that members of minorities strive to maintain their original culture rather than to acculturate, the more threatened they feel, and vice versa: The more majority members perceived that members of ethnic minorities wanted to be in contact with British people or wanted to adopt British culture, the less threatened they felt. This suggests a certain paradoxical situation: Majority members report that they support multiculturalism as long as they perceive that minority members do not wish to maintain their original culture. Or, as the authors of the study put it, support for multiculturalism might be viewed as threatened by a sense of threat itself.

Such problems may be further accentuated by language differences. Those who do not know the generally accepted language or who have low proficiency with it are unable to express their thoughts clearly, which causes tensions to escalate. An inability to understand one another may also obstruct the decision-making process at various levels of city governance. The visions put forward by the central (city) authorities may end up getting treated differently by district councils or other lower-level bodies vested with executive power. Significant differences of opinion within a specific institution may lead to paralysis and an inability to make decisions, leading not only to slower growth but also to possible catastrophes. In addition, considerable cultural diversity may lead to the social exclusion of one or more social groups. Such a group may then become increasingly averse to the surroundings, which provides fertile ground for various kinds of extremism. Of course, such processes are by no means rapid, yet they may prove extremely dangerous. Experience shows that acts of terror are rooted chiefly in religious and cultural differences, rather than being committed for economic reasons.

Without a doubt, a megacity's heterogeneous population and rapid urbanization are conducive to the emergence of a range of social pathologies. Migrants may arrive in such huge numbers that a city cannot absorb them while providing decent living conditions (ensuring places to live and the basic goods related to the urban lifestyle — education, white-collar employment, services, health care, and so on). That is how zones of poverty emerge on the outskirts of cities, areas characterized by ramshackle housing construction, no access to potable water, as well as surging prostitution, crime, and epidemics. When the urban fabric expands in this way, it leads to the ruralization of urban space (giving rise to an intermediate type of space, which cannot be incorporated into the urban community), excluding it from the mainstream of change and by the same token fossilizing and further ingraining the existing social inequalities. Internalizing the urban lifestyle requires that immigrants from rural areas acculturate or partially integrate with their new environment (Szymańska, 2007). Poverty and the lack of access to education and health care often leave entire communities stigmatized, effectively obstructing the aforementioned processes.

Consequently, we can conclude that excessively rapid urbanization, a high population density, uncontrolled settlement, and a considerable cultural and linguistic diversity can make governance of a megalopolis very difficult. Some researchers (Poskrobko, 2014) have even posited that current trends are leading towards a similar social situation as the one seen back in the second latter half of the 19th century, which caused touched off a number of revolutions almost across the whole of Europe and also two world wars. A lack of social stability in the development of megacities could lead to comparable events.

6.3.3. Security threats

A city, even one whose population exceeds 10 million people, is usually part of a larger state entity. For that reason, it wields limited influence over certain political realities affecting it, especially those that stretch across national borders. Consequently, it does not have much of a say in international conflicts, and so it is difficult for a megacity to adopt an adequate strategy for ensuring the security of its own development, in the face of crises that may occur between countries or are rooted in a deeper-seated clash of civilizations.[5]

On the other hand, cities naturally represent attractive targets in the event of a military conflict, as seizing control over urban areas may be crucial for victory. Yet, from the perspective of their military security, megacities are increasingly becoming places where struggles/armed conflicts resemble jungle warfare (the phrase "urban jungle" was coined with good reason). The newly emerging combination of simple, sometimes primitive weapons and state-of-the-art technologies (unmanned military hardware that can both track and directly attack targets) will bring about results that are increasingly difficult to predict. If we add the role of the media to this, we will reach what Münkler (1988: 66) described as follows (in the context of modern conflicts): "The unchaining of violence in the new wars stems not least from a combination of kalashnikov and Hollywood — the simplest Russian weapons technology and the extreme depiction of violence in American feature films." Simple (traditional) armed situations, wherein the two forces that stood against each other on the battlefield had clearly defined potentials and weapons and subscribed to specific rules of engagement, are becoming a thing of the past. This is especially true in the context of megacities.

From the military perspective, megacities are already the subject of extensive analyses, including on the part of the US Army, which is aware that although battles have been waged in cities in the past, even quite recently, military forces nonetheless have never yet faced the challenge posed by warfare in an area whose population exceeds 10 million people. According to the authors of the report Megacities and the United States Army: Preparing for a complex and uncertain future (Harris *et al.*, 2014), published in 2014, the problems that occur in megacities (such as uncontrolled demographic growth, widening social inequalities, growing

[5] We are referring here to Huntington's concept of the inevitable clash between the world's major civilizations (Huntington, 1993, 1996). Countries that belong to a specific civilization will automatically support the side closer to them. Although Huntington's concept has been criticized in numerous publications, it has some power to explain the causes of such events as Islamic terrorist attacks in the Western world.

support for radical political forces) will one day ultimately necessitate the deployment of a land force in such a location. This is a particularly problematic prospect in that the greatest challenges should be expected in megacities situated in developing countries, where — despite growing surveillance capabilities on the part of forces from developed countries (especially the United States) — chaos and the attendant inability to control the situation will be one of the dominant elements of warfare. Traditional military doctrine, treating a city as just another potential scene of battle, calls for such an urban area to be surrounded, cut off from external support and then for the enemy to be gradually eliminated by seizing more and more areas in piecemeal fashion. But as the authors of the report point out, the sheer scale of a megacity rules out operations of this sort, assuming that there will be tens (or even hundreds) of thousands of soldiers involved while the megacity will have a population of at least 10 million people, spread over many square kilometres. The notion of isolating the enemy completely from the virtual world is equally illusory. Hence, it is necessary to develop a new approach to the problem, one that will treat a megacity not in the reductionist way (as a set of elements that can be taken away from the whole and treated separately) but rather as a holistic entity that resists having its components considered in isolation. As already mentioned, each megacity is unique in terms of its development as well as cultural, political, geographic, and many other conditions, and this degree of diversity is seen by the American strategists as precluding any wide-ranging generalizations. Instead, the situation necessitates each megacity being treated as a separate case study. In order to make this task somewhat easier, they propose a variable they call the degree of integration, understood as the presence (or absence) of hierarchical governance (including security) and resultant resilience (ability to absorb stress).

Such military considerations also highlight the complex nature of efforts to ensure security in a large city in the event of riots, unrest, or other disruptions of public order. Such experiences as the riots in London (in 2011) and Paris (in 2013) demonstrate how easy it is for unrest to become unleashed and how difficult it is to regain control of a rebellious crowd. In London, clashes that continued for many days were sparked off by suspicions that a certain female participant had allegedly been subjected to an unjustified police check, during a march against violence staged after an underage drug dealer had been shot dead by the police (although no such check had actually happened). In Paris, the riots were caused by the police's attempt to check the identity of a woman wearing traditional Muslim clothes. Her companions attempted to prevent the police and were arrested, which resulted in many days of riots, clashes with the police, arson, and property damage.

In addition to challenges of a purely military nature, as noted by the US Army and even somewhat earlier by the Australian Army (Modernisation and Strategic Planning Division — Australian Army Headquarters 2014), the list of the most important security threats that may leave megacities largely paralyzed and cause difficulties in their day-to-day functioning should also be extended to include terrorism and organized crime. Although in both cases, perpetrators resort to violence as a primary tool for advancing their goals, these goals are completely different and for that reason the two phenomena need to be analyzed separately.

Undoubtedly, individuals and organizations that resort to terror as a *modus operandi* are attracted by the possibility of easily achieving effects of scale, in terms of the number of victims, the scale of destruction, and media publicity in connection with damage caused or potentially caused (Singh, 2006). The attack on the World Trade Center in New York in 2001 and the subsequent terrorist attacks on other megacities (Moscow in 2002, London in 2005, and Bombay in 2008) reverberated widely across the world. Similar attention was garnered by the more recent attack on the offices of the weekly *Charlie Hebdo* in Paris, but not by the nearly simultaneous events in Nigeria, where people were killed in terrorist attacks. This can be partially (though not exclusively) attributed to the media effect of the Paris story coverage, which dominated the world's major news networks for several days.

In any event, is worth bearing in mind that this phenomena will surely intensify in the future — given that megacities are attractive targets for prospective terrorists due to the high number of people that may be affected, the resultant effect of fear and panic, as well as the ease of hiding and advancing such sinister objectives. In addition, an act committed in a major city, for example, an attack on a police officer or the destruction of a public access building, will have a much greater impact than a similar-scale act committed in the provinces. Such precisely targeted attacks that do not actually cause massive damage to property will be a characteristic feature of acts of terrorism in the future.

Cyberterrorism will also pose a significant threat to the security of megacities. In a society heavily reliant on electronics and electricity, this will pose an important massive-scale danger. For a megacity, a power blackout means a major tragedy, especially in extreme climate conditions (severe hot and cold temperatures generate threats of different sorts, such as epidemics). Bacteriological and chemical attacks are equally dangerous as they may cause massive damage; even the threat alone may cause panic, which may easily lead to chaos and riots, one example being the reactions of people in African cities where entire districts were quarantined against the Ebola virus.

Criminals, on the other hand, naturally avoid publicity because it provokes the public authorities to react. Nonetheless, criminal activities will also intensify in cities for the following reasons:

- the greater scale of expected profits as a result of both greater "demand" for the fruits of organized crime (narcotics, prostitution) and greater "supply" (the number of people and institutions that can be intimidated, and the number of people who can be recruited to become criminals due to poverty and the lack of prospects); recently this phenomena generated great publicity in Brazilian cities (Rio de Janeiro, San Paulo) in connection with the violent measures taken by the police seeking to ensure security during the FIFA World Cup in 2014;
- more chaotic decision-making and communication (i.e. "loosely integrated" megacities in the typology presented above);
- the greater ease of operation for criminal groups, due to the ability to remain anonymous in the "urban jungle" environment and greater access to destitute potential recruits;
- the greater difficulties faced by law enforcement in monitoring such huge areas and masses of people, despite advancements in surveillance and monitoring technologies.

Other security-related threats pertaining to megacities can also be mentioned, such as problems resulting from fragments of the urban space being cordoned off or rendered isolated for security reasons. Examples include gated and closed residential estates, which are becoming an increasingly frequent element of urban landscapes. However, they, too, cause a range of problems, for instance by impairing interpersonal interactions and security services (such as road access for medical and rescue personnel).

In general, this and the previous section have in part sought to show that a number of security-related threats may also have politico-military underpinnings (e.g. military operations) and/or social ones (e.g. terrorism, crime, social unrest).

6.3.4. Environmental threats

The advancement of modern civilization has brought about not only undeniable benefits but also a range of negative phenomena, with environmental threats being regarded as some of the most problematic. Environmental threats are difficult to quantify and measure, and there is a time lag between when their causes occur and when their consequences eventually emerge. These issues have been a subject of numerous studies in recent years, yet there is still not enough concrete data in this field.

The environmental challenges facing megacities include the following groups of threats:

- resource depletion,
- the risk of natural disasters,
- environmental pollution,
- a growing threat of epidemics,

which we will now discuss in turn.

Pressure towards ever-increasing consumption and constant efforts to achieve the highest possible rate of economic growth both entail greater risk of the exhaustion of natural resources. An awareness of such barriers to development is something common among practitioners of the technical sciences, yet this approach is only marginally represented in mainstream economics, with the effect that Malthus's theories are still treated as a sign of catastrophic thinking, not as depicting actual threats. In the 20th century, the problem of the limitations imposed on growth by the depletion of natural resources was touched upon in the Club of Rome's first report (Meadows *et al.,* 1972). The ideas presented there prompted many scholars to start their own studies into resource availability. Although estimates vary significantly (Prandecki, 2013a), many studies raise warnings about the possibility of the exhaustion of certain rare resources starting around 2030.

Megacities are complex entities whose survival depends on the consumption of a large amount of resources. One fundamental resource is energy (especially electricity), necessary for virtually every aspect of a city to function properly: food storage, heating and cooling, transportation (of people and goods, including waste collection), lighting, communication, security, and so on. Other crucial resources include food, water, and nowadays also certain rare metals and elements needed for the construction of modern devices. As a result of their complex structure and lifestyle patterns (with consumption as an element of prestige), metropolitan areas are characterized by greater consumption of resources than small towns and rural areas. Yet, despite such greater consumption, megacities are themselves not especially exposed to the risk of the exhaustion of resources. Contrary to popular belief (i.e. "peak oil" theory), resource depletion is not something that occurs abruptly; rather, it is a process that is spread out over time. When access to certain resources becomes limited (as further extraction grows impossible), the market price of certain goods goes up, which means that only the richest can afford to buy them. Consequently, the poor are left excluded, so the global consumption of such goods declines, causing resources to be available for a longer period (Prandecki, 2014b). Megacities are centres of wealth, so many of their inhabitants should remain able, for longer, to secure access to resources that are running out. On the other hand, it is worth bearing in mind that skyrocketing prices may cause panic, thus leading to the rapid depletion of specific resources. Restoring their supply to a city of more than 10 million inhabitants is no simple task, and this is a risk that needs to be accounted for.

The issue of resource exhaustibility may prove more problematic for large cities in terms of access to resources consumed on a massive scale, with water being at the forefront. First of all, water for human consumption needs to be of high quality, safe for drinking. Moreover, the supply of water requires an infrastructure of relevant capacity and quality. Third, people at large need to have access to this infrastructure. Furthermore, water resources are often also needed in industrial processes, where it nevertheless becomes contaminated and therefore unsafe for human or agricultural use. Hence, access to clean drinking water in megacities is a particularly urgent issue and simultaneously one of the greatest threats facing their inhabitants (Kumar and Saroj, 2014). According to estimates, in some cities as many as 70% of those living in slums and other zones of poverty have no access to clean drinking water today (Szymańska, 2007), which means that such cities are constantly teetering on the brink of an environmental disaster.

Many megacities, such as Delhi, Mexico City, Beijing, and Shanghai, experience abrupt restrictions in their supply of surface and ground water. Consequently, the water necessary to satisfy human demand and industrial needs is transported in from places located farther and farther away, which increases the cost of water and the risk of breakdown (a supply hiatus) or contamination (harmful substances or bacteria).

On the one hand, such high concentration of people in one place leads to greater efficiency in land use and more efficient management of transportation networks (both people and goods, that is, electrical grids and the handling of municipal waste). On the other hand, megacities exert quite a negative impact on their environment. This influence is so great that it entails persistent consequences for their environs, even at relatively large distances. At the same time, as systems, megacities are extremely unstable and constantly evolving. Their high number of inhabitants makes the potential consequences of natural disasters much greater and more difficult to mitigate, especially in megacities located close to coastal areas characterized by considerable seismic activity — which is not a rare situation, given that such locations themselves foster economic growth (De Sherbinin *et al.*, 2007).

The high population densities, buildings that fail to meet basic safety standards, and ramshackle construction practices that are characteristic of zones of poverty in many megacities located in the countries of the poor South, together with the lack of access to medical and rescue services among people living there, entail enormous potential human losses in the event of an environmental disaster. Earthquakes, tornadoes, floods, and tsunamis all claim hundreds, thousands, or sometimes even hundreds of thousands of lives. For example, a landslide in the poor areas of Caracas in Venezuela in December 1999 left 30,000 people dead and over 480,000 destitute (De Sherbinin *et al.*, 2007); such tragedies are a consequence of most of the factors mentioned earlier, chiefly permanent and hereditary poverty, leading to the marginalization of entire communities and their concentration in unfavourably located slums. Note that the risk of natural disasters affecting zones of poverty also pertains to highly developed countries — in August 2005, Hurricane Katrina struck the US state of Louisiana on the coast of the Gulf of Mexico, forcing a significant portion of the city of New Orleans' population to evacuate and leaving over 1,000 dead (De Sherbinin *et al.,* 2007).

Managing the risk of natural disasters is therefore an extremely important field from the perspective of the stable future development of megacities. One example of the difficulties in resolving such problems can be found in Japan's experience with earthquake relief efforts. Studies conducted in the late 1990s demonstrated that, with the introduction of advanced security systems (warning systems, evacuation points, regulations banning entrance to certain zones, and so on), the homeless (informed with considerable delays) and the elderly (finding it difficult to evacuate quickly) were significantly more likely to die or suffer injuries (Takahashi, 1998; Wisner, 1998). This shows that even with very well-organized systems, aspects emerge that lead to certain forms of discrimination and exclusion.

Large cities are "producers" of various forms of pollution, which are side effects of various forms of human activity, generated by industrial centres in producing electricity, by means of transport, by the heating of residential buildings, etc. According to estimates, only 6.5% of the global population lives in megacities, but the impact of their activity of on the condition of the environment is much greater than that figure might indicate. The substances that megacities emit into the atmosphere, especially greenhouse gases, are especially important. However, sulphur oxides, responsible for such phenomena as acid rains, often prove more hazardous, affecting the local and regional condition of the environment in the immediate environs of a megacity to the greatest degree (Folberth *et al.*, 2015). Rapid development in the automotive sector and a high concentration of vehicles in cities are also very important. In this era of economic transformation, as citizens in developing countries accumulate wealth, the number of diesel cars is growing rapidly. Such vehicles cause great atmospheric pollution yet the automotive market in those countries shows no signs of slowing down (Tian *et al.*, 2012; Wang *et al.*, 2014; Xu, 2012).

Liquid and solid waste disposal poses an issue that is often neglected. The level of solid waste generation differs depending on the region, but it is safe to assume around 250 kg per person a year (or even twice that much in Western Europe and the United States). Given the minimum population of 10 million inhabitants, this means that a megacity faces a need for landfill or recycling sites capable of taking in at least 2.5 million tonnes of waste each year. This figure needs to be further augmented by the waste generated by urban renewal (reconstruction, the management of areas of greenery, and so on). Resolving the problem of waste requires waste transportation, sorting, landfill sites, landfill leak protection, and many other measures. If a city lacks adequate municipal systems in this regard, this may increase the risk of various diseases, including those of an epidemiological nature. How complicated such issues may prove is demonstrated by the problems caused by the temporary halting of waste removal in the south of Italy: Although the situation did not affect any megacity, it had far-reaching consequences (D'Alisa *et al.*, 2010). Models for how environmentally safe sewage and waste disposal systems should be devised are so complex that even their designers doubt whether they can be fully implemented in megacities (Rodríguez *et al.*, 2013).

High population densities, poor sanitary conditions, and a limited capacity for controlling the movement of people make megacities especially vulnerable to epidemics. In addition, their dense network of flight connections translates into a high risk of threats being brought in from other regions of the world. According to the WHO (2008), cities are characterized by the presence of three fundamental types of health-related dangers: infectious diseases (including HIV/AIDS, tuberculosis, pneumonia, and diarrheal diseases); non-communicable diseases (such as asthma, cardiovascular diseases, tumours, and diabetes); as well as violence and trauma (i.e. as a result of car accidents). This list shows that the risk of an epidemic is only one of the major factors that pose a danger to the health of urban dwellers, yet the WHO does indicate that many fundamental threats to health are rooted in environmental factors.

The negative impact that large cities exert on the environment is not just a problem for city planners, urbanists, and climatologists to consider for the future. Already now, the quality of life in large cities often fails to meet even basic environmental standards. For example, China's large cities rank among the most polluted places on Earth, with ubiquitous smog making it practically impossible for people to breathe. Since the beginning of the 21st century, the People's Republic of China has spent considerable amounts of money on combating asthma and chronic bronchitis, diseases caused by the inhalation of polluted air (Gawlikowski and Tomala, 2002).

Degradation and pollution of the pedosphere (the Earth's layer of soil), the contamination of rivers and watercourses as well as the noise emitted in large cities have a broad impact, affecting the condition of the natural environment on a local and supra-local scale. The uncontrolled development of megacities entails various threats: Not only the potential intensification of social tensions but also the very real threat of an environmental catastrophe across a whole region.

How can these environmental threats be best approached? One interesting trend of research suggests that we look at major cities as multilayered ecosystems in their own right, considering their consumption of resources and energy, production of goods, and disposal of harmful waste. The urban metabolism (UM) indicator (Kennedy *et al.*, 2014) is one of the multifaceted tools that has been devised to gauge the functioning of a city in this way, reflecting a number of aspects ranging from its territorial borders and population, through climate and the nature of the urban fabric, energy demand, production, and consumption, the heating of buildings, water consumption, water and energy losses, and many others. Adopting such an approach to megacities, viewed holistically as living organisms, could help minimize both the climate risk and the negative impact of urban behemoths on the natural environment.

6.3.5. Infrastructural threats

Cities consist of not only people, but also the infrastructure that enables them to live in such densely populated areas. Forecasts available in the literature often point out that numerous problems may emerge also in this context, including transportation-related challenges (Kumar *et al.*, 2013; Sudhakara and Balachandra, 2012) and, again, problems related to the natural environment (Pattaswamy and Bandarupally, 2014).

One popular trend, in research and in practice, has focused on possible ways of implementing sustainable development concepts in cities (Sorensen and Okata, 2010). In most cases, however, this has been limited to utopian visions for megacity development being posited in the literature, and to only smaller-scale actual attempts to put them into effect in practice.[6] In the planning of major urban agglomerations, such concepts often envision technological advancements and economic growth as factors facilitating positive change, yet they also lead to unrealistic designs, involving the necessity of building infrastructure from scratch. In highly developed countries, such solutions are impossible to implement as a result of the existing structure of the city and the necessity of preserving cultural heritage. Complete urban reconstruction is only possible in centres that do not have such "baggage" to contend with, for example, Shanghai. However, sustainable development in the context of infrastructure is difficult even in such cases, and indeed may even be impossible.

Here again, it becomes clear how interrelated the category of "environmental threats" is with the threats discussed in the previous section (particularly the social and economic aspects discussed there). City planners and urbanists usually focus primarily on infrastructure, under the assumption that it plays the leading role, while unfortunately neglecting the socio-economic aspects of sustainable development (many of which have been discussed in the sections above). It is true, however, that infrastructural issues can have a decisive impact on the future of megacities. One example is the aforementioned access to water. Forecasts and plans must take account of the infrastructure challenges stemming from the information revolution, including growing demand for electricity and data transmission. If such infrastructure is absent or insufficiently developed, this may result in a kind of "digital exclusion" and a decline in the global significance of megacities.

[6]Even the most famous and most advanced project of this sort, Masdar City, remains uncompleted, delayed by many years with respect to initial plans (Prandecki, 2014a). Importantly, by 2015 only several thousand people out of the target 50,000 inhabitants were living and working there.

It should be stressed firmly that the development of urban infrastructure should take account of the needs of inhabitants, which should be analyzed in the three-way configuration typical of sustainable development: simultaneously considering economic, social, and environmental factors. It has been noted that studies of the future of megacities lack relevant tools facilitating such an approach, fostering dialogue between inhabitants and experts (Wuellner, 2011). Taking better account of social needs would help improve the quality of life. That means ensuring not only shelter, transport networks, and work zones but also easy access to elements of social value (such as health care, education, day-care centres) and recreation (parks, playgrounds, sports and cultural facilities) (Snieška and Zykiene, 2014).

The challenge of factoring social, economic, and environmental aspects into plans and forecasts for the development of urban infrastructure is yet another field that demands a critical approach, attempting to assay the possibilities of the occurrence of specific dangers. If such analysis is neglected, certain groups may become non-functional or even face exclusion (i.e. if sports facilities are constructed without access for the disabled). One tragic example of the consequences of the risk of incorrect infrastructure planning being ignored can be found in the collapse of schoolhouses in the aftermath of the earthquake in the Chinese province of Sichuan in 2008 and the disproportionate number of casualties among children. That was caused by the failure to adjust public buildings to the standards necessary in areas of seismic activity (Zhao *et al.*, 2009).

6.4. Conclusions

An analysis of future developmental trends indicates the ever-increasing ubiquity of urbanization processes, leading especially to the further emergence and rise of megacities. Such centres function in highly complex ways, giving rise to a number of threats of various kinds that may, in extreme situations, even lead to their demise.

In this chapter, we have offered a broad overview of the potential threats faced by megacities. While most of these dangers have been recognized elsewhere, the previously existing literature did not provide any comprehensive overview or classification of the risks potentially stemming from the development of megacities. To help fill this gap, in the present study we have classified these potential threats into five fundamental groups: economic threats, social threats, security threats, environmental threats, and infrastructural threats. At the same time, we have sought to underscore the close links between these groups, which in our view must be taken into account in any forecasting work or policy development.

What is to be taken away from the above discussion? One of the main conclusions that follows from the above analysis is predominantly socio-economic in nature: the observation that a megacity's attractiveness as an economic, social, and cultural centre, which may be seen as one of its greatest strengths, may simultaneously and paradoxically pose the greatest threat to its development. The benefits of living in such agglomerations attract many people, but they often fail to actually attain such benefits for themselves, and instead end up joining the ranks of the excluded. This is a result of the rapid pace of urban life and an inability to adjust to rapidly changing conditions. Consequently, zones of prosperity arise in tandem with zones of poverty and dissatisfaction, the latter acting as breeding grounds of internal tension (strikes, riots, and so on) and drawing in those who are dissatisfied. The inhabitants of such areas are also easy tools in the hands of groups who want to destabilize a given megacity (i.e. by recruiting gang members, other criminals, terrorists). Consequently, the greatest threats to the development of megacities are posed by socio-economic factors, in other words by widening income differentials (especially stagnant income levels among the poorest individuals) and cultural differences. The first of these factors causes relative impoverishment, which means that growing income levels, even in real terms, are coupled with a drop in the perceived degree of satisfaction of people's needs and wants (which grow much faster as a result of pressure encouraging ever-greater consumption). That contributes to greater dissatisfaction and mounting social tension. Multiculturalism, in turn, may rest on various foundations, including ethnic differences (race, nationality), religious differences, and/or purely cultural differences (e.g. people identifying with subcultures or specific values). As such, multiculturalism may lead to misunderstandings between individuals and to a lack of acceptance for other people's priorities. In extreme cases, some of them may be completely negated, leading to the alienation of entire social groups. In such situations, tensions escalate, which may lead to the degradation of a given city in the long term.

Social and economic threats are not the whole story, of course. A range of closely related issues like political, military, and environmental security also play a significant role (although, as we have seen, many of these, too, have their social and/or economic dimensions). In their case, however, from the perspective of a given megacity, the possibilities of reacting and reducing the risk of their occurrence are much more limited. As for political problems, including wars, decisions get made between specific states or international organizations, whereas it is megacities that mainly bear the brunt of those decisions, being strategic targets of various operations (both classic warfare operations as well as cyberattacks and terrorism). Here, measures may be limited to aiming to be prepared for faster and better-tailored responses and educating inhabitants to mitigate tensions and extremist attitudes.

As concerns purely environmental problems, however, the most important ones are threats of a global nature, such as climate change and the depletion of resources. A megacity may therefore collaborate with other similar centres and countries to counter such threats, but it is unable to resolve the problem alone — the only effective way forward here involves attempting to adjust to the new conditions. But much better effects may be achieved in efforts to counter phenomena that occur on a local scale yet also have global consequences (i.e. water consumption and air pollution). Proper waste management is another such problem: The size of a megacity means that the disposal of waste in landfill sites and possible recycling initiatives must be undertaken on an enormous scale and therefore require complicated solutions.

Another over-arching conclusion is that, perhaps not surprisingly, most of the problems facing megacities result from their sheer scale. A perhaps less-obvious corollary is that creating relevant institutions capable of monitoring threats and reacting quickly are, for megacities, a particularly fundamental instrument for minimizing future risks. For instance, a problem like a water supply system failure can make it necessary to provide alternative access to water to tens or hundreds of thousands of people (or even millions in extreme cases), certainly no easy task. One of the most fundamental ways of countering the risk posed by stagnation in the development of megacities is the construction of relevant infrastructure, adequate to tackle existing problems. If such infrastructure fails to take account of local factors, it may even turn into an additional threat itself.

In closing, let us reiterate that the overarching objective of our review of the threats to the development of megacities, as presented in this chapter, has been to render the potential consequences of ongoing changes easier to understand and help raise awareness of the attendant challenges — and thereby to help prevent dangerous trends from becoming a reality in the future.

References

Arasaratnam, L.A. (2013). A review of articles on multiculturalism in 35 years of IJIR. *International Journal of Intercultural Relations*, 37(6), 676–685.

CS (2014). *Global Wealth Report 2014*. Zurich: Credit Suisse AG.

D'Alisa, G., D. Burgalassi, H. Healy, and M. Walter (2010). Conflict in Campania: Waste emergency or crisis of democracy. *Ecological Economics*, 70(2), 239–249.

Davis A. and L. Mishel (2014). *CEO Pay Continues to Rise as Typical Workers Are Paid Less*. Washington: Economic Policy Institute.

De Sherbinin, A., A. Schiller, and A. Pulsipher (2007). The vulnerability of global cities to climate hazards. *Environment and Urbanization*, 19(1), 39–64.

Easterlin, R.A., L. Angelescu, and J.S. Zweig (2011). The impact of modern economic growth on urban–rural differences in subjective well-being. *World Development*, 39(12), 2187–2198.

Folberth, G.A., T.M. Butler, W.J. Collins, and S.T. Rumbold (2015). Megacities and climate change — A brief overview. *Environmental Pollution*, 203, 235–242.

Fromm, E. (1976). *To Have Or To Be?* New York: Bantam.

Gawlikowski, K. and K. Tomala (2002). Chiny. *Rozwój społeczeństwa i państwa na przełomie XX i XXI wieku*. Warszawa: Trio.

Harris, M., R. Dixon, N. Melin, D. Hendrex, R. Russo, and M. Bailey (2014). *Megacities and the United States Army. Preparing for a Complex and Uncertain Future*. Arlington: Chief of Staff of the Army, Strategic Studies Group.

Huntington, S.P. (1993). The clash of civilizations? *Foreign Affairs*, 72(3), 22–49.

Huntington, S.P. (1996). *The Clash of Civilizations and the Remaking of World Order*. New York: Simon & Schuster.

IMF. (2014). *An Uneven Global Recovery Continues* (*World Economic Outlook Update*). Washington DC: IMF.

Inayatullah, S. (2011). City futures in transformation: Emerging issues and case studies. *Futures*, 43(7), 654–661.

Jiang, S., M. Lu, and H. Sato (2012). Identity, inequality, and happiness: Evidence from urban China. *World Development*, 40(6), 1190–1200.

John, W.B. (2013). Intercultural relations In plural societies: Research derived from multiculturalism policy. *Acta de Investigación Psicológica*, 3(2), 1122–1135.

Kabaj, M. (2014). Problemy współczesnego rynku pracy. In Z. Strzelecki, E. Kryńska and J. Witkowski (Eds.). *Kryzys jakości życia*. Warszawa: Komitet Prognoz "Polska 2000 Plus" przy Prezydium PAN, pp. 150–174.

Kasarda, J.D. and G. Lindsay (2011). *Aerotropolis: The Way We'll Live Next*. New York: Macmillan Publishers.

Kennedy, C., I.D. Stewart, N. Ibrahim, A. Facchini, and R. Mele (2014). Developing a multi-layered indicator set for urban metabolism studies in megacities. *Ecological Indicators*, 47, 7–15.

Kleer, J. (2012). Zagrożenia globalne: Próba identyfikacji. *Przyszłość Świat-Europa-Polska*, 2(26), 14–29.

Knoblauch, D. and M.A. Chase (2015). Rural, suburban, and urban schools: The impact of school setting on the efficacy beliefs and attributions of student teachers. *Teaching and Teacher Education*, 45, 104–114.

Kołodko, G.W. (1984). *Cele rozwoju a makroproporcje gospodarcze*. Warszawa: SGPiS.

Kopczuk, W. (2014). What Do We Know about Evolution of Top Wealth Shares in the United States? *NBER Working Paper No. 20734*. Cambridge: National Bureau of Economic Research.

Kumar, P. and D.P. Saroj (2014). Water-energy-pollution nexus for growing cities. *Urban Climate*, 10, Part 5, 846–853.

Kumar, P., S. Jain, B.R. Gurjar, P. Sharma, M. Khare, L. Morawska, and R. Britter (2013). New Directions: Can a "blue sky" return to Indian megacities? *Atmospheric Environment*, 71, 198–201.

Machnik, K. (2013). Megamiasta — nowe oblicze globalnej urbanizacji. *Dialog Międzykulturowy*. Retrieved from http://www.dialogmiedzykulturowy.org.pl/numer-2-2013-megamiasta-nowe-oblicze-globalnej-urbanizacji [access: 23.03.2014].

Meadows, D.H., D.L. Meadows, J. Randers, and W.W. Behrens III (1972). *The Limits to Growth*. New York: Universe Book.

Midouhas, E. and L. Platt (2014). Rural–urban area of residence and trajectories of children's behavior in England. *Health & Place*, 30, 226–233.

Modernisation and Strategic Planning Division — Australian Army Headquarters. (2014). *Future Land Warfare Report 2014*. Canberra. Retrieved from http://www.army.gov.au/~/media/Files/Our%20future/Publications/FLWR_Web_B5_Final.pdf [access: 12.03.2015].

Münkler, H. (1988). *The New Wars*. Cambridge: Polity.

Naisbitt, J. (1984). *Megatrends: Ten New Directions Transforming Our Lives*. New York, N.Y.: Warner Books.

Nawrot, K.A. (2013). Kryzys światowego system finansowego a rynki azjatyckie. In E. Mączyńska, J.J. Michałek and J. Niżnik (Eds.). *Kryzysy systemowe*. Warszawa: Polska Akademia Nauk, Komitet Prognoz, "Polska 2000 Plus," pp. 279–293.

Nawrot, K.A. (2014). *Kraje rozwijające we współczesnej gospodarce światowej. Przyczynek do ekonomii rozwoju*. Warszawa: Wydawnictwo Naukowe Scholar.

OECD (2011). *Divided We Stand: Why Inequality Keeps Rising*, Paris: OECD Publishing.

Oxfam. (2015). *Wealth: Having it all and Wanting More* (Oxfam issue briefing). Oxford: Oxfam International.

Oxfam. (2017). *An Economy for the 99%*. Oxford: Oxfam International.

Pattaswamy, B.S. and S. Bandarupally (2014). Tree-like structures for addressing carbon capture in megacities charged with anthropogenic carbon-di-oxide. *Procedia Engineering*, 95, 518–527.

Porwit, K. (2009). *O warunkach sprostania "wyzwaniom współczesnosci" w obliczu schorzeń i kryzysowych zagrożeń gospodarki*. Warszawa: Polskie Towarzystwo Ekonomiczne. Retrieved from http://www. pte.pl/pliki/2/11/konpte09.pdf [acces: 03.04.2014].

Poskrobko, B. (2014). Kształtowanie odporności jednostek organizacyjnych na zagrożenia globalne. *Ekonomia i Środowisko*, 2(49), 10–28.

Prandecki, K. (2012). Rola megatrendów w przewidywaniu przyszłości. *Przyszłość Świat-Europa-Polska*, 2(26), 75–94.

Prandecki, K. (2013a). Wyzwania globalne. In *Perspektywy nowego ładu światowego*. Warszawa: Adam.

Prandecki, K. (2013b). Zmiany w globalnym układzie sił gospodarczych w świecie. In K. Rybiński (Eds.). *Polska w niestabilnej gospodarce europejskiej i globalnej. Problemy polityki gospodarczej i rozwoju*. Warszawa: Vistula.

Prandecki, K. (2014a). Jakość życia w perspektywie 2050 roku. In Z. Strzelecki, E. Kryńska, and J. Witkowski (Eds.). *Kryzys jakości życia*. Warszawa: Komitet Prognoz "Polska 2000 Plus" przy Prezydium PAN, pp. 115–130.

Prandecki, K. (2014b). Perspektywy ograniczenia konsumpcji zasobów naturalnych do 2050 r. In *Czy kryzys światowych zasobów?* Warszawa: Komitet Prognoz "Polska 2000 Plus" przy Prezydium PAN, pp. 137–163.

Prandecki, K., A. Kafara, E. Kirejczyk, M. Fronia, and M. Wawrzyński (2012). Polityka a przesunięcie centrów gospodarczych w świecie. In *Innowacyjność, Kreatywność a Rozwój*. Warszawa: Komitet Prognoz "Polska 2000 Plus" przy Prezydium PAN, pp. 127–169.

Prandecki, K., K.A. Nawrot, and M. Wawrzyński (2013a), Nowe centrum i nowe peryferia połowy XXI wieku. *Przyszłość Świat-Europa-Polska*, 28(2), pp. 58–81.

Prandecki, K., K.A. Nawrot, M. Fronia, and M. Wawrzyński (2013b), Megatrends and sustainable development. *Problems of Sustainable Development*, 8(2), 49–61.

Prandecki, K., M. Hacaga, W. Kazanecki, and S. Śmietanko (2015). Rewolucja informacyjna a społeczeństwa połowy XXI wieku — punkt widzenia młodego pokolenia. In J. Auleytner and J. Kleer (Eds.). *Rewolucja informacyjna a kryzys intelektualny*. Warszawa: Komitet Prognoz "Polska 2000 Plus" przy Prezydium PAN, pp. 204–226.

Rodríguez, J.P., N. McIntyre, M. Díaz-Granados, J.P. Quijano, and Č.M. Vic, (2013). Monitoring and modelling to support wastewater system management in developing mega-cities. *Science of The Total Environment*, 79–93, pp. 445–446.

Royo, M.G. (2007). Well-being and consumption: Towards a theoretical approach based on human needs satisfaction. In L. Bruni and P. L. Porta (Eds.). *Handbook on the Economics of Happiness*. Cheltenham: Edward Elgar, pp. 151–169.

Saez, E. and G. Zucman (2014). *Wealth Inequality In The United States Since 1913: Evidence From Capitalized Income Tax Data*. NBER Working Paper No. 20625. Cambridge: National Bureau of Economic Research.

Shi, L. and L. Chuliang (2010). Re-estimating the Income Gap between Urban and Rural Households in China. *Procedia — Social and Behavioral Sciences*, 2(5), 7151–7163.

Singh, K.T. (2006). Terror trends: Mega cities, maximum impact. *Strategic Analysis*, 30(3), 655–661.

Snieška, V. and I. Zykiene (2014). The role of infrastructure in the future city: Theoretical Perspective. *Procedia — Social and Behavioral Sciences*, 156, 247–251.

Sorensen, A. and J. Okata (Eds.). (2010). *Megacities: Urban Form, Governance, and Sustainability*, 2011 edn. Tokyo; New York: Springer.

Sudhakara, R.B. and P. Balachandra (2012). Urban mobility: A comparative analysisof megacities of India. *Transport Policy*, 21, 152–164.

Szymańska, D. (2007). *Urbanizacja na świecie*. Warsaw: PWN.

Takahashi, S. (1998). Social geography and disaster vulnerability in Tokyo. *Applied Geography*, 18(1), 17–24.

Tian, L., W. Zhang, Z.Q. Lin, H.S. Zhang, Z.G. Xi, J.H. Chen, and W. Wang (2012). Impact of traffic emissions on local air quality and the potential toxicity of traffic-related particulates in Beijing, China. *Biomedical and Environmental Sciences*, 25(6), 663–671.

Tip, L. K., H. Zagefka, R. González, R. Brown, M. Cinnirella, and X. Na (2012). Is support for multiculturalism threatened by threat itself? *International Journal of Intercultural Relations*, 36(1), 22–30.

Treiman, D.J. (2012). The "difference between heaven and earth": Urban-rural disparities in well-being in China. *Research in Social Stratification and Mobility*, 30(1), 33–47.

UNDP (2009). *Human Development Report 2009. Human Mobility and Development*. New York: United Nations Development Program.

UN-HABITAT (2010). *Hidden cities: Unmasking and overcoming health inequities in urban settings*. World Health Organization, The WHO Centre for Health Development, Kobe, and United Nations Human Settlements Programme.

United Nations. (2014). World Urbanization Prospects: The 2014 Revision. New York: United Nations Department of Economic and Social Affairs/Population Division.

Wang, S., J. Gao, Y. Zhang, J. Zhang, F. Cha, T. Wang, Ch. Ren and W. Wang (2014). Impact of emission control on regional air quality: An observational study of air pollutants before, during and after the Beijing Olympic Games. *Journal of Environmental Sciences*, 26(1), 175–180.

Wawrzyński, M. (2012). Urbanizacja, komunikacja lotnicza, cyfryzacja człowieka — kluczowe megatrendy zmian XXI. *Przyszłość Świat-Europa-Polska*, 2(26), 95–116.

WEF (2013). *Global Risks 2013*. Geneva: World Economic Forum.

WHO (2008). *Our cities, our health, our future. Acting on social determinants for health equity in urban settings*. Kobe: WHO Commission on Social Determinants of Health.

Wierzbicki, A.P. (2011). *Tehnen: Elementy niedawnej historii technik informacyjnych i wnioski naukoznawcze*. Warszawa: Komitet Prognoz, "Polska 2000 Plus" przy Prezydium PAN i Instytut Komunikacji.

Wisner, B. (1998). Marginality and vulnerability: Why the homeless of Tokyo don't "count" in disaster preparations. *Applied Geography*, 18(1), 25–33.

Wuellner, F.C. (2011). Beyond economic and value wars: Mythic images of future cities. *Futures*, 43(7), 662–672.

Xu, J.H. (2012). Online news reports of air quality issues in Beijing. *Telematics and Informatics*, 29(4), 409–417.

Zhang, Z., and D.J. Treiman (2013). Social origins, hukou conversion, and the wellbeing of urban residents in contemporary China. *Social Science Research*, 42(1), 71–89.

Zhao, B., F. Taucer, and T. Rossetto, T. (2009). Field investigation on the performance of building structures during the 12 May 2008 Wenchuan earthquake in China. *Engineering Structures*, 31(8), 1707–1723.

7

MEGACITIES AND THREATS TO HUMAN HEALTH

Agata Penconek

7.1. Introduction

In 1900, only 13% of the world population lived in urban areas. One hundred years later, the urbanization rate was 47% (Gurjar and Leliveld, 2005). Since 2014, more than a half of the world's population (54%) lives in cities, and it is estimated that in 2030 the urbanization rate will reach 61%. The level of urbanization depends on the region of the world. In 2014, its highest level was recorded in North America (80.1%), Latin America (79.5%), Europe (73.4%), and Oceania (70.8%), and the lowest in Asia and Africa (47.5% and 40%, respectively). However, Asia and Africa have the highest growth rate of urbanization (World Urbanization Prospects, 2014). The consequence of the ever-growing level of urbanization was the emergence of megacities, that is, homogeneous areas with a total population in excess of 10 million people. In 1950, there were two megacities, namely New York and Tokyo, with a population of 12.4 and 11.3 million inhabitants, respectively (Gurjar and Leliveld, 2005). In 1990, there were already 10 megacities recorded. According to forecasts of World Urbanization Prospects, there will be 41 megacities in 2030. And 28 megacities are currently (as of 2014) being home to 453 million people (12% of the world's population). The high level of urbanization contributes to the economic development of the region. However, the city infrastructure very often does not keep pace with the rising rate of urbanization, which leads to problems of access to clean water and sanitation, transport, or electricity. Gurjar and Leliveld (2005) indicated, as an example, an increase of the length of roads in Delhi. Between 1971 and 2001, the length of the roads increased from 8,380 km up to 28,508 km (more than a three-fold), while the number of cars in the same time grown twenty-fold, from 0.18 million to 3.46 million. The megacities' development causes that more people travel by car over greater distances and for a long time, literally spending hours in traffic jams. The road transport and car traffic jams are the biggest sources of air pollution in megacities (Mage *et al.*, 1996). An increase in urbanization entails an increase in the level of air pollution caused not only by the road transport, but also by energy production and industrial activity. Although megacities are the driving force of economic growth, they are also a huge source of anthropogenic air pollutants that not only affect the local environment, but — through easy spreading — have a global impact (Lawrence *et al.*, 2007). This problem concerns mainly the megacities located in the developing countries, although other megacities also participate in global air pollution (but on a smaller scale). For example, Asia's megacities cover about 2% of the continent's area, but contribute to 16% of anthropogenic emissions of sulphur into the atmosphere (Gurjar *et al.*, 2008). Therefore, the interaction of megacities' rise on human quality of life and health should be also taken into consideration and this is the aim of this work.

7.2. Air Pollution and Health of the Megacities' Population

Air pollution in Europe and North America has decreased gradually over the last decade. We owe to the systematically implemented greenhouse gas regulations and particulate emission standards. In addition, the growing environmental awareness of societies, as well as the researches on air quality and the effects of pollution on human health contribute to this decrease. Nevertheless, the overall and local air pollution level in the world is still high. There are two sources of air pollution: man and nature. The burning of fossil fuels in transport, industry and domestic use, industrial processes (e.g. the chemical industry), waste disposal, and agriculture are the main sources of anthropogenic air pollution. Volcanic eruptions, dust storms, and the emission of volatile compounds (organic and inorganic) from the depths of the earth are the natural sources of air pollution. European Environment Agency (EEA) defines eight air pollutants: sulfur dioxide (SO_2), nitrogen oxides (NO_x), particulate matter (PM), ozone (O_3), ammonia (NH_3), non-methane volatile organic compounds (NMVOCs), carbon monoxide (CO), and methane (CH_4). Table 7.1 presents the impact of each pollutant on the human body.

The main sources of air pollution according to the European Environment Agency (Air pollution fact sheet 2013) are summarized in Fig. 7.1.

Table 7.1. The effects of air pollutants on human health

Compound	The effect of human health
Sulfur dioxide (SO_2)	SO_2 limits lung function, leads to the inflammatory changes in the airway epithelium, can cause the headache, and cough.
Nitrogen oxides (NO_x)	NO_x affect the functioning of liver, kidney, spleen and blood. NO_x can damage the airway epithelium, which increases the susceptibility to infection.
Particulate matter (PM)	PM cause the heart problems and lung diseases. They can penetrate into the different areas of the body (depending on PM size) and cause the inflammation. They are defined as possible carcinogenic to humans.
Ozone (O_3)	O_3 contributes to the problems with the respiratory and circulatory systems.
Ammonia (NH_3)	Exposure to high concentrations of ammonia leads to the irritation of skin, eyes, and respiratory tract, and can cause coughing.
Non-methane volatile organic compounds (NMVOCs)	Due to the large amounts of organic compounds, which may have carcinogenic effect, NMVOCs can also be mutagenic for people.
Carbon monoxide (CO)	It can cause heart disease and damage of the nervous system. Excessive exposure to high concentrations leads to death by suffocation.
Methane (CH_4)	There are no data on the direct effect of methane on human health.

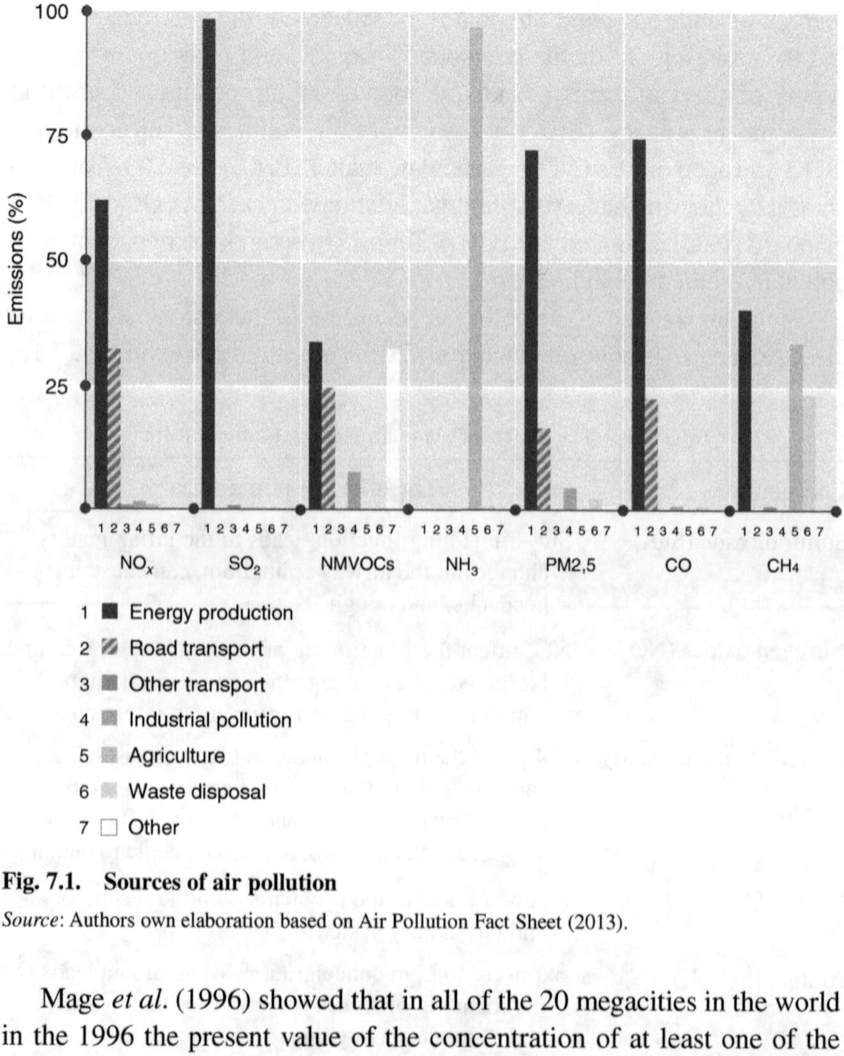

Fig. 7.1. Sources of air pollution

Source: Authors own elaboration based on Air Pollution Fact Sheet (2013).

Mage *et al.* (1996) showed that in all of the 20 megacities in the world in the 1996 the present value of the concentration of at least one of the components of air pollution exceeded norm recommended by the WHO health protection guidelines. The PM concentration was exceeded more than twice in Bangkok, Beijing, Mumbai, Cairo, Kolkata, Delhi, Jakarta, Karachi, Manila, Mexico, Seoul, and Shanghai and was exceeded less than twice in Buenos Aires, Los Angeles, Moscow, New York, Rio de Janeiro, and San Paulo. The SO_2 concentration was exceeded more than twice in Beijing, Mexico, and Seoul and less than twice in New York, Rio de Janeiro, and Shanghai. The CO concentration was exceeded less than twice in Cairo, Jakarta, London, Los Angeles, Moscow, New York, and San Paulo. The NO_x concentration was exceeded less than twice in Los Angeles, Mexico, Moscow, New York, and San Paulo. The O_3 concentration was exceed more than twice in Los Angeles, Mexico, San Paulo, and Tokyo and less than twice in Beijing, Jakarta, and New York.

The high concentration of solid particles (PM) present in the air is the biggest problem for humans, not only in megacities. In 1996 the norm of PM concentration was exceeded in 17 megacities (of all 20 megacities), and in 12 megacities the standard was exceeded more than twice. A report, published by the WHO Department of Public Health and the Environment in 2011, showed that after 25 years, the situation has not much changed (Fig. 7.2). The concentration of particulate matter with an aerodynamic diameter of less than 10 microns (PM10) is exceeded in 11 megacities (the measurements were taken in 16 megacities). The maximum permissible concentration of PM10 was marked as black line

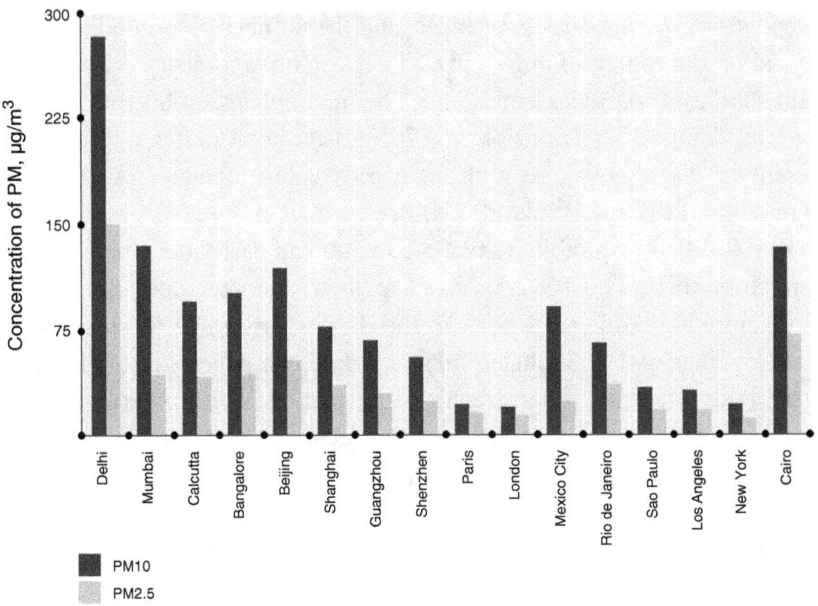

Fig. 7.2. The average concentration of particulate matter (PM10 and PM2.5) measured in selected megacities in the years 2009–2011

Source: Authors own elaboration based on urban outdoor air pollution database (WHO, 2014).

in Fig. 7.2. The concentration of particles with an aerodynamic diameter of less than 2.5 microns is exceeded or is on the verge of standards in 13 megacities. The maximum permissible concentration of PM2.5 is marked as grey line in Fig. 7.2. Only in New York, Los Angeles, and San Paulo have concentrations of particulate matter has fallen within 25 years.

Environmental pollution of particles has two sources. First — natural phenomena like volcanic eruptions; second — anthropogenic sources such as manufacturing processes and road transport. Cairo, Beijing, Mexico City, and Los Angeles are mainly exposed to particles emitted into the atmosphere by natural processes due to their proximity to the desert or active volcanoes. The toxicity of natural particles is smaller than the anthropogenic particles, but they can also lead to irritation of the respiratory system and infection once they enter into the lungs. Anthropogenic particles are emitted into the atmosphere by combustion of fossil fuels. They consist of a carbon core and organic and inorganic substances adsorbed on their surfaces. The particles' sizes, the type and amount of compounds present on their surfaces, and the number of emitted particles depend on the source of emissions. The automotive industry is one of the main sources of particles emissions. The incomplete combustion of fuels in diesel engines is responsible for 70% of the total number of particles present in the atmosphere with an aerodynamic diameter of less than 10 microns (PM10) (Weinhold, 2002).

PM10 called respirable particulate matter can easily penetrate into the respiratory tract. The PM2.5 particles (their diameter does not exceed 2.5 microns) are able to deposit in the deepest region of the respiratory tract (together with the inhaled air), and they can penetrate to all tissues of the body view the bloodstream. In megacities like Bangkok, Manila, and Seoul where a large share of vehicles are equipped with diesel engines, the problem is particularly important (Mage *et al.*, 1996). Emissions of particulate matter and other air pollutants (e.g. CO, NO_x) generated by modern engines manufactured or admitted to trading in the EU are subjected to scrutiny. The first emission standard for cars and light trucks was introduced in 1993. Currently, Euro 5 emission standard is in force for light passenger and commercial vehicles. Euro 5, as compared to the first emission standard, lowered the maximum permissible emissions by about 86% (newly manufactured engine cannot emit more than 5 mg of particles per km). In 2014, Euro 6 was introduced for heavy vehicles. Euro 6 forced the use of Diesel Particulate Filter (DPF) in all new cars equipped with diesel engine. Efficient DPFs reduce nearly 99% of particulate emissions (Ulrich *et al.*, 2012). Nevertheless, still more than 77% of cars on for example, Polish roads are more than 10 years old (and 10% of them are more than 30 years old) (PZPM, 2013). It means that they are not equipped with DPF and, therefore, they are still one of the major sources of particulate matter in the atmosphere. The particulate matters are composed of primary particles with diameter of 10–70 nm (Arai *et al.*, 2005). Primary particles are connected together and form the fractal-like aggregates with diameters ranging from 10 nm to 10 microns. They can cause necrosis of lung epithelial cells (Matsuo *et al.*, 2003), DNA strand breaks and mutations. They enhance the production of inflammatory factors like TNF-α, IL-6, IL-8 (Dybdahl *et al.*, 2004). The environmental pollution caused by particles' matters is responsible for 6% of annual deaths (Künzli *et al.*, 2000). Half of them are consequences of exposure to particles generated by automotive engines. The determination of visibility, that is, the distance from which the observer is able to see a black object situated on the horizon is a way to assess the level of particulate air pollution. The high concentration of particles in the air decreases significantly visibility, because light rays are refracted on particles. Admittedly visibility is also affected by weather conditions. For example, an increase in the temperature and wind speed improves visibility, whereas high humidity and high pressure causes visibility reduction. However, the impact of weather conditions on visibility can be easily determined. In urban areas with high population, visibility is worse than in rural areas (Tsai *et al.*, 2007). This problem particularly affects megacities. Che *et al.* (2007) observed that from 1990 to 2005 the visibility in major cities in China declined by an average of 2.1 km per year. Chang *et al.* (2009) measured that the number of days in the year in Beijing and Shanghai with visibility less than 10 km increased from 68 in 1973 to 180 in 2007 and from 210 to 310, respectively. The high concentration of airborne particulate matter with an aerodynamic diameter of less than 2.5 microns (PM2.5) is mainly responsible for these effects (Song *et al.*, 2006). Sand and dust storms appearing in the spring contributed to the growth of dustiness especially in Beijing (Mahowald *et al.*, 2007). However, the relationship between the concentration of dust in the air and visibility is not linear. When the dust concentration in the air is high the change in particles' level does not change the visibility, but when the dust concentration in the air is low, the changes in particles' level significantly influence the visibility (Deng *et al.*, 2008). The problems of dust and air pollution are identical for megacities in developing and developed countries, but megacities in the developed countries overcame them earlier. The worst air-pollution event in the history of the United Kingdom took place in December 1952 and was known as Great Smog of '52 or Big Smoke. Windless weather and high humidity combined with huge particles' emissions caused that within a few December days nearly 4,000 people died due to acute respiratory failures (and another 8,000 over the next few months). The law on air quality and emissions' standards introduced in 1956 saved the London against subsequent, similar incidents. The report about air quality in London from 1996 showed that only the level of carbon monoxide was elevated above normal. The level of particulate matter was below normal, similar as in the report from 2011. In 1984, in Los Angeles one of the highest concentrations of ozone in the atmosphere was recorded, and after that strict standards were introduced and the ozone level began to decline. Similar standards were introduced in China, after the hitherto low concentrations of ozone in Beijing grew in 2008 to an ozone level in Los Angeles in 1984 (Parrish and Zhu, 2009). The level of contaminants in the air should be monitored and emission standards and regulations should be enforced to protect residents of megacities against the health effects of exposure to airborne contamination. The efficient and effective monitoring of the air conditions in megacities poses problems. The air monitoring system in New York, London, Paris, Tokyo, Los Angeles, San Paulo, Osaka, and Seoul runs smoothly and provides reliable data, which can be useful to protect the residents. Unfortunately, in Dacca or Lagos or in other megacities in developing countries, air monitoring does not exist. Gurjar *et al.* (2010) created a megacities' ranking with highest number of deaths caused by air pollution (based on the mathematical model, which predicts the risk of health problems due to the exposure on air pollution in megacities). Karachi (15,000 deaths per year) took the first infamous place, followed by Dhaka (14,700), Cairo (14,100), Beijing

(11,500), and Delhi (10,500). Osaka, San Paulo, Los Angeles, New York, and Tokyo, with 60–500 deaths per year were at the bottom of the list. Gurjar *et al.* (2010) showed that the number of deaths depends on the concentration of particulate matter in the air (the higher the particulate matter concentration, the higher mortality). Studies conducted in 21 countries in Europe have shown that the 10 mg/m^3 increase in particle concentration of PM10 in an atmosphere increases mortality rate by 0.6% per day, and increases the incidence of chronic obstructive pulmonary disease (COPD) in people over 65 years by 10%, and also increases the risk of heart disease by 11%. Studies conducted in the United States showed an increase in mortality by 0.5% per day, and the risk of the occurrence of COPD was 15% and 11% of heart disease (Brunekreef and Holgate, 2002).

The World Health Organization reported that in 2012, nearly 7 million deaths were caused by air pollution (WHO, 2014). The highest numbers of death — 2.8 million and 2.3 million — were recorded in the area of the Western Pacific and Southeast Asia (Fig. 7.3).

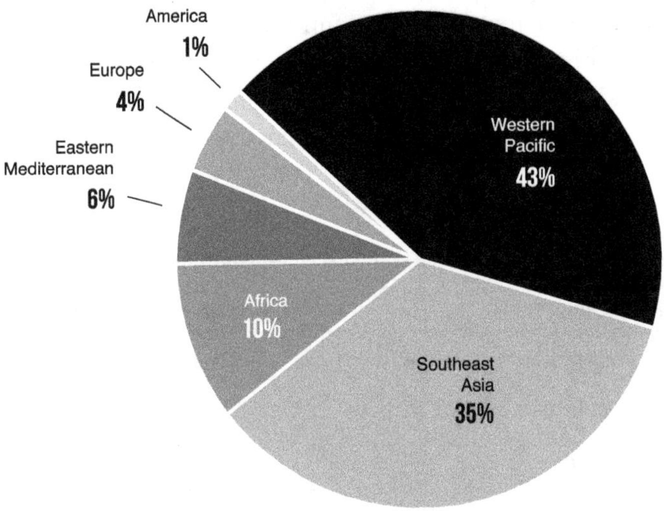

Fig. 7.3. The percentage of deaths caused by air pollution in various areas of the world

Source: Authors own elaboration based on WHO (2014).

The most common cause of death covered ischemic heart disease (36%), stroke (33%), COPD (17%), acute lower respiratory infections (8%), and lung cancer (6%). Men, over 25 years old, were more likely to die (49%), than women of the same age (42%) and children (9%).

In European Union, 91–96% and 85–88% of people in urban areas may be exposed to concentrations of particulate matter (PM2.5 and PM10, respectively) higher than those recommended by the World Health Organization (Table 7.2). For ozone, nitrogen dioxide, and sulphur dioxide, these values are, respectively, 97–98%, 5–13%, and 46–54% (EEA, Air quality in Europe — 2013 report).

The latest report of the European Environment Agency about the level of particulate matter (PM10 and PM2.5) air pollution of the European Union puts Poland, Czech Republic, Slovakia, Italy, and Bulgaria in the first place among the countries where the concentration of particulate matter increased — comparing to the measurements of 2010 (EEA, 2013) although there are no megacities there. That is why we should take care of our own health and safety and eliminate, or at least limit, the exposure to harmful agents no matter where we live — in a megacity or in a small town. We should follow the instructions to stay at home in case of high dust concentration recorded in our cities. We should also avoid walking or running near busy roads, particularly highways (intensive breath during exercises increases the deposition of particulate matter in the airways (Penconek and Moskal, 2013)).

Table 7.2. WHO recommendations

Compounds	WHO recommendations
Particulate matter, PM2.5	10 $\mu g/m^3$*
Particulate matter, PM10	20 $\mu g/m^3$*
Ozone	100 $\mu g/m^3$**
Nitrogen dioxide	40 $\mu g/m^3$*
Sulphur dioxide	20 $\mu g/m^3$***

Explanations: * annual exhibition; ** 8 hours exposure; *** daily exposure.

However, if you are not able to avoid particulate matter exposure, additional, properly selected respiratory protective equipment should be considered (Penconek *et al.*, 2013).

The megacities' rise is an inevitable process, which entails consequences for both local and global economy. It is not only a great opportunity for the region but also a huge risk. The risk is mainly due to the lack of solutions to the environmental issues associated with excessive emissions by the sprawling city. An increase in the incidence of respiratory and circulatory diseases and increased mortality is the consequence of the process. The sooner this will be realized, the better for our health.

References

Air pollution fact sheet 2013 — EU27 (available online: https://www.eea.europa.eu/.../air/air-pollution...fact-sheets/eu-27-a...).

Arai, M., K. Amagai, T. Nakaji and S. Hayashi (2005). Primary and aggregate size distributions of PM in tail pipe emissions from diesel engines. *JSME International Journal,* Series B 48, 639–647.

Brunekreeff, B. and S.T. Holgate (2002). Air pollution and health. *Lancet*, 360, 1233–1242.

Chang, D., Y. Song and B. Liu (2009). Visibility trends in six megacities in China 1973–2007. *Atmospheric Research*, 94, 161–167.

Che, H., X. Zhang, Y. Li, Z. Zhou and J.J. Qu (2007). Horizontal visibility trends in China 1981–2005. *Geophysical Research Letters*, 34, L24706.

Deng, X., X. Tie, D. Wu, X. Zhou, X. Bi, H. Tan, F. Li and C. Hang (2008). Long-term trend of visibility and its characterizations in the Pearl River Delta (PRD) region, China. *Atmospheric Environment*, 42(7), 1424–1435.

Dybdahl, M., L. Risom, J. Bornholdt, H. Autrup, S. Loft and H. Wallin (2004). Inflammatory and genotoxic effects of diesel particles *in vitro* and *in vivo*. *Mutation Research*, 562, 119–131.

EEA — European Environment Agency, Air quality in Europe — 2013 report, No 9/2013.

Gurjar, B.R. and J. Leliveld (2005). New direction. Megacities and global change. *Atmospheric Environment*, 39, 391–293.

Gurjar, B.R., A. Jain, A. Sharma, A. Agarwal, P. Gupta, A.S. Nagpure and J. Lelieved (2010). Human health risk in megacities due to air pollution. *Atmospheric Environment*, 44, 4606–4613.

Gurjar, B.R., T.M. Butler, M.G. Lawrence and J. Lelieveld (2008). Evaluation of emission and air quality in megacities. *Atmospheric Environment*, 42, 1593–1606.

Künzli, N., R. Kaiser, S. Medina, M. Studnicka, O. Channel, P. Filinger, M. Herry, F. Horak, P. Qenel, J. Schneider, R. Steethaler, J. Vergnaud and H. Sommer (2000). Public health impact of outdoor and traffic-related air pollution: A European assessment. *Lancet*, 256, 759–801.

Lawrence, M.G., T.M. Butler, J. Steinkamp, B.R. Gurjar and J. Lelieveld (2007). Regional pollution potentials of megacities and other major population centers. *Atmospheric Chemistry and Physics*, 7, 3969–3987.

Mage, D., G. Ozolins, P. Peterson, A. Webster, R. Orthofer, V. Vandeweerd and M. Gwynne (1996). Urban air pollution in megacities of the world. *Atmospheric Environment*, 30(5), 681–686.

Mahowald, N.M., J.A. Ballatine, J. Feddema and N. Ramankutty (2007). Global trends in visibility: Implication in dust sources. *Atmospheric Chemistry and Physics*, 7, 3309–3339.

Matsuo, M., T. Shimada, R. Uenishi, N. Sasaki and M. Sagai (2003). Diesel exhaust particle-induced cell death of cultured normal human bronchial epithelial cells. *Biological & Pharmaceutical Bulletin*, 26(4), 438–447.

Parrish, D.D. and T. Zhu (2009). Clean air for megacities. *Science*, 326, 674–675.

Penconek, A. and A. Moskal (2013). Deposition of diesel exhaust particles from various fuels in a cast of human respiratory system under two breathing patterns. *Journal of Aerosol Science*, 63, 48–59.

Penconek, A., P. Drążyk and A. Moskal (2013). Penetration of diesel exhaust particles through commercially available dust half masks. *The Annals of Occupational Hygiene*, 57(3), 360–373.

PZPM — Polski Związek Przemysłu Motoryzacyjnego, Raport (2013) — Branża Motoryzacyjna (pobrano ze strony: http://www.pzpm.org.pl/Publikacje/Raporty/Raport-branzy-motoryzacyjnej-2013).

Song, Y., Y. Zhang, S. Xie, L. Zeng, M. Zheng, L.G. Salmon, M. Shao and S. Slanina (2006). Source apportionment in PM2,5 in Beijing by positive matrix factorization. *Atmospheric Environment*, 40, 1526–1537.

Tsai, Y.I., S.C. Kuo, W.J. Lee, C.L. Chen and P.T. Chen (2007). Long-term visibility trends in one highly urbanized, one highly industrialized and two rural areas in Taiwan. *Science of the Total Environment*, 382, 324–341.

Ulrich, A., A. Wichser, A. Hess, N. Heeb, L. Emmenegger, J. Czerwinski, M. Kasper, J. Mooney and M. Mayer (2012). Particle and metal emissions of diesel and gasoline engines — Are particle filters appropriate measures?

Retrieved from http://www.exisab.com/Docs/Conferences/ETH_Nanoparticle_2012/Ulrich.pdf [access: 12.01.2017].
Weinhold, B. (2002). Fuel for the long haul: Diesel in America. *Environmental Health Perspective*, 110, A458–A464.
WHO (2014). Department of Public Health and Environment, Urban outdoor air pollution database, 2011.

8

THE IMPACT OF MEGACITIES ON HUMAN NATURE

Maria Szyszkowska

8.1. Introduction

Architecture is the kind of art that has constant impact on human nature, although not everyone is aware of it. Moreover, the hard work of urbanites, and thus the build-up of the cities, the width of the streets, and the height of the buildings combined with the population and transport do influence our psyche. Sadly, it is not the above-mentioned factors, but rather the pursuit for profit that has become the major objective of our epoch. Similarly — speaking the language of Kant — man ceases to be the aim in itself, so the highest value. My polemic, as defined in the title of this chapter, is a result of the deep concern that the concept of megacities implies.

8.2. Human Nature and the Progress of Civilization

Every human being is a part of nature's microcosm and has to abide by its rules. Notwithstanding, we are also the co-creators of culture and civilization, which differentiates us from the world of animals. It does not mean we are better, just different. Moreover, some human beings exist not only on the biological and cultural plane but also on the ideological one and so are commanded by higher values, which should be reflected in the world of culture and civilization.

We remain under the influence of various ideological views and opinions, which we barely verify. Even Bacon in 17th century, while forming the Theory of Idols, pointed out that human mind is not expository enough towards the functioning notions and views, including those that derive from tradition. One of the stereotypical attitudes is the admiration of progress. Unfortunately, in Europe, progress is often referred to as the development of widgets and gadgets. It is, however, very typical that, while appreciating the progress of civility, one ignores the negative results that this process entails.

From the ancient times, sages and scholars acknowledged progress, but in the sense of spiritual development of a man. They pointed out that neither the bloom of science and education, nor the inventions of civilization would lead to the spiritual development of the humankind. It is the progress, however, that should be understood as a versatile development of the human nature.

The inventions of civilization, which, in a sense, lead to the formation of megacities, serve mainly the purpose of comfort of a man and, to a considerable extent, promote indolence. Moreover, they cause isolation of individuals, who very often tend to choose for example, internet contact rather than face-to-face relationship.

When creating megacities, one does not take into account that contact with nature facilitates the inner harmony and, as a result, alleviates aggression. In terms of unconventional medicine, the healing process requires all four elements, namely water, fire, air, and earth, in order for it to be successful. Certain psychotherapeutic methods also recommend contact with nature. Rebuilding the bond with nature makes sense in the healing process. I would like to refer here to the Teatr Laboratorium (Laboratory Theatre) by Jerzy Grotowski in Wroclaw, Poland, and his "paratheatrical" shows directed to teach the spectators how to re-bond with the world of nature. Similarly, not long ago, Valuliso walked the streets of Vienna for several years demanding respect for earth and air as a condition for the survival of humankind. The apostle of peace, as he liked to call himself, was also invited to other countries.

8.3. Isolation and Aggression

It is common knowledge that not only lack of contact with nature but also overpopulation can intensify conflicts and increase aggression among people. Surely, at the beginning of the world — as the theory of the state of nature poses — humankind did not create society. It all rather resembled a gathering of hermits. Man by nature is an asocial creature. This view is as convincing as the Aristotle–Thomistic Theory on social human character functioning for example in Poland. The coexistence is possible thanks to the result of mutual agreements.

Nobody is self-sufficient, therefore we had to build a society. We depend on others. Life in society, thus, is not natural but necessary. This fact needs to be emphasized if we predict an increase in creating megacities and, subsequently, increase in population. Overpopulation intensifies conflicts and aggression.

Growing megacities will facilitate the state of isolation and loss of an individual thought. Living among people who exist in a virtual reality may lead to depression. Even as we speak, the majority choose to contact other people via internet rather than in the real world. Mobile phones are overrated, we tend to stay in the circle of people that we have already met, and we do not want to make new relations in a different environment. One simply expects a phone call only from somebody already existing in one's phone book.

The number of residents in megacities will progressively cause a dislike for another person, reluctance caused by overpopulation rather than race, religion, or views. As can be predicted, intolerance will be replaced by indifference towards the notions that divide humankind at present. Racism and religious or political animosity will come second after the excess of people living in the megacities isolated from the natural environment.

Aggression caused by overpopulation, rather than the differences among people which trigger conflicts nowadays, will be enhanced by material disparity. The division of the society into rich producers and bankers and the poor consumers will increase because the middle-class group will perish. Predictably, the rich will soon inhabit the outskirts of the cities, which in majority are slums now. They will be able to afford the need to sustain the contact with nature. It is possible, thus, that as a result of this move, the present city centres will turn into slums.

8.4. The Results of the Economic Liberalism

Human nature is to always strive for comfort, and enhancing the comfort will lead to such an indolence that activity will only be a result of conflicts. Silent consent to a world wrongly organized by economic liberalism will become overpowering. The right for citizen disobedience will remain a non-executed declaration.

The growth of population on the scale unheard of so far will not be accompanied by any considerable improvement of the quality of social services. I assume that the economic liberalism will be sustained for the next half of the century despite the oncoming crises. We should bear in mind that this liberalism reduces the protective function of the country. The state will not fulfil even the subordinate role in the event there are no roads, train tracks, post offices, viaducts, or hospitals. The turn from the 19th century economic liberalism is already very evident. Consequently, we should expect an increase in material disparity, which I have mentioned above, and a large group of people made redundant. The group will comprise of the elderly, sick, disabled, mentally ill, intellectually challenged, and, certainly, the creators of the higher values. We can observe the onsets of this process even now, and it will only gain in strength in megacities. Reading, going to classical music concerts, or visiting art galleries will be replaced by poor-quality Americanized media culture. Megacities will produce highly qualified specialists in a narrow discipline who will be employed in for example, top-rank clinics. The theory of holism will not play any significant role in education anymore. Humanities, especially Philosophy, will be considered irrelevant for the job market. Therefore, the intellectual group will start to decline. Learning goals of the scientific research will be abandoned in favour of education, fulfilling the expectations of the allegedly objective power of the labour market. The value of wisdom will be forgotten in favour of the management and usefulness of knowledge for practical purposes.

The emphasis in education on the intellectual development of an individual with exclusion of the development of higher-level feelings as well as ignorance towards sensitivity and imagination will lead to mass production of psychopaths. Lack of contact with natural environment will facilitate the process. An existence deprived of contact with nature, which is being destroyed by the pursuit for profit, will minimize the role of intuition in the process of cognition. It is expected that the characteristic for the Sokratesian–Kartesian–Hegl rationalism will increase in large European cities as well as continents depended on Europe, such as Australia, South America, and North America. Lack of intuition in the process of cognition may impede formation of innovative theories, for it is intuition that triggers new theoretical solutions, to mention only Einstein's Theory.

The highly promoted innovation will be accompanied by the stagnation of the spiritual process (It is the versatile development of an individual that I have in mind, which is broader than the notion of the intellectual one). It will come as a result of isolation of humankind from nature, for the inventions of civilization will become a kind of a fence closing in on the individual in the world created by them.

8.5. Spread of Diseases

One should expect an increase of ill people in megacities for a number of reasons. I will only mention the basic ones.

The air-conditioned places, in which many people will be spending most of their lives, are one of the pathogenic factors. Other innovations such as mobile phones or microwave ovens fall into the same category. The research on the harmful effects of these has been suspended for now. The noise pollution coming from various sources and devices will also have considerable effect on our health. At present, because of noise pollution, not everybody can differentiate half tones; in the future, we can expect other senses such as eyes to be affected by the inventions of man. One can expect an "invasion" of adverts distorting the reality and affecting the subconscious in order to manipulate the freedom of an individual. New medications, different from those recommended by non-academic medicine, will be introduced to the market. Their side effects, however, will be treated with other medications, and the vicious circle will lead to the degradation of human health.

Reflecting on the issues here, I somehow remember the words of the Polish professor of medical studies Kazimierz Dąbrowski, who predicted that the world in the 21st century would so much deviate from the human nature that it would be an honour to be in the psychiatric unit. What he probably wanted to say is that the psychopaths will consider feelings, imagination, and sensitivity of individuals a mental disorder. Sensitive intellectuals, though, will not resign to living in the world of civilization progress.

8.6. Unemployment and Migration

It is predicted that people will begin to suffer from anxiety caused by unemployment, which will result from the mass replacement of human power by machines. The world of robots will take over the reins. It will hardly be possible to maintain a positive attitude towards not only overpopulation but also the world of the machines that would make us merely passive observers in those large cities. The anxiety will also be caused by lack of social security resulting from unemployment. A man will only be human capital.

It has to be noted that unemployment is likely to cause boredom. An individual degraded by the market and robots will feel the dearth of the virtual reality. It is highly improbable that there would be people whose responsibility would be to organize time for the unemployed, or people who would encourage the contact with and broaden the mind about cultural material. I base my assumption on the fact that even today one can observe symptoms of total ignorance towards the cultural material of the past generations.

An increase in immigration and emigration caused by false expectations can also be predicted. The flow of immigrants will not, however, be triggered by the curiosity to learn about different cultures or by positive attitude to anything that is different. Perhaps, the quest to conquer the universe will rise in order to find space to build megacities. Paradoxically, moving there would not change anything, for we would only take there problems and conflicts unsolved here on Earth.

Approval of what statistically might seem mediocre, as well as the impact of the poor-quality media culture on human conscience, will cause a decrease of distinctive individuals. It would be worth mentioning here, that one of the creators of the 19th century liberalism J.S. Mill called for special respect and unrestricted freedom for sensitive intellectualists. The voice of Mill is being ignored these days.

In such an "anthill," one must expect a boost in the number of criminals, for it will become apparent that incarceration does not bring the expected results. Non-custodial sentences will become more popular. One of the promoters demanding them for the last several years has been Polish Professor Andrzej Bałandynowicz. Should that ever occur, a specific society of non-criminals and criminals will form, but such an integration will not include the rich or the poor. The police will efficiently tackle anticipated conflicts among them, as the invigilation of personal life will thrive.

In the above discussed conditions, the attention of individuals will be focused on satisfying basic needs. What follows then are general egoism, indifference towards the others, and aggression, which will rise. We should not expect disputes leading to the establishment of the right views. Should they ever occur, they will take place in virtual reality.

8.7. Transpersonalism

It can be expected that the idea of transpersonalism will start to flourish. Transpersonalism is a notion formed in 20th century by German philosopher and politician from Weimar Republic — Gustav Radbruch. He pointed out the paradox occurring from the beginning of the world, namely, that existing generations remain under the influence of individualism and super-individualism. In other words, people of every epoch are encouraged either to freely develop their individualism or — by the definition of super-individualism — to devote their lives to the State, society, or the Nation. The past epochs, with their masterpieces of cultural heritage, are being cherished; however, the present generations are not encouraged to create any new ones. This paradox expressed in the fact that whatever is demanded from the living, the past generations are evaluated according to different criteria, which made Radbruch form the idea of transpersonalism. The core of the notion is for the man to create cultural masterpieces. It is probable that, in the future, transpersonalism will help to shape the psychological stamina of the unemployed in megacities and, perhaps, will distract them from the world of virtual reality.

8.8. Conclusion

We have come to live in the times of civilization boom, so — as Oswald Spengler says — in times when our culture has exhausted its possibilities.

The moral degradation is expressed through the focus on profit, which, among others, shows itself in the need to build megacities and in the rejection of the ideals as a guide. Megacities adversely affect human psyche, which effectively causes more diseases, for our psychosomatic balance is being degraded. The danger is in the fact that megacities are like a dam isolating us from the natural environment and its energy.

Part II

Opportunities in the Development of Megacities — Regional, National, and Multidisciplinary Perspectives

9

RURAL–URBAN MIGRATION, URBANIZATION, AND MEGACITIES IN CHINA

Feng Wenmeng

9.1. Introduction

The past four decades have witnessed the rapid urbanization and emergence of megacities in China, the most populous country in the world. This chapter aims to provide a comprehensive analysis regarding China's urbanization. In particular, by exploring the similarities and differences of China's urbanization when compared with other countries of the world, this chapter tries to answer the following three questions: (1) What are the characteristics of China's urbanization at the current stage? (2) Has the emergence of megacities provided opportunities or posed challenges to China? (3) What are the characteristics of China's megacities as compared with other countries of the world?

9.2. History of China's Urbanization Since 1949

9.2.1. China's urbanization in world history

Although the appearance of cities in China could be traced back thousands of years,[1] China's urbanization had remained on a comparatively low level before the 20th century. In 1500, 1600, 1800, and 1890, China's urbanization ratio was 3.8%, 4.0%, 3.8%, and 4.4%, respectively much lower than that of Western Europe at the same period.[2] Even compared with Japan, one of China's neighbouring countries in Asia, the development of China's urbanization over the past 5 centuries has been slower. In 1500, Japan had a lower urbanization ratio than China, while its urbanization development later on was much faster.[3] In 1800, China's *per capita* income was $600 and its urbanization ratio[4] was 3.8%. In contrast, in the same year, Japan's *per capita* income was $570 and its urbanization ratio was 12.3% (Maddison, 2013: 43).

The reason why China maintained a comparatively low urbanization level in the global context, according to the explanation offered by Angus Maddison, was that China had been run by an imperial bureaucracy which raised income from taxes on the peasantry and so fostered rural development (Maddison, 2013: 43). However, this argument only provides part of the story. In fact, a more important reason for the comparatively slow development of urbanization in China has been the priority given to agriculture resulting from considerations besides taxation. In most times of world history, China has always had the largest population. Starting from this basic fact, the issue of how to provide enough food for the people is of great importance for maintaining basic order in society. In order to obtain enough food, fostering the development of agriculture should undoubtedly be given the highest priority.

---

[1] Debates still exist regarding the exact time for the city's appearance in China. The current evidence provided by archaeology shows that cities first appeared physically in China more than 5,000 years ago and cities with markets, one key element of urban life, appeared around 2,500 years ago.

[2] The corresponding urbanization ratios for Western Europe as at the year 1500, 1600, 1700, 1800, and 1890 were 5.8%, 7.9%, 9.5%, 10.2%, and 20.6%, respectively.

[3] The urbanization ratio for Japan in 1500 was only 2.9%.

[4] The definition of "urbanization" here refers to the percentage of population living in cities with 10,000 persons and above. For details, see Maddison (2013: 43).

In fact, not only China but also other parts of the world with long history had witnessed slow development of urbanization. Urbanization is a modern phenomenon accelerated by the industrial revolution since the mid-18th century. In history, China's rapid urbanization first appeared in the southern part of the country in the Ming and Qing Dynasties, around the late 14th century (Shiji, 1987; Fan, 1990). Given its importance in China's urbanization history, this period has been called the period of "original urbanization" by some Chinese researchers (Zhiqiang and Chen, 1994). However, without support from industrialization, urbanization in this period lacked momentum and sustainability (Weiping, 1999). Since 1840, China has become involved in the global system gradually, modern cities began to appear, and the functions and characteristics of cities have been changing accordingly. After 1949, the establishment of the People Republic of China introduced new economic and social institutions into Chinese society, and urbanization entered a new stage.

9.2.2. Trajectory of urbanization since 1949

As shown in Fig. 9.1, urbanization in China since 1949 can be divided into four phases. The first phase is the 1950s, characterized by rapid development. In this period, the urbanization ratio increased from 10.6% in 1949 to 19.8% in 1960. The second phase is from 1960 to 1978. In this period, with the introduction of the *Hukou* (Household Registration) System, urbanization stagnated for almost 20 years and the urbanization ratio stood at around 17% for this whole period. The third phase is from 1978 until the first half of the 1990s, characterized by the appearance of an enormous "floating population"[5] and rapid urbanization. In this period, with reforms starting from rural areas and the later rapid development of small- and middle-sized township enterprises, lots of labourers left their villages and settled down in nearby towns. The small town strategy[6] was

[5]"Floating Population" is one particular term used in China's social context, referring to these people who live in places different from their *hukou* registered place. For more details regarding "floating population," see Wenmeng (2009).

[6]The importance of the Small Town in China's urbanization was first proposed by one famous sociologist, Fei Hsiao-tung, in 1983. Based on field investigations in Jiangsu

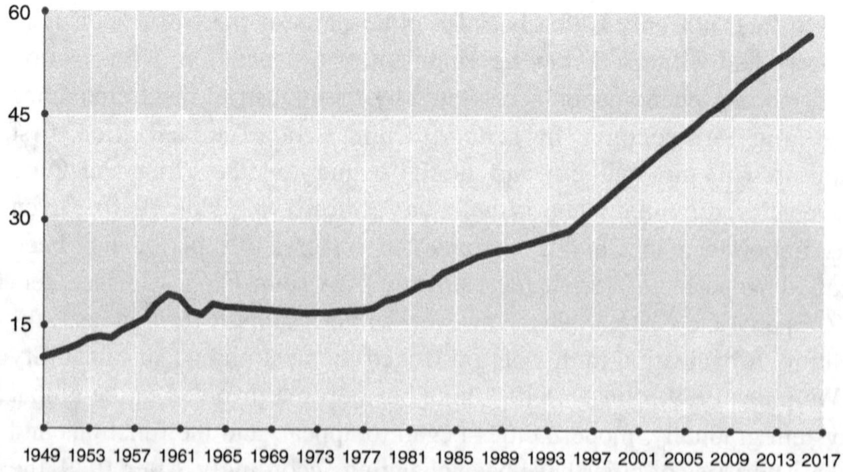

Fig. 9.1. China's urbanization rate in 1949–2016 (in %)

Source: compiled by the author based on National Bureau of Statistics of China (2017).

once regarded as China's particular pathway to industrialization and urbanization. The fourth phase is from the late 1990s until now. This period has witnessed rapid urbanization as well, but with a different path. In this period, the change in the economic driving force and the pressure from pollution concerns have made the development of small- and middle-sized township enterprises much harder than before. Under these circumstances, big cities have demonstrated more and more potential in driving economic growth and accumulating population. Thus, since the late 1990s, the development of metropolitan areas has become the main trend in China's urbanization.

9.2.3. The *Hukou* system and its changes

The most important aspect in discussing China's urbanization since 1949, especially after the 1960s, is the *Hukou* System. As one of the three measures meant to implement the "heavy industry first" strategy in 1950s,

province, Fei described the potential for these small towns in absorbing the surplus labour force from the rural side and in realizing industrialization and urbanization. For more details see Fei (1999).

China introduced the *Hukou* System in 1958 (Wenmeng, 2009). Under this system, each individual is given one registered place, namely, their *hukou*. In addition, the individual's *hukou* was categorized into one of two types: "agricultural" or "non-agricultural." Given the fact that the provision of education, employment, social security, housing, and almost all welfare benefits have been associated with the individual's *hukou*, this division is of great importance. With the introduction of the *Hukou* System, rural-to-urban migrations in China were basically forbidden during the 1960s and 1970s. As a result, a large amount of surplus labourers were limited to rural areas and China's agricultural productivity had been much lower than its potential. In 1978, agriculture accounted for 28.1% of GDP and the sector employed 70.5% of China's labour force (National Bureau of Statistics of China, 2004).

Starting from the 1980s, with the introduction of the household land contract system, peasants became free to choose their activities. In order to seek additional income from non-agricultural activity, these surplus labourers began to leave their villages and enter the cities. Faced with increasing numbers of migrants, the government began to show a softer stance towards migration. In 1984, the state council released a notice acknowledging the movement of peasants to small towns, on condition that these migrants should resolve their food supply by themselves. The release of this notice became the first step in initiating the *Hukou* System reform (Li, 2005).

It should be pointed out that the government's attitude towards migration has been changing gradually since then. In the 1980s, the government was reluctant to push forward reform regarding the *Hukou* System, and the release of the notice mentioned above was only one measure to address the already existing enormous migrations. However, with passing time, the government began to realize the great benefits brought by the migrations and became more positive in pushing forward the reform regarding the existing *Hukou* System. In 2001, the state council approved the Act on Opinions Concerning Pushing Forward the Reform of the *Hukou* System in Small Cities and Towns, which was proposed by the Ministry of Public Security. Based on experiences concerning *Hukou* System reform in more than 400 small cities and towns, this act declared that from October 1, 2001, the *Hukou* System reform would expand to more than 20,000 small cities and towns within the whole country. In addition, this act also clarified two conditions to obtain the destination city's *hukou*: securing stable residence and legal income.[7]

In addition to the 2001 reform expansion within the small cities and towns, further reform initiatives were taken to change the situation in middle and big cities. Starting from 2003, the government began to tackle the issue of migrant children's education and released a notice in 2006 in that regard. In it, the central government made it clear that it should be the destination city's responsibility to provide equitable education opportunities to migrants' children during their compulsory education period. In 2014, the government took a further step — the state council released the Act on Opinions Regarding Furthering the *Hukou* System Reform, declaring that the division of agricultural vs. non-agricultural *hukou* would be eliminated. Under the guidance of this act, actions have been taken by local governments. To date, in most parts of China, the division of "agricultural" and "non-agricultural" *hukou* has been replaced by a single term — "residential."

9.2.4. Strategies of different stages over the past six decades

A closer look at China's urbanization trajectory since 1949, especially after the 1950s, shows that as compared to other countries' urbanization, one feature of China's urbanization is the whole process has been influenced dramatically by the government policies. Before the introduction of the *Hukou* System in 1958, domestic migrations had been basically free. People could almost go everywhere they wanted. During this period, the Chinese government realized the importance of urbanization and even took actions to accelerate the development of urbanization. In the second plenary session of the 7th CPC committee held in March 1949, the Communist Party of China decided to "shift its focus from rural areas to

[7] In fact, during the reform starting from 1980s, in addition to the notices mentioned above, much more measures have been taken simultaneously. There are two targets in implementing these measures: on the one hand, providing more room for migration, on the other hand, establishing good framework to address migration-related problems in destination cities. For more details concerning the *Hukou* System reform refer to Wenmeng (2009: 21–44).

urban areas." Free migrations had brought rapid development of China's urbanization during the first decade after the establishment of the P.R.C.

However, things changed dramatically after the introduction of "Heavy Industry First" strategy, especially after the implementation of the *Hukou* System in 1958. From 1958 to 1978, rural-to-urban movements were basically forbidden. China's urbanization had stagnated during these two decades. China's urbanization ratio had been kept around 17% during the whole period.

In 1978, the implementation of reform and opening-up policy brought new changes to China, and rural-to-urban migrations have become more and more active since then. Accordingly, the government changed its policies gradually. In the 1980s and early 1990s, the government softened the control on migration and permitted free movements of labourers from the countryside to urban areas. However, the government's main target during the 1980s was to develop the small cities and towns. In this period, the government took an active role in pushing the peasants to "leave their land without leaving their hometown." With the rapid development of township enterprises in this period, the government proposed that the labourers could leave the countryside without going too far. Therefore, the policies in this period have shown two contradictory sides. On the one hand, the government had been taking measures to soften controls on migration; on the other hand, the government had been trying to make migrations happen within short distances. In the late 1980s, the proposal of controlling "aimless migration" to big cities was regarded as one important component in the social management framework.

The 1990s witnessed both the prosperity and the declination of township enterprises. As the result, the potential of small cities and towns in absorbing the surplus labourers from countryside has declined dramatically. Instead, big cities began to show more and more potential in sustaining economic growth, providing job opportunities, and creating better living conditions. Accordingly, migrants began to concentrate in big cities since the later 1990s. Concerning the urbanization strategy in this period, new considerations have been involved in the government's policy framework. On the one hand, facing the increasing floating population, the government has shifted its attitude from "manage" to "serve." In practice, the central government required the local governments to take measures to meet the needs of this floating population. Among them, ensuring migrant children's equitable opportunities to compulsory education has become one of these many measures taken to address the migration-related issues. On the other hand, the government has changed its urbanization strategy from emphasizing the importance of "small cities and towns" exclusively to emphasizing the importance of balanced development of cities with different scales.

In 2012, by acknowledging the importance of metropolitan areas in China's economic and social developments, the Chinese government proposed the "Beijing–Tianjin–Hebei" Coordinated Development Strategy. The purpose of proposing this strategy was to explore the mechanism to achieve a coordinated development among one metropolitan area and provide one model for China's future development in its urbanization.[8] The proposal of this strategy shows that the Chinese government has been paying more and more attention to the development of its metropolitan areas during the urbanization. On April 1, 2017, the Chinese government declared that in addition to Shenzhen and Pudong special areas, China will establish a third national special area — the "Xiong An New Area." This proposal has been regarded as another new step towards realizing the coordinated development strategy of Beijing, Tianjin, and Hebei province.

9.3. Characteristics of China's Urbanization at the Current Stage

The past three decades have witnessed the rapid development of China's urbanization. From 1978 to 2014, China's urbanization ratio increased by 1% on average for each year. Permanent residents living in urban areas have increased from 170 million to 750 million. The number of cities has increased from 193 to 653. Among them, 6 cities had more than 10 million by 2010 (National New Urbanization Plan, 2014: 8). Urban areas have increased from 7,000 km^2 in 1981 to 49,000 km^2 in 2014. From 2000 to 2014, the newly added population in urban areas reached 21 million on average for each year.

[8] For details regarding the "Beijing–Tianjin–Hebei" Coordinated Development Strategy refer to Wenmeng (2014).

Nowadays, urban areas have been playing a big role in China's economic and social development. In 2011, China's urbanization ratio reached 51.3%, signalling the first time in China's history that there were more people living in urban areas than those living in rural areas. By the end of 2016, China's urbanization ratio had reached 57.4%, among them people with local *hukou* accounting for 41.2% of the total population. Meanwhile, the number of "floating population" in that year was 245 million (National Bureau of Statistics of China, 2017). In December 2015, more than 80% of the national economic output was produced in urban areas, 51% of the labour force was working in urban areas and 86% of consumption was carried out in urban areas, more than 90% of the investments and 66% of the loan activity was happening in urban areas. In 2014, *per capita* disposable income of the urban residents was 2.75 times of that of rural residents, and *per capita* expenditure of the urban residents was 2.38 times that of rural residents.

Over the past three decades, with rapid economic growth and dramatic social transition, the macro context surrounding China's urbanization has changed completely. Facing the new circumstances, the Chinese government redesigned its urbanization strategy and in March 2014 released the National New Urbanization Plan (2014–2020). This plan illustrates the blueprint for China's urbanization by 2020. The key messages from this plan include the following two aspects: on the one hand, to accelerate China's urbanization so that cities can play a more important role in China's economic and social developments; on the other hand, urbanization needs to take a new model to achieve a balanced and sustainable development and with higher quality. In particular, this plan proposed five targets concerning China's future urbanization: (1) to improve the ratio and quality of urbanization; (2) to establish a better structure for urbanization[9]; (3) to formulate a more scientific and reasonable development model for cities; (4) to make the urban life more attractive and environmentally friendly; (5) to improve urbanization related institutional arrangements. With the proposal of the above five targets, it is expected that China will pursue a rapid urbanization with

[9]A better structure here means that the location, size, function of each city will be more balanced and well connected.

higher quality in the coming years. In the future development, the concepts of “green,” “smart,” “humanistic” will be given more priority.

Another thing that needs to be pointed out in the above plan is its clarification of the guidelines concerning the *Hukou* System reform. By considering the different situations faced by cities with different scale, this new plan elaborated different guidelines for migrants to obtain local *hukou* in different cities. Based on the mutual conditions that the migrants should have legal and stable job and residence, it articulated the following criteria for different scaled cities: for small cities and towns, eliminate all the limitations; for cities with population of 0.5 million to 1 million, eliminate the existing limitations in an orderly way; for cities with population of 1 million to 3 million, eliminate the limitations in a reasonable way; for cities with population of 3 million to 5 million, determine the conditions in a reasonable way; for cities with population of more than 5 million, strictly control the city’s scale.

Historically, the following judgements could be drawn regarding China’s urbanization at the current stage.

Firstly, China is still in the middle of its rapid urbanization. In other words, in the coming years, China’s urbanization is expected to maintain a high speed. A close look at what has happened during these developed countries’ urbanization history demonstrates that without drastic interventions from outside, once kicking off, a country’s urbanization will continue at a high speed until its urbanization ratio reaches 70%. As shown in Fig. 9.1, China’s urbanization ratio was 57.4% by the end of 2016. In fact, in the National New Urbanization Plan (2014–2020) released in 2014, China proposed that by 2020 it expected its urbanization ratio would reach 60% and people with local *hukou* in urban areas would account for 45% of the total population. The actual development of the past 3 years has shown that the actual speed of China’s urbanization since 2014 has been higher than expected. In addition, the Chinese government also released another target in that plan — it expected that by 2020 another 100 million migrants would settle down in urban areas (National New Urbanization Plan, 2014: 3). Taking all the above information together, it is highly possible that in the coming years China’s urbanization will proceed at a high speed.

Secondly, China is in the second stage of its urbanization and metropolitan areas have been playing a more active role in its economic and social developments. As revealed in the first part, since taking off in the late 1970s, a dramatic policy shift has happened in China's urbanization strategy. The proposed "small cities and towns" strategy did bring the rapid development of the small cities, especially the towns in the 1980s and early 1990s. China's number of towns has increased from 2,173 in 1978 to 19,410 in 2010, accordingly. However, since the late 1990s, big cities have shown much more potential in driving economic growth and providing job opportunities for migrant workers. In fact, the natural accumulations of people into big cities in China have formulated three big metropolitan areas from south to north: the Pearl River Belt centring on Guangzhou and Shenzhen, the Yangtze River Belt centring on Shanghai, and the Beijing–Tianjin–Hebei Belt centring on Beijing, respectively. Under these circumstances, to explore a coordinated development model for the cities among the three metropolitan areas is of great importance and many policies have been made accordingly. It is no doubt that in the coming years and even in the long run, small cities and towns are expected to play an important role in China's economic and social developments; however, at least over the short term, accumulation of people into the metropolitan areas is unavoidable. At the current stage, the development of metropolitan areas and the development of megacities should be given enough attention.[10]

Thirdly, impacts of the *Hukou* System are still very strong. In spite of the continuous reform regarding the *Hukou* System, migrants' lives are still strongly influenced by their *hukou* status. As shown above, by the end of 2016, there was 16.2% gap between urban permanent residents and people with local *hukou* in terms of urbanization ratio. The entitlements to medical insurance, pension, housing, and many other public services are still connected with the individual's *hukou* status. Especially after the releasement of the National New Urbanization Plan (2014–2020), in order to control the population growth, many megacities have tightened their control on *hukou*. Meanwhile, the latest reform concerning China's land system carried out in rural area has increased the value of land and village membership. These two factors have added complexity to China's *hukou*

[10] Over the past years, China's megacities have been continuously growing. By the end of 2016, Beijing's population reached 22 million and Shanghai's population reached 24 million.

system reform in the future. However, it should be pointed out that the *Hukou* System, combined with the land system in China, contribute to the nonexistence of slums in megacities and as a result, unlike some countries in the world, China's rapid urbanization has been accompanied with the rapid decrease of poverty and the absence of slums in cities. This is one feature in China's urbanization.

9.4. Implications of Megacities for China: Challenge or Opportunity?

In China, cities are divided into several ranks based on their population size. The current criterion was proposed in November 2014, as a result of the releasement of the Notice on Adjusting Standards Regarding the Division of Cities. According to this notice, China's cities are divided into five categories: small city with population of less than half a million, middle-sized city with population of from half a million to 1 million, big city with population of 1 million to 5 million, megacity with population of 5 million to 10 million, super megacity with population of more than 10 million (The State Council, 2014). Table 9.1 shows the numbers of cities of different scales. It is plain to see that the numbers of cities of different sizes have all surged dramatically over the past three decades.

By the end of 2015, the 10 largest cities in China in terms of population size were Shanghai, Beijing, Chongqing, Shenzhen, Tianjin,

Table 9.1. Numbers of cities and towns in China: 1978 vs. 2010

Categories of urban settlement	1978	2010
Cities	193	658
City with population of more than 10 million	0	6
City with population of 5–10 million	2	10
City with population of 3–5 million	2	21
City with population of 1–3 million	25	103
City with population of 0.5–1 million	35	138
City with population of less than 0.5 million	129	380
Towns	2,173	19,410

Source: National New Urbanization Plan (2014).

Guangzhou, Wuhan, Xi'an, Nanjing, and Chengdu, respectively. Among them, three cities had more than 20 million population — Shanghai 24 million, Beijing 22 million, and Chongqing 21 million. In addition, Shenzhen's population was 11 million, and it has the highest population density among China's cities. The population of the other six cities ranged from 5 million to 10 million, respectively.

In fact, the above 10 cities are the most attractive places for the migrants in China. Over the past decades, especially during this century, the inflows of migrants have enormously exceeded these local governments' expectations. This momentum has forced these cities to update their city plans continuously. Figure 9.2 shows the yearly increment in population of Beijing from 2000 to 2014. The average increase is 538,000 per year. In other words, on average, half a million people were added to Beijing from 2000 to 2014 per year. Among these additions, most are migrants.[11] The enormous rapid inflow of migrants has forced the local government to update its city planning frequently. In 2004, when Beijing's City Planning (2004–2020) was approved by the state council, the target of population was set at within 18 million by 2020. However, by the end of 2009, the population of Beijing had reached 18.6 million, exceeding the 2020 target 11 years earlier. This has forced Beijing to change its population target. In 2015, before the 13th Five-Year Plan was made, the population target was set at within 23 million (Beijing 13th Five-Year Plan, 2015) by 2020. By the end of 2016, Beijing's population was 22 million, among them being 8 million migrants, accounting for 37.2% of the total population. This means that in the coming 4 years, Beijing still needs to make great efforts to control its population growth. Under these circumstances, not only Beijing but also other megacities in China have renewed their measures to control the inflows of migrants and made great efforts to redistribute their population within the city.[12]

In regard to migration, enormous research has been done worldwide and many theories have been proposed to provide explanations for this

[11] The number of migrants was 2.56 million in 2000 and reached 8.19 million in 2014.

[12] In 2015, the number of migrants in Shanghai has declined for the first time, a decrease of 147,000.

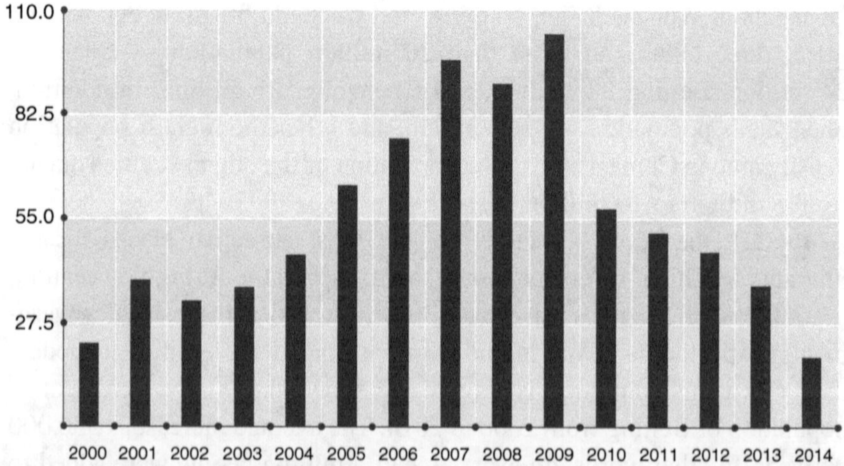

Fig. 9.2. Yearly added population of Beijing: 2000–2014 (in ten thousands)

Source: Compiled by the author based on Beijing Bureau of Statistics (2017).

economic and social phenomenon.[13] Although the existing theories have provided different explanations regarding the reasons behind migrations, they share one thing in common — in most cases migrations have provided great benefits to the migrants and their households. In fact, proof could be found more easily in the case of migration to the megacities. What has happened and is happening around the world has shown that megacities are so attractive that enormous numbers of people have left their hometown and gathered there, even if they have to overcome lots of difficulties in their movement.

In China, as in most parts of the world, the emergence of megacities has proven to be a two-edged sword: on the one hand, it has provided great contributions to China's economic and social development; on the other hand, it has also brought great challenges to China's city planning and social governance.

[13]These theories include the rule of Ravenstein, Lee's migration direction and choice, push and pull theory proposed by Bogue, the transition hypothesis proposed by Zelinsky, and others. For more details regarding the discussion of migration related theory, see the first chapter of Wenmeng (2009).

In fact, the emergence of megacities over the past decades has provided opportunities not only to the individuals involved at the micro-level, but also for economic growth and social transition at the macro-level.

The first sort of benefits involves the contribution to China's economic growth. In particular, two types of advantages have been provided by cities and especially by megacities. The first advantage is the power of economies of scale. By accumulating a large amount of people into one place, urbanization has provided not only enough labour supply for massive production but also enormous markets for products. As pointed out in the first part of this chapter, in history China has paid great attention exclusively to fostering its agricultural development, and this biased approach has impeded the development of China's industrialization and urbanization. However, this situation began to change in the start of the 20th century. Following 1949, rapid industrialization led by the heavy industry first strategy transformed China's economic structure completely. Figure 9.3 shows the changing structure of China's GDP since 1949. In 1952, the primary industry, namely, agriculture, accounted for a 50.5% of China's GDP but by 2016 that share had declined to 8.6%. In contrast, the share of secondary industry has increased since the 1950s and peaked in 2006, accounting for 47.6% of China's GDP in that year. Tertiary industry started taking off in the 1980s, now accounting for more than half of China's GDP.[14] This breakdown shows that nowadays most production activities are carried out in urban areas.

The second advantage lies in innovations stimulated in urban areas, especially in the megacities. Figure 9.4 shows the breakdown by different sectors since the 1980s. It is clear that over the past three decades, secondary industry has been the main driving force for China's economic growth. It is the gradually free movement of labour since the 1980s and the fast urbanization that have worked together to prompt the development of China's secondary industry over the past three decades. Furthermore, a closer look at Fig. 9.4 shows that in 2015, the tertiary sector contributed 53.7% of China's GDP growth. This number, combined with the tertiary sector's share in China's GDP, demonstrates that tertiary industry, namely,

[14] In 2015, the share of the tertiary industry reached 50.2%, and in 2016 its share increased to 51.6%.

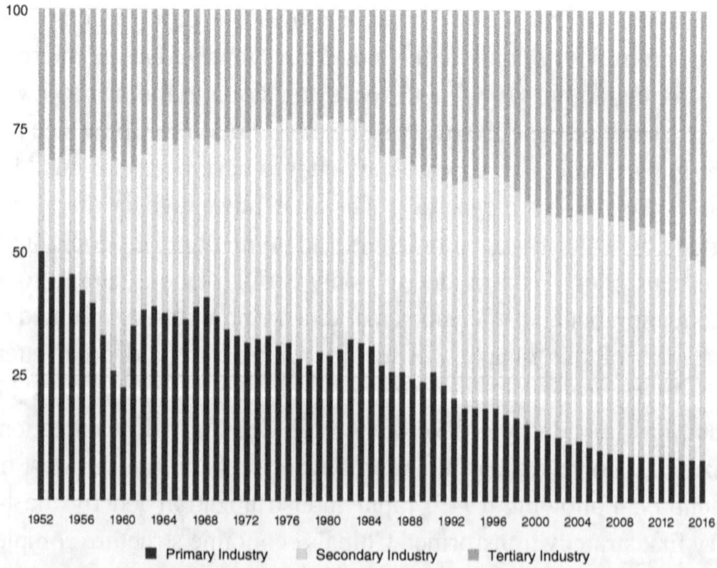

Fig. 9.3. China's GDP composition by industry: 1952–2016 (in %)

Source: Compiled by the author based on National Bureau of Statistics of China (2017).

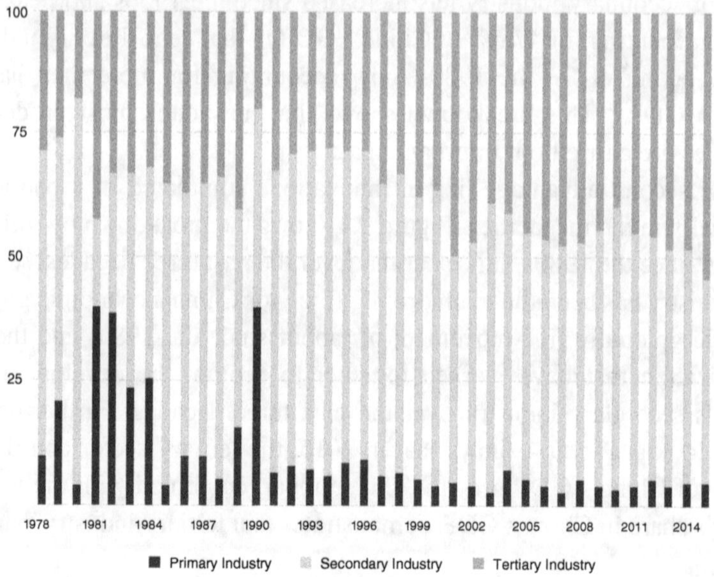

Fig. 9.4. Industry contribution to GDP growth: 1978–2015 (in %)

Source: Compiled by the author based on National Bureau of Statistics of China (2017).

the service sector, has in recent years been emerging as the driving force of China's GDP growth. Given the fact that most tertiary-industry activity has been carried out in urban areas, especially in megacities, it is obvious that urban areas, especially megacities, are expected to play a more active role in China's economic development in the coming years.

In fact, the role played by megacities has been illustrated by China's recent shift in its economic growth strategy as well. Since 2012, China's economic growth rate has been in the double digits and has entered into a middle-upper speed.[15] This change has been called the entrance of the "New Normal." In this new phase, China's economic growth model is expected to change from the traditional low-cost based, scale-expansion model to a quality- and effectiveness-oriented model, driven by innovation. In the coming years, China's economic growth will depend more heavily on innovation. Megacities, by accumulating numerous intelligent people together, with support from the well-developed infrastructure, are expected to play the key role in this new phase.

The second sort of benefits is improvement of people's living conditions. In the global context, one of the main achievements that China has accomplished over the past several decades is its great success in antipoverty. Although by the end of 2016 China still had 43 million people living in poverty,[16] around 700 million people had been helped out of poverty over the past three decades. Among the many contributors to antipoverty, the contribution of vast-scale migration accompanied by rapid urbanization has been extremely remarkable. Historically, there have been great income gaps between China's rural areas and urban areas. In most parts of the history, China's rural residents' income has been less than that of urban residents and this gap even exists today.[17] Under these circumstances, the relocation of labourers from the countryside to an urban area is usually accompanied their obtainment of higher income and an improvement in living standards over their original households. Thus, in

[15] China's GDP economic growth rates for 2012, 2013, 2014, 2015, and 2016 were 7.7%, 7.7%, 7.3%, 6.9%, and 6.7%, respectively.

[16] This number is calculated based on the current criteria set in 2011, namely, yearly 2,300 RMB per person (at constant value).

[17] In 2016, *per capita* disposable income of China's urban residents is 33,616 RMB, 2.72 times of that of rural residents.

addition to reshaping China's urban and cultural landscapes (Fan, 2008; Wenmeng, 2009; Sun, 2014) and providing enough labour supply to China's expending manufacturing sector and service sector, enormous migration has contributed remarkably to China's rural development through the large amount of remittances sent back by the migrant workers. Figure 9.5 shows the changing share of income from salaries among rural residents' *per capita* income from 1983 to 2013. It is obvious that the share of salaries among the rural residents' income has increased steadily since the 1980s, the same period when large amount of migrants began to move from rural areas to urban areas. In 1983, income from salaries only accounted for 18.6% of rural residents' *per capita* income, while in 2013 this share increased to 45.2%. In other words, nowadays almost half of rural residents' income is derived from employment as a labourer. Through these remittances, the rural households' living conditions have improved remarkably. After basic needs such as food and clothing have been met, rural residents have used the remittances to repair and rebuild their houses. This has helped a lot in improving China's rural living conditions and landscapes over the past three decades. Furthermore, after years of accumulation of capital and knowhow in the urban areas, some migrants

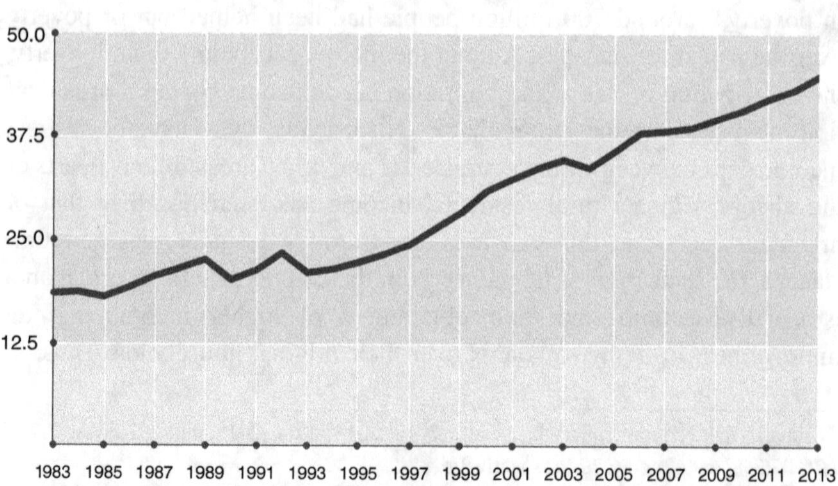

Fig. 9.5. Share of salary earnings in rural residents *per capita* income: 1983–2013 (in %)

Source: Compiled by the author based on National Bureau of Statistics of China (2017).

have returned to their hometown. With the obtained wealth and knowledge in urban areas, the returned migrants have introduced new ideas, technologies and business models into China's rural society. This has translated into the accelerated modernization of China's agriculture.

In improving the living conditions of the residents, another important benefit that has been provided by urbanization is the increased efficiency and effectiveness of the provision of public services. Before the reform of taxation and fee system that started beginning in 2000, financing the provision of public services in China's rural areas has been basically the responsibility of the peasants themselves (China Development Research Foundation, 2014). Due to the lack of public financial support from the government, the development of public services such as infrastructure, education, and basic health care has long been lagging in China's rural areas. As a result, the educational attainments and health conditions of rural residents have been much worse in China's rural areas. Faced with this enormous gap in the provision of public services between rural areas and urban areas, the sixth plenary session of the 16th CPC committee proposed the idea of pushing forward equality in the provision of public services between rural areas and urban areas in 2006. However, the broadness of China's rural areas, combined with the sparse distribution of rural residents, has made the achievement of this target much more difficult than expected. Through migration and urbanization, lots of rural residents have transferred to urban areas and accumulation of population has facilitated the provision of public services to a large extent. Furthermore, the megacities, given their more dense accumulation of people, have been proven to be more efficient and effective in the provision of public services and people living there accordingly have higher educational attainments and longer life expectancy.[18]

The third sort of benefits provided by migration and urbanization is the acceleration of social transition. With enormous inflows of people from the countryside to urban areas, over the past several decades China has experienced a dramatic social transition from an agricultural, traditional

[18] For example, in 2010 the sixth national census showed that Shanghai and Beijing were with the highest life expectancy, reaching 80.3 years and 80.2 years, highly above the national average of 74.9 years.

society to a non-agricultural, modern society. In other words, through enormous migration and rapid urbanization over the past decades, China has been successfully accelerating the process of its modernization. Nowadays, no one can deny that the lifestyle in the megacities such as Beijing and Shanghai has become quite similar to that of New York, Tokyo, and London. In megacities, people have been building a society based on rules and contracts instead of personal relations which had been the core in Chinese villages and traditional society. Nowadays, communities have become the basic block in China's urban areas, and even in some rural areas the traditional villages have been replaced by the newly established communities.[19]

In addition to the above changes, China has also witnessed the rapid development of the third sector over the past three decades. Figure 9.6 shows the rapid expansion of social organizations in China. By 2015, the number of social organizations had reached 662,425. These social organizations have been playing active roles in different fields. Rapid

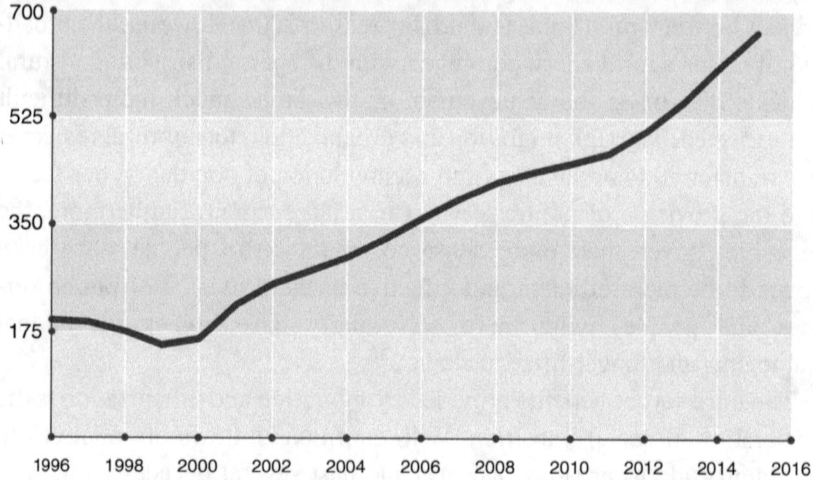

Fig. 9.6. Number of China's Social Organizations: 1996–2015 (thousands)

Source: Compiled by the author based on National Bureau of Statistics of China (2017).

[19] Related examples could be found in provinces of Shandong, Hebei, etc. For details, please refer to Wenmeng (2017).

urbanization, especially the emergence of megacities over the past decades, has accelerated China's social transition remarkably.

Despite the enormous contributions mentioned above, urbanization and the emergence of megacities are by no means without their challenges. In particular, three sorts of challenges have been displayed in China's megacities.

The first challenge is traffic. With the unexpectedly rapid urban expansion, traffic has become a big challenge for most of China's megacities. In contrast to those public transportation system based megacities such as Tokyo, up to now the role played by public transportation system has been quite limited in China. In 2011, in the cities with more than 1 million population, people using the public transportation system in their daily traffic only accounted for 45%. Under these circumstances, in 2014 the government proposed to increase this ratio to 60% by 2020. The underdeveloped public transportation system, combined with the separation of people's living places and their working locations, has resulted in the long commute time in megacities. One report published in 2015 shows that the average commute distance in China's cities in 2014 was 9.18 km, taking 28 minutes on average. Among the 300 cities surveyed, Beijing had the farthest average commute distance of 19.2 km and the longest commute time of 52 minutes, while Shanghai had the second farthest commute distance of 18.8 km and longest commute time of 51 minutes (Travel.People, 2015). In order to resolve the traffic congestions, most megacities have accelerated their constructions of railway system. By the end of 2016, Beijing's railways had increased to 19 lines, totalling 574 km. In addition, new railways under construction reached 300 km. In April 2016, the daily usage of railways in Beijing reached 12 million passengers per day. Now, in downtown Beijing passengers using the railway have accounted for more than half of the pubic traffic transportation system.

The second challenge brought by rapid urbanization and the emergence of megacities is the environmental problem. Rapid accumulation of too many people into one place has caused many cities, especially these megacities, to approach the limits of their environmental carrying capacities. In 2012, among the cities above county level, only 40.9% had reached the air quality criteria set by the government. This situation has forced more and more Chinese citizens to pay attention to the air quality of their living cities in their daily life. Nowadays, in megacities such as Beijing and Shanghai, to check the air conditions has become one necessary action for citizens in the morning. Accordingly, the performance in addressing environment related issues has become one indispensable aspect in the yearly evaluation of city managers.

The third challenge brought by urbanization is its negative impact on China's rural development. It is true that the enormous outflows of migrant workers have provided enough labour supply for urban development. However, with a large amount of loss of labour, to ensure enough labour supply in carrying out agricultural activities has become a critical problem in some rural areas. In addition, without the active participation of young residents, the effectiveness of village governance has decreased remarkably.

To summarize, the emergence of megacities in China have provided great opportunities for China's economic growth, social transitions, and the improvement of individuals' and households' living conditions, yet meanwhile it has also brought new challenges to residents, the government and the society. When making any judgement regarding the roles that have been played by megacities in China, both of the above two sides need to be noticed.

9.5. Characteristics of China's Megacities within the Global Context and the Prospects of China's Megacities

World history over the past three centuries has been characterized by expanded industrialization and rapid urbanization. Compared with other developed countries that had experienced rapid urbanization earlier, China after 1949 has demonstrated great similarities during the process of its urbanization: enormous labour resources left countryside for urban areas; urban areas expanded quickly; agriculture's share of the GDP was gradually replaced by the manufacturing sector and the service sector; with higher income people's living conditions improved dramatically; the traditional culture emphasizing informal relations of kinship was replaced by an urban culture that pays attention to formal relations and social contract. In spite of the above similarities, China's urbanization and the development of megacities have shown certain distinctive features when compared with other countries in the world. These features are partially caused by China's historical emphasis on agriculture, but more importantly, these features have been brought by the strong influence of China's policies.

There is no doubt that during the process of rapid urbanization, most countries have worked out certain policies to shape the direction, the speed, and the distribution of their urbanizations.[20] However, it is rare to see such a country like China where the policies have shaped the country's urbanization so strongly.

As far as the expansion of urban areas, the emergence of megacities and the greater concentration on megacities as time passes are concerned, China shows great similarity to other countries. However, when compared with the main feature of other selected countries, such as in the case of India, the security threat in the case of South America, the alteration of the public sphere in the case of African cities, it is the strong impact of government policies that has characterized China's urbanization over the past six decades.

To date, there are two sets of policies that have shaped China's urbanization. Both of them have shown both negative and positive impacts during the process of China's urbanization. The first set is the *Hukou* System. As shown in the previous analysis, the *Hukou* System has resulted in the three phases of China's urbanization over the past six decades. In addition, this system has caused the obvious difference in public service access and welfare entitlements between migrants and residents with the local *hukou*. This difference has engendered conflicts between the original local population and the migrants. Under these circumstances, the social integration of the migrants into the destination cities has become an important issue for city managers. Given the various problems encountered by migrants due to the *Hukou* System, China's urbanization could be called a "Half Urbanization." Here half means that although the migrants have physically moved to urban areas and started working there, they have not become citizens in the real meaning, since great differences still exist between them and citizens with local *hukou*.

---

[20] For example, in order to achieve a balanced development during the rapid urbanization, Japan has worked out five National Comprehensive Development Plans. For details, refer to Wenmeng and Nie (2017).

On the other hand, the *Hukou* System has also shown its positive impacts as well. Given the fact that land in rural areas is basically owned by villages, being a member of one village is indispensable in obtaining a piece of residential land and cultivating agricultural lands. Under the *Hukou* System, even if individuals have left their villages and moved to the cities as migrants, their village membership still remains. Therefore, when the migrants are experiencing hardships in urban areas, they can choose to return to their hometown and engage in agricultural activities again. This option has provided a certain resort for the migrants and has become a key contributing factor in the migrants' safety net. After the 2008 financial crisis, in spite of the shocks from outside, unemployment did not become a serious problem in China. Part of this success should be attributed to this special institutional arrangement of the *Hukou* System. Furthermore, thanks to this arrangement, slums are absent in China's cities, which is quite unique in world urbanization history.

The second set of polices includes those proposed in the National New Urbanization Plan released in 2014. It should be pointed out that these policies have included many of the latest advanced concepts such as "green city," "smart city," and "humanistic city." Under the guidance of these new concepts, great changes have been happening in China's urbanization. What is more, this plan has paid enough attention to the development of metropolitan areas. In addition to the three existing metropolitan areas in China, this plan has proposed developing new metropolitan areas in China's central and western parts. By implementing related policies, it is expected that the development of megacities will be accelerated and more metropolitan areas will appear in China in the coming years.

On the other hand, with the clear proposal of controlling the population scale of cities with more than 5 million population, many megacities in China have worked out detailed plans to control or even decrease the population of their cities in the coming years. This population controlling strategy will undoubtedly impact the movement of migrants. As already shown in Beijing and Shanghai, this strategy is expected to effect changes in the population distribution in the city as well. Meanwhile, it will also change the structure in megacities, since in most of the megacities' migrants with higher educational attainments and skills are usually welcomed at the expense of the dispersion of the migrants with low skills and educational attainments. However, in spite of the pushing power generated by this population controlling strategy, the higher incomes, abundant job opportunities, and colourful lifestyles continue to attract the young generation to come to megacities. Under these circumstances, the development of China's megacities will be jointly influenced by both the pushing power and the pulling power in the coming years, and the results will be more complex than anticipated.

After two decades of engaging in pushing forward the development of small cities and towns, China has realized the importance of developing its megacities. At the current stage and in the long run, megacities have been playing and will continue to play a more important role in the pursuit of economic growth, social transition, and environmental protection. As a result, megacities will experience even more rapid development in China's future.

At the current stage, two improvements are particularly needed in pushing forward the development of China's megacities. The first is to improve the efficiency of megacities. The achievement of this target relies heavily on the construction of well-connected transportation systems inside and outside the megacities. Inside, more railways need to be constructed and transfers between railways, buses, and other means of transportation should be well designed and quickly connected. Outside, railways and highways need to be built between cities. Only after quick connections have been well established, fast movements of goods, people and services can be realized, can a metropolitan area then be seen as a powerful body.

The second is to improve the quality of megacities. Megacities never mean only large accumulations of buildings and populations. The more important role played by megacities lies in the fact that they can provide more convenient and comfortable living places for human beings. Thus, the focus in developing megacities in the future should also shift from only paying attention to their economic efficiencies to paying more attention to the life qualities of residents living there. By all means, a better life for humans should be the ultimate target in the development of megacities.

References

Beijing Bureau of Statistics (2017). Retrieved from http://www.ebeijing.gov.cn [access: 12.03.2017].

Beijing Municipal Government (2015), Beijing 13th Five-Year Plan.

China Development Research Foundation (2014). *China Development Report 2013/14: Achieving a Prosperous Society in Chinese Rural Areas.* Beijing: China Development Press.

Fan, S. (1990). *Exploring Cities and Towns of the South in Ming and Qing Dynasties.* Shanghai: Fudan University Press.

Fan, C. (2008). *China on the Move: Migration, the State, and the Household.* London & New York: Routledge.

Fei, H.-T. (1999). Small town big issue. *Fei Hsiao-Tung Synthesis*, 9, Beijing: Qunyan Press.

Li, S. (2005), Institutional innovation regarding peasants movement to cities. *China's Population in Transition.* Beijing: China Statistics Press.

Maddison, A. (2013). *Contours of The World Economy, 1-2030AD.* Oxford: Oxford University Press.

National Bureau of Statistics of China (2004). *China Statistical Yearbook.* Beijing: China Statistics Press.

National Bureau of Statistics of China (2017). *Statistical Press of 2016 National Economic and Social Development.* National Bureau of Statistics of China, February 28, 2017. Retrieved from http://www.stats.gov.cn/tjsj./zxfb/201702/t20170228_1467424.html [access: 12.03.2017].

National New Urbanization Plan (2014). *National New Urbanization Plan (2014–2020).* People Publishing House Beijing.

Shiji, L. (1987). *Cities and Towns of the South in Ming and Qing Dynasties.* Beijing: China Social Sciences Press.

Sun, W. (2014). *Subaltern China: Rural Migrants, Media, and Cultural Practices.* New York: Rowman & Littlefield.

The State Council (2014). Notice on Adjusting Standards Regarding the Division of Cities, October 29, 2014.

Travel.People (2015). Retrieved from http://travel.people.com.cn/n/2015/0128/c41570-26463574.html [access: 12.03.2017].

Weiping, W. (1999). Urbanization of the South in Ming and Qing Dynasties. *Academic Monthly*, 12 p. 69–76.

Wenmeng, F. (2009). *China's Migration and Social Realities.* Tokyo: Mineruba Press.

Wenmeng, F. (2014). Experiences and Lessons from the Tokyo Metropolitan Area Development. China *Development Research Foundation (CDRF) Internal Working Paper.*

Wenmeng, F. (2017). China's Land System Reform. *CDRF Internal Working Paper*, February 2017.

Wenmeng, F. and H. Nie (2017). The development of Tokyo metropolitan area, *Journal of Northeast Asia Studies*, 2017(5), p. 49–54.

Zhiqiang, Q. and Y. Chen (1994). Original urbanization of cities and towns in the south. *Shanxi University Journal*, 4, p. 13–19.

10

MEGACITIES IN INDIA: WHERE ARE THE OPPORTUNITIES?

Gaurang Rami and Yogesh N. Vansiya

10.1. Introduction

Megacities are increasingly a developing countries' phenomenon that will affect the future prosperity and stability of the world economy. Megacities contain a rich mix of coexisting inhabitants with their distinctive ethnic, community, culture, and lifestyle values. Around 54% of the world's population now live in urban areas, and it is expected to increase to 66% by 2050 as per UN report "World Urbanization Prospects 2014." The largest of these are Tokyo and New Delhi with a population of over 25 million inhabitants (UNDESA, 2014). Majority the world's megacities, as defined as urban areas with a population more than 10 million, falls within so-called "Valeriepieris circle." In 2011, India's total population was 1.23 billion, of which 31.17% lived in urban areas, and it is projected that urban population of India will reach 590 million (38%) by 2030. India currently, as for 2016, has five megacities namely New Delhi, Mumbai, Kolkata, Bangalore, and Chennai. Rural-to-urban migration will result in two more urban areas (Hyderabad and Ahmedabad) becoming megacities by 2030, according to the UN. The major problems of megacities in India are slums, homelessness, illegal construction, traffic congestion, pollution, socio-economic disparities, internal security threat, affordable housing, availability of pure and safe water, solid waste management, sanitation, urban public transport, environmental concern, urban crime, etc. The Indian government has taken various steps to improve urban development in megacities such as the Constitution (74th Amendment) Act, National Urban Transport Policy, National Urban Renewal Mission, introduction of metro trains, Smart city concept, and Clean India (*Swachh Bharat*) mission among others. The megacities of India, confronted by nearly intractable problems, have a pervasive and crucial need for policies and socio-technological and socio-economic approaches that must be devised in a different context than that of the developed world. This chapter thus explores various problems and challenges megacities in India are facing, while shedding the light on opportunities derived from ongoing and speeding urbanization processes for the country and its people.

10.2. Megacities as Areas of Opportunities and Challenges

Megacities are undergoing economic boom times, often generating considerable opportunities as well as strong pressures for change accompanied by environmental degradation. They allow convenience and opportunities to find work, but they are also fraught with complicated problems. As the city's population swell, these megacities are struggling to cope. Thus, the megacities in India are struggling to keep up with their increasing size. As they are developing at an incredible rate, they are facing various numerous challenges.

Rapid urbanization has become the hallmark of the 21st century, and it is expected that existing megacities will continue to grow, as there are few takers for new cities to take excess or overflow populations — just look at the number of new "ghost" cities dotting China, built at great cost and still unoccupied. Therefore, governments must learn to live with megacities and do their best to enhance quality of life.

There is one school of thought in the emerging economies that urbanization must be seen as a positive force and harnessed for national development, rather than curtailed. The present Indian government subscribes to this view and is enthusiastic about building infrastructure to support industry, develop industrial corridors, and foster old and new "smart" cities across the land — with the major beneficiaries of all this "development" being the domestic and foreign private sector.

Little attention is being paid to the inexorable increase in urban populations, particularly in very low income countries. Instead of focusing on the issues involved with coordinating a coherent policy response to this demographic trend, the development agenda has focused on how coordination problems in supporting industry can be overcome. This has resulted in increasingly dysfunctional cities, especially within the Valeriepieris circle,[1] where paucity of land makes pressure on population (Buckley, 2015).

Furthermore, analysis of the evidence indicates that urban growth in the megacities is no longer a result of "pull" migration, where the newcomer can make his fortune in the city of opportunity, but rather a sad consequence of distress or "push" migration from an unbearable life in the countryside in developing countries.

The situation is exacerbated by planning practices, often learnt from colonial times, which are totally out of sync with the predominant village or tribal culture from which these migrants increasingly originate. With cities now being planned after their occupants have arrived rather than in anticipation of its growth, this "pathological urbanization" results in chaotic cities without sufficient public space to realize agglomeration economies with dense, fetid slums and huge informal economies — untaxed and unregulated.

While there is no gainsaying that Indian cities need development planning on a massive scale, especially in the housing and services sector; we need to stem this distress migration at its source — through the tertiarization of the rural economy in emergency mode. After all, despite the proliferation of towns and cities, India is still only 31% urbanized and we cannot afford to go on neglecting the remaining 69%, who still have a decisive role to play in nation building.

[1]Valeriepieris circle is located at 106.6° East and 26.6° North, visible on the Winkle Triple Projection of the Earth. This conjectural circle is difficult to go unseen because of the amazing realities associated with it. The Valeriepieris circle encompasses more than half of the world's population within a diameter of just 4,100 km. The circle pulls all of this off while being mostly water and including the most sparsely populated country on earth, that is, Mongolia. There are more Muslims in the circle than outside of it. There are more Hindus in the circle than outside of it. There are more Buddhists in the circle than outside of it. There are more people living inside this circle than outside of it. 24 of the world's 38 megacities in 2016 falls within this Valeriepieris circle (Siddiqui, 2015; Facts, 2013).

10.3. Indian Scenario

According to the UN 54% of the world's population now lives in urban areas and it is expected to increase to 66% by 2050 (UNDESA, 2014). The UN further highlights the emergence of 29 megacities, that is, urban areas with 10 million inhabitants, around the world, compared to 10 megacities in 1990. Currently, Tokyo (Japan) is the world's most crowded city with 38 million inhabitants, followed by New Delhi (India) (25 million), Shanghai (China) (23 million), and Mumbai (India) (21 million) (UN, 2014; Singh, 2015). The UN predicts there will be 41 megacities by 2030 (UNDESA, 2014).

The total number of people living in India has been estimated at 1.21 billion, of which 31.17% lived in urban areas, and it is projected that urban population of India will reach 590 million (38%) by 2030 (Census India, 2011). The cities are expanding in terms of boundaries and attracting people from other parts of the country for a better life. Rapid urbanization is creating lots of challenges such as housing, sanitation, utilities, and transportation for these cities. Mobility is emerging as the key challenge for policy makers around the world and India. The UN takes into account urban sprawl and measures populations beyond official city limits. On these criteria, India currently has five megacities, namely (Tokington, 2016):

(1) **New Delhi**: The capital city has a population of 26.5 million people;
(2) **Mumbai**: India's financial hub has a population of 21.4 million people;
(3) **Kolkata**: An important trading hub, with 15 million people living in urban area;
(4) **Bangalore**: The "Silicon Valley" of India; 10.5 million people call it home;
(5) **Chennai**: Home of the Indian motor industry, as well as 10.2 million people.

Other urban areas in India are growing rapidly as people look to cities for jobs and financial security, as well as the chance of a better education for their children. This rural-to-urban migration will result in two more urban areas becoming megacities by 2030, according to the UN:

(1) **Hyderabad**: A strong information technology (IT) hub and tourism centre. It may be home to 12.8 million by 2030;

(2) **Ahmedabad**: The heart of the textile industry is expected to house 10.5 million by 2030.

Big cities "create wealth, generate employment, and drive human progresses." On the downside, megacities are also responsible for driving climate change, inequality, and exclusion, as well as the breakdown of traditional family structures, which leaves elderly people isolated and vulnerable (UN-Habitat, 2013). As stressed by Kotkin (2014) megacities grow because "globalization" and "technological change" have increased the return of being smart.

Delhi and Mumbai are the two key megacities of India with a 20 million plus population. These two cities attract more than 200 migrants every day in search of livelihood. By 2030, the population of Delhi and Mumbai is expected to reach 36 and 27 million, respectively (Singh, 2015).

Delhi is ranked as the most polluted city in the world. It has the most extensive road network in the country, but still does not enough space for its traffic (WHO, 2014). The Victoria Transport Institute concluded that half of the increased roadway capacity is consumed by added traffic in just 5 years. Interestingly, according to the study conducted by Urban Emissions, Delhi's cars are no faster than pedestrians for 20% of their running time (Singh, 2015).

These two cities with a high urban population are looking to find sustainable transport solutions and underground is seen as one of the key public transport system. Delhi is leading with longest operational length, whereas, Mumbai is the latest entrant in the league of Metro System in India.

Delhi has made significant investment in metro network and created a network of 190 km carrying more than 1.7 million passengers a day. The city is expanding its existing network, adding more than 140 km within Phase-III. The system has carried 3.7 billion passengers in last 12 years. The metro system has helped to put 117,249 vehicles off the road daily and helped to save 106,493 tones of fuel by providing commuters with an alternative to motorized vehicles, resulting in savings of Rs. 16 billion *per year*. Furthermore, the metro has helped in reduction of emission of harmful gases into the city's atmosphere in Delhi, helping to save 786 g per passenger per trip, leading to a reduction of 457,615 CO equivalent tonne annually. Mumbai has completed first phase of metro construction and launched the commercial operation on September 2014. Mumbai metro has been completed on public–private partnership basis. The first line is the 11.4 km-long Versova–Andheri–Ghatkopar corridor and has 12 stations on the elevated line. The system carried more than 30 million passengers in the first 100 days. The economic and environment impact of Mumbai metro is positive, but it is not quantified yet (Singh, 2015).

The main reason of the rapid growth of the cities is the migration from the surrounding areas of the cities, not the natural growth. So its outcome is countless types of problems in the city region. To cater to such problems planning is essential. Problems including environmental challenges, demographic surge, socio-economic tensions, and administrative issues arise (Kaushik, 2013).

Large proportions of the Indian population live in megacities (e.g. Delhi, Mumbai, and Kolkata), which are vibrant centres of economic opportunities and offer better quality of social life. Due to increasing migration to these cities, Indian megacities are constantly expanding, which subsequently leads to strain on the environment with a range of impact at local, regional, and global levels. During the last few decades the anthropogenic emissions of greenhouse gases (GHGs) and other air pollutants have increased substantially, resulting in worsening ambient air quality of these cities. With respect to time span, the concern over air pollutants has also changed in Indian megacities. Concern over particulate matter, black carbon, NO_x, and ozone has heightened recently due to their local and regional impacts on air quality, environment, and public health and also because they contribute to global climate change. Although authorities have implemented several measures to reduce air pollution and its impacts in Indian megacities, much more is yet to be done to improve their ambient air quality (Bhola and Nagpure, 2015).

10.4. Major Problems of Megacities in India

Due to the rising population, the absolute number of slum dwellers in Indian megacities is rising. This is due to massive migration from rural areas and from semi-urban areas to large agglomerations. The settlements in slums often have minimal or no access to pure drinking water, sanitation, health care facilities, education, or the urban economy. Acute shortage of affordable housing is the cause of such legal and illegal slums in megacities. These slum areas unfortunately form the repositories of urban crimes. Megacities often have significant numbers of homeless people. In a city like Mumbai and its suburbs, we observe people living on railway stations, footpaths, or under the flyovers. Many slum dwellers are not protected with tenant's rights, so they can be easily evicted or forced out and become homeless.

The rapid growth of a city like Mumbai has led to the illegal construction of buildings with poor quality of sanitation, drinking water, and other facilities on government as well as on private lands. Traffic congestion is a condition on road network that occurs as its usage has increased and is characterized by slower speeds, longer trip times, and rising vehicular queuing. The air quality in the megacities has deteriorated due to heavy traffic on the roads. More cars and more congestion have led to increasingly poor air quality but also residential heating, and cooking leads to air pollution. Toxic chemical spread into the atmosphere has triggered acute respiratory illness. Water contamination and frequent outbreak of epidemics has become the feature of megacities.

In megacities, we can recognize a wide range of social standards and social fragmentation, and sociocultural conflicts because of the different background of the migrants. Many cities and megacities in India have experienced the tensions between the different communities during religious festivals. Internal security threat in India's biggest cities is emerging as the greatest challenge for the security managers. Some cities in India had witnessed the ethnic and communal tensions in the past. Riots of that kind that happened in Ahmedabad, Delhi, and Mumbai between the communities were the main challenges faced by the Indian Police. Besides, Mumbai in 1993, Jaipur, Surat, Bangalore, Pune, and New Delhi have witnessed terrorists' attacks along with serial bomb blast. Terrorism is therefore a clear and present-day challenge for Indian megacities.

There is no doubt that India's future is in the cities. What is happening in India is a part of the worldwide challenge. Megacities are sprouting around the globe. But in India, it seems that the urban local governments have failed to cope with the problems of people living in cities, as these cities are growing without any proper planning. A shortage of affordable housing in Indian cities has led to rampant illegal construction by developers using cheap materials and shoddy methods in order to offer low-cost homes to low-paid workers. Despite several promises by the government to build homes for India's poor in densely populated cities, the country's urban housing shortage is estimated at nearly 19 million households (Urbanization and its issues, 2016). That lack of affordable housing is especially acute in Mumbai, India's financial capital and home to some of worlds costliest real estate, where an estimated 6 out of 10 people live in slums. Large number of households in cities do not have access to one of the most basic human needs — a safe and reliable supply of drinking water. Rural areas contain the largest number of people without access to safe drinking water, but like in many developing countries, even urban and semi-urban areas face the problem of adequate and safe drinking water. The average availability of water is reducing steadily with growing population, and it is estimated that by 2020 India will become a water stress nation. The urban water supply and sanitation sector in the country is suffering from inadequate levels of service, an increasing demand–supply gap, poor sanitary conditions, and deteriorating financial and technical performance. Some 35 Indian cities with more than a million residents provide water distribution for only a few hours a day. Waterborne diseases cause an estimated 90 million days of lost productivity annually.

Solid waste management is one of the major environmental problems in Indian cities. Improper methods of solid and liquid waste management in many urban areas pose a great threat to urban ecology and environment. Average waste generation ranges from 1,000 to 2,500 metric tons/day in the urban area. Various studies have revealed that 40% of waste is disposed of unscientifically in open dumps, landfills creating problems to public health and environment. The suitable facilities to treat and dispose of the waste are absent in all most all mega cities. Lack of financial resources leads to low quality of service provision, which leads to fewer people willing to provide for such services. Due to the expansion of cities, disposal sites have now come amidst the thick population, thereby posing threat to health of the residents.

Big Indian cities like Mumbai have huge slums like Dharavi, which is to be replaced by modern metropolis, but there is no plan for rehousing of the slum and its slum dweller. There is also tension between industry vs.

agriculture, for example, in Bengal it is Tata Nano vs. farmers, in Maharashtra it is between Reliance Special Economic Zone and farmers in the Konkan area.

10.5. Challenges in Urban Development

Insights (2014) has highlighted the following institutional, infrastructural, and other challenges faced by megacities and urban areas in India.

10.5.1. Institutional challenges

Urban Governance: The 74th amendment act has been implemented half-heartedly by the state, which has not fully empowered the Urban local bodies (ULBs). ULBs comprise of municipal corporations, municipalities, and *Nagar Panchayats*, which are to be supported by the state government to manage the urban development. For this, ULBs need clear delegation of functions, financial resources, and autonomy. At present, urban governance needs improvement for urban development, which can be done by enhancing technology, administrative, and managerial capacity of ULBs.

Planning: Planning is mainly centralized, and till now the state planning boards and commissions have not come out with any specific planning strategies and depend on planning commission and now on *NITI Aayog* for it. In fact, for big cities the plans have become outdated and do not reflect the concern of urban local dwellers, these need to be take the care of by metropolitan planning committee as per provisions of 74th amendment act. Now, the planning needs to be decentralized and participatory to accommodate the needs of the urban dwellers. Also, there is lack of human resource for undertaking planning on full scale. State planning departments and national planning institutions lack qualified planning professional. There is a need to expand the scope of planners from physical to integrated planning — land use, infrastructure, environmental sustainability, social inclusion, risk reduction, economic productivity, and financial diversity.

Finances: A major challenge is the revenue generation by the ULBs. This problem can be analyzed form two perspectives. First, the states have not given enough autonomy to ULBs to generate revenues, and second in some cases the ULBs have failed to utilize even those tax and fee powers that they have been vested with. There are two sources of municipal revenue, that is, municipal own revenue and assigned revenue. Municipal own revenue is generated through taxes and fee levied by them. Assigned revenues are those which are assigned to local governments by a higher tier of government. There is a growing trend of declining ratio of own revenue. There is poor collection of property taxes. Use of geographical information system to map all the properties in a city can have a huge impact on the assessment rate of properties that are not in tax net. There is need to broaden the user charge fee for water supply, sewerage, and garbage disposal. Since these are the goods which have a private characteristic and no public spillover, so charging user fee will be feasible and will improve the revenue of ULBs, along with periodic revision. Once the own revenue-generating capacity of the cities will improve, they can easily get loans from the banks. At present, due to lack of revenue-generation capabilities, banks don't give loans to ULBs for further development. For financing urban projects, municipal bonds are also being implemented, which work on the concept of pooled financing.

Regulator: There is exponential increase in the real estate, encroaching the agricultural lands. Also the rates are very high, which are not affordable, and there are other irregularities in practice. For this, we need regulators, which can make level playing fields and will be instrumental for affordable housing and checking corrupt practices in the real estate sector.

10.5.2. Infrastructural challenges

Housing: Housing provision for the growing urban population will be the biggest challenge for the government. The growing costs of houses in comparison to the income of the urban middle class has made it impossible for majority of lower income groups who are residing in congested accommodation, and many of those are devoid of proper ventilation, lighting, water supply, sewage system, etc. For instance, in Delhi, the current estimate is of a shortage of 500,000 dwelling units in the coming decades.

The United Nations Centre for Human Settlements (UNCHS) introduced the concept of "Housing Poverty" (UN-HABITAT, 2017) which includes "individuals and households who lack safe, secure, and healthy-shelter, with basic infrastructure such as piped water and adequate provision for sanitation, drainage and the removal of household waste."

Safe drinking water: The safe drinking water sources are also found to be contaminated because water in the cities are inadequate, and in the future, the expected population cannot be accommodated without a drastic improvement in the availability of water. The expenses on water treatment and reuse will grow manifold.

Sanitation: The poor sanitation condition is another gloomy feature in urban areas, and particularly in slums and unauthorized colonies of urban areas. The drainage system in many unorganized colonies and slums either do not exist, and if they exist they are in a bad shape and in some areas resulting in blockage of waste water. This unsanitary condition leads to many sanitation-related diseases such as diarrhoea and malaria. Unsafe garbage disposal is one of the critical problems in urban areas, and garbage management always remained a major challenge.

Health and education conditions: The important indicators of human development are education and health. The health conditions of the urban poor in some areas are even more adverse compared to rural areas. As many as 20 million children in the developing countries are dying due to contaminated drinking water. About 600,000 persons are losing their lives because of indoor air pollution (WHO, 2014). The National Family Health Survey (NFHS, 2007) has envisaged that a lot of women and children are suffering from nutritional anaemia and diseases like tuberculosis and asthma. Providing health care services to the growing urban population is major challenge for the government health care delivery system. They have to take the help of private players as public health facilities are poor. In case of migrants, they cannot take the benefit of government policies, so they must pay very high charges, which keep them in the vicious cycle of poverty. Urban education system also is becoming elite in private institution due to limited seats and high charged fee. The condition of public educational institutions is dismal.

Urban public transport: Individuals with high income in India buy more private vehicles and use less public transport. Such huge number of vehicles in cities is causing more traffic jams, which in turn decreases the efficiency of public transport. Also, the penetration of public transport is less, which makes people use private vehicles. Public transport is less disabled friendly. There is also a lack of infrastructure and poor maintenance of existing public transport infrastructure.

10.5.3. Other challenges

Environmental concern: According to UNDP (2004) 70% of the Indian population is at risk to floods and 60% are susceptible to earthquakes. The risks are higher in urban areas owing to density and overcrowding. Urban areas are becoming heat islands, ground water is not being recharged, and water crisis is persistent. Compulsory water harvesting will be beneficial.

Urban crime: Prevention of urban crime is another challenge for the governments having more number of urban areas and particularly metropolitan cities. The megacities are facing increased criminal activities because of unchecked migration, illegal settlements and diverse socio-cultural disparities, organized groups, and gangsters, and professional criminals for wishing a lavish life in metropolis. The cities of Delhi, Mumbai, and Bangalore have accounted for 16.2%, 9.5%, and 8.1%, respectively, of the total crime reported from 35 mega cities. Prevention of crime in megacities is thus a huge challenge for the government of India and authorities of megacities.

Poverty: Roughly a third of the urban population today lives below the poverty line. There are glaring disparities between haves and have-nots in urban areas. The most demanding of the urban challenges unquestionably is the challenge posed by poverty; the challenge of reducing exploitation, relieving misery, and creating more human condition for urban poor. Urban inequality is on the rise — according to the UN-HABITAT (2010), urban inequality in India rose from 34% to 38% based on consumption in period of 1995–2005.

Provision of employment: Providing gainful employment to the growing urban population is a major challenge. It is generally observed that the literate and semi-literate migrants are absorbed with minimal works, having lower wage and more hours of work. The UN-HABITAT report (UN-HABITAT, 2013) has rightly remarked "The cities have become a dumping ground for surplus population working in unskilled, unprotected and low wage informal service industries and trade." As the rural agricultural sectors are shrinking day by day, the challenges before the urban sector to provide viable employment to migrating population will be a daunting task in the coming year.

10.6. Steps Taken by Indian Government to Improve Urban Development

The following initiatives and activities by the Indian government have been undertaken in order to improve urban development.

The Constitution (74th Amendment) Act: Came into effect in 1993, emphasizes to strengthen urban planning, regulation of land use, roads and bridges, and providing urban amenities (India Code, 2017).

National Urban Transport Policy, 2006: Its main purpose is to provide affordable, comfortable, safe and rapid, and reliable and sustainable urban transport system for the growing number of city residents. Integrated land use and transport planning in all cities is encouraged so that travel distances are minimized and access to livelihoods, education, and other social needs, especially for the marginal segments of the urban population, is improved (NUTP, 2006).

National Urban Renewal Mission (NURM), 2005: The primary objective of the JnNURM is to create economically productive, efficient, equitable, and responsive cities. The JnNURM consists of two sub-missions: Urban Infrastructure and Governance (UIG) and Basic Services for Urban Poor (BSUP). The mission focuses on: integrated development of infrastructure services; securing linkages between asset creation and maintenance for long-run project sustainability; accelerating the flow of investment into urban infrastructure services; planned development of cities including the peri-urban areas, out growths, and urban corridors; renewal and re-development of inner city areas; universalization of urban services so as to ensure their availability to the urban poor (NURM, 2005).

Introduction to metro trains: Megacities like Delhi, Mumbai, Kolkata, or Bangalore are part of above-mentioned initiatives. Recently, cabinet has also passed a proposal for the second phase of Bangalore Metro (*Namma Metro*). In addition, governments have ordered many feasibility studies in Tier-II and Tier-III cities. Now, 1 million plus cities can go for metro projects according to new urban policy.

India's first monorail: It will be thrown open to the public, 8 years after it was first proposed, with the Maharashtra government. With this, India will join countries like the United States, Germany, China, Japan, Australia, and Malaysia that have monorails.

Smart city concept: In the budget of 2014, it was projected to launch "one hundred Smart cities," as satellite towns of larger cities and the existing mid-sized cities. In a broader definition of smart city, it may include creative, cyber, digital, e-governed, entrepreneurial, intelligent, knowledge, harnessing the power of information and communication technology (ICT). Smartness must be there with respect to governance and service delivery. Its feature can be e-governance (through Digital India initiative, National e-governance plan, National Optical fibre network, e-*panchayat* project of Ministry of Rural Development, Government of India, etc.).

Clean India (Swachh Bharat): Clean urban areas will attract tourists and can increase the economic diversity of the urban dwellers, and it will be also source for revenue generation for ULB (PMIndia, 2017).

10.7. Policy Implications

The attention in Indian megacities should be focused on integrated development of infrastructure services covered under the mission of the government. Furthermore, there should be establishment of linkages between asset-creation and asset-management through a slew of reforms for long-term project sustainability. Green building concepts should additionally be implemented. Along the lines suggested by the administrative reforms commission over 7 years ago, states should undertake "activity mapping" for municipal governments to be clear about which activities are essential for them to manage, which require them to act as agents for higher tiers of government, and which involve sharing responsibility with other tiers of government. There is no "one size fits all here" — the answer will vary across municipalities. The office of an empowered mayor (instead of the municipal commissioner) must take responsibility for administrative coordination internally between municipal departments, and externally with the state and central government agencies. Urban planning mechanisms need an overhaul to unify land record keeping, integrate land use with transport planning, and embed municipal plans into district and regional plans.

Finally,

- local bodies should fill vacancies;
- time-tested master plans should be strengthened instead of preparing quick-fix city development plans;
- populist policies and reforms should have their logical conclusion and should be not done in great haste;
- land development should be the part of planning of urban development;
- project management skills need to be enhanced;
- timely completion of projects needs to be applied;
- more projects in public–private partnership should be encouraged.

10.8. Conclusions

No phenomenon reflects more the sheer power and appeal of urbanism than the rise of megacities. In conclusion, the large urban agglomerates are increasingly a developing-world phenomenon that has affected the future prosperity and stability not only of its own inhabitants, but of the world economy at large. It is important for India to understand megacities' dynamics, their immense problems and needs, and the economic and market development opportunities they may offer. The evolution of megacities in the country has shaped patterns of national and global economies and will continue to affect the settlement of vast populations, and social and political dynamics. Megacities play a key role on the global stage by virtue of their very size. The megacities of India, confronted by nearly intractable problems, have a pervasive and crucial need for policies and socio-technological and socio-economic approaches that must be devised in a different context than that of the developed world — a context with different settings, different needs, different challenges, and different opportunities.

References

Bhola, G. and A. Nagpure (2015). Indian megacities as localities of environmental vulnerability from air quality perspective. *Journal of Smart Cities* 1(1), 15–30, Retrieved from http://ojs.whioce.com/index.php/jsc/article/view/01.003./53 [access: 08.12.2016].

Buckley, R. (2015). Urbanization & Demographics: The Coordination Problem. Retrieved from https://unhabitat.org/urbanization-demographics-the-coordination-problem-robert-buckley-the-new-school-2/ [access: 25.02.2017].

Census India (2011). Retrieved from http://censusindia.gov.in/ [access: 15.01.2017].

Facts (2013). Unbelievable facts. Valeriepieris: A Circle Housing Majority of the World's Population. Retrieved from http://www.unbelievable-facts.com/2013/06/valeriepieris-circle-housing-majority.html [access: 20.12.2016].

India Code (2017). Retrieved from http://indiacode.nic.in/coiweb/amend/amend74.htm [access: 15.03.2017].

Insights (2014). Urbanization in India: Facts and Issues. Retrieved from http://www.insightsonindia.com/2014/10/29/urbanization-in-india-facts-and-issues/ [access: 08.12.2016].

Kaushik, I. (2013). Challenges and issues in mega city planning in India. *International Journal of Scientific Engineering and Research*, 1(3), 128–132. Retrieved from http://www.ijser.in/archives/v1i3/SjIwMTM2MQ==.pdf [access: 08.12.2016].

Kotkin, J. (2014). The problem with megacities. Retrieved from https://www.chapman.edu/wilkinson/_files/MegaCitiesUPDATED%20VERSION.pdf [access: 08.12.2016].

National Family Health Survey (NFHS) (2007). The National Family Health Survey. Retrieved from http://rchiips.org/nfhs/NFHS-3%20Data/VOL-1/India_volume_I_corrected_17oct08.pdf [access: 15.03.2017].

NURM (2005). Retrieved from http://moud.gov.in/cms/JNNURM.php [access: 15.03.2017].

NUTP (2006). Retrieved from http://www.urbantransport.kar.gov.in/National%20Urban%20TransportPolicy.pdf [access: 15.03.2017].

PMIndia (2017). Retrieved from http://www.pmindia.gov.in/en/government_tr_rec/swachh-bharat-abhiyan-2/ [access: 15.03.2017].

Siddiqui, N. (2015). Are megacities really the key to India's future? Retrieved from https://nasrinsiddiqui.wordpress.com/2015/02/13/are-megacities-really-the-key-to-indias-future/ [access: 20.01.2017].

Singh, J. (2015). Growing Indian Mega-Cities — Sustainable Future? Retrieved from http://www.india.uitp.org/articles/indian-mega-cities [access: 10.01.2017].

Tokington, S. (2016). India will have 7 megacities by 2030. World Economic Forum. Retrieved from https://www.weforum.org/agenda/2016/10/india-megacities-by-2030-united-nations/ [access: 02.03.2016].

UN (2014). World Urbanization Prospects 2014. Retrieved from http://www.india.uitp.org/articles/indian-mega-cities [access: 20.01.2017].

UNDESA (2014). *World Urbanization Prospects*. Retrieved from https://esa.un.org/unpd/wup/publications/files/wup2014-highlights.Pdf [access: 20.01.2017].

UNDP (2004). A Global Report: Reducing Disaster Risk — A Challenge for Development. Retrieved from http://www.preventionweb.net/files/1096_rdrenglish.pdf [access: 15.03.2017].

UN-HABITAT (2010). *Annual Report*. Retrieved from http://mirror.unhabitat.org/pmss/getElectronicVersion.aspx?nr=3105&alt=1 [access: 17.03.2017].

UN-HABITAT (2013). *State of World's Cities*. Retrieved from http://mirror.unhabitat.org/pmss/getElectronicVersion.aspx?nr=3387&alt=1 [access: 20.01.2017].

UN-HABITAT (2017). Retrieved from https://www.habitat.org/stories/7-things-you-should-know-about-poverty-and-housing [access: 17.03.2017].

Urbanization and its issues (2016). Retrieved from http://dspace.vpmthane.org:8080/jspui/bitstream/123456789/4178/1/FC%20Sem%204%20URBANISATION%20%20AND%20%20ITS%20ISSUES.pdf [access: 10.12.2016].

WHO (2014). *Air Quality Report*. World Health Organization. Retrieved from http://www.who.int/phe/health_topics/outdoorair/databases/AAP_database_results_2014.pdf [access: 15.01.2017].

11

AFRICAN MEGACITIES AS EMERGING INNOVATION ECOSYSTEMS

Katarzyna A. Nawrot, Calestous Juma, and James Donald

11.1. Introduction

The unprecedented population growth in Africa and its projections followed by a high rate of urbanization are resulting in a growing number of huge urban agglomerations — cities and megacities. That phenomenon creates opportunities for the continent, but it also raises concerns about low levels of development and diminished quality of life among the majority of urban residents. African cities are characterized by overcrowding, poor infrastructure, and limited connectivity to the international economic system. They are essentially underperforming as potential centres of creativity and innovation. This chapter argues that despite these challenges, Africa's emerging megacities can unleash their potential as drivers of economic transformation if they can be viewed and managed less as static administrative regions and more as dynamic innovation ecosystems rather than a collection of discrete geographical enclosures that encroach on each other and neighbouring regions without adequate urban planning.

To support this argument, the chapter first briefly examines Africa's economic prospects. The chapter then advances the concept of megacities as innovation ecosystems that drive economic transformation. This is followed by an analysis of the population growth and urbanization trends, focusing on the rise of megacities and their challenges and opportunities. The chapter uses case studies of Lagos and Johannesburg to illustrate the importance of reforms in urban governance in repositioning megacities to become an innovation ecosystems. It concludes with lessons learned from the cases for emerging megacities leaders, who are interested in shaping megacities as innovation ecosystems.

11.2. Africa's Economic Prospects

The first decade of the 21st century marked the beginning of the new African economic narrative. The dynamics of economic growth and development observed in numerous African countries showed discernible potential, generating interest and discussion among researchers and policy makers worldwide (Aryeetey *et al.*, 2012; Nawrot, 2014a; Monga and Lin, 2015a, 2015b; Rynarzewski *et al.*, 2017).

While the average rate of economic growth in sub-Saharan African countries during 1988–1997 amounted to 2.3%, it rose to 4.3% in the next decade. Economic growth intensified after 2004, when the rate exceeded 7%. This acceleration of economic growth in sub-Saharan Africa persisted in the years 2004–2014 at a level of about 5.7%, a more than two-fold increase in growth compared to the average from the previous decade. In many African countries, from 2007 to 2014, the economic growth exceeded 5% (Zambia, Nigeria, Mozambique), and even maintained a level of 7–10%, for example in Angola or Ethiopia (IMF, 2006, 2012, 2015).

Sub-Saharan Africa's GDP growth in the years 2007–2014 was more than five times the average for developed countries. The region recorded higher rates of economic growth than the Middle East and North Africa, South America, and the Caribbean. It came second to Asian countries, fluctuating around an average of 8% (the last three decades remain unchanged, see IMF (2015)). The dynamics differed depending on the region of Africa, as well as across countries. The increase in GDP and in GDP *per capita* was further recorded in the last decade, compared to the rather stagnant situation in both 1980s and 1990s (see Fig. 11.1).

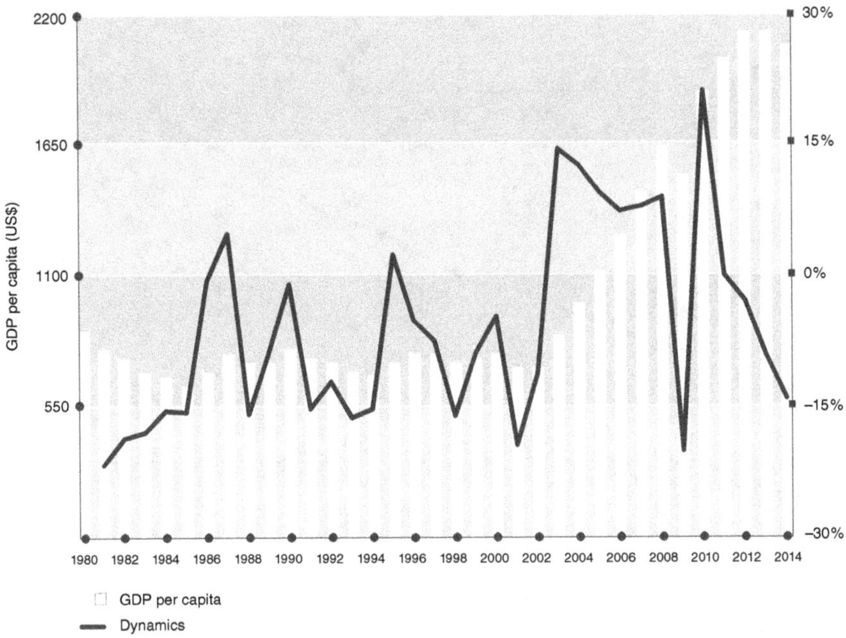

Fig. 11.1. GDP *per capita* and its dynamics in Africa in 1980–2014 (US$ and %)

Source: Authors' own calculations based on WDI (2016).

Despite the observed changes, sub-Saharan African countries remain at a very low level of development. The least developed countries are almost exclusively on the continent of Africa. Changes in world GDP and GDP of Africa show a growing development gap (see Fig. 11.2), mainly due to progress in developed economies and emerging markets, predominantly in Asia.

The unprecedented increase in the level of knowledge and new technologies contributed to the current transformation of the global economy, as well as to the widening gap between countries. The key question is how Africa can use its potential as a latecomer to catch up in economic performance using technological innovation. This raises additional questions about how to utilize the potential of demographics, rising urbanization, natural resources, and relations with developed countries and emerging markets. Answering these questions requires a better understanding of the continent's urbanization dynamics. Of particular interest is the role of cities in general and megacities in particular.

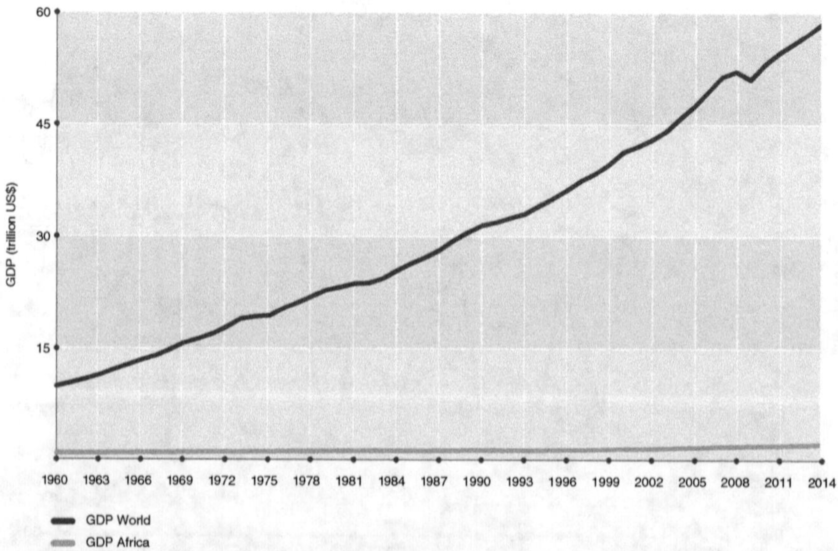

Fig. 11.2. Evolution of the world GDP and GDP of Africa in 1960–2014 (trillion US$)
Source: Authors own calculations based on WDI (2016).

11.3. Cities as Innovation Ecosystems

Cities have always been hubs and sources of productivity, innovation, economic growth, and development. Megacities encompass a larger share of the cumulative population, not only bigger number of people, but also more talent, ideas, innovative thoughts, and possibilities. They offer space for more communication, interaction, cooperation, and competition between different cities stakeholders, cumulating and accelerating the knowledge, while creating the space for vast capabilities for creativity and innovation. Following an evolutionary economics approach pioneered by Joseph Schumpeter (1934), innovation refers to both a result, as well as a process leading to the result, and associated with the formation of a new product, an innovative method of production or delivery, new markets, acquiring new resources, or implementing new organizational solutions. Based on that, the definition of innovation used by OECD in the Oslo Manual categorises innovation into technological (including product and process innovations) and non-technological applications (containing organizational and marketing innovations) (OECD, 2003).

The innovation literature refers to management research and the level of an enterprise or industry (Fan and Gao, 2016; Lee and Lim, 2001; Mu and Lee, 2005). Numerous researchers have also explored innovation capabilities of nations, including technological change, and the resulting possibilities of leapfrogging or catching up (Gerschenkron, 1962; Abramovitz, 1986; Minami, 1986; Kleer *et al.,* 1989; Hobday, 1994; Wang, 2007; Fagerberg and Srholec, 2008; Suehiro, 2008; Fu *et al.,* 2010; Juma, 2010; Lee, 2013; Juma, 2011a, 2014, 2016; Nawrot, 2014b, 2014c). In the case of cities, social innovation is also important as discussed, among others, by Heden and King (1984) or Mulgan (2006).

Glaeser (2011) points out that, despite numerous challenges, cities enable their inhabitants to learn from each other in a complex world, building on each other's ideas and powering humanity's progress. Richard Florida (2002) shows that cities are characterized by high levels of diversity, social mobility, and tolerance. When combined with the stock of talent and advanced technologies, cities create a background for creativity for its communities, determining the comparative advantage of urban networks at both national and international levels. He defines a paradigm of a creative class, arguing — in favour of cities's potential — that this class contains individuals who, through their creativity, add value to the place they live. The creative class refers to the social and cultural preferences associated with consumption, buying behaviour of goods of daily use, through favourites of spending free time. The creative class is defined as those seeking prosperous, diversified societies, and a place with rising employment opportunities and more inhabitants. The characteristic feature of a creative class is its engagement in creating new useful forms, usages, and services. Thus, the creative class should be perceived not in terms of a welfare status but of intellectual potential (Florida, 2002).

Florida defines a creative class through two components: a super creative core and creative professionals. In the first category belong: scientists, engineers, academic scholars, writers, architects, artists, and researchers, among others. Their role refers, beyond their work, to a constant search for innovative solutions. The second category includes professionals whose occupation is based on the use of diversified and interdisciplinary knowledge and combining standard solutions in non-conventional manner.

The group includes technicians, financial advisors, medical personnel, managers, or entrepreneurs (Florida, 2002).

The concept of the creative class underlies the changing character of the global economy and the growing supremacy of services. Therefore, those creating new ideas are also active participants of a daily life, accelerating creativity and innovativeness of a place they live, which mostly refers to cities.

Domański (2012) points out that the diversity of a space extends the possibilities and with a higher degree of freedom of behaviour creates a mechanism that generates micro-diversity of its elements. This in turn accelerates the development of the existing structure of the system, wherein the new structures are further formed, and a system becomes one with varying structural diversity. These changes are a source of new behaviours that can lead to sudden, abrupt transformations. In this way, the system is enhanced with new features, which allow it to move into new dimensions.

The potential of cities and megacities shows their growing political power and comparative advantage compared to nation states. This tendency was underpinned by Ohmae (1995), indicating the dominant role of regions and megaregions. The emergence of such structures is largely determined by transportation and communication networks. This led to the definition of megalopolis (Gottman, 1961) as cities corridors — e.g. Boston–New York–Washington; and of megapolitan areas as networks of clusters around metropolis exceeding 10 million inhabitants (Lang and Dhavale, 2005) or even megaregions. All the above-mentioned structures benefit from the growing concentration of talented people, which is further enhanced and enabled by transportation and connectivity.

As megacities become growing hubs for knowledge, information, and innovation, they determine their own productivity and competitiveness. The process of creating and accelerating knowledge use as well as the role of education become important. Human capital very much depends on the education system that exists in a particular location, which in turn influences the productivity and welfare of that location. Consequently, products of an education system determine and are determined by the quality and character of the education of the population and workforce.

High qualification of a workforce builds capabilities of a local economy and increases its effectiveness, influencing the structure of employment and further spurring the demand for qualified workforce. Further synergies can be observed as the process continues to accelerate the upgrading of the existing education system.

Innovations can be used in megacities in numerous dimensions to spur their sustainable development. On the other hand, cities — as concentrating people, talents, as well as technology parks, institutes, corporations, and universities can further enhance innovativeness. Cities attract more talents and creative individuals if they provide an enabling environment, which includes education possibilities, business environment, culture, air quality, transportation, and connectivity. That leads to the view that megacities can be perceived not only as grounds for innovation and innovation ecosystems but as innovation ecosystems themselves.

Though the "ecosystem" concept was originally derived from the biological sciences, it can be applied in a variety of contexts, including management research or innovation (Dongson *et al.,* 2015; Dalohoun *et al.,* 2009; Chaturvedi, 2007). The notion of "ecosystems" provides a suitable metaphor for describing and analyzing a range of value creating interactions and relationships between sets of interconnected organizations (Autio and Thomas, 2015). Even more broadly participants, actors, and elements within boundaries of a defined construct interact to constitute an ecosystem.

In management research the term "ecosystem" usually refers to a network of interconnected organizations that are linked to or operate around a focal firm or a platform (Moore, 1996; Teece, 2007). Building on that concept and relating it to innovation Autio and Thomas (2015) define innovation ecosystem as a network of interconnected organizations, connected to a focal firm or a platform. The network incorporates both production and use-side participants and creates and appropriates new value through innovation. In addition, a number of researchers apply innovation system or ecosystem to the analysis of nations (Ebner, 2007; Ramstad, 2009; Fageberg and Srholec, 2008;) or a region (Arvanitis and Jastrabsky, 2006).

A megacity innovation ecosystem can be defined as a *network of interconnected institutions, actors, and participants connected to a defined platform of an urban agglomeration of a megacity with ability to interact, adopt, and evolve within its diverse environment by creating new structures, forms, and value that enable the system to evolve to new levels.* Given the diversity of megacity ecosystems, the high degree of freedom of behaviour of its participants and interactions, the system is enhanced with new features that allow it to move to new dimensions, as desired direction of megacities development. This definition shares a number of attributes with the broader concept of "clusters of innovation" as described by Engel (2014).

There are at least five interconnected dimensions that form the structure of a megacity innovation ecosystem and determine the quality in terms of its attractiveness and innovation potential. They are: entrepreneurship, education, environment, culture, and connectivity. Thus, megacity ecosystems should function as self-accelerating their own creativity and innovativeness, and as magnets for attracting talents and innovation.

There are two interconnected hypotheses that apply to the African context. First, innovation can enhance the sustainable development of megacities. Second, megacities can stimulate the growth of innovation.

Participants in cities are crucial aspects of the ecosystem function. They include: city authorities, the private sector, academia, non-governmental organizations, and other institutions and individuals/citizens. Relationships among participants in ecosystems are symbiotic, as they coexist and coevolve with the system. Significant interdependence between different participants is observed, determining stability and advancement of an ecosystem. Thus, megacity ecosystems are dynamic constructs, whose participants coexist and interact creating a new value and further evolution of the construct. Megacity innovation ecosystem dynamics arise from relationships and interactions between the participants. All megacity participants are active agents and depend on the dynamics arising from relationships and interactions between ecosystem participants. This sets the stage for creativity and innovation. As Basole (2009) notes, the characteristics of innovation ecosystems include their ability to adopt and evolve based on internal and external influences. This ability, as shown in the next section, requires purposive intervention aimed at aligning various institutions with innovation objectives.

11.4. Urbanization Trends

While analyzing urbanization in Africa, a short overview of population growth on the continent draws particular attention. The population of the continent was estimated in 1950 at around 228.9 million. According to the United Nations, it is expected to exceed 2.4 billion in 2050. Furthermore, Africa's proportion of the world population is gradually increasing. It is expected to exceed 25% by mid-century. By the end of 21st — according to the medium variant of estimates — it will reach about 4.4 billion, accounting for 39.1% of the expected world population (UNDESA, 2015). Africa is recording the highest rate of population growth, which in 2010–2015 was around 2.5%. This is mainly a result of high birth rates. The countries with the highest population growth rate include Nigeria, Zambia, Mali, Uganda, Gambia, Burundi, Tanzania, Chad, Somalia, and Angola. It is expected that in 2050 the most populous countries on the continent will include Nigeria (440 million), Ethiopia (188 million), Democratic Republic of the Congo (155 million), Tanzania (129 million), Egypt (122 million), and Uganda (104 million) (UNDESA, 2012).

In 2015, the population of Africa exceeded 1.22 billion, while the population of sub-Saharan Africa was about 1 billion, and of North Africa exceeded 223 million (WDI, 2016). This represented 13.6% and 3% of the world population, respectively. The projected estimates mean that the African population will double by 2050, and further increase by 2 billion until 2100 (UNDESA, 2015).

Africa is a young continent, with 60% of population under the age of 25 and 29% between 25 and 49 years old (UNDESA, 2015). In this regard, the proportion of the working age population of Africa is expected to exceed the same indicators for India and China in 2035. Moreover, according to estimates by the UN, Africa's share in the working age population is expected to reach 18% by 2030 and 25% by 2050 (UNDESA, 2012). It means that the labour resources of African countries will double between the years 2010 and 2050. As a result, consumer demand will increase, especially from the growing middle class. Such projections indicate the high potential of the region, but also raise concerns. While it creates opportunities for economic growth, consumer demand, and potential markets for the goods and services of the world's producers, it can lead to a deepening of poverty, unemployment instability, and population movement and migration within and outside the continent.

Along with the rise of population, the level of urbanization in Africa is growing, including a number of large agglomerations, cities, and megacities. This is another challenge for development opportunities observed in the 20th and 21st centuries, not only in Africa but in developing countries at large. The process of urbanization in developed countries, leading to the growth of welfare of the people was incremental. At present, however — particularly in developing countries — we observe galloping urbanization. What this means is that providing the public goods in fast-growing agglomerations takes place much more slowly. Cities are simply not logistically prepared for such a massive influx of people. It leads to a deepening of the developmental problems associated with social exclusion, the increase in urban poverty and crime. Furthermore, it deepens the negative impact on the quality of life of the population arising from factors such as congestion and pollution.

Africa is projected to lead in the world urbanization of the 21st century. Cairo, Lagos, and Kinshasa are ranked as megacities, with estimated populations in 2015 of 18.8 million, 13.1 million and 11.6 million respectively. The projections show that the numbers will increase to 24.5 million in Cairo, 24.2 million in Lagos, and 19.9 million in Kinshasa. Furthermore, by 2030 the populations of Dar es Salaam, Johannesburg and Luanda are projected to exceed 10 million. For Dar es Salaam and Luanda it will mean doubling of the actual size of the cities inhabitants (UNDESA, 2014).

The level of urbanization for the continent is growing constantly and reached 40% in 2015, compared to 15% in the 1960s. The number of people in urban areas is expected to be equal to that in rural areas by around 2040, and exceeding 80% by the end of the century (UNDESA, 2015).

There are significant disparities in economic development and the distribution of wealth in Africa between urban and rural areas. As a consequence, there is growing migration to cities. This gives hope for improving the wellbeing of the people. But it also contributes to the expansion of slums and deterioration in living conditions.

One of the key problems from urban development is growing urban poverty and the increasing number of slums. Africa ranks highest in the world with urban people living in poverty. Over 60% of the people in sub-Saharan African urban areas live in slums. This number increased in the first decade of the 21th century, in particular in the Central African Republic, Ivory Coast, Malawi, Mozambique, Zambia, and Zimbabwe. For comparison, in East Asia the number of people in urban areas living in slums was estimated at around 28.2%, in South Asia at 35%, and in developing countries on average, at 32.7% (UN-HABITAT, 2012).

The above-mentioned issues raise the dilemma of whether the projected population growth along with urbanization will be a dividend or a curse. Whether governments will manage to provide jobs, education, and the infrastructure needed to take advantage of emerging opportunities and productivity of the young and growing population remains an open question. Finally, the other question is whether cities and megacities will evolve into centres of creativity and prosperity contributing to the national wealth or will remain points of chaos and pathologies, rather than progress.

One of the reasons behind the sluggish growth of African cities is their lack of connectivity to the rest of the world in terms of goods and services for trade on regional and international markets (Lall *et al.*, 2017). This, along with low capital investment caused by Africa's relative poverty and lower levels of GDP *per capita* at the acquired stage of urbanization subsequently leads to a deepening of developmental problems and degradation of the public sphere of growing urban agglomerations.

African cities are not adequately serving as engines of innovation spurring technological change and entrepreneurship. What is more, the crucial role that innovation can play in transforming African cities falls short in policy and academic discussions thus far. One of the reasons for this might be the perception of the continent as being predominantly a consumer of imports and not a contributor to global manufacturing. It is therefore important to explore the potential of innovation in African megacities and to map the possible solutions areas arising from an increasingly urbanizing region.

11.5. Illustrations from Lagos and Johannesburg

11.5.1. Lagos

11.5.1.1. *Overview*

The State of Lagos, which is distinct from the Lagos Metropolitan Area, is located in the southwestern zone of Nigeria. Despite being the smallest of Nigeria's 36 states, it is the most important state in the country and in West Africa. If it were a country it would rank as the seventh largest economy in Africa, bigger that Kenya or Ivory Coast. Its GDP is estimated at US$90 billion. The state includes the city of Lagos, the largest urban centre in the country. It was the capital of Nigeria until 1991, when the federal administration was relocated to Abuja. The population of the city of Lagos was estimated at 16 million in 2015.

Despite the relocation of the federal capital to Abuja, Lagos has remained the country's main economic, social, and financial hub. It continued to serve as the Nigeria's centre for international and national communications. Most of the foreign corporations operating in the country are located in Lagos. It is a vibrant commercial and industrial centre with two seaports, an international and local airport, and industrial estates located in Apapa, Ikeja, and Ilupeju. The economic base of Lagos includes manufacturing, service industries, banking, and telecommunications. It also includes fishing, mining, agriculture, forestry, and quarrying.

Lagos State is rich in resources such as bitumen, clay, crude oil, silica, and wood. It accounts for nearly 30% of Nigeria's GDP. Five terminals and ports account for nearly 50% of the country's port income. This agglomeration of economic activities is mainly due to the relatively well-developed air, sea and land transportation infrastructure. Lagos is also a major educational hub housing several federal, state, and private institutions of higher learning. This enables it to provide highly skilled manpower to the various industries.

The concentration of economic activities in Lagos State, its vibrant entrepreneurial culture, and connectivity with the rest of West Africa makes it a natural hub for innovation (Ogbu and Adeoti, 2010). But more importantly, it has the key elements needed to shift from being an administrative unit of the country to an innovation ecosystem. In fact, Lagos State has historically functioned as an implicit innovation ecosystem by virtue of the density of and connectivity between the various economic activities. Being the country's main gateway with the rest of the world, it serves as a receptacle for new ideas as well as an outlet of innovative products originating from the country. The rise of the Nollywood film industry in Lagos is an illustration of the prospects of the state as a leading innovation ecosystem.

11.5.1.2. *Governing innovation*

One of the most important elements in repositioning a megacity into an innovation ecosystem should be attributed to city governance. Important lessons in that respect can be drawn from the office of Babatunde Fashola, Governor of the city-state of Lagos from 2007 to 2015.

During his first term Governor Fashola undertook, important projects regarding city and state infrastructure, transport and connectivity. The government have launched public works programs, which have included the construction of new highways, a commuter rail metro system, a bus rapid transport system with new bus routes, and West Africa's first suspension bridge (Kaplan, 2012). Other initiatives also included improvements in slums and demolishing shanty towns while encouraging occupants to return to their rural villages (Rice, 2012). Also, Fashola's government dedicated substantial funds to sanitation, affordable housing, and "beautification projects" involving the planting of trees and creation of public parks and installation of scores of solar-powered traffic lights across Lagos (Wernick, 2016).

Among numerous initiatives we would like to focus on the InnovateLagos project initiated in 2011. The project was a result of a meeting between Governor Fashola and Calestous Juma at Harvard Kennedy School. In 2010 Governor Fashola visited Harvard Kennedy School to explore how to move Lagos State to a next level of performance after helping it improve its infrastructure and several other services. It is notable that, the history of Lagos from the colonial period had been largely a footnote on failed efforts and ensuring that infrastructure and other urban services kept up with population increase and influx. One of the responses to the pressure was to relocate the federal capital from Lagos to Abuja with the hope that this would result in the decongestion of the city. While federal functions moved to Abuja, Lagos remained the financial capital of Nigeria.

The Governor raised three important topics. The first was how a financial capital like Lagos could enhance its place on the global scene as a commercial gateway for Nigeria given the fact that the federal government controlled foreign relations. This question led to a discussion on how different cities or states around the world work with their federal ministries to establish their presence internationally. This is a common practice in the field of commercial diplomacy and did not represent a challenge to the authority of the federal government to conduct international diplomacy. Lagos is formidable economic force not just in Nigeria but in the region. If it were a country it would rank as the eight largest economy in Africa and the fifth in sub-Saharan Africa.

The second topic was about how to measure the achievements made during the Governor's tenure. The fact that the performance of urban services in Lagos had dramatically improved during the previous 3 years was widely acknowledged. The question was whether to spend the next few years working on performance impact without a clear characterization of baseline conditions. The third topic was how to find a solution to the piracy problem facing Nollywood, Nigeria's film industry. In 2009, Nollywood surpassed Hollywood as the world's second-largest feature film producer after Bollywood. Nollywood is the second-largest Nigerian employer and its combined box office revenue was US$11.5 million in 2016, with about a third of ticket sales coming from Nigerian movies (Corrigan, 2017).

The discussions concluded with the suggestion that 2010 be considered a baseline against which to shift Lagos from its initial focus on infrastructure to becoming a regional innovation hub building on the country's scientific and technological base (Ogbu and Adeoti, 2010). This proposal could also address the first theme related to economic diplomacy.

11.5.1.3. *Fostering institutional innovation*

In charting a way forward, it was decided that the best approach was to help build capacity among the leadership of Lagos State Government to manage the transition from infrastructure to innovation. Harvard Kennedy School ran an executive education program in Lagos in October 2010.

It was led by Calestous Juma and included Professor Henry Etzkowitz of Stanford University and Professor John Adeoti of the Nigerian Institute of Social and Economic Research in Ibadan. The program was attended by 42 participants including State Government Commissioners (ministers), private sector executives, academia, and federal government representatives. It was preceded by a meeting between Calestous Juma and Nigerian President Goodluck Jonathan, who pledged his support for greater functional autonomy by states, a point that was reinforced at the executive training program by his designated representative.

The program was designed as an exploration and was not convened with presumption of outcomes. The curriculum included: innovation systems and development; states and regions as economic actors (Rodríguez-Pose, 2008; Cooke, 2007); regional innovation systems (Etzkowitz and Dzisah, 2008); technology and regional development; emerging technologies and regional development; slum upgrading; policy and institutional innovation (Lakshmanan and Chatterjee, 2009; Wu, 2007); and an open discussion on the way forward. Early in the program consensus emerged that shifting from the focus on infrastructure to innovation would require adjustments in the governance structure of Lagos State with the Governor's office play a key role in serving as a coordinator of the institutional adjustments.

It was agreed that the starting point would be to create the Lagos Innovation Council (LIAC), which would comprise representatives from government, business, academia, and relevant civil society. The body would report directly to the governor for action. Other organs were also envisaged to work on technology development and financing. An extensive exploration of how different countries structured their innovation systems was conducted and it was concluded that some of the elements of the Finnish system would serve as a good role model and source of heuristics. It became evident from the search that no major city in the world had created analogous organs so Lagos would have to proceed in an experimental manner knowing it did not have other examples to emulate.

11.5.1.4. *InnovateLagos*

The council met regularly and its first major task was to recommend the creation of the InnovateLagos as a partnership of the Lagos State

Government and the private sector. Its goal was to nurture a sustainable innovation ecosystem across all sectors in Lagos with a mission to inspire and promote enterprise, research, and skills for innovation. The main target was to champion technological innovation, promote entrepreneurship, and technological dynamism (Juma, 2011b). The immediate objectives were crafted to build entrepreneurship and a favourable business environment, and climate that would spur innovation across the city-state. These objectives included: developing an economic and business climate that rewards innovation; creating and supporting initiatives that took innovative ideas to the market; crafting enabling legislation and policies for innovation (covering human, physical, and technological resources, strong networks to facilitate the flow of ideas, expertise, and knowledge for innovation); and investing in research and innovation via grants, equity funding, and match funding (Rhodes, 2017).

To help implement the project, InnovateLagos Secretariat was founded and located in the Office of the Deputy Chief of Staff, Office of the Governor of Lagos under Ms Moji Rhodes. Two crucial bodies continued to support implementation of the project were LIAC and the Lagos Research & Development Council (LRDC) which started their operations in 2011 and 2012, respectively. The principal goal of the LIAC — a 21-member body of government, private sector leaders, and academia — was to provide high-level advice to better target and generate effective programmes to focus and improve governments and industry support for innovation (Rhodes, 2017).

The starting point in the terms of reference of the LIAC was to develop an innovation strategy and plan for Lagos State that the InnovateLagos office would execute. In particular, the strategy focused on elaborating and influencing policy initiatives to accelerate innovation in public service delivery. It was further critical to identify and review the major obstacles to innovation and to provide solutions that would enhance the economic and social development of a city-state. The crucial aspect of an effective implementation of the strategy was to link the private sector, public sector, and academia to raise their current levels of innovation performance and create the value added from the synergies of their collaboration. The Lagos State innovation agenda was to develop and champion both locally and abroad. Thus, a multidisciplinary and globally competitive approach to innovation was encouraged. To further support it the leadership identified opportunities to work with other states and countries to influence and integrate prospective aspects to the national innovation agenda (Rhodes, 2017).

The crucial pillars of the strategy included policy frameworks (Lagos Innovation Policy, Lagos Broadband Policy); building networks and collaboration through stakeholder mapping exercise and events; facilitating enabling infrastructure for spaces and broadband access (incubators and accelerators, co-working spaces, maker space); targeting education and capacity development through coding and robotics sessions for schools; technical, and mentoring support for innovators and entrepreneurs; industry collaboration with secondary and tertiary institutions and R&D; and funding was provided (Angel Funding, Lagos Innovation Fund).

Among the successful activities, the Council supported the launch of the Lagos Innovation Hotspot Map in collaboration with Co-Creation Hub (CcHub), providing investors and policy makers with data on innovation clusters within the city, ranging from fashion to creative photography, tech start-ups, or financial services. Another initiative — Lagos Angel Network linked entrepreneurs with potential investors to give impetus to businesses, while "Made in Lagos" was supporting Lagos innovators via grants for prototyping, testing and scaling, along with business support and mentoring. The initiative targeted tertiary institutions with industry-linked training programmes and secondary schools with innovation competition programme — IDEASLAGOS. These initiatives, as pointed out by Moules (2014) have encouraged a wave of technology start-ups, earning Lagos the reputation of "Africa smartphone app capital."

Besides these activities, the LIAC addressed culture, in particular the Nollywood movie industry through grants, capacity development, and distribution. One of the guiding principles for the selection of activities discussed at the 2010 executive program was to upgrade existing activities where Lagos could provide regional or international leadership. One obvious case was the film industry. Lagos, the home of Nollywood, views its film industry as an opportunity to promote its tourism and serve as Africa's premier hub for multimedia entertainment. Nollywood filmmakers, however, lost up to 80% of their profits through piracy. Attempts to find technical fixes to the problem were fruitful, so one way forward is to upgrade the technical capacity of Nollywood to stay ahead of the pirates rather than seek to eliminate the problem.

At the heart of Nollywood's woes lay the lack of professional training opportunities for filmmakers to increase their revenue and distribution. Access to continually improving digital equipment, evolving production techniques, and cutting edge distribution strategies were needed to improve film production. In 2012 Lagos State (through InnovateLagos and the Living Labs Global) partnered with Nollywood Workshops to design and implement the Nollywood Upgrade Project (Nollywood UP). The goal was to address the piracy challenge through training, capacity building, and innovation. It trained 150 Nigerian filmmakers in its inaugural five-day workshop. The Nollywood UP training team facilitated intensive workshops in cinematography, directing, production design, film and distribution business, screenwriting, editing, and acting. The workshops were designed by filmmakers for filmmakers, and they took into account the complex realities of filmmaking in Nigeria. The trainers included experts from Nollywood and Hollywood in the United States. To ensure that the training workshops met industry standards, the Nollywood UP team partnered with Boston University's Center for Digital Imaging Arts. The Nollywood UP Training illustrated enormous demand for technical media training in Lagos. Curriculum lectures, handouts, videos, equipment guides were created as resources made available to the Lagos State University for the development of its own film program (Corrigan, 2017).

The second body, the Lagos Research & Development Council (LRDC), including ten members mainly from academia, was inaugurated by Governor Fashola in September 2012. Its aim was to strengthen R&D in tertiary institutions in Lagos through the administration of the Tertiary Institutions R&D Fund, whose purpose was to support research and development emanating from tertiary institutions ranging from arts and humanities, to medicine and pharmacy, engineering and transportation, science and technology, environmental science and climate change, housing, agriculture, and other agro-allied projects. Furthermore, the fund provided higher education institutions with a platform to transform their ideas into commercial products and services for Lagos and facilitate collaborative partnerships with government, the private sector, and domestic and international research institutions.

The LRDC aimed to strengthen tertiary institutions' R&D capabilities through funding both ideas that will lead to the introduction of commercial products and projects that will foster strong domestic and international industry and academic partnerships. It led to further growth of new start-ups born out of tertiary institution R&D labs. Supporting various activities that help to develop the innovative capabilities of tertiary institutions for the private and public sector formed the partnership among the three stakeholders within the Triple Helix collaboration mode. Innovation capabilities and culture in higher education were gradually improving and along with various innovation programs stemming in the quality of learning, teaching, and graduate employability.

A notable LRDC initiative was a call for research proposals to tertiary institutions in Lagos State in November 2013. The call was published to meet the developmental goals of the state in line with its 2012–2025 Development Plan produced by the Ministry of Economic Planning and Budget. The ministry received 137 proposals, mainly from the fields of health (21%), education and training (16%), agriculture and agro-allied industries (10%), environmental science (9%) and power and energy (7%), among others (Rhodes, 2017).

11.5.1.5. *Ecosystem activities*

The active agent of innovation and a crucial component of innovation ecosystems is private sector itself with entrepreneurs adopting new technologies and information systems while providing new products and services for customers. One to mention is Jumia, initiated and founded in Lagos in 2012 and formerly known as Africa Internet Group (AIG). Jumia could be described as an ecosystem itself, embracing online commerce, marketplaces, and classifieds websites and applications. As internet start-ups and e-tailer, gradually expanding business both geographically across Africa, as well as regarding products and services offered to the modern age consumers Jumia is the leading actor of online commerce in Africa.

Besides, a wide variety of facilitation institutions is playing a critical role in innovation and innovation ecosystems (Wernick, 2016). They range from nonprofit organizations, multinational corporations to innovation hubs and tech accelerators. Already mentioned Co-Creation Hub (CcHub) serves as an important platform in that respect in Lagos and Nigeria at large. Established in 2010 with a support of Omidyar Network and UK-based nonprofit Indigo Trust CcHub is catalyzing innovation and creating solutions through a number of activities, including brainstorming sessions, workshops, lectures, and mentoring services for entrepreneurs transforming their ideas into marketable products or solutions (Udonkang, 2014).

As a result of these initiatives and its tangible results, Fashola's governance is considered and characterized as "innovative governance" (Wernick, 2016) and Lagos labelled as a role model for African cities (Kaplan, 2012; Rice, 2012). We can conclude here, that although the InnovateLagos project was in fact targeted at building innovation at the micro- and industry-level across Lagos State, Governor Fashola oversaw an inspirational experiment that sought to reposition the Lagos megacity as an innovation ecosystem. Trained as a lawyer, Fashola brought a culture of science and technology advice to his leadership. When Lagos was hit by the Ebola virus crisis in 2014, he appointed Dr. (Ms.) Adekemi Oluwayemisi Sekoni as his Chief Scientific Adviser to focus on controlling infectious diseases. At the time, Governor Fashola was possibly the only African head of state or federal government supported by a chief scientific advisor.

InnovateLagos activities moved to the Lagos Ministry of Science and Technology and the Lagos Ministry of Establishment, Training, and Pensions in 2014, ahead of the end of the Governor's term in May 2015. In November 2015, Fashola was appointed by President Muhammadu Buhari as the Federal Minister of Power, Works and Housing.

11.5.2. Johannesburg

Johannesburg is the capital of South Africa's Gauteng Province and the seat of the Constitutional Court. We provide a history of the city and the region to show how economic analysis must be cognizant of history, context, and theory to be of practical use (Pieterse, 2016). The history of the City of Johannesburg (CoJ) and current efforts at the city, regional and nationals levels do foster an innovation ecosystem.

11.5.2.1. *Overview*

By 2013 the region had produced 40% of all gold extracted globally to date (valued at $8 trillion). Capabilities built up in this endeavour have provided a platform for ongoing innovation and strong institutions such as the University of the Witwatersrand (Wits), originally a mining school; the South African Bureau of Standards (SABS); and the Council for Scientific and Industrial Research (CSIR) (Harrison and Zack, 2012). The capital-intensive nature of the extraction created a robust financial sector that produced 56% of GVA in 2013 (CoJ, 2015). The finance sector's contribution had increased from 22% in 1996 to 32% in 2013; manufacturing had decreased proportionally from 20% to 16% but was still growing strongly. The financial and business services sectors had also become primary innovators in the digital technology space, though institutions such as the CSIR had developed software development expertise and a national Technology and Innovation Agency funded the commercial links between research and commercialisation (Gauteng Department of Economic Development, 2012).

In recognition of the strong linkages between Johannesburg and the surrounding urban area, the Gauteng Province coordinated strategic planning and policy beyond the three top metros area under the Gauteng City Region (GCR) framework. The GCR reflected an understanding of the innovation and other agglomeration benefits of cities and ranked as the 30th largest in the world. The GCR's total population of 12.9 million produced 11% of Africa's total GDP and hosted 65% of Africa's total market capitalization on local exchanges (AfDB *et al.*, 2016). Population and GDP *per capita* were expected to double before 2050. By these measures, it is clear that a significant portion of Africa's knowledge, capability, and capital stocks were in and around Johannesburg.

A 2015 Brookings Institute Report compared the GCR with eight global peers such as the so-called "gateway cities" of Istanbul, Mexico City, and Shenzhen (Parilla and Trujillo, 2015). The report labelled the GCR the powerhouse of African business and the de facto African capital of finance and technology. The report also pointed to the high presence of multinational corporation headquarters as evidence of gateway status.

11.5.2.2. *History*

Paul Kruger, the President of the Afrikaner republic, declared Johannesburg (also now often referred to as Jozi, Joburg, and eGoli), a gold mining village in 1887, 1 year after local farmers discovered gold. The scientific community today agree that humankind had its origins in the area (a major driver of tourism in 2016). When the farmers discovered gold, the region had a small population of Afrikaner and Bafokeng farmers. The Bafokeng people had been indigenous to the area since at least the 1500s and were farmers and metal workers with trade ties as far away as China. A period of ethnic warfare with the Ndebele had depopulated the area in the 1820s and Afrikaner settlers fleeing the British Cape Colony declared a republic in 1840, driving the Ndebele to present day Zimbabwe. The founding constitution of the Afrikaner republic stated that "blacks and whites are not equal before God or state" and that foreigners could not own land.

The region of present-day South Africa was a patchwork of Afrikaner states; Basutho, Swazi and Zulu Kingdoms; and British colonies. The discovery of gold renewed interest from the British who had already fought against the Afrikaner and Zulu nations in separate wars. Johannesburg grew to a tented city of over 100,000 people within 10 years of the discovery of gold attracting fortune-seekers from across Southern Africa and as far afield as Australia, California, China, and Russia. Much of the early growth was driven by speculation on the Johannesburg Stock Exchange, and British financial interests led to an ugly war that ended with the British taking control of Johannesburg in 1903.

Factors out of Johannesburg's control such as the size of gold deposits, global demand for the metal, and events such the World Wars contributed to the unlikely rise of an isolated industrial "city of gold." However, through an innovation ecosystem lens, we see how early Johannesburg developed a particular culture of innovation and enterprise that drove growth from the bottom up. This rough but open culture persists to the present day and often stood in stark contrast to the closed tribal and nationalism of the rest of South Africa throughout its history. Harrison and Zack's (2012) paper, "The Fall of Gold and the Rise of Johannesburg," and Van Onselen's (1982) "New Babylon New Nineveh," are rich accounts of this history and document a vast array of technological, social, and industrial innovations from all sectors, races, and socio-economic groups. These range from the structure of the stock exchange and local property development to mining innovations in chemicals and explosives and labour unions and associations. The development of rapid integration of systems for sanitation, labour, electricity, transport, and even the "underworld" networks of taverns and brothels created a platform on which Africa's leading urban economy could develop. These authors also highlight the diversity of the early city, and the proximity in which people lived and worked.

The labour-intensive quality of the industrialization created persistent labour shortages until the 1970s, and the ability of the local industry to keep wages low shifted disproportionate value to profits rather than workers, and much of these profits were passed on to international capital. This labour dynamic and pervasive racism in European settler, colonial, and then apartheid political systems produced high inequality in development outcomes between residents. Migrant labour was attracted to Johannesburg from around the world; labourers were recruited from neighbouring countries or coerced off communal lands through rural tax schemes. Black Africans, in particular, faced racially targeted wage ceilings, restrictions on land ownership and business ownership, inferior public health and education, and no voting rights for the first 100 years of the city's development (Harrison and Zack, 2012). The nationalist government of the post-second World War II era compounded these effects through forced removals of black residents from areas near the urban centres and development of segregated and undercapitalized housing and social infrastructure.

Without romanticizing early Johannesburg, it is clear that as racism and segregation policies intensified, they strangled innovation, particularly in the social structures of the city. For example, a British parliamentary report into labour shortages in Johannesburg in 1904 conducted over 50 indepth interviews with business, union, and education leaders. The report's recommendations and the policies it led to were primarily around incentivizing black labour yet only two of the testimonies were from black participants. Similarly, at the end of the World War II South Africa's highly respected

Prime Minister, Jan Smuts, turned down advice from his staff to engage the leaders of the black community and political movements in finding a lasting solution to resolve racial tensions achieve and equal rights. Ironically Smuts had built his international reputation on negotiating tensions between the "white races of Africa" and advocating for a rights-based new world order. The nationalist government that ousted him campaigned on apartheid as a policy solution to devastating long-term effect. The Group Areas Act of 1950 further limited rights of black residents, and forcibly removed whole communities to the margins of the city. In one example over 60,000 people were moved at gunpoint overnight. The city made extremely limited social housing investments in the 1960s and 1970s for black residents, and these were often men-only dormitories, with property rights limited to leases.

Johannesburg began to ease the implementation of these policies in the early 1980s, culminating in national democratic elections in 1994. When the first democratically elected government took control in 1994, it inherited not only the challenge of underinvestment in the black communities but the overall downturn of the city; slower economic growth, capital flight, and urban sprawl accelerated by "white" flight. A wave of urbanization of over 1 million people in less than 10 years caused an influx that sprouted informal settlements around the city.

Colonial and apartheid land use and subsequent underinvestment in well-located housing mean poverty is concentrated in densely populated areas spatially, or socially, removed from employment. Low wages and poor education contribute, but the location and undersupply of housing are the defining features of poverty in Johannesburg as they replicate the current economic environment.

The apartheid-planned black townships of Soweto and Ivory Park appear on the far Eastern and Western edges. The previously middle-class high-rise apartment districts near the inner city are now mostly poor and have become one of the most densely populated urban areas in the world. Having survived forced removals, one neighbourhood-Alexandra appears in the economic zone but is separated by a freeway and light industry from Sandton, Africa's wealthiest square mile. The residents of these areas spend 20% of their income on transport and 46 minutes per trip (Kelly, 2014).

This concentration of poverty is a drag on individual upward mobility and regional growth. Poor access to social systems, markets, and institutions are both the cause and consequence of poverty, and the resultant inequality has severe social (disease, crime, civil unrest) and economic (constrained growth) consequences (Galster and Killen, 1995). In Hillbrow density has soared to over 67,000 people per km^2, which is five times higher than the poorest neighbourhoods of New York City. This density puts huge pressure on local government services and negates the positive social effects of living closer to economic opportunity. The over-populated and poorly maintained and managed environment means residents do not feel at home there; only a significant improvement in the management of the area will realize the opportunities that are present (Silverman and Zack, 2007).

This reality shows the importance of context in understanding economic data. Poor planning and historical legacy often negated agglomeration benefits. The city estimates that doubling employment density would improve productivity by up to 5% (CoJ, 2016).

The transition of governance created a period between 1990 and 2000 with limited local public spending, and a retraction of management. As South Africa opened to global markets the city experienced rapid population growth and neoliberal economic forces drove growth and private development thus creating splintered urbanism (gated communities and malls), urban sprawl, and a transition to a service economy that exacerbated inequality.

Even in this environment, Cartwright and Marangane (2016) document the city of Johannesburg's (CoJ's) remarkable turnaround from bankruptcy in 1998. This turnaround arguably did little for the city's poor as inequality accelerated but they recognize a rapid rise to international standing, culminating symbolically with the hosting of the 2010 FIFA World Cup Final in Soweto. High-speed rail, bus rapid transit, mega-scale freeway improvement projects, and private investments such as one of the world's largest malls have boosted the city's image and economy. Other high-profile events such as a failure in city billing systems (even though SAP rated the integration successful), massive construction collusion on World Cup projects, and a contested open road tolling system to pay for the upgrades have countered some of the improved perceptions. Business, adventure, and regional shopping tourism have become a primary source of income, and the economy has grown at a far higher rate than the country as a whole.

In 2016, like in many African cities, there existed two starkly different Johannesburg's, one of poverty and exclusion that "from below" and another of global competitiveness and consumer excess "from above." Almost half of Johannesburg's population was not born in the city, and 1 in 10 was not born in South Africa (Palmary *et al.*, 2015).

11.5.2.3. *City government response*

Under the leadership of Executive Mayor Parks Tau (2012–2016), Johannesburg city government for the first time began to exert a progressive influence on the urban economy that at least partly lived up to the rhetoric of South Africa's claimed developmental state. Tau focused on innovation in local government and created space for the experimentation, risk, and the additional budget this required to reposition the city as a platform of competitiveness and urban renewal (Cartwright and Marrengane, 2016).

The CoJ now supplements national health care, education, and social transfers with its clinics and a food security program, thus reducing income inequality and poverty levels over the past 5 years. These improvements are recognized primarily as the result of transfers, and the attention has shifted to policies that will drive equal growth.

In this context, the CoJ adopted the 2040 Growth and Development Strategy. The city aimed to transform the economy and improve competitiveness through industrial transformation, spatial rejuvenation, and institution and global identity building (CoJ, 2011).

In 2013, CoJ announced the largest local capital program in post-apartheid South Africa with plans to "re-stitch" the city and create "quality of life" for all. The latest statutory 5-year Integrated Development Plan (2016–2021) includes these investments as well as the local economic development strategy. The Johannesburg Development Agency, responsible primarily for targeted property development, is tasked with implementing the Corridors of Freedom project (JDA, 2016).

Corridors of Freedom is rooted in transit-orientated development theory, using public transport and infrastructure investments along existing transit routes between the densest residential neighbourhoods and the employment centres of the city. This strategy, while top-down, is designed to direct the present trends using an ecosystem view of the city that is complementary to an innovation ecosystem approach. While densifying work, residential, activity and recreational activity along transport corridors the city will also provide broadband wireless internet access. Johannesburg has identified investment precincts with creative economy focuses such as the fashion district, the film district, the diamond district, and the digital innovation district. In partnership with local banks, the CoJ runs six small-to-medium-sized enterprise hubs that streamline services for small businesses, while the city's policies work to reduce the cost of doing business, the cost of data, the cost of transport, and the cost of financial services (Adams, 2016).

A further institutional response to the spatial challenges was the creation of the Gauteng City-Region Observatory (GCRO), a research partnership between the Gauteng Provincial Government and the Universities of the Witwatersrand (Wits) and Johannesburg (UJ) (Mubiwa and Annegarn, 2013). The GCRO improved the integrating capacity of local government by, for example, commissioning an interactive GIS system from the Johannesburg Centre for Software Engineering (JCSE), a partnership between Wits and the CoJ (JCSE, 2015).

The JCSE partnership was extended in 2016 to create the Tshimologong Digital Innovation District that used corporate tax rate credits to attract firms and encourage the growth of Johannesburg's software cluster in a district of the inner city that has been experiencing urban renewal. Early investors included an IBM research laboratory and the innovation offices of provincial government agencies such as Treasury (e-government services Design and Validation Services) and the Innovation Hub (South Africa's only accredited innovation centre). The World Bank reported that Johannesburg hosted three digital technology hubs, including venture capital lead hubs in the Fintech environment (Kelly, 2014).

In 2016 the University of the Witwatersrand appointed Professor Ronald Wall as the Johannesburg City Chair of Economic Development. Professor Wall, also the head of Urban Competitiveness and Resilience at Erasmus University Rotterdam, mapped trade flows to determine

Johannesburg's relative position in the increasingly connected network of global cities. This data was used to guide urban planning within changing economic demands (AfDB *et al.*, 2016).

While the authors identified innovation as a relative strength with industry and university collaboration, they warned that declining patent filing rates and an under-investment in venture capital should be noted. The South African National Innovation System was conceptually sound but poorly integrated with the efforts of Johannesburg, the nation's economic engine (Raphasha, 2015).

Recent judgements of the Constitutional Court in city matters, including local street vendors and zoning approvals, have caught the attention of researchers. Researchers were studying the perspective of judges on cities in South Africa, India, and Colombia. Judgements affect the right to the city, and we encourage similar work on judgements that impact local innovation systems (Coggin, 2017).

Each of these actions has combined to create an ecosystem with dispersed governance and increasing interconnectivity towards an innovation ecosystem in Johannesburg. With its financial strength, commercial activities, and intellectual resources, the CoJ has great potential to emerge as a strong innovation ecosystem. It has sufficient local institutions that can serve as centres for the absorption of internationally available technologies. To move in this direction Johannesburg will need to review the available technologies and make the necessary adjustments in its institutions to foster technological catch-up and to leapfrog.

11.6. Lessons for Emerging Megacities

Emerging megacities in developing countries have a chance to become innovation ecosystems. Galloping urbanization and negative externalities and pathologies — including overpopulation, urban poverty, poor living condition, congestion, pollution, social exclusion, and ethnic conflicts, among others — do not negate the opportunity. Thus, the urban potential is to reposition cities toward innovation ecosystems. To reposition, a city needs to be governed in an innovative way to spur and enhance the creation of an innovation ecosystem. Transforming urban areas of developing countries into well-managed, modern, and innovative areas require activities and actions in all identified dimensions of a megacity innovation ecosystem, including entrepreneurship, education, environment, culture and connectivity, and by all cities participants through symbiotic and value-creating interactions.

Authorities play a crucial role in a megacity in terms of how they coordinate the dimensions and how they manage and govern it.

Successful public–private partnerships (PPPs) have emerged in an array of areas. PPPs have been used to promote enterprise and entrepreneurship, support and build capabilities for innovation, launch and fund initiatives to transmit ideas into practical solutions and take them to the market, support human development, and build transportation and infrastructure. Public authorities together with entrepreneurs can further spur the emergence of innovative districts across given urban agglomeration and technological and industrial clusters as well as enhance the clustering of cities neighbourhoods in an innovative way.

Whether innovation takes the from of a product or process, or is organizational or social it can be applied in the analysis of a megacity and utilized in the city context. Thus, by analyzing the potential use of innovations at the megacity level, we can identify various dimensions of their use, which can include people (including individuals, the level of a household and enterprise); infrastructure (transportation, housing, management and distribution of energy, energy use of electricity, heating, renewable resources); environment (pollution, climate, haze); communication (ICT, early warning systems, cities management, among others); and urban planning.

The role of the government would include elaborating on spatial planning, legislation procedures and policies for a progressive legal framework where entrepreneurs can freely develop and innovation usher in.

Another important aspect is governments support for education. In that respect, all level of education is crucial, but from innovation and megacities point of view secondary and tertiary education seems decisive. Further, collaboration between government, the private sector, and academia — thus enhancing Triple Helix — is necessary to spur innovation ecosystems through common research, funding, grants, and other initiatives designating and targeting crucial areas for sustainable development of a city.

The activities undertaken — whether at the level of city authorities, or in collaboration with private sector and academia while leading to creating a megacity as an innovation ecosystem — will naturally attract talents and creative people into that system. Additional initiatives could be undertaken in that respect, whether through city-branding, promotion, joint university programmes, internships, joint corporation internships, conferences and summits, sports, and culture events, among other incentives.

One of the most important aspects attracting creative people into a city is its cultural potential. The authorities of the city have a particularly important role in that respect, as culture very often requires public funding and assistance.

The environment is another crucial aspect in the sustainable development of a megacity and quality of live for its inhabitants. This area seems especially problematic for fast emerging megacities, facing problems of pollution and congestion. Environmentally targeted activities can be undertaken at the governmental city level, but they can also be encouraged through sustainable entrepreneurship, civil society, and individual citizens themselves.

Finally, regarding connectivity, there are two critical dimensions. The first is connectivity within a megacity itself and the second connectivity with the world economy at large. Both dimensions are crucial and interconnected. One aspect to be mentioned here is the importance of public-private partnerships in transportation building and planning, including public transportation, roads, as well as if possible harbours, and airports, as important gateways in today modern and globalised world economy.

Another significant aspect of megacity connectivity is its connection with the global economy whether through industries and corporations (i.e. services, global value chains), international institutions and organisations, and other forms of networking and cooperation (collaborative initiatives, forums, platforms). The later dimension of connectivity underlines the importance of external actors in repositioning a megacity into an innovation ecosystem, and here we consider support of research and academic institutions from abroad; assistance of knowledge and expertise of diaspora and experiences, and learning lessons from other states, cities, megacities, and smart cities.

Above all, clear and long-term vision and strategy of megacity authorities are necessary, followed by practical solutions and sustainability of undertaken projects and strategies. Thus, problems resulting from the vast population in megacities can be alleviated with good governance and by governing cities as innovation ecosystems resulting in significant improvements in numerous areas of megacity structure and functioning of its inhabitants.

Growing urbanization with rising urban agglomerations of megacities can also drive growth and creativity at the national level, contributing to country's GDP. Central governments should acknowledge the impact of megacities on national economy as well as on megacities participants and encourage their governance in an innovative manner as innovation ecosystems. What is more, as the Lagos and Johannesburg case studies show, a megacity can play a significant role in the developing world to promote development and address developmental problems. From that standpoint, the clear division of competencies between the central government and authorities of a megacity is crucial, as is the empowerment of megacities for a wider range of competencies along with funding.

Addressing all megacity dimensions (including entrepreneurship, education, environment, culture, and connectivity) and creating value added from synergies between cities authorities, the public and private sector, as well as academia with an active and collaborative involvement of all cities participants allow a city to be repositioned into innovation ecosystem. It should be further supported and encouraged by central government and other external agents and institutions for better outcomes.

Shifting the focus of city management from regional administration to innovation involves experimentation and institutional reforms based on lessons learned. These lessons can hardly be sustained over time without corresponding reforms in the laws and regulations governing the functioning of cities. This is not just a matter for the cities but involves legislative coordination with federal authorities. The absence of such legal entrenchment could lead to tensions between established administrative approaches and the new objectives to focus on innovation. When such conflicts arise it is likely the incumbent institutional arrangements are likely to win the day because they are supported by existing laws. The only way to counter such resistance to change is to codify the lessons learned in law, which also means engaging other branches of government such as the legislature and the judiciary.

11.7. Conclusions

A growing population in Africa with rapid urbanization, followed by a rising number of both cities and megacities create a great challenge for the continent, but also a vast opportunity for its development. Urbanization along with a young generation of Africans and an emerging middle class can significantly contribute to the growth of GDP and result in the prosperity of societies. Urban agglomerations of megacities as areas concentrating people, talents, academic institutions, the private sector, technology parks, and innovation hubs can be perceived as promising ground for innovation and innovative ecosystems but also as innovative ecosystems themselves.

Furthermore, megacities will attract more talents and creative individuals, as well as innovative entrepreneurs if they provide an attractive environment, what include security, education possibilities, business climate, culture, air quality, transportation, and connectivity. In that sense, innovative governance of a city is necessary to retrieve it towards an innovation ecosystem, which participants will be able to evolve and adapt in a way, so the system will be self-accelerating its creativity and innovativeness moving to the new dimensions, as the desired direction of megacities development.

The case studies further show that developmental problems associated with overpopulation, urban poverty, city congestion, pollution, or security can be substantially alleviated if not eliminated at the city level. This point further underpins that urban areas consisting of both cities and megacities might be more efficient places than central governments to address developmental issues if properly governed. Thus, as Kaplan (2012) notes big cities could be a basis for a new urban-based development model, which should be considered by numerous developing countries in Africa and worldwide.

Note

This chapter is an expanded version of a discussion paper accepted for publication by the Harvard Kennedy School; Nawrot, Katarzyna A. and Juma, Calestous and Donald, James, African Magacities As Emerging Innovation Ecosystems (August 16, 2017). HKS Working Paper No. RWP17-031. Available at https://SSRN.com/abstract=3020109.

References

Abramovitz, M. (1986). Catching up, forging ahead, and falling behind. *Journal of Economic History*, 46, (2), 385–406.

Adams, S. (2016). "Joburg positioned as hub for entrepreneurs," *Destiny Magazine*. Retrieved from http://www.destinyconnect.com/2017/03/14/joburg-positioned-hub-entrepreneurs/ [access: 30.03.2017].

AfDB, OECD, and UNDP (2016). *African Economic Outlook 2016: Sustainable Cities and Structural Transformation*. Retrieved from http://www.oecd.org/countries/namibia/1826046.pdf [access: 28.03.2017].

Arvanitis, R. and E. Jastrabsky (2006). A regional innovation system in gestation: Guangdong. *China Perspectives*, 63.

Aryeetey, E., S. Devarajan, R. Kanbur and L. Kasekende (Eds.) (2012). *The Oxford Companion to the Economics of Africa*. Oxford: Oxford University Press.

Autio, E. and L.D.W. Thomas (2015). Innovation ecosystems. Implications for innovation management? In M. Dongson, D.M. Gann and N. Phillips (Eds.). *The Oxford Handbook of Innovation Management*. Oxford: Oxford University Press, pp. 204–228.

Basole, R.C. (2009). Visualisation of interfirm relations in a converging mobile ecosystem. *Journal of Information Technology*, 24, 144–159.

Cartwright, A. and N. Marrengane (2016). *Urban Governance and Turning African Cities Around: City of Johannesburg*. Nairobi, Kenya.

Chaturvedi, S. (2007). Exploring interlinkages between national and sectoral innovation systems for rapid technological catch-up: Case of Indian biopharmaceutical industry. *Technology Analysis & Strategy Management*, 19(5), 643–57.

City of Johannesburg (CoJ) (2011). *Joburg 2040: Growth and Development Strategy "A promising future*." Retrieved from http://www.joburg.org.za [access: 28.03.2017].

City of Johannesburg (CoJ) (2015). Economic Development Strategy of the City of Johannesburg. Retrieved from http://www.joburg.org.za [access: 28.03.2017].

City of Johannesburg (CoJ) (2016). *Spatial Development Framework 2040 City of Johannesburg Metropolitan Municipality*, City of Johannesburg, Department of Development Planning. Retrieved from http://www.joburg.org.za [access: 28.03.2017].

Coggin, T. (2017). Urban Law Lab. Retrieved from https://www.urbanlawlab.org/ [access: 02.04.2017].

Cooke, P. (2007). To construct regional advantage from innovation systems first build policy platforms. *European Planning Studies*, 15(2), 179–194.

Corrigan, A. (2017). *Personal Communication*, Cambridge, MA, USA.

Dalohoun, D.N., A. Hall and P. Van Mele (2009). Entrepreneurship as driver of "self-organizing system of innovation": The case of NERICA in Benin. *International Journal of Technology Management and Sustainable Development*, 8(2), 87–101.

Domański, R. (2012). *Ewolucyjna gospodarka przestrzenna*. Poznań: Wydawnictwo Uniwersytetu Ekonomicznego w Poznaniu.

Dongson, M., D.M. Gann and N. Phillips (Eds.) (2015). *The Oxford Handbook of Innovation Management*. Oxford: Oxford University Press.

Ebner, A. (2007). Public policy, governance and innovation: Entrepreneurial states in east asian economic development. *International Journal of Technology and Globalisation*, 3(1), 103–124.

Engel, J.S. (2014). What are clusters of innovation. How do they operate and why are they important? In J.S. Engel (Ed.). *Global Clusters of Innovation: Entrepreneurial Engines of Economic Growth around the World*. Northampton, MA, USA: Edward Elgar Publishing.

Etzkowitz, H. and J. Dzisah (2008). Rethinking development: Circulation in the triple helix. *Technology Analysis and Strategic Management*, 20(6), 653–666.

Fagerberg, J. and M. Srholec (2008). National innovation systems, capabilities and economic development. *Research Policy*, 37(2008), 1417–1435.

Fan, P. and H. Gao (2016). Catching up and developing innovation capabilities in China's telecommunication equipment Industry. In Z., Yu, W. Lazonick and Y. Sun (Eds). *China as an Innovation Nation*. Chapter 8, Oxford: Oxford University, pp. 215–239.

Florida, R. (2002). *The Rise of the Creative Class*. New York: Basic Books.

Fu, X., C. Pietrobelli and L. Soete (2010). The role of foreign technology and indigenous innovation in the emerging economies: Technological change and catching-up. *World Development*, 39(7), 1204–1212.

Galster, G. and S. Killen (1995). The geography of metropolitan opportunity: A reconnaissance and conceptual framework. *Housing Policy Debate*, 6(1), 7–43.

Gauteng Department of Economic Development (2012). Gauteng Innovation and Knowledge Economy Strategy. Retrieved from http://www.saine.co.za/wordpress/wp-content/uploads/2012/10/gauteng_innovation_and_knowledge_economy_strategy.pdf [access: 29.03.2017].

Gerschenkron, A. (1962). *Economic Backwardness in Historical Perspective.* Cambridge: Harvard University Press.

Glaeser, E. (2011). *Triumph of The City: How Our Greatest Invention Makes Us Richer, Smarter, Greener, Healthier, and Happier.* London: Macmillan.

Gottman, J. (1961). *Megalopolis — The Urbanized Northeastern Seaboard of the United States.* New York: The Twentieth Century Fund.

Harrison, P. and T. Zack (2012). The power of mining: The fall of gold and rise of Johannesburg. *Journal of Contemporary African Studies*, 30(4), 551–570.

Heden, C.G. and A. King (Eds.). (1984). *Social Innovations for Development.* Oxford: Pergamon Press.

Hobday, M. (1994). Technological learning in Singapore: A test case of leapfrogging. *The Journal of Development Studies*, 30(3), 831–858.

IMF (2006). *World Economic Outlook 2006. Financial systems and economic cycles.* IMF: Washington DC.

IMF (2012). *World Economic Outlook 2012. Growth resuming, dangers remain.* IMF: Washington DC.

IMF (2015). *World Economic Outlook. Adjusting to lower commodity process.* IMF: Washington DC.

JCSE, JCSE Annual Report 2015/2016. Retrieved from https://www.jcse.org.za [access: 29.03.2017].

JDA (2016). *Johannesburg Development Agency 2016/2017 Business Plan.* Retrieved from https://www.jda.org.za [access: 29.03.2017].

Juma, C. (2010). *Science, Technology and Innovation for Development*, Presentation to the Policy Organs of the Common Market for Eastern and Southern Africa, 21 August to 1 September, The Royal Kingdom of Swaziland.

Juma, C. (2011a). *The New Harvest. Agricultural Innovation in Africa.* New York: Oxford University Press.

Juma, C. (2011b). "Africa's New Engine." *Finance and Development.* New Africa. Retrieved from http://www.belfercenter.org/sites/default/files/legacy/files/juma_finance_and_development_dec-2011.pdf [access: 15.03.2017].

Juma, C. (2014). Complexity, innovation, and development: Schumpeter revisited. *Policy and Complex Systems*, 1(1), 4–21.

Juma, C. (2016). *Innovation and it's Enemies: Why People Resist New Technologies.* New York: Oxford University Press.

Kaplan, S. (2012). City Development States: Why Lagos Works Better than Nigeria. Global Dashboard. Retrieved from http://www.globaldashboard.org/2012/05/10/city-development-states-why-lagos-works-better-than-nigeria/ [access: 22.03.2017].

Kelly, T. (2014). Tech hubs across Africa: Which will be the legacy-makers? | Information and Communications for Development. Retrieved from http://blogs.worldbank.org/ic4d/tech-hubs-across-africa-which-will-be-legacy-makers [access: 14.03.2017].

Kleer, J., M. Perczyński and Z. Dobosiewicz. (1989). *Z doświadczeń rozwoju skokowego*. Warszawa: Państwowe Wydawnictwo Ekonomiczne.

Lakshmanan, T.R. and Chatterjee, L. (2009). New governance institutions in the entrepreneurial urban region. *Innovation — The European Journal of Social Science Research*, 22(3), 371–391.

Lall, S.V., J.V. Henderson and A.J. Venables (2017). *Africa's Cities. Opening Doors to the World*. Washington DC: The World Bank.

Lang, R.E. and D. Dhavale (2005). *Beyond Megalopolis: Exploring America's New "Megapolitan" Geography*, Metropolitan Institute Census Report Series, Census Report 05:01.

Lee, K. (2013). *Schumpeterian Analysis of Economic Catch-up. Knowledge, Path-Creation, and the Middle-Income Trap*. New York: Cambridge University Press.

Lee, K. and Ch. Lim (2001). Technological regimes, catching-up and leapfrogging: Findings from the Korean industries. *Research Policy*, 30, 459–483.

Minami, R. (1986). *The Economic Development of Japan: A Quantitative Study*, 1st Edn. Basingstoke: Macmillan.

Monga, C. and J.Y. Lin (Eds.). (2015a). *The Oxford Handbook of Africa and Economics. Volume I: Context and Concepts*. Oxford: Oxford University Press.

Monga, C. and J.Y. Lin (Eds.). (2015b). *The Oxford Handbook of Africa and Economics. Volume II: Policies and Practices*. Oxford: Oxford University Press.

Moore, J.F. (1996). *The Death of Competition: Leadership and Strategy in the Age of Business Ecosystems*. New York: Harper Business.

Moules, J. (2014). "Apps mean jobs for young nigerians." *Financial Times*. Retrieved from https://www.ft.com/content/77df79a8-c716-11e3-889e-00144feabdc0 [access: 21.03.2017].

Mu, Q. and K. Lee (2005). Knowledge diffusion, market segmentation and technological catch-up: The case of the telecommunication industry in China. *Research Policy*, 34, 759–783.

Mubiwa, B. and H. Annegarn (2013). Occasional Paper 4: Historical spatial change in the Gauteng City-Region. Retrieved from http://www.gcro.ac.za/

sites/default/files/reports/mubiwe_occasional_paper_new.pdf [access: 29.03.2017].

Mulgan, G. (2006). The process of social innovation. *Innovations. Technology, Governance and Globalization*, 1(2), Spring, 145–162.

Nawrot, K.A. (2014a). *Kraje rozwijają ce we współczesnej gospodarce światowej. Przyczynek do ekonomii rozwoju*. Warszawa: Wydawnictwo Naukowe Scholar.

Nawrot, K.A. (2014b). Capabilities of leapfrogging and catching up of a developing country — policy implications from theory and practice. *International Economics Letters*, 3(4), 115–123.

Nawrot, K.A. (2014c). The role of innovation in development — experiences in leapfrogging and catching up through regional clustering: East Asian perspective. *Actual Problems of Economics*, 11(161), 73–82.

OECD (2003). *Oslo Manual, Guidelines for Collecting and Interpreting Innovation Data*, 3rd edn. OECD Publishing.

Ogbu, O. and Adeoti, J. (2010). Science and technology development in Nigeria: Past experiences and the imperative of an innovation driven economy. In S. Akande and A. Kumuyi (Eds.). *Nigeria at 50: Accomplishments, Challenges and Prospects*. Nigerian Institute of Social and Economic Research, Ibadan, Nigeria.

Ohmae, K. (1995). *The End of a Nation State — The Rise of Regional Economies*. New York: McKinsey & Company.

Palmary, I., B. Hamber and L. Nunez (2015). *Healing and Change in the City of Gold*. Retrieved from http://link.springer.com/10.1007/978-3-319-08768-9 [access: 28.03.2017].

Parilla, J. and J. Trujillo (2015). *South Africa's Global Gateway: Profiling the Gauteng City Region's International Competativeness and Connetions*. Retrieved from https://www.brookings.edu/research/south-africas-global-gateway-profiling-the-gauteng-city-regions-international-competitiveness-and-connections/ [access: 28.03.2017].

Pieterse, E. (2016). "Parks Tau's second act is reward for a job well done in Joburg," *Daily Maverick*. Retrieved from https://www.dailymaverick.co.za/article/2016-10-24-parks-taus-second-act-is-reward-for-a-job-well-done-in-joburg/#.WOIrkRjURo4 [access: 28.03.2017].

Ramstad, E. (2009). Expanding innovation system and policy — and organizational perspective. *Policy Studies*, 30(5), 533–553.

Raphasha, P.I. (2015). Integrating National and Regional Innovation Policy : The Case of Gauteng in South Africa. University of the Witwatersrand.

Rhodes, M. (2017). *Personal communication*, Abuja, Lagos, Nigeria.

Rice, X. (2012). "Africa: Lessons from Lagos," *Financial Times*. Retrieved from https://www.ft.com/content/8b24d40a-c064-11e1-982d-00144feabdc0 [access: 22.03.2017].

Rodríguez-Pose, A. (2008). The rise of the "City-Region" concept and its development policy implications. *European Planning Studies*, 16(8), 1025–1046.

Rynarzewski, T., K.A. Nawrot, K. Zajączkowski and E. Cieślik (2017). *Potencjał gospodarczy i możliwości rozwojowe Afryki. Polska perspektywa*. Warszawa: Polskie Wydawnictwo Ekonomiczne.

Schumpeter, J. (1934). *The Theory of Economic Development*. Cambridge: Harvard University Press.

Silverman, M. and T. Zack (2007). *Land Management and Democratic Governance Issues in Hillbrow/Berea, an Inner City Area of Johannesburg*, Commissioned by Planact and CUBES, Ford Foundation Project.

Suehiro, A. (2008). *Catch-up Industralization. The Trajectory and Prospects of East Asian Economies*. Singapore: NUS Press.

Teece, D.J. (2007). Explicating dynamic capabilities: The nature and microfoundations of (Sustainable) enterprise performance. *Strategic Management Journal*, 28, 1319–1350.

Udonkang, N. (2014). Co-Creation Hub (CCHub) — Transforming Ideas to Products or Solutions. Retrieved from https://course.novoed.com/venture1-2014-2/reports/256479 [access: 22.03.2017].

UN-HABITAT (2012). *State of the world's cities 2012/2013: Prosperity of cities*, New York.

UNDESA (2012). *World Population Prospects: The 2012 Revision*, New York.

UNDESA (2014). *World Population Prospects: The 2014 Revision*, New York.

UNDESA (2015). *World Population Prospects: The 2015 Revision*, New York.

Van Onselen, Ch. (1982). *New Babylon New Nineveh. Everyday Life on the Witwatersrand, 1886–1914*. Johannesburg: Jonathan Ball Publishers.

Wang, J.-H. (2007). From technological catch-up to innovation-based economic growth: South Korea and Taiwan compared. *Journal of Development Studies*, 43(6), 1084–1104.

WDI (2016). *World Development Indicators*. World Bank Database.

Wernick, D. (2016). Innovation in Africa: A view from the peaks and hilltops of a spiky continent. In J. Haar and R. Ernst (Eds.). *Innovation in Emerging Markets*. New York: Palgrave Macmillan.

Wu, W. (2007). State policies, enterprise dynamism, and innovation system in Shanghai, China. *Growth and Change*, 38(4), 544–566.

12

A SMART FUTURE FOR ENERGY IN MEGACITIES

Jessen Page

While international negotiations continue to make incremental progress, C40 Cities are forging ahead. Collectively they have taken more than 5,000 actions to tackle climate change, and the will to do more is stronger than ever. As innovators and practitioners, our cities are at the forefront of this issue — arguably the greatest challenge of our time.

Michael Bloomberg, C40 President,
Mayor of New York City from 2002 to 2013

12.1. Energy and the City

Megacities, and cities in general, are hubs of dense social interaction and economic activity. As such they consume, compared to national averages, a disproportionately large amount of resources and produce an equally large amount of national income. From a purely material point of view, cities are essentially an aggregation of buildings and infrastructure: buildings to shelter inhabitants and their economic and social activities, infrastructure to provide the services (e.g. mobility, water, waste management, lighting, and power) required to fulfil those activities with a minimum level of efficiency and comfort. Independently of the climate zones they live in, urban inhabitants will expect the buildings which they spend time in to offer comfortable indoor climatic conditions, thereby requiring heating, cooling, ventilation/air-conditioning, and lighting. In most cities, these services represent a large part of final energy consumption.[1] The provision of potable water, management of waste (and wastewater), availability of public lighting, access to public transport as well as to roads and railways for private and logistical transport are all services provided in cities whose infrastructure requires massive amounts of energy for its construction and operation. The provision of "power"[2] is not only a core service in its own right but a prerequisite for the operation of all the above services. Power is mostly distributed in the form of electrical energy with electrical grids underlying its distribution. In other words, without energy cities do not function: buildings are no longer comfortable (or even inhabitable), economic activity comes to a standstill, and social activity becomes extremely limited.

This has not always been the case. Indeed cities, and even megacities such as ancient Rome, 10th century Baghdad, or 19th century London, have been around for centuries, but only recently have their inhabitants enjoyed the comfort and empowerment provided by ubiquitous energy supply. Queen Victoria, possibly the richest and most powerful person of the 19th century, only enjoyed the comfort provided by electricity and central heating in the latter years of her life,[3] all services available today to a majority of the world's population. While an essential asset to our daily lives, energy is taken for granted in most megacities, and sometimes even *literally* by the inhabitants of informal urban settlements, commonly known as slums, where illegal connections to the electricity grid can account for up to half the city's electricity consumption (T&D World Magazine, 2015).

---

[1] The distribution of final energy consumption, at national level, in developed countries can be broadly approximated by 1/3 for transport, 1/3 for industrial activity and 1/3 for energy consumption in buildings.

[2] Power is meant here as the energy available for the operation of mechanical or electrical devices.

[3] Electricity was first installed in Buckingham Palace in 1883 but only in 1902 did it enjoy modern heating, ventilation and electric lighting.

Megacities can arguably be divided into those belonging to developed countries and those belonging to developing countries.[4] In the former case, we are dealing with cities with existing, but often ageing, energy production and distribution infrastructure, a mainly service-based economy (these cities underwent de-industrialization during the 20th century) and a gently increasing population causing a gently rising energy demand.[5] In the latter case, we are dealing with cities that are attracting large swathes of population migrating from mostly rural environments to an unacquainted urban environment and the promise of work opportunities. Their settling in the city is unprepared and often unwanted by the city authorities who do not wish to legitimize these settlements by providing them with decent services (e.g. provision of water, electricity and mobility, management of waste) and the infrastructure that supports them. While economic arguments are frequently used against the provision of these services, that is, the cost of building infrastructure overweighs the guaranteed payment of services by poor consumers, it has been shown that this reasoning is ill founded (Parikh and Parikh, 2008). Slum-dwellers usually already pay a substantial amount of money for surrogate solutions to the lack of infrastructure in order to ensure a minimum of well-being. Not only would the provision of decent services improve the living conditions (e.g. health, level of education) of a substantial fraction of a city's inhabitants and avoid the social disparities and ensuing tensions between the more fortunate and less fortunate inhabitants of a same city, it would also promote economic development within these settlements and potentially the city as a whole.

12.2. In a Nutshell

Modern cities depend on energy to provide the services required by their economic activity and the quality of living aspired by their inhabitants; the greater the size and complexity of the city, the greater the dependence.

[4]The distinction between cities from developed and developing countries is admittedly overly simplistic yet it highlights two challenges faced by cities, namely sustaining or increasing the quality of life of its inhabitants.

[5]The increasing energy efficiency of appliances is often compensated by the increase in appliance ownership and in total population.

Cities of the developed world are mainly concerned by guaranteeing current living standards with its population while reducing the environmental impact[6] associated with the underlying energy consumption. In the developing world, the main concern is managing, politically as well as technically, a massive exodus towards already huge cities while *increasing* the living standards of its inhabitants. We will argue that the attainment of these objectives relies on economical as well as political prerequisites (discussed respectively in the sections "Urban energy economics 101" and "Political will and power") and on adopting "the Smart City" approach, an integrated approach to urban planning, infrastructure design, and operation supported by Information and Communication Technology (ICT), in particular Internet of Things (IoT)[7] solutions. In "Contrasting perspectives on Smart Cities," we will see that a variety of countries and cities around the world (e.g. in Europe, India, and South Korea) have embraced the concept of the Smart City and adapted it to their own needs and context. Yet, before talking about "smartness," it is important to first understand the current status of energy sources, networks and markets and how these are about to change.

12.3. Sources of Energy

In 2014, the world primary energy consumption (i.e. the raw energy resource converted into a final energy consumed by consumer) was dominated by more than 80% of fossil fuels (coal, oil, and gas), 13% renewable energy, and 5% of nuclear energy (IEA, 2016). Attitudes towards this energy mix vary greatly from one region of the globe to another. For example, in the United States, security of supply for the needs of the nation's economy and military essentially trump environmental concern. Major fossil fuel exporters primarily consume fossil fuels but are trying to diversify both energy resources (e.g. Saudi Arabia with solar

[6] Be it climate change due to greenhouse gas emissions, local pollution of the air and water due to particulates, sulphur oxides or nitrous oxides, or radioactive pollution due to nuclear waste.

[7] The term IoT covers the inter-networking of devices (referred to as "smart" devices) embedded with electronics, software, sensors, actuators, and network connectivity that enable these objects to collect and exchange data.

energy and Iran with nuclear energy) and sources of national income. South American countries (especially those with limited fossil fuel reserves) see renewables (e.g. hydropower, solar, and wind power) as potential cost-effective means of being independent of foreign imports. Rapidly growing economies such as China and India, while installing massive amounts of both renewable and nuclear energy production capacity, are still struggling to reduce their dependence on imported fossil fuels. Finally in Europe, while most national policies agree on the necessity of increasing renewable energy production[8] the effective implementation of that policy varies greatly from country to country. In addition, their stance on nuclear energy is far from univocal, as some countries have banned nuclear energy (e.g. Austria and Italy), others currently plan a phase-out of nuclear energy (e.g. Germany and Switzerland), while others see it as a core instrument towards a climate-change free energy mix (e.g. Sweden and France).

The obvious issues regarding fossil fuel are the environmental impact of its combustion (for the production of electricity, for transportation, and for heating purposes) due to the release of greenhouse gases and possibly other pollutants and the geopolitical impacts of depending on foreign imports of such an essential motor of economic and social activity available in relatively limited quantities. Issues related to nuclear energy are actually quite similar. While the combustion of nuclear fuel (e.g. uranium) does not produce greenhouse gases, the waste product that ensues needs to be treated and stored securely, thereby resulting in possible damage to the environment. In addition nuclear fission reactors require a nuclear fuel (e.g. uranium ore) that needs to be mined, transported, and processed into a final combustible material. The raw material is found in limited amounts in a limited number of countries and its exploitation is already the source of geopolitical issues.

Renewable energy comes in various forms such as biomass (provided the source of the biomass is replanted), hydropower, wind power, geothermal, and solar energy. While not entirely exempt of environmental and geopolitical

[8]The 20–20–20 objective of the European Union has a target of installing 20% renewable energy production, reducing greenhouse gas emissions by 20% and improving energy efficiency by 20% by 2020.

impacts,[9] these technologies are considered to be less damaging to our environment and climate. Because they rely on the exploitation of natural resources (wind, water, sun, and biomass), their production is linked to the variations of Nature itself: while hydropower will have seasonal variations depending on rainfall, solar and wind energy production can vary from one minute to the next due to rapid changes in weather conditions. This volatility in production can heavily impact the operation of electricity networks and the cost of electricity. Counteracting the volatility of a large production of renewable energy, as planned in some national policies, requires the use of large capacities of energy storage such as pump-and-storage in dams, electro-chemical batteries, or the conversion of electricity to other forms of energy easier to store such as natural gas (so-called "power-to-gas"). Another option is to manage energy demand to synchronize it with energy supply (so-called "demand-side management"), thereby reducing the need for expensive storage capacities. "Smart grids" use ICT to optimize the production, distribution, and consumption of energy (so far this concept is restricted to electricity grids) in regions where the stochastic production of renewable energy has an impact on the distribution network and energy market.

Finally, what distinguishes renewable energy production is the broad range of its possible scale: for example, solar energy production can range from a single PV panel (<1 kWp[10]) on a building rooftop to a "solar farm" producing over 700 MWp, that is, 700,000 times more. As its roofs become covered in solar PV panels, the city moves from being an end consumer to a hybrid system of consumption and production. This has a technical and a socio-economical impact on the nature of the urban energy system. First of all, it is disturbing the current hierarchy of the energy (especially electrical) network; a grid that once trickled energy from the top (production) down to the bottom (consumption) now has to deal with absorbing production at its lowest levels. While this is physically possible, it remains a great challenge in terms of real-time operation of the network,

---

[9] Dams will typically impact local fauna. Solar photovoltaic (PV) panels and wind turbines require rare earths that are mined in a handful of countries.

[10] A kilowatt-peak (kWp) is the maximal power, expressed in kilowatts (kW), which can be provided by a production facility. A facility providing a constant power of X kW for one hour will produce energy of X kilowatt-hours (kWh).

a challenge to be met by smart grids. Secondly, the production of energy has become democratized with individual citizens becoming "prosumers," both producers and consumers, expecting the energy network to absorb their production and still meet their needs in consumption.

To close this tour of energy production technologies, one should mention possible breakthroughs in the near future. Those used today (nuclear fission, combustion processes, thermal machines, electrical machines, solar PV, wind, and hydro turbines) all rely on technologies developed between the late-18th and mid-20th centuries. The near past has indeed seen crucial innovations in production and operation processes that have made certain technologies economically competitive (e.g. exploration, automation, materials sciences, and process optimization), yet no essentially new production technologies have appeared in the market. Nor are any future breakthroughs expected to radically modify the current energy landscape and trends over the next couple of decades. In addition, one should keep in mind that the transfer of technology from research to market typically takes over a decade, and the assessment of their environmental impact often even longer.

12.4. Urban Energy Economics 101

Energy is sold in various forms, called "energy vectors"; the physical nature of each vector determines the networks required to distribute the energy and markets selling it. Fuels for mobility are typically transported in liquid form by trucks and sold in petrol stations operated by a petrol company. Gas has its own networks (pipelines) for its distribution stretching across national borders from the points of extraction to the points of consumption. Mid- and low-pressure network branches providing the final consumer in a city are typically managed by a local utility, while the high-pressure network of pipelines across countries and country borders is managed by large companies. Thermal networks, and district heating and cooling networks and distribute heat and/or cold by using a medium such as steam, water, or a refrigerant within a network of pipes. The points of production and consumption usually lie within a city's boundaries[11] (or

[11] Denmark's countrywide network of inter-connected district heating networks is a unique exception and a key component of the country's successful energy strategy.

even a district of the city), with each network managed by a single company. National electricity grids are often interconnected forming complex international high voltage networks (this is especially the case in Europe). Given the nature of electricity, supply and demand need to be equal at all times; any difference between the two results in variations of voltage, of which only very slight amplitudes can be tolerated by the network. Maintaining this balance is done by transmission system operators (TSOs) for the national high voltage grid and by distribution system operators (DSOs) for the mid- and low-voltage networks that supply cities by connecting them to the national grid.

The need to perfectly balance supply and demand at all times distinguishes electricity from all other energy vectors and requires it to have "imbalance markets" to patch discrepancies between forecasted demand and last minute deviations from those forecasts. The rapid increase in stochastic renewable (mainly wind and solar) electricity production and the fact that it has priority over all other means of production when injected into the grid[12] has shaken the foundations of electricity markets, especially in Europe. In addition the fact that other energy vectors such as petrol for mobility and oil for heating are increasingly being replaced by electricity (e.g. electric vehicles and heat pumps) add extra strain on an infrastructure that while currently robust will venture ever closer to the limits of its capacity if not updated. This will require expensive investment in reinforcing the network itself. An alternative at a significantly lower cost is the use of smart grid hardware and software solutions to synchronize production with consumption. Future electricity grids will most probably adopt a combination of grid refurbishment and the use of smart grid technology.

Recent deregulation of the electricity market in some parts of the world (e.g. Europe) has forced a separation between those companies that manage the networks, TSOs and DSOs, and those that use the network to buy and sell electricity, the power utilities. In deregulated markets, both system operators and power utilities are private companies, though many are still fully owned by municipal, state or national authorities. In countries where deregulation has not taken place electric power generation,

[12]This is a matter of national legislation.

transmission, and distribution is usually provided by a state controlled organization. Deregulation has also affected natural gas markets and often pushed single vector energy utilities together to form multi-energy utilities[13] capable of improving the overall efficiency of their multi-energy system by using the diversity of vectors they control (electricity, natural gas, heat, and cold).

In addition to these traditional market players, electricity markets are witnessing the arrival of new players from the field of ICT with companies such as Google (with its subsidiaries GoogleEnergy, an energy utility, and Nest Labs, a home automation company), IBM, or Cisco (selling IoT solutions for smart grid management, and efficient energy consumption), or telecommunications providers such as Swisscom (Swisscom Energy Solutions proposes smart grid storage solutions). It is also worth noting the role that current consumers (either private individuals or non-energy companies) can play in the future as prosumers either by distancing themselves from the urban energy system in the search for maximal autonomy or by acting as local market players selling decentralized production, storage, and flexibility services to a citywide energy utility.

A final mention should be made of the goods sold by energy markets. Energy is currently sold as commodity with kWh as its unit and a specific market for each energy vector. An energy consumer connected to a specific network will pay a one-off fee for its connection to a network as well as a regular fee (energy bill) for the total units of goods consumed over a period of time. New business models are being proposed to sell *energy services* to their clients, such as thermal comfort, indoor lighting or private mobility,[14] rather than kWh. Clients would no longer acquire a gas boiler, a heat pump, solar PV panels or electrical storage but rather allow the energy utility to install their own energy conversion and storage technologies best adapted to the urban energy infrastructure they manage. Clients would pay a fee for the services provided much like current mobile phone contracts. The ingenuity of these business models is to displace the

[13]Or even multi-utility companies offering multimedia services in addition to energy services.

[14]Tesla Motors already proposes this by including the electricity consumption of their cars over the lifespan of the vehicle within the price of their cars.

motivation for energy efficiency from the consumer to the energy utility and thereby motivate energy suppliers in getting more output per kWh of primary energy consumed rather than selling as many final energy kWh as possible. It also reduces the massive redundancy in production technologies allowing for more effective and streamlined design and operation. This type of business model is a core economic factor for a successful implementation of the Smart City concept. Even more important are the political will and power required to embrace the concept and set it in motion.

12.5. Political Will and Power

While international agreements on climate change[15] and national energy strategies define a framework for the transition of energy systems at a national level it is cities that are taking the most active and interesting role in planning and implementing the change of their energy system. Totalling approximately 60% of the world's energy consumption and 70% of its greenhouse gas emissions (UN-Habitat, 2011) concentrated on a limited territory they possess a political and administrative structure well adapted, in theory at least, to implement such a change. The most prominent examples of the initiatives taken by cities over the past decade are the C40 Cities Group (C40.org, 2017) and Covenant of Mayors (CovenantofMayors.eu, 2017). The C40 Cities Climate Leadership Group is a "network of the world's megacities committed to addressing climate change." It connects over 80 of the world's major cities, representing about 600 million inhabitants and a quarter of the global economy, helping them exchange experience and know-how in order to mitigate and adapt for climate change. The Covenant of Mayors for Climate & Energy comprises over 7,000 signatory towns and cities in Europe[16] (corresponding to about 250 million inhabitants) who commit themselves to meet the

[15] Such as the Kyoto Protocol, the Paris agreement of the 21st Conference of Parties or the 20–20–20 targets of the European Union's 2020 Climate & Energy Package.

[16] As of the January 1, 2017 the EU Covenant of Mayors and the Compact of Mayors merged to form the Global Covenant of Mayors for Climate and Energy the largest global coalition of cities committed to climate leadership, including 7,100 cities from 119 countries and six continents, representing more than 600 million inhabitants.

European Union's 20–20–20 targets (signatories of a new covenant pledge to reduce CO_2 emissions by at least 40% by 2030). Their first step after signing the covenant is to produce, within a year of their membership to the initiative, a Sustainable Energy Action Plan (SEAP) approved by the municipal council. The SEAP serves as a roadmap for the activities to be implemented by the city in order to meet its objectives as well as a framework defining the responsibilities and procedures set up by the municipality to ensure its implementation.

While cities show a strong desire to make a difference their actual success will depend on the actual power, both political and economical, they have to implement their plans. The political power of cities essentially depends on their autonomy in terms of defining and implementing legislation. With this in mind those most apt at implementing energy plans will be city-nations such as Singapore, followed by city-states such as Vienna in Austria, Hamburg and Berlin in Germany, the "municipalities" of Beijing and Shanghai in China or the union territory of NCT Delhi in India.

While not a megacity by size, the Swiss city-canton of Geneva provides a telling example of a city-state making use of its political and economical power to fulfil its energy-related objectives. It has its own law on energy[17] that, for example, makes mandatory the measurement of a building's annual heat consumption, based on which the cantonal energy service (www.ge.ch/energie, 2017) can force its owners to invest in the energy refurbishment of their building. It also uses this information in combination with energy infrastructure data for the purpose of spatial energy planning ("planification énergétique territorial"), that is, "the integration of energy aspects into all of the city's spatial planning projects in order to reduce energy consumption and increase the use of local renewable energy sources." This translates into the obligation of each municipal development plan ("plan directeur communal"), and at a lower level each neighbourhood plan ("plan localisé de quartier"), to include a spatial energy concept ("concept énergétique territorial") enabling a progressive reduction of fossil energy consumption and the development of strategies

---

[17] Swiss cantons are asked to implement the national strategy but have the final say on how to translate it into cantonal laws.

for the refurbishment of the most polluting heating systems. The city government can impose the construction of a district heating network and oblige buildings under construction or refurbishment to be equipped for a future connection to the network. In addition to restrictive measures, the canton manages a generous budget of subsidies for the installation of renewable energy production and energy efficiency measures in buildings.

Finally, the greatest asset of the canton of Geneva is its ownership of its energy utility (Services Industriels de Genève), allowing them to work hand-in-hand for a successful implementation of the city's spatial energy plans. It cannot be stressed enough that cities that control their utilities, for energy but also mobility, waste and water, or that have enough leverage to control private companies building and operating these infrastructures have a real chance at impacting the city as a whole; others will be mainly limited to assets under their own influence, typically the stock of municipal buildings.

12.6. The Smart City

There are almost as many definitions of the term "Smart City" as there are proponents advancing a Smart City agenda or selling Smart City products.[18]

In an age of smart phones and smart homes, it is easy to grasp a sense of what a smart city could mean: The unfathomable possibilities provided by IoT solutions that could enable cities to be more sustainable by improving (or sustaining) their citizens' quality of life and promoting economic activity while reducing their environmental impact. It is true that the Internet has produced changes in our everyday lives that were neither planned nor foreseeable, yet the belief that simply adding ubiquitous technology will automatically make our cities better is simplistic. ICT and IoT technologies are very powerful tools for the support of collaborative processes, decision-making and the automation of system operation but not solutions as such.

[18]The first mentions of the term "Smart City" can be associated to IBM's "Smarter Cities" services, to the pioneering article of Rudolf Giffinger (Giffinger and Pichler-Milanovic, 2007) and to the European Innovation Partnership on Smart Cities and Communities.

At the foundation of the Smart City concept lies the necessity of conceiving the city as a whole and creating bridges between disciplines, within city administrations and between city administrations and urban utilities in order to *plan*, *design* and *operate a city* and its infrastructure in the most effective possible way that can meet the city's objectives. In the field of energy this translates into (1) integrated urban energy planning, (2) integrated energy infrastructure design, and (3) integrated energy system operation (Jakutyte-Walangitang *et al.*, 2015). While each of these activities rely on ICT and IoT they do so in different ways that we will now describe.

12.7. Integrated Urban Energy Planning

Energy demand and energy production in a city (e.g. the availability of renewable energy) are closely linked with many other of its aspects, such as mobility, waste and water management, building regulations, refurbishment subsidies or the provision of public services (e.g. schools, sports centres), each falling within the authority of a specific department of a city's administration. Urban planning typically encompasses many of these aspects but even when urban planning is done in an integrated manner its department lacks the overarching authority required for producing plans that apply to all departments of the administration. In addition there is rarely a concerted collaboration between the city administration and its utilities when such plans are made, even more so in cities where utilities are no longer in public hands. In other words the integrated urban planning expected from a Smart City requires a horizontal administrative structure that reports to the highest city authority (e.g. mayor) while collaborating with all departments and all utilities concerned. Vienna offers an example of a city that has come close to this objective by setting up an internal steering group including the heads of the city's chief executive offices ("Magistratsdirektionen") reporting to the mayor to produce, in 2014, the Smart City Wien Framework Strategy (Smartcity.wien.gv.at, 2017). It also created an energy-planning department ("Magistratsabteilung fuer Energieplanung — MA20") affiliated to its urban planning department and collaborating with the city's utility company (Wiener Stadtwerke).

While the successful implementation of integrated urban energy planning relies above all on effective public administration management and collaboration between public administration and private utilities, ICT can play a decisive role too. A successful framework requires a strategy with objectives quantified into key performance indicators (KPIs) that can be monitored over time, and an action plan of measures with predicted quantifiable impacts on those KPIs. Estimating the impact of measures relative to KPIs requires more or less sophisticated calculation methods applied to large sets of data, typically in the hands of a variety of stakeholders, different departments of the city administration but also national agencies and private utilities. Merging data from these various databases and using these data for analysis and calculations requires various ICT tools and techniques (e.g. CityGML database models, Big Data analysis techniques, and energy systems simulation). Data acquisition itself for example, from smart meters, utility Supervisory Control And Data Acquisition (SCADA) systems, even mobile phones, is growing exponentially with the arrival of IoT technologies providing ever more data to process and an ever greater need for tools and methods to process them.

12.8. Integrated Energy Infrastructure Design

Energy utilities offering energy services by exploiting the multi-energy infrastructure of a city would arguably be the most efficient way to meet the energy efficiency, renewable energy production and greenhouse gas emission reduction targets cities have given themselves. Indeed the utility would be able to design an integrated system with the objective of making best use of the different energy vectors, different levels of scale, different levels of centralized vs. decentralized production and storage, to deliver on the above targets while optimising overall costs (capital investment, operational, and risk-associated costs) and ensuring system resilience. ICT can support this by basing the design of the whole system, that is, the choice of production, distribution and storage technologies and size of their components, on computer-aided decision-making tools (such as energy system modelling, optimization algorithms, quantitative risk assessment). Collecting large amounts of historical data thanks to IoT technologies can help to refine the models used for simulating these complex energy systems and therefore the decision support provided in optimal system design and future operation.

12.9. Integrated Energy System Operation

Once integrated urban energy planning processes are in place within the city administration, once the infrastructures relative to the different energy vectors distributed within the city are connected to ensure maximal efficiency and resilience, then ICT and IoT technologies can deliver their most powerful impact, namely in the operation of the urban energy system. By seamlessly connecting building, mobility, and industrial automation systems to energy distribution networks, energy storage, and production units, themselves linked to weather and even human behaviour forecasting algorithms, future *smart energy grids*[19] will optimally operate the urban energy system while sparing the investment costs of having a redundancy of infrastructure (e.g. power lines, production capacity, and storage capacity). Strangely enough it is this aspect of the Smart City, the most expensive in terms of financial and energy costs (ICT and IoT technologies consume energy too!), that is the most liable to materialize in the future. Yet without the fundamental steps of integrated planning and the integrated design of the urban energy system an invasion of ubiquitous technology will provide little positive impact on how effectively we manage our cities in meeting the global challenges they have given themselves, in particular in the field of energy.

12.10. Contrasting Perspectives on Smart Cities

Be it a concept embodying integration in the planning, design, and operation stages or simply the embedding of ICT and IoT technologies into urban infrastructure, the idea of Smart City is being used around the world with different objectives in mind. In the developed world there is a growing consensus that cities need to play a central role in meeting sustainable development objectives, in particular those related to climate change. It is this moral obligation, often supported by the need to increase their attractiveness in an increasingly global competition over tourists, international companies, and a young educated workforce, that motivates their transition towards becoming a Smart City.

---

[19]The term "smart energy grid" is used here to extend the "smart grid" concept beyond electricity networks to multi-energy (gas, heat/cold, electricity) networks.

Cities in the developing world face a variety of other incentives for becoming a Smart City that often depend more on national policy than municipal authority strategy. What they often have in common is, given their fast rate of growth, the opportunity to leapfrog from little or no energy infrastructure to smart grid infrastructure avoiding problematic decisions and the costs related to system refurbishment. The investment in new technology attracts international companies and investors eager to test concepts and products that, if conclusive, they will later advertise and seek to roll out globally. This is especially apparent in India's Smart Cities Mission (Smartcities.gov.in, 2017), where each Smart City is often sponsored by a partner country, bringing with it foreign investment and companies (Make in India, 2016). A notable aspect of India's mission is its objective to create new centres of economic development along industrial corridors between India's existing megacities.[20] This offers the advantages of providing a clean canvas for the implementation of innovative Smart City concepts and state-of-art infrastructure and relieving the strain on megacities by redirecting migration flows towards these new developments. By providing high-end infrastructure, including the reliable energy and communication networks needed by high-tech and service-based companies (e.g. banks), it hopes to attract foreign companies and investment and the qualified Indian labour these would employ locally.

The case for building new Smart Cities completely from scratch (on so-called "greenfield developments") or almost from scratch (on "brownfield developments") is an attractive concept as it avoids the need for retrofitting and provides planners and designers with a blank sheet for conceiving and building the smart city of their dreams. Masdar City in the Emirate of Abu Dhabi and New Songdo City in South Korea are examples of modern Smart City (greenfield) developments relying on high-tech ICT-heavy infrastructure. In many cities around the (developed and developing) world, receding industrial activities, decommissioned airports, and railway stations, leave huge urban areas available for building new city districts, thereby testing Smart City concepts and technologies. This is the

[20]The Smart City Mission also includes retrofitting and redevelopment amongst its core strategic components and the 60 cities selected so far also include megacities such as Mumbai and New Delhi.

case of the Aspern Seestadt district in Vienna, the Smart City Wilhelmsburg district in Hamburg and some of the projects of the United Kingdom's Eco-town program.

12.11. Megacities — Future Smart Cities?

As they enter the 21st century megacities face tremendous challenges: managing immigration, urban sprawl, and informal development (slums); sustaining economic development; offering decent standards of living to their citizens by providing them with accommodation, access to education, healthy living conditions and protection from crime. Energy underpins every single one of these challenges and as the world wakes up to the impact its energy consumption has on the environment, managing wisely the energy used to meet them becomes essential. The Smart City concept, as presented here, offers cities with a solution that, far from relying blindly on technology, proposes an integrative approach to the planning, design and operation of the urban energy system.

Integrated planning requires the departments of a city administration to work together and in collaboration with the city's energy utility (or utilities) in producing a Smart City Framework that defines long-term objectives and the roadmap to be followed to meet these objectives. This undertaking, impacting many of the city's planning and strategy documents, needs to be managed by a committee, reporting directly to the city's highest authority, with the responsibility of implementing the roadmap and monitoring its progress.

Integrated energy system design considers the urban energy system as a whole, covering all of its energy vectors from production to consumption, via storage and distribution. Its objective is to provide a system design and operation strategy capable of meeting the city's targets (e.g. for energy efficiency, renewable energy production and greenhouse gas emissions' reduction) while minimizing costs and ensuring system resilience. It will do so by exploiting the possible combinations of different energy vectors, of levels of scale and of centralized vs. decentralized energy production and storage.

The final level of integration, integrated energy system operation, corresponds most to the common understanding of a Smart City — a city relying on IoT solutions for its operation — where interconnected "smart" devices exchange and process information for an optimal automated operation of the complex multi-energy infrastructure.

A successful transition towards becoming a Smart City will depend on the city's power over its legislation and budget, the ability of its administration to introduce and manage an overarching program over a long period of time, its authority over the energy utilities operating on its territory and their adoption of a service-based business model. Given their size, the complexity of their administration and the complexity of their energy infrastructure and its ownership this will be a great challenge for megacities. Yet, the past decade has clearly seen the emergence of megacities in the global leadership on climate change. The will is there. The process is in motion. The Smart City concept offers an opportunity for cities to make a change.

References

C40.org (2017). *C40 official website*. Retrieved from http://www.c40.org [access: 13.02.2017].

CovenantofMayors.eu (2017). *Covenant of mayors official website*. Retrieved from http://www.covenantofmayors.eu/index_en.html [access: 13.02.2017].

Giffinger, R. and N. Pichler-Milanovic (2007). Smart Cities: Ranking of European Medium Sized Cities, *Vienna University of Technology, University of Ljubljana and Delft University of Technology*. Retrieved from http://www.smart-cities.eu [access: 13.02.2017].

IEA (2016). Key World Energy Statistics 2016. *International Energy Agency*. Retrieved from https://www.iea.org/publications/freepublications/publication/key-world-energy-statistics.html [access: 13.02.2017].

Jakutyte-Walangitang, D., J. Page, O. Pol, R.-R. Schmidt and U. Mollay (2015). Contribution to the knowledge development for smart cities. In W. Leal Filho, A. Ubelis, and D. Berzina (Eds.). *Sustainable Development, Knowledge Society and Smart Future Manufacturing Technologies*, 1st edn. Springer, Switzerland, pp. 149–161.

Make In India (2016). Smart Cities. *Make in India*. Retrieved from http://www.makeinindia.com/article/-/v/internet-of-things [access: 13.02.2017].

Parikh, P. and H. Parikh (2008). Slum networking — a paradigm shift to transcend poverty with water, environmental sanitation and hidden resources. In *Water and Urban Development Paradigms: Towards an Integration of Engineering, Design and Management Approaches*, CRC Press, pp. 357–370.

Smartcities.gov.in (2017). *Official website of Smart Cities Mission of India's Ministry of urban Development.* Retrieved from http://smartcities.gov.in [access: 13.02.2017].

Smartcity.wien.gv.at (2017). *Official website of the Smart City Wien program.* Retrieved from https://smartcity.wien.gv.at/site/en [access: 13.02.2017].

T&D World Magazine (2015). "India to spend $21.6 billion on smart grid infrastructure by 2025," *Transmission & Distribution World Magazine*, Feb. 12, 2015. Retrieved from http://tdworld.com/smart-grid/india-spend-216-billion-smart-grid-infrastructure-2025 [access: 13.02.2017].

UN-Habitat (2011). *Cities and climate change: Global report on human settlements 2011, GRHS 2011*, UN-HABITAT. Retrieved from http://unhabitat.org/books/cities-and-climate-change-global-report-on-human-settlements-2011 [access: 13.02.2017].

www.ge.ch/energie (2017). *Official website of the Office Cantonal de l'Energie (OCEN) — Geneva.* Retrieved from http://ge.ch/energie [access: 13.02.2017].

13

WHAT FUTURE LIES AHEAD FOR MEGACITIES IN EUROPE?

Jerzy Kleer and Katarzyna A. Nawrot

13.1. Introduction

Megacities first occurred in the latter half of the 20th century. They represent a complex phenomenon that emerged under the influence — and confluence — of globalization, the information revolution, consecutive transitions from one stage of civilization to another, and booming population growth. Megacities already fulfil a broad array of functions: political, economic (especially in the context of financial centres), and of course social. Moreover, they continue to take on still more functions, becoming major centres of not only scientific and technological but above all political and cultural thought, irrespective of their status as capital cities of their respective countries. It is difficult to speculate about the future administrative and political status of megacities, but it cannot be ruled out that they will strive to gain a certain degree of independence, or even the capacity to make sovereign decisions of their own, within or indeed outside their countries of origin. As such, megacities are certainly a quintessentially modern-day phenomenon, a force to be reckoned with in the modern world, and at the same time a subject that demands serious intellectual consideration, in-depth academic research, and cautious socio-economic scrutiny.

In this chapter, we will consider the past, present, and future of megacities on the European continent. We begin by considering which megacities already exist in Europe, the commonalities of their histories, and the differences between their more recent trajectories of development. We then proceed by considering the general factors underlying the rise of megacities globally, before turning some more specific attention to the distinctive developmental, demographic, and globalization-related characteristics of the European continent, as they influence its major urban regions. Next, we try to sum up the factors underpinning the rise of a new, knowledge-based civilization, and then examine how Europe's megacities can be expected to fare in the face of booming global population growth — mainly outside Europe — and the emergence of a knowledge-based civilization. In closing, we conclude that the question of what lies ahead for the continent's megacities is on one level an easy question, while on another it is a question fraught with great complexity.

13.2. Does Europe Already Have Megacities?

The common definition, applied in this volume, states that a megacity is an urban area whose population exceeds 10 million inhabitants. By this definition, the European continent does indeed have megacities — as of 2015, there were four: Istanbul (with 14.164 million inhabitants), Moscow (12.166 million), Paris (10.843 million), and London (10.313 million) (UNDESA, 2014). However, aside from some variation in terms of population numbers, these cities also differ quite fundamentally in terms of their political and economic importance, their place in the history of Europe and the world, their dominant cultural systems, as well as their degree of influence over the history of Europe and the world, both in the short term and in the long run. Although space prevents us from comparing and contrasting these four existing European megacities in great detail here, a brief outline of their commonalities and differences will nevertheless be useful in laying the groundwork for answering the question posed in the title of this essay.

What these four cities have in common lies largely in their histories. All were once capitals of major empires, *albeit* very different ones: Istanbul as the capital of the Ottoman Empire; Moscow as the hub first of the Grand Duchy of Moscow, then of the Soviet Union, now of Russia; London as the capital of what was once the world's largest-ever colonial empire; and Paris as the centre of a colonial empire that was not as extensive as the British one, but the city itself was to a large degree the capital of enlightened thinking and the spiritual capital of Europe.

All those empires ultimately crumbled, each in its own way, and as such far-reaching differences emerged between the political and economic significance of their erstwhile capitals as well as between each of these cities' role in and influence over global politics in Europe and in the world. Each of the capitals has pursued different political concepts and interests, in terms of both the challenges facing the present-day world and the capacity for collaboration within the European framework. Moscow is striving to regain its former influence as a superpower from the Cold War era, whereas Istanbul wants to occupy a significant place on the periphery of Europe and become an important factor in the Middle East. London's policy is now not fully clear in the wake of the Brexit vote, as is Paris' after French elections. All four cities also differ considerably in terms of their dominant cultural systems, as is especially visible from the perspective of their respective dominant religions: Islam in Turkey, Orthodoxy in Russia, Protestantism in the UK, and Catholicism in France. Substantial differences are also to be found in how the relationship between society and state plays out in each of them.

This outline of differences has not, of course, exhausted even the most fundamental problems that pertain to Europe's megacities. We will revisit certain of these issues below.

13.3. Origins of Megacities and Reasons Behind Their Development

Let us now take a step back and look more generally at the past factors that have underlain the emergence of today's megacities, wherever they are located on the globe. For this, we need to take as our point of departure the modern-day transitions from one stage of civilization to another, or "civilizational turning points." Such a perspective is crucial because it makes it clear that we are in fact dealing on the one hand with a transition from the industrial stage of civilization to the knowledge-based civilization, especially in the developed countries from the Euro-Atlantic region, and on the other one with a very fast and therefore distinctive, yet also heterogeneous, degradation of the agrarian stage of civilization, especially in Asia, Africa, and South America.

Such degradation is largely attributable to globalization and the dissemination of the market economy on a global scale, as well as the emergence of over a hundred new countries in the aftermath of de-colonization and the fall of socialism. Once those newly established countries started to open up to external capital (a process that lay firmly in the interests of multinational corporations and financial markets, which have dominated the modern system of economics), they witnessed the accelerated development of capitalism and the market economy.

The process has been accompanied by booming population growth, especially in the economically underdeveloped countries, notably in Africa and Asia, as more and more people move to newly formed and rapidly developing cities. An important factor facilitating this process is the very rapid pace of emerging infrastructural links as a consequence of the market economy and the information revolution. The latter has contributed to the growing significance of the service sector as a fundamental manifestation of different forms of business activity and employment: There is every indication that services will be the main form of economic activity in the emerging knowledge-based civilization. Huge masses of people unleashed by the degradation of the agrarian civilization have looked to cities as their hope and chance to find employment, potential social assistance from the state, the city, and various social organizations.

A gigantic global influx of people to both existing and newly established cities has resulted in an accelerated disruption of the public sphere and numerous negative externalities such as corruption, organized crime groups, xenophobia, human trafficking, and the escalation of terrorism. Another phenomenon that is equally important is the fast growth of slums (Nawrot, 2014: 108). The various negative phenomena related to megacities, especially in less developed countries, are a profound issue not only for the present but also for the near and distant future. So far, neither theory nor practice have found a way to mitigate the existing and emerging conflicts and threats in these constantly growing urban agglomerations.

13.4. Distinctive Characteristics of European Development

In order to properly understand the particular characteristics of modern capitalism, we need to look back to its origins in Europe. Although the market economy has a long history, the system in its capitalist form originated in Europe, and its emergence was particularly closely tied, though not exclusively so, to the United Kingdom. The industrial revolution provided a major and fundamentally important stimulus spurring the development of the market economy, which not only altered the forms of production in a gradual way but also affected the organization of markets, the interrelations between market players, and brought fundamental changes in the structure of employment, in market demand, and equally importantly, in the forms of human relations.

Without analyzing more broadly the interrelations between such economic changes and the changes in the role of politics, it is important to stress here that a market economy may develop not only when the citizens of a specific country enjoy full freedom, but also within the framework of various kinds of subjugation. Although the French Revolution and the Napoleonic Wars altered the structure of power in Europe to a serious degree, those processes spread gradually and continued until the 20th century and the end of World War I. For that reason, we can conclude that the emerging economic and political institutions of capitalism became widespread. One exception in this regard was Russia, which experienced a socialist revolution that gradually introduced non-market economics as a basis for economic activity.

What is decisive for our considerations here, however, is the gradual and variegated development of cities and industrial centres in the emerging civilization, initially in connection with areas rich with natural resources and trade centres, chiefly on the coasts. Those centres not only provided a major impulse for business activity but also determined social and political development to a considerable degree.

The evolutionary and slow-paced development of European cities had its roots particularly in the slow and highly diversified development of capitalism in Europe, which was considerably faster in Western Europe than in Eastern Europe. The factors underlying this situation in the east of the continent certainly varied, but the most important ones were linked to the relations within the feudal order, the dominance of the nobility and, by the same token, the slower development of the bourgeoisie, especially the middle class, the more gradual development of education, a lower level of imitation, and above all the more limited capital-related potential of the class associated with the emergence of the industrial civilization. City dwellers were not very affluent in relative terms, which also translated into the more sluggish development of the domestic market. Another important factor behind the slower advancement of the industrial civilization in Eastern Europe was the dominance of powers that were still quite deeply rooted in the old social order, such as the Austro-Hungarian Empire and Russia, not to mention the Ottoman Empire.

Cities in Europe developed slowly yet in a highly non-uniform way, chiefly for economic reasons as well as a result of political and demographic factors. As a case in point, note that in the year 1800, London had 1 million inhabitants, more than Paris, which had a mere 600,000 inhabitants, despite having been more populous than London just several decades earlier. To put this into perspective, Vienna then had 250,000 inhabitants, Berlin 172,000 (Hohenberg and Lees, 1985) and New York 60,515 (US Bureau of the Census, 1998). Population growth in cities was generally very slow, except for in the United Kingdom, where a majority of the population had already been residing in cities and towns since about 1850 (UNDESA, 1980: 7). In other European countries, the share of the urban population was lower, as a result of very slow transformations in rural areas and gradual changes in the forms of interdependencies between their inhabitants. The reasons for this lay in state policies, the conservative attitudes of landowners, as well as a shortage of capital to facilitate the modernization of agricultural production. This was particularly true in Eastern Europe, whereas in Western Europe, in turn, both agriculture and non-agricultural sectors of the economy developed quite intensively. The gap between Western and Eastern Europe kept widening, with consequences that continue to be seen until the present day.

Differences between the west and the east of Europe also widened in other important spheres such as political models, especially in the model of education and the scope of its dissemination in society. Although Eastern Europe contributed significantly to Europe's spiritual (cultural) and enlightened development in the 19th and 20th centuries, the process failed to bring widespread effects in the east, which was hindered by the problem of illiteracy, particularly common among those living in rural areas.

13.5. The Demographics of Europe

Europe practically never experienced booming demographic growth, despite providing a major impulse for the emergence of the industrial stage of civilization and its expansion. Nevertheless, Europe, especially some countries in Western Europe, experienced fundamental changes in the economic as well as political, mental, and social sphere. That was particularly, or even exclusively, due to the urban population, which grew slowly yet surely and engendered a highly diversified society in terms of wealth and culture.

From the beginning of the 19th century onwards, urban growth was driven by the developing industry and related sectors, including public administration, as well as education centres, in particular the relatively fast development of higher education, especially universities. Those factors were fundamentally important not only for urban growth but also for the dissemination of industrial civilization. Gradually and very slowly, its influence became visible also in rural areas, in particular through the supply of goods and industrial tools and products for agriculture and the imitation of certain forms of urban life, above all as a result of the development of transportation and road infrastructure, which brought cities closer to rural areas.

A fundamental stimulus propelling Europe's economic expansion, at least in some countries in Europe, was provided by the increasing colonial expansion of both existing and emerging European powers. It is difficult to overestimate the contribution of those conquered regions or countries to the economic and industrial development of Europe and its civilizational and financial potential. That held true in particular for colonial powers, not only the United Kingdom and France but also the Netherlands, Germany, and Belgium. Here, we should note, however, that Russia's expansion in Asia was based on somewhat different principles, chiefly because the political system in Russia and the class structure within Russian society differed fundamentally from those found in the countries of Western Europe.

The important consequences of the industrial revolution included growing multiculturalism, which was nonetheless to a certain degree attributable to the way Europe developed before the industrial revolution (human migrations had taken place also in the Late Middle Ages, though the scale of that phenomenon was not very significant). Nevertheless, trade between specific countries, or strictly speaking between urban centres, played a role, not only by providing a supply of hitherto unknown products but above all by enabling people to familiarize themselves with "the Other" (i.e. people from other cultures). Multiculturalism in Europe is an old phenomenon, *albeit* one rather limited until the arrival of the industrial revolution. Nevertheless, people from other cultures played a very positive role from the perspective of development by bringing and showing new products, new forms of activity as well as new behaviours and different mentalities.

The fundamental changes wrought by the industrial revolution coincided with the liberation of rural inhabitants from the system of relations imposed by serfdom. The process resulted in the large supply of workers, who migrated from rural areas to cities in search of work and better living conditions. However, finding satisfactory work was not an easy process. Those especially brave and willing to take risks found an outlet by contributing to the colonial expansion of European powers, especially the United Kingdom, with the surplus of labour being channelled to colonies and subsequently to such countries as the United States, Australia, and New Zealand. A population exodus to those countries and the newly formed colonies was observed not only from relatively developed countries, which chiefly means colonial powers, but from the whole of Europe, including Eastern Europe.

13.6. What Does Globalization Change in Europe from the Perspective of Megacities?

It is important to stress that technological advancement, the arrival of the information revolution, and the dissemination of the market economy are no longer observed only in European countries, or in the European powers, as was the case in the past. North America has moved to the forefront of those processes, a situation that was a result of World War II, the damage suffered by many European countries, and the expansion of the socialist experiment to the countries of Eastern, Central, and Southern Europe. For half a century, those countries were excluded from active participation in the development of modern technologies and science as a result of their isolation from global thinking.

In turn, de-colonization processes became increasingly widespread. However, they often took the form of armed conflicts or even wars. With de-colonization processes coming to an end mostly in the 1960s and 1970s, the world appeared to consist of sovereign states, especially after the breakup of the Soviet Union and Yugoslavia. Importantly, the world then witnessed the emergence of more than a hundred new sovereign states of various sizes that differed in terms of their economic development, their political systems, and obviously their interests as well as their hostility towards other countries, often their neighbours. As we signalled earlier, the important consequences of that process included the dissemination of the market economy, which became universal in its nature: The rules of the game were similar or even identical everywhere. By contrast, the cultural systems in place in specific countries remained diverse and likely to cause conflicts with other countries or societies and groups, often neighbouring ones. Political systems in Europe were likewise highly diverse, ranging from democracies to autocracies, or even dictatorships.

At the same time, Western Europe launched integration processes, gradually transforming into the European Union, a body drawing together 28 member states at its peak, with several more countries waiting in line to become members. Multiculturalism entered another stage of its expansion, in particular in Western Europe. The process, which started after the end of World War II, was initially linked to the new order in Europe, the new delimitation of state borders, and the imposition of the arrangements made at the Conference in Yalta and the socialist model with the domination of the Soviet Union on the countries of Central and Eastern Europe. The expulsion of ethnic Germans from socialist countries was coupled with an exodus of the groups that were threatened in the socialist model, either because they did not accept it for political and ideological reasons or because they had belonged to privileged groups in the past. However, the strong mixing of people and the emergence of multiculturalism was related in particular to de-colonization, as the most active individuals or larger groups were willing to take risks and look for good jobs or achieve success, so they moved to former metropolitan areas, especially as some of them had opened their gates to migrants. Two decades later, that process would be accompanied by the exodus of groups of various sizes from former socialist countries in search of fair or better-paid employment, education opportunities, prosperity, or even a financial or scientific success in Western Europe. That process has never been halted or interrupted. At best, some limitations may have been placed on immigration, but they disappeared when the Schengen Area was established, at least for EU nationals. That was when multiculturalism gathered pace, especially in the more affluent countries.

Irrespective of the processes described above, Europe's position has remained unchanged from the perspective of its population resources. When we compare population growth in Europe to that witnessed in other continents, we can see that this growth was globally the lowest in the years 1960–2015. The booming population growth that has gradually affected the world elsewhere was not observed in Europe. An even more dramatic conclusion may be drawn from population forecasts: by 2050, Europe will be the only continent whose overall population will drop compared to the situation in 2015, whereas the overall global population will surge by nearly 2.4 billion over the same period (UNDESA, 2015). Without overdramatizing the consequences of this trend, we nevertheless need to recognize that Europe will most certainly not avoid numerous problems related to booming population numbers in the world, in the face of the decline in Europe's own indigenous population.

13.7. Will Europe Become Marginalized?

Any answer to this question, which logically follows from what was stated above, can only be hypothetical, because marginalization can assume different forms. From the perspective of the Europe's indigenous population, most countries will witness a decline, also in terms of the supply of labour, at least in a majority of countries, for reasons related to the significance of population aging. The post-reproductive population will be growing rapidly. Based on existing forecasts, we can assume that Europe's economic potential, measured by the continent's share in the world's GDP, will fall significantly. This is indeed an assumption reflected in all important development forecasts, both comprehensive and partial ones.[1]

[1] See Prandecki *et al.* (2013) and Nawrot (2013).

However, these two fundamental components cannot be used as a basis for drawing overly far-reaching conclusions, as they merely reflect decisive metrics that are characteristic of the industrial stage of civilization yet are not crucially important in the emerging knowledge-based civilization. It is not out of the question that Europe, in the light of a gradual decline in its economic potential, may manage to reconfigure its development pattern to be more in tune with new fields specifically related to the knowledge-based civilization. It certainly has a sufficient pool of skilled individuals as well as the technological, innovative, and above all cultural potential necessary for such a shift to be possible. Making any forecasts on this basis, however, requires us to consider how much we actually know about what shape this new stage of civilization will take.

13.8. What Will the Emerging Knowledge-based (Post-modern) Civilization be Like?

There is, as yet, no sufficiently clear and rigorously defined vision of what the emerging knowledge-based (post-modern) civilization will ultimately be like, but it is nonetheless possible to pin down some of its important components. While presenting them here we will not attempt to evaluate their relative significance, on the grounds that for our purposes they should be considered together, as a coherent whole comprised of intertwined factors. In addition, it is safe to assume that the importance of each of those components will change over time. The system sketched out below probably does not reflect the full picture, yet it does show with sufficient clarity the substantial differences between the emerging knowledge-based civilization and the system typical of and prevalent in the industrial stage of civilization.

Overall, we claim, the emerging system of the knowledge-based civilization can be described quite well in terms of the following 10 interrelated components:

(1) A good system of high-quality education that covers a vast majority of society, especially the two youngest generations, which will act as anchors of this civilization. More importantly, they will also eliminate the

components of industrial civilization that will be hindering the development of the emerging knowledge-based civilization;

(2) A significant share of society (over 80%) will live in urban areas, most of which have relatively long traditions as well as a good and modern public sphere, in addition to offering relatively full employment and a relatively high level of security compared to urban agglomerations on other continents;

(3) An important component determining the system's adaptation capabilities will be the relatively long period of generational continuity, with members of specific generations living in urban areas characterized by a relatively good pace of development;

(4) In the conditions of a knowledge-based civilization, cities will be most probably inhabited by social groups characterized by a relatively high level of economic and technological innovation;

(5) An important role in the dynamics of the new civilization will most probably be played by groups characterized by a relatively high level of cultural creativity, those capable of influencing the spiritual culture, as well as various ideologies that serve not only economic but above all social development. This may translate into the creation of a political system that represents a consensus that is relatively beneficial for everyone, or at least most of the groups that live in cities;

(6) Although the modern-day model of the state is a product of the industrial stage of civilization, it will still most probably remain in place for a relatively long time. Nevertheless, the ruling elite must skilfully cultivate the functions of that model to meet the challenges posed by the knowledge-based civilization, which were either absent in the past or may have been to some degree unnecessary in the conditions of industrial civilization. The longer the continuity of a specific state, the more effectively it should adapt to new challenges or threats. Arguably, such threats will be first of all much broader in scope compared to the past and secondly largely universal in their nature;

(7) The difficulties societies will have adjusting to the new civilization may be, and most probably will be, linked to differences between cultural

systems that fall into an interrelated five-way configuration. These are according to Kleer (2016: 217): language, tradition, history, religion, as well as society's attitudes with respect to the state and the state's stance with respect to society. Minimizing the possibility of conflicts with other cultural systems will pose a fundamental problem, because the knowledge-based civilization will necessitate close or even very close contacts with other societies (as well as other countries). In all likelihood, this will be one of the most difficult challenges facing the main institutions of the knowledge-based civilization and their societies;

(8) An important condition for a knowledge-based civilization involves shaping the ability of various groups of people to work together to create common goods that impact significantly on the functions of the new civilization but were not created by the industrial civilization, reliant on the market economy and efforts to maximize individual interests and benefits. This will require not only the emergence of new rules of cooperation and coexistence but, equally importantly, the abandonment of some of the rules that have been applied so far;

(9) One of the fundamental goals of the knowledge-based civilization will involve the development of positive attitudes to relatively fast changes of an economic, social, and political nature;

(10) Finally, the knowledge-based civilization must create an at least positive attitude of society to multiculturalism, which will arguably become increasingly common in social communication and the system of mutual relations, also in the light of the increasingly universal nature of future challenges.

The model presented above — as a proposed system systematizing and summarizing what we know about the emerging knowledge-based civilization — also needs to be supplemented a certain corollary commentary, a certain caveat of sorts. Namely, this model is certainly linked to booming population growth, a process that is temporally related to the emergence of the knowledge-based civilization, yet this is not inherently a cause–effect relationship. We can approximately treat the year 1950 as the starting point of the global population explosion, since which we have observed extremely rapid growth in population numbers. As mentioned earlier, forecasts show that the world's population will surge to nearly 10 billion (9,725 million) by 2050 (UNDESA, 2015). This population expansion has various causes, but we must not forget about two that should be regarded as fundamental: Socio-economic progress and human migrations from rural areas to cities. Irrespective of the problems of poverty and famine that still continue to affect the world, the substantial progress that has been made in terms of raising people's living standards. Such progress is a result of numerous factors, ranging from improvements in food quality and housing conditions to advancements in medicine and education, which have allowed people to take advantage of those changes to a large degree, even if not globally than undoubtedly in numerous regions. In developed countries, a significant contribution to these better standards of living has been made by the state, especially in the period dominated by the model of the welfare state. Those processes first manifested themselves in cities, and they were indeed very visible there. On the scale of the whole globe, the share of the urban population rose from 30% in the first half of the 19th century to 54% in 2015, which works out as a five-fold increase in numerical terms. According to existing forecasts through 2050, the share of the urban population will vary from 55% to nearly 80–90%, depending on the continent (UNDESA, 2014). Little wonder, then, that megacities will grow so rapidly on the continents characterized by a high or very high rate of natural increase. This does not mean, however, that these major agglomerations will be characterized by general prosperity. We could even say that rapid growth in urban population numbers, especially in large urban agglomerations, comes coupled with poverty, high unemployment, and the disruption of the public sphere. However, these problems result from the excessive rate of population growth coupled with a much slower pace of adjustment to this growth.

13.9. How Will Europe's Megacities Fare in the Face of Booming World Population Growth and the Emergence of a Knowledge-based Civilization?

With these characterizations of megacities and their interrelationship with global processes now firmly in hand, we are now ready to close by addressing the leading theme of this chapter: The future of Europe and its major urban areas. First, however, note that when we talk about Europe, often conceived of as a rather homogeneous whole when viewed from a global perspective, we are at the same time referring to a group of countries that nonetheless differ quite widely in terms of their population and economic potential, their political systems, and above all their cultures.

When describing the knowledge-based civilization, in turn, we could likewise present a comprehensive vision or a fragmentary one. So far, the considerations we have presented above have focused on a comprehensive vision. In the context of Europe, however, such a vision can be presented either "from within" or from a bird's eye view, in a comprehensive and simultaneously diversified way. In fact, both approaches need to be taken into account, to facilitate understanding of the question posed in the subtitle of this section and to present at least the outlines of an answer.

The relationship between booming population growth, its impact on Europe, and the emergence of the knowledge-based civilization has numerous, mutually interrelated dimensions, which we will now examine. Firstly, note that the various colonial systems fell apart for various reasons. The mechanisms by which their breakup played out were likewise quite diverse, ranging from more or less peaceful ones to more tragic armed conflicts. Relations between the newly-formed countries and the former colonial powers were beneficial to various degrees. In addition to numerous economic links, one form of such interrelations involved the possibility, though a limited one, for people to migrate to former metropolitan areas. This phenomenon gathered momentum over time, when reports of much better standards of living among the emigrants started to reach their families or affiliated groups back home. For the dynamic societies of the former colonies, emigration became a goal in life. As such, it turned out that, for the former colonies, attaining the status of an independent state alone failed to resolve most of their economic and social problems, and living conditions often failed to address even people's most basic needs. Indeed, the emergence of post-colonial statehood was in numerous cases not a peaceful process, as a result of conflicts not only with the former colonial powers but also with the institutions and authorities of the nascent state itself, further inflamed by various ethnic groups, often hostile towards one another. Almost all of the factors likely to provoke conflicts made themselves manifest relatively quickly: ethnic and religious differences, the delimitation of new borders, corruption, exploitation on the part of foreign corporations from both the old and the newly-formed states, which had in the past no links to a given area or population.

The information revolution, in turn, brought in its wake the widespread visibility of the way of life prevalent in European countries. Europe therefore became a dream place to live for numerous groups of people, chiefly from countries stricken by numerous wars on various scales, that have recently taken on more dramatic dimensions together with the rise of the Islamic State and the toppling of old dictators. At that time, booming population growth had been strongly felt for decades, especially in Africa.

Migration into Europe started to gain momentum as a phenomenon in the 1970s and 1980s, whereas the end of the 20th century and the beginning of the 21st century witnessed a growing wave of immigration from two completely different regions: from the former colonies, especially Africa and the Middle East, and from the post-socialist countries. Western Europe became increasingly multicultural. However, this multiculturalism differed fundamentally from what had been observed in the past, became hostile over time, and its conflict-prone nature took on increasingly dramatic dimensions, suddenly turning into important, sometimes even dominant, element of policy, especially within the EU. Such multiculturalism was to a certain degree linked to terrorism, and some elements of religious warfare emerged. In connection with this phenomenon, which gathered momentum rapidly in the second decade of the 21st century, we may be tempted to formulate the hypothesis that religious warfare is something inherently linked to modern-day civilizational turning points in general, not merely to the transition to the industrial civilization.

In recent years in Europe, a phenomenon that could be described as an invasion of refugees has revealed, or more strictly brought to light, various previously unapparent differences or even conflicts between European countries. Such differences have a long history and are related to the emergence of the old and the new European countries. We will not explore these factors in-depth here, but merely note that many of them lost the continuity of their statehood, on numerous occasions at that, even if we only restrict ourselves to what has happened since the beginning of the 20th century. Disrupting the continuity of statehood in practice entails a change of the legal order and institutions, and often — as was the case after the end of World War I and after the Yalta Conference — the national borders themselves also underwent fundamental changes. Some countries re-emerged on very different territories, others came into existence for the very first time. Such a situation sparked off numerous new conflicts and revived old and unsettled animosities and disputes, in addition to reinvigorating nationalism.

The latter had been almost always present in societies to a smaller or larger degree; although it was sometimes mitigated to a certain extent, new circumstances often emerged that provided additional stimuli conducive to the development of nationalism. One example in the present-day world is the emergence of hundreds of thousands of immigrants to Europe from the Middle East and Africa, in particular North Africa. This has had numerous consequences for the functioning of the European Union.[2] From the perspective of its history, the EU is the best concept of a united Europe based on the principles of peace and social solidarity. Yet, the deep-seated reservoirs of nationalism that have been always present in most or almost all countries in Europe have been recently revived. In addition, we have witnessed explosive growth in populism and xenophobia, supported by an important set of tools newly offered by the information revolution. It turned out very quickly that the only true value was that embodied by one's own sovereign nation-state, rather than the abstract notions of collaboration or joining forces in the conditions of globalization offered by the EU, especially for small- or medium-sized countries on the continent.

13.10. Conclusions

First of all, if we refer to demographic projections for Europe, we should conclude that the number of European megacities will not grow in the foreseeable future. Namely, Istanbul, Moscow, London, and Paris can be expected to retain their status as megacities through 2030, while at the same time Europe (unlike other continents, Asia and Africa in particular) should not be expected to see any new contenders for the status of

[2] More discussion on migration, see Nawrot *et al.* (2016).

"megacity" rise within its confines (UNDESA, 2014). This general projection still holds even if we assume a continued influx of people from other continents (the forms and nature of such migrations may be largely or even completely different from those observed so far). Such migrations will surely continue and what is more, this continuance is desirable for Europe, for at least two reasons. There is, after all, every indication that the indigenous population of the European continent will itself not be large enough to sustain economic growth, if not across the whole of Europe then arguably in most of its countries, and this is additionally coupled with aging population on the continent. What seems crucial in this regard is the ability to more effectively harness the potential of immigrants and refugees, and to a smaller or larger degree to control their scope and destinations. Finally, in this respect job creation and social integration are essential for ensuring the integral social fabric and sustainable growth of major cities — where the majority of the population influx can be expected.

As for the European megacities, London and Paris will most probably play a growing role in Europe, whereas the importance of Istanbul and Moscow will likely dwindle. Regardless of possible growth in their economic potential (perhaps also military potential in Moscow's case), their links to Asia will become stronger, not only because they are partially anchored in Asia and linked territorially to that continent, but also in view of the growing opportunities for economic and possibly also political expansion in these regions.

Furthermore, European megacities should be perceived through the significant role they have to play in the development of the modern-day world. Depending on their size, character, and resources, as well as a number of additional factors, cities form a network of interrelations that grow in strength as these cities develop and become established. We could look at this network through the prism of not only population numbers but also other principal components that determine the nature of the present-day world. The later underlines the importance of not only megacities but also of urban agglomerations that are smaller in size but have great influence, which is particularly characteristic for Europe.

Numerous researchers from the late 20th and early 21st century have analyzed the connectivity of cities from different perspectives, including their emerging networks that may or will play a decisive role in the world economy. In Taylor's (2001) extensive work on such connectivity, he identified a network of 10 global cities crucial in the supply of advanced services. These 10 cities include four European cities (namely London, Paris, Frankfurt, and Milan), three in the United States (New York, Chicago, and Los Angeles), and three in Asia (Tokyo and the city-states of Singapore and Hong Kong). All of them are situated in highly developed and highly technology-advanced economies. Interestingly, among these 10 cities, only five can be described as megacities both now and from the perspective of 2030: London, Paris, New York, Los Angeles, as well as Tokyo. Extensive research has also been conducted by the Globalization and World Cities (GaWC) Research Network, categorizing world cities into Alpha, Beta and Gamma tiers, based upon their international connectedness. According to the 2012 GaWC (2012) classification, the Alpha cities — apart from those already mentioned above — included another 12 European cities — Moscow, Madrid and Amsterdam, followed by Vienna, Istanbul, Zurich, Warsaw, Barcelona, Dublin, Munich, Stockholm, and Prague. The presented categorizations very much relate to the potential of European cities as hubs of knowledge, new technologies, innovation, and creative ideas, which has been always a principal advantage of Europe (for instance, from perspective of the prestige of the various world leading academic centres across the continent).

Such forecasts underscore the role that the knowledge and service sector will play in the modern-world civilization, and also help us to understand which urban areas will not rank among the megacities of the future but will nonetheless play a significant role in the system of the global economy.

From these deliberations, another important question emerges: What may happen within Europe itself? Here is where the answer becomes difficult, because everything will depend on what happens to the European Union in the near future, to what extent the centripetal trends towards degradation become strengthened and gather speed. This is because we can observe a tendency in some countries towards the idea of leaving the EU or weakening the process of integration. If such trends grow in intensity, then Europe's future may become marginalized on a global scale. Over time, however, this process may be reversed, and the ties between specific countries as well as leading economic, technological, scientific, and cultural centres may play a stronger role. If this happens, the kind of relations that are in a sense supranational will grow in strength. Such pro-development functions may be taken over by rapidly developing urban centres from specific countries, thus leading to the emergence of new systems of interrelations and connectivity.

At this point, it is difficult to say which of these trends will ultimately prevail. From the perspective of the long history of Europe and its ability to overcome challenges, however, we can posit the assumption that the common sense and creativity of the Europeans will nevertheless once again allow for the transformative revival of Europe's position in the world.

References

GaWC (2012). Globalization and World Cities (GaWC) Research Network. Retrieved from http://www.lboro.ac.uk/gawc/world2012t.html [access: 24.03.2017].

Hohenberg, P.M. and L.H. Lees (1985). *The Making of Urban Europe*, 1000–1950. Cambridge: Harvard University Press.

Kleer, J. (2016). Związki między myśleniem strategicznym a wielokulturowością. In J. Kleer, P. Szukalski and K. Prandecki (Eds.). *Dokąd zmierza Europa: Państwo-Gospodarka-Społeczeństwo-Finanse*. Warszawa: Polska Akademia Nauk, Komitet Prognoz "Polska 2000 Plus," pp. 208–232.

Nawrot, K.A. (2013). Kryzys światowego system finansowego a rynki azjatyckie. In E. Mączyńska, J.J. Michałek and J. Niżnik (Eds.). *Kryzysy systemowe*. Warszawa: Polska Akademia Nauk, Komitet Prognoz "Polska 2000 Plus," pp. 279–293.

Nawrot, K.A. (2014). *Kraje rozwijające się we współczesnej gospodarce światowej. Przyczynek do ekonomii rozwoju*. Warszawa: Wydawnictwo Naukowe Scholar.

Nawrot, K.A., M. Rybicka and W. Wieszczycka (2016). Nierówności społeczno-ekonomiczne i przemieszczanie się ludności, a katastroficzne wizje rozwoju współczesnego świata. *Przyszłość. Świat-Europa-Polska*, 2(34), 75–108.

Prandecki, K., K.A. Nawrot and M. Wawrzyński (2013), Nowe centrum i nowe peryferia połowy XXI wieku. *Przyszłość. Świat-Europa-Polska*, 28(2), 58–81.

Taylor, P.J. (2001). Urban hinterworlds: Geographies of corporate service provisions of contemporary globalization. *Geography*, 86(1), 51–60.

US Bureau of the Census (1998). *Population of the 33 Urban Places: 1800.* Retrieved from https://www.census.gov/population/www/documentation/twps0027/tab03.txt [access: 23.03.2017].

UNDESA (1980). *Patterns of urban and rural population growth.* Population Studies, No. 68. United Nations, Department of International Economic and Social Affairs. New York: United Nations.

UNDESA (2014). United Nations, Department of Economic and Social Affairs, Population Division. *World Urbanization Prospects: The 2014 Revision,* CD-ROM Edition. New York.

UNDESA (2015). United Nations, Department of Economic and Social Affairs, Population Division. *World Population Prospects: The 2015 Revision,* Data Booklet. New York.

Part III

Case Studies of Selected Megacities

14

TOKYO AND DELHI — A COMPARATIVE ANALYSIS OF ASIAN MEGACITIES

Katarzyna A. Nawrot

14.1. Introduction

The rise of megacities has been particularly visible in Asia, which is currently home to eight out of the world's 10 largest urban agglomerations, according to Demographia (2016). However, as we will seek to show here, it would be incorrect to lump all the Asian megacities together (or, *a fortiori*, to assume that the world's megacities are largely alike). The most populated of Asia's megacities is Tokyo–Yokohama, which has consistently remained the world's most populous metropolitan area since the mid-1950s. Delhi, on the other hand, is a notable example of a fast-emerging, relatively new megacity in Asia, one that did not even rank among the world's 30 largest cities just half a century ago, but has since risen to become one of the world's most populous cities. Delhi is even projected to become the largest agglomeration on the globe around 2030 (UNDESA, 2014). These very distinct developmental trajectories motivated the choice of Tokyo and Delhi as the study sample for this chapter, as representing two very different examples of megacities in Asia.

In what follows, we will first examine some of the demographic and economic indicators of the two cities themselves and trends evident in their home countries. Next, using the preliminary insights from this comparative analysis as a springboard, we propose a way of classifying the world's megacities in terms of their model of urbanization and stage of development. Lastly, we look again more closely at Tokyo and Delhi in terms of the developmental opportunities and challenges they face, pointing out how these are linked to their differing models of urbanization and stages of development.

14.2. A First Snapshot: Growth Trajectories and Population Density

Tokyo–Yokohama, which covers an area of 8,547 km^2, displaced New York to become the world's largest megacity in 1954. It has since then consistently retained that title, now with a population of 37.75 million people, making up almost 30% of Japan's population and labour market and generating over 35% of the country's GDP. Its population rose gradually from around 7.6 million in 1920 to 15.4 million in 1955, first exceeding 30 million back in 1985 (Statistics Bureau of Japan, 2010). Delhi, by contrast, is a newly emerged megacity that had just 1.5 million inhabitants in the 1950s, yet at present has a population of more than 25.7 million people (Demographia, 2016). Moreover, covering an area of just 2,163 km^2 (see Table 14.1), Delhi is estimated to have a population density of 11,900 inhabitants per km^2 in 2016, which is an approx. around 24% increase compared to 2014 and is almost three times higher than in Tokyo. Despite being the world's most populous megacity, Tokyo does not have intensely dense central areas. Therefore, the centre of Japan's capital is in fact less densely

Table 14.1. Tokyo–Yokohama vs. Delhi: A comparison of basic figures, 2016

Urban agglomeration	Country	Population	Area (km^2)	Population density (per km^2)
Tokyo–Yokohama	Japan	37,750,000	8,547	4,400
Delhi	India	25,735,000	2,163	11,900

Source: Compiled by the author based on Demographia (2016).

populated than that of a number of smaller megacities, including Manhattan and downtown Paris. Tokyo's *ku* wards have a density of 14,400 per km^2, compared to 27,000 in Manhattan and 21,000 in the ville de Paris. Only one of the *ku* (Toshima) exceeds the density of Paris (Cox, 2012).

14.3. The Broader Backdrop: Urbanization in Japan vs. India

In the broader perspective, the two cities are also situated in countries with distinctively different demographic situations and trends. In the coming decades, urbanization can be expected to continue in both countries, *albeit* more intensely so in India. Japan is already highly urbanized, and the country's population as a whole will decline as a result of depopulation, in both urbanized and non-urbanized areas. However, the population shift to urban areas will continue in Japan, and as such the relative share of those living in urbanized areas, already high, will continue to rise to 98% (see Fig. 14.1). In other words, the drop in population numbers in Tokyo

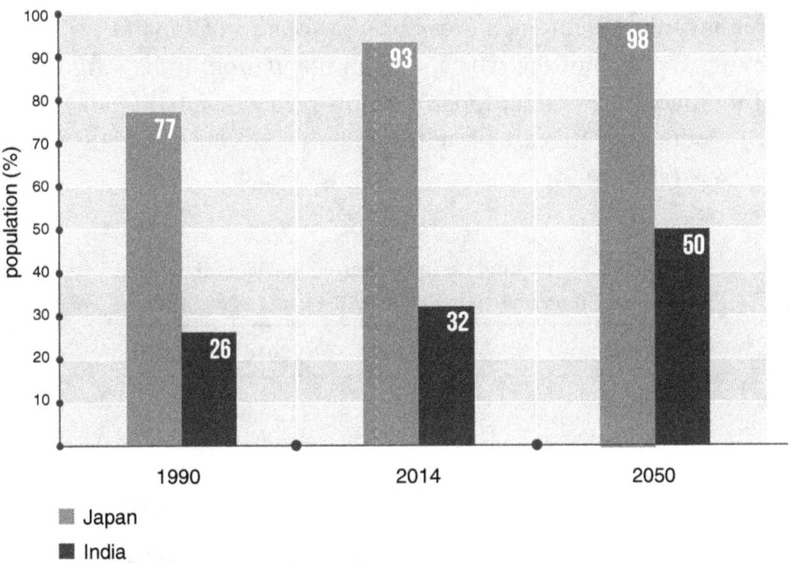

Fig. 14.1. Overall share of population in urbanized areas in Japan and India in 1990, 2014, and 2050 (%)

Source: Compiled by the author based on Demographia (2014).

will be smaller in relative terms than for the whole of Japan, indicating that the agglomeration will be the main driver behind the country's economic growth.

India, in turn, presently has a sizeable share of its population (858 million people) living in rural areas. However, the population of the country's urbanized areas is projected to increase more than two-fold by 2050, to exceed 800 million, which will mean more than half of the country's population then living in urban areas (Table 14.2). In addition, as a country India ranks second in the world, after China, in terms of the number of emerging megacities. India's four existing megacities, namely Delhi, Mumbai, Kolkata, and Bangalore, are expected to be joined by three more over the coming 15 years: Chennai, Hyderabad, and Ahmedabad, with still others likely to follow thereafter (UNDESA, 2015).

Of the world's thousand-odd urban areas, about half are found in Asia. Japan, however, is home to just 23 of them (just 2.5% of the number of urbanized areas in the world), and they are inhabited by only 4.4% of the global urban population. India, on the other hand, has 93 urbanized areas accounting for 10.6% of the world urban population. The highest number of such areas can be found in China (194), inhabited by nearly 20% of the world's urban population. India's figures are therefore much higher than Japan's in this respect, but still half those of China — although it must be noted India is exhibiting strong upward trends (see Table 14.3).

Table 14.2. Population in urbanized and non-urbanized areas in Japan and India in 1990, 2014, and 2050 (million)

Country	1990	2014	2050
Japan			
Urbanized areas	94.55	118.14	105.78
Non-urbanized areas	27.70	8.87	2.55
India			
Urbanized areas	221.98	410.20	814.40
Non-urbanized areas	646.91	857.20	805.65

Source: Compiled by the author based on Demographia (2014).

Table 14.3. Urbanized areas in selected regions and countries, 2014

Country/ region	Number of urbanized areas	Population of urbanized areas	% of world's urbanized areas	% of world population in urbanized areas
World	922	1,917,558,000	100	100
Asia	473	1,073,840,000	51.3	56.0
Africa	103	198,429,000	11.2	10.3
China	194	370,639,000	21.0	19.3
India	93	203,614,000	10.1	10.6
Japan	23	84,902,000	2.5	4.4

Source: Compiled by the author based on Demographia (2014).

In addition to depopulation, Japan is experiencing a pronounced shift in its population structure towards having a greater proportion of individuals over 65 (around 23%), and also a growing number of single-person households (Statistics Bureau of Japan, 2011: 4).

Juxtaposing the basic indicators of economic growth and development for the two countries (see Table 14.4) illustrates how Tokyo and Delhi are situated in economies that differ quite significantly in terms of such factors as *per capita* income, poverty level, economic growth rate, and structure of population. These differences certainly affect urbanization processes in the two countries, the nature of their megacities, and the related developmental challenges that they face, all of which we will consider in more detail in what follows.

14.4. The Dynamics of the Development of Urban Agglomerations of Tokyo and Delhi

Both Tokyo and Delhi rank high among the top three on the list of the world's largest megacities according to both UNDESA (2014) and Demographia (2016) figures. The modern-day dominance of Asian megacities on this list is a result of rapid changes in population growth in recent decades and ongoing economic transformations taking place in the region. Of the list of the world's largest megacities in 2016, as many as eight of the top 10 are situated in Asia (Demographia, 2016).

Table 14.4. Japan vs. India: Basic indicators of economic growth and development, 2015

Country	Japan	India
GDP (billion, current US$)	4383.1	2095.4
GNI *per capita*, Atlas method (current US$)	38,840	1,600
GNI *per capita*, PPP (current US$)	42,310	6,030
GDP growth (annual, %)	1.2	7.6
HDI	0.891	0.609
GINI	32.1	33.6
Poverty gap at $1.25 a day (%)[a]	..	23.6
Poverty gap at $2.00 a day (%)[a]	..	59.2
Poverty gap at national poverty line (%)[a]	..	21.9
Urban poverty — national poverty line (% of population in urbanized areas)[a]	..	13.7
Rural poverty — national poverty line (% of population in non-urbanized areas)[a]	..	25.7
Populations living in slums (% of urban population)	..	24
Urban population growth (annual, %)	0.4	2.4

Explanation: (..) — insignificantly small levels; [a]figures from 2014.
Source: Compiled by the author based on World Bank (2015); World Bank (2017); UNDP (2017).

However, despite both seemingly being part of this same "Asian megacity trend," Tokyo and Delhi do differ fundamentally as megacities chiefly because they are at different stages of urbanization, having developed at different paces over the past century. Tokyo, after a period of rapid development in the 20th century, has begun to experience the effects of stagnation, low or zero growth, depopulation, and population aging. Delhi, in turn, is an example of a fast-growing, newly developing megacity in an emerging economy whose population is 10 times larger than that of Japan.

To underscore the fundamental differences between the two cities under scrutiny here, let us cite three tell-tale facts. Firstly, over the past decade alone, the population of the Delhi agglomeration has risen by 38.2%, while Tokyo's population increased only slightly, by 7%, over the same period (small by comparison to other megacities, although still considerable when viewed against the backdrop of Japan as a whole). Secondly, while Tokyo accounts for 30% of Japan's population, Delhi is one of India's four megacities at present, when *taken together* account for around 10% of the country's population. And thirdly, having emerged as a megacity only quite recently, Delhi is projected to become the world's largest megacity around 2030, whereas Tokyo's population is actually expected to decrease in the coming years. As this short list of facts illustrates very well, the two cities are on very different trajectories in terms of their population growth, the broader environment in which they function, and their future prospects.

Note, too, that the difference between the two developmental patterns can be viewed in terms of a much broader trend: namely, the growth of megacities can nowadays be observed chiefly in developing countries, including those characterized by low level of development. This is illustrated by Table 14.5, listing the world's top megacities in terms of the population growth rates they experienced in the years 2000–2010.

Table 14.5. The fastest-growing urban agglomerations in 2000–2010

Urban agglomeration	Country	Population in 2016 (million)	Growth rate in 2000–2010 (%)
Karachi	Pakistan	22.8	80.5
Shenzhen	China	12.2	56.1
Lagos	Nigeria	12.8	48.2
Beijing	China	20.4	47.6
Bangkok	Thailand	15.3	45.2
Dhaka	Bangladesh	16.2	45.2
Guangzhou–Foshan	China	18.8	43.0
Shanghai	China	22.7	40.1
Delhi	**India**	**25.7**	**38.2**
Jakarta	Indonesia	31.3	34.6
Istanbul	Turkey	13.5	25.3
Tokyo	**Japan**	**37.7**	**7.0**

Source: Compiled by the author based on Demographia (2014, 2016).

14.5. Urbanization Models: A Preliminary Classification

The above brief review of basic facts about Tokyo and Delhi against the backdrop of the economies of Japan and India has led us to the conclusion that the two megacities have distinctly different models of urbanization and development and, by the same token, diverse characteristics. Tokyo and Delhi develop at fundamentally different paces and function within economies at deferring levels and patterns of economic development. For that reason, they experience different problems related to spatial development, depending on selected aspects of the pace of urbanization and standards of living as well as the history of urbanization, economic policy, and involvement on the part of civic society.

Tokyo can be described as a mature megacity characterized by evolutionary urbanization. The agglomeration's development has largely gone hand-in-hand with Japan's industrialization. The city's spatial structure emerged together with the development of railroads and has been concentrated around the intensively growing rail network since the 1930s. Consequently, inhabitants of Tokyo usually travel by public transport, with the average commute time of approx. 48 minutes. Commuters in Delhi, on the other hand, a megacity characterized by chaotic and disorderly yet extremely rapid urbanization, need 1.5–2 hours on average to get to work in the morning.

These observations suggest the beginnings of a framework for classifying megacities. New York, for instance, with a population of over 20 million people and a growth rate of less than 10%, could be seen as belonging to the same category of megacities as Tokyo. Cities like Karachi and Jakarta, on the other hand, with growth rates in excess of 30% and populations exceeding 20 million, fall roughly into the same group as Delhi. We can then flesh this classification out further by recognizing that individual megacities differ in terms of spatial planning and the state's involvement in such planning. The proposed classification system is presented in Table 14.6. Note, however, that this is an initial and intuitive proposal that requires more data and an explanatory methodology, which will be the subject of further research.

Table 14.6. Proposed classification of megacities

Category	Population size and growth rate[a]	Examples of megacities	Type of urbanization
Mature	≥20 million <10%	Tokyo, New York	Evolutionary
Mature	<20 million <10% <20 million >10%	Paris Moscow	Evolutionary
Growing	<20 million <30%	Los Angeles	Moderate/sustainable
Fast-growing	≥20 million >30%	Karachi, Delhi, Jakarta	Galloping
Fast-growing	<20 million >30%	Lagos, Dhaka	Galloping
Emerging	≈10 million >30%	Kinshasa, Lima	Galloping

Explanation: [a]Data concerning population size and the pace of urban agglomeration growth in 2000–2010 taken from Demographia (2014).

14.6. Developmental Opportunities and Challenges Faced by Megacities

Differing levels of economic development, determined to a significant degree by the level of urbanization, affect the nature of urbanization and the challenges faced by megacities. It is no surprise, therefore, that Tokyo and Delhi, falling into very different niches in the above classification, face very different developmental opportunities and challenges in the years ahead.

After a period of rapid growth, Tokyo, a mature megacity, is now grappling with such problems as depopulation, population aging, effectiveness of the city management, including transportation, the proper management of its subcentres (suburbs), and efforts to improve living standards on the periphery. We can expect Tokyo's population growth (currently around 7%) to continue to fall. As a result of ongoing processes, downtown Tokyo is observing gradual depopulation and progressive de-industrialization. This means that it will be necessary to take measures aimed at proper management of the abandoned areas, including those characterized by soil contamination, and at revitalizing both post-industrial areas and the outskirts and suburbs, with emphasis being placed on their use for the purposes of research centres, institutes, light industry, housing as well as culture, commercial, and business space. The directions of Tokyo's further development therefore follow from the city's distinctive characteristics and Japan's socio-economic situation and are visible in development plans for the region. We should expect the authorities to make efforts to stimulate the megacity's further development around existing transport routes, to prevent the urban sprawl and the city's borders from being shifted, and to make maximum use of existing resources. In addition, an aging population will mean growing depopulation in the outskirts. We can therefore expect a population shift from the suburbs to downtown Tokyo. Undoubtedly, problems posed by the maintenance of the existing advanced urban infrastructure will be further aggravated.

Yet, despite evident stagnation and extant challenges, Tokyo remains one of the world's leading megacities in terms of its economy, the opportunities it offers, its international character and connectivity, and the quality of life, as confirmed by numerous indices such as the Global Metro Monitor Map (Brookings), the Global Financial Centres Index (Z/Yen), the Global City Competitiveness Index (*The Economist*), the Global Cities Index (A.T. Kearney), the City Prosperity Index (United Nations) — see Table 14.7. Moreover, in the context of the area's development, we can observe measures aimed at increasing the number of green areas and the design of public spaces in order to improve the quality of life of Tokyo's inhabitants.

According to the collective Global City Economic Power Index, compiled by researchers from the Martin Prosperity Institute based on the evaluation of business activity, the finance and banking sector, competitiveness in the global market, the quality of life, and all the measurements listed above, Tokyo ranked third in 2015, surpassed only by New York and London. The world's 10 most economically powerful cities also included such megacities as Paris (5),[1] Los Angeles (7). Other Asian megacities that

[1] The number in parenthesis indicates the position in the ranking.

Table 14.7. Megacities and cities in rankings, 2015[a]

Position	Global City economic power index	Global metro monitor map	Global financial centres index	Global city competitiveness index	Global cities index	City prosperity index
1	New York	Tokyo	New York	New York	New York	Vienna
2	London	New York	London	London	London	New York
3	Tokyo	Los Angeles	Hong Kong	Singapore	Paris	Toronto
4	Hong Kong	Seoul	Singapore	Hong Kong	Tokyo	London
5	Paris	London	Zürich	Tokyo	Hong Kong	Stockholm
6	Singapore	Paris	Tokyo	Sydney	Los Angeles	Helsinki
7	Los Angeles	Osaka–Kobe	Seoul	Paris	Chicago	Dublin
8	Seoul	Shanghai	Boston	Stockholm	Beijing	Oslo
9	Vienna	Chicago	Geneva	Chicago	Singapore	Paris
10	Stockholm	Moscow	San Francisco	Toronto	Washington	Tokyo

Explanation: [a]Figures from 2015 or the most recent available data.

Sources: Compiled by the author based on CityLab (2015); The Brookings Institution (2015); Z/Yen Group (2014); Citi (2015); A.T. Kearney (2015); UNHSP (2012).

made it into the top 20 were Osaka–Kobe (16), Beijing (18), and Shanghai (also 18).[2] Note how Tokyo ranks high, or at least in the top 10 for the world, in all of the rankings cited in Table 14.7.

Given all of the above, we must conclude that Tokyo is undoubtedly one of the modern world's leading metropolitan areas, whose experience on the road to urbanization offers valuable lessons in many fields.

Delhi, on the other hand, serves as a clear example of the principle that quality of urbanization does not necessarily go hand-in-hand with its speed. Here, galloping urbanization has engendered many problems with the provision of basic services related to housing, social protection, access to safe water resources, and public transport. According to India's National Institute of Urban Studies, water is available for an average of 2.9 hours per day and 40–60% of water supplies are not safe for use. Among

[2]The Global City Economic Power Index is published every year on the website CityLab, founded by Richard Florida, director of the Martin Prosperity Institute at the University of Toronto and professor at New York University; CityLab (2015).

households, 30–50% have no sewage system access and less than 20% of waste is subject to purification.[3] Monopolies on the provision of basic services result in organizational inefficiencies. In addition, the city authorities are not legally authorized to accept devolved authority. Delhi has only 2.7 m^2 of open space *per capita*, compared to 6 m^2 in Tokyo and 14 m^2 in Beijing, a factor that worsens the quality of life of the city's inhabitants. An uncontrolled influx of people is continually being recorded, which increases social pressure, leading to social exclusion, the expansion of poverty areas and, consequently, growing urban poverty. According to estimates, 20–30% of Delhi's inhabitants live in slums. In addition, there are cases involving the expropriation of land. Consequently, Delhi's problems can be identified in the following dimensions:

- city transport and its dysfunctionality,
- water supply, sewage system, city cleaning,
- the natural environment,
- human interactions,
- urban poverty,
- institutional solutions at the level of megacity governance.

In Delhi's case, it is important that the city make even greater strides towards resolving such problems as poverty and slums and effectively including migrants into the job market, in addition to providing them with relevant social protection. It will be necessary to take steps aimed at improving the standards of living in informal settlements and the quality of sociocultural, interpersonal interactions, thereby countering social exclusion and building a sense of community in the city. First and foremost, however, transportation links need to be developed to prevent the exclusion of the megacity's periphery and hamper the emergence of ghettos. Ensuring a relevant infrastructure requires effective solutions in such fields as housing, public spheres, the establishment of hospitals, kindergartens, and schools as well as adequate education to improve job market inclusion. Attempts have been made to provide education, including vocational training, to those living in slums. In addition, numerous

[3] Figures pertain to the national average of urbanized areas in India, after: Johnson (2011: 24).

micro-initiatives have been taken and efforts have been made to raise public awareness on health issues and social responsibility for public goods.

Surging population numbers and galloping urbanization give rise to infrastructural shortages. Negligence in spatial planning at the early stages of megacity development — as in the case of Delhi — significantly hinders its current and future establishment and enlargement of an effective transport network. Insufficient infrastructure and low-cost housing, often coupled with a failure to ensure safety standards, and also a high population density all contribute to Delhi's greater vulnerability to the consequences of a catastrophic risk occurring.

Consequently, existing transport links and public transport services pose a major challenge for Delhi. Dysfunctional transportation results from the city's inadequate transportation infrastructure as well as inconsistent spatial development plans and plans to develop the transport network. The growing wealth of the population is raising people's mobility and the number of cars on the road. If public transport remains ineffective and efforts to improve its quality bring little effect, this will prevent the existing infrastructure from being optimally used, in addition to causing further traffic problems in the megacity.

Moreover, the intensive nature of globalization processes tends to be conducive to its uncontrollability, and this should be prevented by spatial development planning. Strategic long-term planning nonetheless proves difficult to implement in such a rapidly changing urban environment. On the other hand, there has been some recognition of the effectiveness of measures developed *ad hoc*, which often assume the form of interventions and make use of public-private partnerships. Examples can be found in the revitalization of the historical network of sewers, called *nullah*, or new ways of utilizing the unused railroad tracks surrounding Delhi. Proposed solutions include creating an alternative system of transportation, for example, bicycles, implementing a system conducive to environmental renewal, and developing a system of historical and cultural routes (Johnson, 2011).

Megacity governance is a crucial issue that will require effective institutional solutions in the context of funding, management, and planning. The most important issues that require intervention include security, the judiciary, the tax system, water quality and access to water, efforts to attract talented people, and city sanitation. In addition, the de-centralization of administrative power seems crucial, which in Delhi's case will require constitutional amendments. At the same time, it will be necessary to ensure the consistency of programs at local, regional, and national level and clearly define tasks and competences at individual levels of central and local government. Issues that are important in the context of funding include choosing the right financing instruments and earmarked funds as well as harnessing the mechanisms of public–private partnerships.

Such challenges, in both developed and developing countries, give rise to a certain dilemma concerning what the optimum size of a megacity is. At the same time, we can see the limits continually being stretched in terms of being able to maintain the effective functioning of megacities through the application of new technologies, innovation, and more effective governance.

14.7. Conclusions

Ongoing research indicates that we may expect a growing number of megacities to be affected by major developmental problems in the coming decades. As the present contrastive analysis of two major megacities in Asia has shown, however, the various megacities of today and tomorrow may face very different developmental opportunities and challenges, linked to their differing models of urbanization and stages of development.

In this context, Tokyo's experience is invaluable, not only for Delhi but also for other emerging megacities in developing countries (especially those classified in groups similar to that of Delhi in the above classification). These megacities similarly face the challenge of creating effective and multifaceted governance mechanisms combining spatial planning, urban infrastructure, the labour market, transportation and communication, the natural environment, social protection, and access to basic services and common goods by using new information technologies, and helping build a sense of community in major complex human settlements.

At the same time, planners must remain mindful that the forthcoming challenges in the development of megacities will differ depending on their level of urbanization. They will pertain to the following areas:

- the megacity's development vs. the conservation of the natural environment, soil, and agricultural land,
- transportation and its effectiveness,

- the provision of basic services,
- the provision of common goods,
- central areas of megacities and their developmental dynamics,
- the revitalization of suburban areas,
- the protection and conservation of cultural and historical heritage areas,
- the improvement of housing conditions in informal settlements,
- the improvement of housing conditions in suburban areas and on the periphery,
- security,
- ethnic tensions,
- the improvement of the quality of life of inhabitants and social interactions.

The increasingly city-centric model of the world's economy gives rise to a need for efforts by state administration focused on better guiding the development of megacities, for instance, by establishing chambers of industry and commerce or representative offices in megacities. At the same time, there is a need for collaboration between authorities of megacities and the states; cities and megacities, and not only within a given region or country but at the level of the whole world economic system.

Note

This chapter is the result of the research project "East Asia in regional cooperation and governance" financed by the National Science Centre, Poland (decision no. DEC-2013/09/B/HS4/01147).

References

Citi (2015). *Hot spots 2025. Benchmarking the future competitiveness of cities*. A report from the Economist Intelligence Unit, Commissioned by Citi. Retrieved from http://www.citigroup.com [access: 12.11.2015].

CityLab (2015). *CityLab*. Retrieved from http://www.citylab.com [access: 12.11.2015].

Cox, W. (2012). *The Evolving Urban Form: Tokyo*. Retrieved from http://www.newgeography.com/content/002923-the-evolving-urban-form-tokyo [access: 20.10.2015].

Demographia (2014). *Demographia World Urban Areas*, 10th Annual Edition, March.

Demographia (2016). *Demographia World Urban Areas*, 12th Annual Edition, April.

Johnson, Ch. (Ed.). (2011). *Indian Cities: Managing Urban Growth*. A Metropolis Research Publication in Association with India's National Institute of Urban Studies, Mumbai.

Kearney, A.T. (2015). *A.T. Kearney Global Cities Index and Emerging Cities Outlook*. Retrieved from http://www.atkearney.com [access: 12.11.2015].

Statistics Bureau of Japan (2010). *2010 Japan Census*. Retrieved from http://www.stat.go.jp [access: 10.11.2015].

Statistics Bureau of Japan (2011). *2010 Japan Census*, October 26.

The Brookings Institution (2015). Global Metro Monitor 2014: An uncertain recovery, Metropolitan Policy Program.

UNDESA (2014). *World Urbanization Prospects: The 2014 Revision*. United Nations, Department of Economic and Social Affairs, Population Division. CD-ROM Edition. New York.

UNDESA (2015). *World Urbanization Prospects: The 2014 Revision*. United Nations, Department of Economic and Social Affairs, Population Division. New York.

UNDP (2017). UNDP Database. Retrieved from http://www.undp.org [access: 08.02.2017].

UNHSP (2012). *State of the world's cities 2012/2013: Prosperity of Cities*. United Nations Human Settlements Programme, Nairobi.

World Bank (2015). World Bank Database. Retrieved from http://www.worldbank.org [access: 10.11.2015].

World Bank (2017). World Bank Database. Retrieved from http://www.worldbank.org [access: 08.02.2017].

Z/Yen Group (2014). The Global Financial Centres Index 16, Z/Yen Group, September. Retrieved from http://www.zyen.com [access: 12.11.2015].

15

SHANGHAI — THE FIRST MEGALOPOLIS ON THE GLOBE?

Bogdan Góralczyk

15.1. Introduction

One of the more important, although not much explored, processes in the Chinese transformation, happening since 1979 under the slogans *gaige* — reform and *kaifang* — openness to the world, is fast urbanization. When China was getting ready for war, there was only 17% of urbanization there. After over three decades of reforms, in 2011, China, for the first time in their history, had more citizens in the cities than in the villages. In 2016, the level of urbanization exceeded 55%, and the aims of the administration of "the fifth generation of leaders" were more ambitious than ever. The Prime Minister Li Keqiang had declared that by 2030 as much as 70% of China population was expected to live in the cities.

In this context, the aim of this study is to explore the largest Chinese agglomeration — Shanghai, which, in the past decades, transformed into a megalopolis by merging with other nearby cities.

After a short introduction to the history of the city, the author will try to explain what has led to the fast modernization of the city, and why and when it has taken place. He will also present how the process has been conducted, providing evidence that it has constantly been directed from above and regulated to meet the latest demands and trends of the agglomeration process. A key impulse for modernization was for Shanghai the EXPO 2010 exhibition. Separate interesting issue is the so-called Pudong zone, which, presently, is the shopping window for China. A lot of attention is paid to some of the unique architectonic objects in this particular area, such as Shanghai Tower. The aim of this study, thus, is to present the dynamics of the development of Shanghai — the largest agglomeration of the biggest rising market, which China has become.

15.2. Shanghai — Basic Data

According to the official data, the territory of Shanghai in 2014 was 6,340 km², with a population of 17.2 million excluding the immigration rate (*liudong renkou*), which has been difficult to estimate and oscillates between 5–9 million (Fact Sheets, 2017). It needs mentioning here, that all the data regarding the population of the metropolis are mostly estimations, for in the last 10–15 years Shanghai has transformed into a large city cluster. It can easily be checked by taking a fast train to for example, Nanjing. All the cities passed on the way such as Kunshan, Wuxi, Suzhou, or Changzhou, which used to be separate cities, have now merged into one huge cluster with agreed borders. Shanghai and the neighbouring areas are the most urbanized regions of the Republic of China, together with Chongqing in the province of Sichuan, the capital Beijing, and the Pearl River Delta including Guangzhou.

As Shanghai is already surrounded by large cities, it is getting popular among urbanites to refer to the area not only as Shanghai but as Yangtze River Delta (Changjiang). Formally, it consists of 16 cities from the provinces of Zhejiang and Jiangsu (and partially Anhui). Towards the end of the first decade of 21st century, (The Economist, 2017) this region comprised 6% of the Chinese population, and 19% of the GDP. We are, thus, dealing with a very strong and dynamic megalopolis in the country considered as the first economy in the world.[1] It is clear that without the powered economic mechanism as Shanghai, China would not be able to reach its aim and position. It is Shanghai, according to the central government in

[1]About the Chinese economical ambitions and possibilities, for example, Acharya (2014: 27) and Hu (2011: 1, 4, 28).

Beijing, that will be the head of quickly rising Chinese Dragon pertaining not only to be the power as China already has become, but superpower which they want to be, not only in the financial aspect but as an example of a modern state for other countries.[2]

15.3. Short, Chequered History

It has not always been like that. At the dawn of the 19th century, China, that had for centuries been the world power, started to lose their leading position.[3] However, Shanghai's position was slightly different form the position of the rest of the country. It belonged, at that stage, to the harbours taken over by foreign capital and colonial countries during the infamous Opium Wars (1839–1842 and 1856–1860). Officially, thus, Shanghai, like the whole Middle Kingdom, was at the losing end. In fact, however, the entry of the foreign capital and executives made Shanghai the shop window for the world and gave it the opportunity to develop. The problem was that, in the eyes of many Chinese people, Shanghai had become a symbol of subordination to foreign rules and colonial dependency. It remained like that practically throughout the entire period of the so-called "century of national humiliation" (*bainian guochi*),[4] until the proclamation of the Republic of China on the October 1, 1949.

The bourgeois and colonial past did not suit the new orthodox communist central government. Nevertheless, these authorities, despite the ideological bond with the communistic schemes, including the prejudice towards capital and property, did not ruin the effects of the first "Golden Age" of urbanization and modernization of Shanghai that the Huangpu River Wharf called Bund (Chinese: *Waitan*) became in the 1920s and 1930s. This region still exists in good shape, with 33 addresses and 52 buildings collectively, nearly all of them recognized for their architectural value, both

[2]This Chinese stream can be found in the works of a famous political scientist and strategist from Tsinghua University — Yan Xuetong (Yan, 2011).

[3]According to classic calculations by Angus Maddison from OECD, in 1800 China was generating 1% of the global GDP whereas Great Britain only 4/3%. In 1890 China's contribution to the global GDP dropped to 13.2% and constituted a mere 5.2% in 1952. Maddison (1998); see also Ye (2011: 36–37).

[4]A more in-depth analysis of this subject see Wang (2012).

the ones built in the gothic revival style and those in neo-baroque style, but all of them being the most interesting collection of art deco in the world.[5] Shanghai at that stage was not only a huge industrial city, but was largely taking advantage of its location — a big harbour that boosted the financial and banking services. It was not the industry (mainly light one), but the financial activity that became Shanghai's trademark and gave it a reputation of an affluent city.

The Communist Party of China did not destroy Bund. However, they let the citizens who did not flee to Taiwan with Jiang Jieshi, or Hong Kong feel their strong aversion to the "ill past" of the region. This animosity was specifically expressed during over two decades of the left wing incidents, especially the "grand leap forward" (1958–1960) and "cultural revolution" (1966–1976). Despite the fact that it was in Shanghai that the Communist Party of China was created in July 1921, the city was not favoured by the party. On the contrary, it became the centre of the extreme left wing group Jiang Quing, associated with the last wife of the chief and dictator Mao Zedong, which, after the death of Mao (September 1976) and the fall of his wife a month later, was named "the Gang of Four" (*si ren bang*).[6]

The fall of the left wing unfortunately did not mean getting back to favours for Shanghai. American sociologist and political scientist Lynn T. White III from Princeton University for decades studied the situation of Shanghai. He proved that the new authorities, led by Deng Xiaoping, first of all had only good intentions to rebuild China as a global power, and, at the beginning of the reform period, at least in the field of agriculture, trusted the initiatives of the peasantry, who gave rise to those changes in the Yangtze Delta near Shanghai (White, 1998, 1999).[7]

It can be, thus, posed that Chinese reforms were initiated by pragmatic vision of Deng Xiaoping in the peripheries and suburbs of China,

[5]Architectonic details can be found on: Shanghai (2017).

[6]There is a detailed study of the eyewitness to those events, a correspondent in Beijing in those days Ludwik Mysak, see Mysak (1990).

[7]The process was initiated by the farmers form the village Xiaokang, Anhui province by signing a special cerograph stamped with thumbs dipped in their own blood. See details Li *et al.* (2014: 145). White (1998, 1999: 86–89) using source material proves that the first reforms were initiated in that area in the years 1971–1973, so still in the middle of the cultural revolution.

especially in the Yangtze Delta. Moreover, the dynamic changes pleasingly surprised the authorities. Deng Xiaoping himself admitted he did not expect such a success and commented:

> "Generally speaking, the reforms in villages were happening very fast and the peasants were very enthusiastic. It is not the achievement of our central government. Small and medium companies in towns and villages were registering 20% increase yearly. I did not expect that, similarly to the other companions. This is something that surprised us very much."[8]

As for Shanghai, the economical successes of the first decade of reforms, especially in agriculture and in villages, did not help much. Of course, in the context of fast development and the success of the first four economic zones, capitalistic enclaves of the communist giant that Shenzhen, Zhuhai, Xiamen, and Shanton became, there were 14 more zones opened, mainly in the harbour cities and on the coastline, including Shanghai. However, in the 1980s, the taxes in the entire Yangtze Delta remained high (White, 1998, 1999), whereas the government, at first concentrated on the success in agriculture that was in its prime, and then on the ideology connected with not fully successful process of profound reforms in the cities still ignored the potential of Shanghai. The attitude changed — gradually as always for China — in the years 1988–1990. Only then did Shanghai return to its classic position, namely a strong economical and financial hub and pioneer and leader of changes and modernization. The city finally began to take on not only the new challenges coming from deep transformation, but also more financial means from the government for urbanization. In terms of the circumstances of contemporary China, this phenomenon should be perceived if not as a synonym of modernization, reform programme, and openness to the world, then definitely as one of its most successful effects.

[8] Motto to the volume White (1998, 1999). The author adds that at the very beginning of the process of reforms "central government in Beijing did not have any clear, unified reform plan" (White, 1998, 1999: 3). This thesis seems to be right, there was a will and a vision on how to rebuilt China but there was no detailed outline or agenda for there was no precedence (Mikhail Gorbachev's reforms took place 7 years later), and the Chinese science completely destroyed during the "cultural revolution" was not fit for presenting reform programmes.

15.4. The Biggest Urbanization Process on a Global Scale

When China entered the "epoch of reforms and openness to the world" (*gaige, kaifang*) at the end of the 1970s, about 83% of Chinese society still lived in the villages. It was, thus, mainly a society of peasants and farmers. The Mao Zedong era (1949–1976) had not changed much in this respect. It is estimated, for there were no exact registers made in those days, that in 1949, when the Communist Party of China was coming to power, the percentage of Middle Kingdom citizens living in the villages was 88–92% (Tálas, 1991: 24–25). The industrial campaigns, so livid in those days, did not really change anything, and so farming and peasantry still dominated the country. The success of the reforms was due to the fact that the Chinese agriculture was made communist only in 1958, which meant that the work ethos of Chinese villagers did not die out in one generation, that it did not change it into the working farmers who had completely different mentality (a peasant would work on its plot day in day whereas a farmer only when necessary). Paradoxically, it was the conservative peasantry that became the spark for creativity and initiative that Shanghai used to be famous for and now could get back to it using the rural contract system (*baochan daohu*) — the first impulse for commercialization and privatization of the country.

In the first decade of the reforms, they used a system called *hukou*, which was a special identification number representing a personal ID on one hand, and documentation of the Tekst family on the other. It was nothing more than a method of complete tying the citizen, specifically the peasant, to the place of living.

According to the very good analysis presented by Jason Young, different cities had a different attitude towards *hukou*. Beijing, for example, was doing everything to stop the flow of the migrants from villages called *nongmin'gong*, whereas the largest at present metropolis in China — Chongqing with over 33 million citizens — was trying to attract them. It seems that Shanghai, which was not a subject of the author's study, was somewhere in-between; officially, they did not try to attract the migrants from villages, but at the same time they were using them largely, which was especially noticeable during the investment outburst right before the EXPO exhibition (Young, 2013).

Despite the difficulties connected with *hukou*, and officially propagated policy of *litu, bu lixiang* (leave the land, but do not leave the village), which was meant to distance from monoculture of cultivation while staying in the home village, many peasants quickly understood that big cities, where large building sites started to emerge, offered new prospects. The chance for better money was far from one's home village. Peasants, thus, started to mass-migrate to the cities.

This gave rise to the migrants, especially the above-mentioned *nonmin'gong,* who, until now, were unheard of in Republic of China. They were coming from villages and working mainly on the building sites, usually without any social security, because, after leaving their homes, they were losing *hukou,* so all benefits (and so did their children if they went with them, therefore it was uncommon for the peasants to take the whole family with them). Despite all that, the chance for better money was so tempting that this category of new citizens in the city, devoid of nearly all legal rights, was constantly increasing.

According to the official data of the National Bureau of Statistics of the Republic of China, the category of migrants was first registered in 1982 with 7 million people, so under 1% of the whole population. In 1990, the number increased to 22 million and the whole process gained on speed after 1992 when Deng Xiaoping, having drawn the correct conclusions from the fall of USSR, commanded China to go into globalization, open markets, and grow richer and richer.[9] In the meantime, China, that so far tried to reform the communist system, went into a different stage by many observers called the era of building national capitalism. It was then, after 1992, that the notions such as market, globalization, or urbanization gained a new, positive connotation both in the eyes of the authorities and citizens.

Because of taking on the new approach and pushing towards marketing and full exposure of the economy to the world, openness to the foreign

[9] It was so-called inspection in the south (*nan xun*) in January and February 1992 which was at the same time a kind of a political will of Deng. His strongly edited thoughts can be found in the third volume of "Selected Works" by Deng Xiaoping, see Deng (1993: 370–383). Detailed analysis of this key event in contemporary China, see Vogel (2011: 669–677).

market and capital, the number of people migrating to large cities increased considerably in comparison to the previous decade of "changes within the schedule."[10]

According to the same data of the National Bureau of Statistics, the number of migrants increased to 79 million in 2000, and further to 163 million in 2012.[11] It has been estimated that currently the number of migrants in China amounts to 265 million (Lardy, 2014: 17), so more than the McKinsey Institute predicted in 2009 (according to them, the population of migrants was meant to increase to 240 million by 2025). McKinsey prepared one of the best reports on Chinese urbanization entitled "Preparing for China's urban billion," in which they postulated that by 2025 the urban population of the Middle Kingdom would exceed 350 million and would be further aided by the above mentioned 240 million migrants. Moreover, they posed that in the Republic of China would by then be 221 cities with population over 1 million, and 23 megacities with population of over 5 million (McKinsey, 2009: 6–7). It seems all the predictions will be largely exceeded because the central authorities in Beijing are still putting fast urbanization as the key factor in the modernization process of the country. McKinsey report confirmed the unprecedented, biggest, and fastest urbanization process in history that happened in China after 1978, and certainly after 1992. Within the process, in 2011, for the first time in the history of that civilization (which was always mainly agricultural), the population in the cities exceeded the population of the villages. The plan of the fifth generation of the leaders, headed by Xi Jinping and Prime Minister Li Keqiang assumed that by 2030 the population of the cities in China would have made 65–70% of the population of the whole country.[12]

[10] It is a paraphrase of the title of one of the most important economic studies about the early stage of Chinese economic reform by Barry Naughton, see Naughton (1995).

[11] Data based on the "Report on the 2012 National Migrant Worker Investigation Survey," 27th of May 2013, Available at: www.stats.gov.cn [access: 02.12.2014].

[12] These urbanization aims were put forward by the Prime Minister Li Keqiang in his speech on the subject delivered on September 7, 2012. English version of the speech Available at: http://www.primeeconomics.org/wp-content/uploads/2013/06/Li-Keqiang-China-urbanization-speech.pdf [access: 06.09.2014].

15.5. Shanghai's Modernization — Phase 1

In the light of such tendencies, there has come time for yet another "Golden Age" for Shanghai. The greatest researcher of Shanghai and Yangtze Delta, the above-mentioned Lynn T. White III, has rightly concluded that the main reason for the central government in Beijing to pay more interest in Shanghai in the second half of the 1980s was resource deficiency. The city was needed not only as a port, but also as a source of additional capital. At first, the decision was made to limit the compulsory deliveries (their number dropped from 150 categories of material in 1984 to 35 3 years later) (White, 1998, 1999: 171–174) and move fast to the contract system based on the one introduced in villages earlier. This movement obviously brought the old traditions of banking back and made Shanghai again an important financial centre of the entire Republic of China (White, 1998, 1999: 313). It would be worth mentioning that the Yangtze Delta had already been richer than other regions in 1985. Income *per capita* there at that stage was 1,174 Yuan, whereas the national rate was only 529 Yuan (White, 1998, 1999: 235). That gave rise to one of the biggest problems of China in that era, namely rapid social division and deep income disparities. The first decisions about the necessary development of the city were made already in 1988, but implementation of those was partially halted due to the incidents on the Tiananmen Square in spring 1989. Despite this, though, the first development plan of the city for the years 1989–2008 was agreed in exactly 1989. According to this plan, a decision to create a special zone and built the most modern district in the world using the so far neglected area of Pudong was made. Thanks to this, a completely new urban fabric in areas so far desolate began to form.

The realization of the first spatial building layout of the city gained on speed after the encouragement Deng Xiaopang gave to his successors in 1992, calling for people of Shanghai to open their minds and keep the hard work of developing the city. In Chinese culture, nearly always ruled from above, Xiaopang's encouragement was nothing less than an order. From then on, Shanghai began to develop rapidly. The major points of this development were as follows:

- it was decided to destroy the housing tissue, which was mainly in very bad condition and failing to fulfil any criteria of a modern urban built-up.

From 1992 until 2000, 650,000 flats and dwellings were demolished, all of which were in the areas considered by the international standards as slums;

- in place of the destroyed architecture, new skyscrapers began to be erected, modelled on the shop window, which, at that time, was the Pudong district. It is estimated that until 2008 there had been 4,000 skyscrapers built, so twice as many as in Manhattan;
- apart from modernization of the housing tissue, it was decided on increasing the housing space *per capita* (from 6 m² to 22 m²), and at the same time, decrease the density of the city, which was very high (c. 280 people per hectare, whereas in USA and western Europe the rate oscillates between 15 and 35 people per hectare). In addition to that, it was also agreed to increase the area of green space per citizen (to c. 10 m² per person);
- Since the opening of the first high technology zone in 1990 called Caoheng, they began the process of building special high-technology parks in the city. This project has been gaining on speed and so far, there have been 26 of these parks created.

15.6. Shanghai Modernization — Phase 2, and the Second "Golden Age"

At the end of the first decade of the 20th century, after the crash on the western markets (starting with USA), when it began to perspire that China is growing as a new global power, the plans concerning Shanghai's future became even more ambitious. The proof of that can be found in the programme document "Plan of the city development" from 2008, which was an amendment to the "Master city plan of the megalopolis of Shanghai" from 1999. Earlier on, the emphasis was put on the EXPO world exhibition in 2010, which was the real incentive for the modernization of the city.

The EXPO, held on 528 hectares on the bank of Huangpu river from May 1, till October 31, 2010, helped both the city authorities and the central government in Beijing to realise the master project to transform Shanghai into a global city for its infrastructure and solutions (architectonic, technological). The cost of organizing this huge exhibition (73 million visitors as comparing to the one held in Osaka in 1970 where only 64 million people visited the place) was estimated for nearly 12 billion Yuan. This undoubtedly boosted the city's growth.

It was then, during the preparations for the EXPO, that it was agreed to make Shanghai the Dragon Head (*Long Tou*) of the whole Yangtze Delta, and subsequently the whole China understood as a new global power. Therefore, more, hard to estimate, means were spent on various architectonic experiments specifically in the Pudong area. The greatest architects and architectonic companies were invited to China to work on the project. Therefore, at the beginning of the 21st century, Shanghai became an architectonic laboratory on a global scale. The latest architectonic project in the Pudong area, namely the construction of the tallest building in China — the Shanghai Tower serves as evidence for that. The project was prepared by the international company Gensler. The construction works ended in October 2014, and the building was commissioned in 2015. It is 632 metres high and consists of 121 floors, above which there are additional nine "sky lobbies" fitted with stage rooms, restaurants and clubs. The whole building is covered with a double glazed facade to save the energy. During the construction works that began in November 2008, and cost estimated $4.2 billion, they used — according to the main project manager of Gensler, Jun Xia — 43 modern technologies designed to reduce the use of energy and save the natural environment. Moreover, the entire building rotates around its own axis, which, according to the constructors, guards it against strong wind power (one must not forget Shanghai's coastal location makes the city prone to typhoons).

The pace and character of the urbanization process in the Pudong area is defined by the fact that, as the constructors wanted, Shanghai Tower stands next to the two other skyscrapers, which are symbols of the Pudong panorama. One of them is erected in 1999 Jin Mao tower (architect: Adrian Smith from renowned company Skidmore, Owings, and Merrill), the other is, commissioned in 2008 and run by the Japanese, the Shanghai's World Financial Centre (architects: American company Kohn, Pedersen, Fox), commonly known as "the bottle opener." The abovementioned Jun Xia explains that the three objects are a kind of a trinity with the Jin Mao symbolizing China in the past, World Financial Centre — contemporary China, and Shanghai Tower — China in the future. The trinity manifests the fast architectonic and urban changes and reforms happening in China. What was modern a decade ago is now obsolete or requires deep reconstruction.

According to the mentioned planning programme documents, Shanghai as the Dragon Head was meant to be not only the centre of urbanization with futuristic architecture, but most of all a key economic and world financial centre equal if not better to the most important ones in this field such as New York, London City or Hong Kong. The paramount decisions concerning this plan were made during the meeting of the central government in Beijing on March 25, 2009, which was China's answer to the crisis on the global markets. According to them, Shanghai is to become a double financial centre (*shuang zhongxin*), and a large port. The unexpected success of the EXPO would soon prove that the ambitious plans of Shanghai's development were further expanded.

It was presumed then, that a "multifunctional centre within the global financial system" would have to be created. It was meant to happen not only through the 1990 exchange (one of the two existing in China, the second functioning in Shenzhen), but also through the headquarters of big investment funds, insurance corporations, hedging funds, and, of course, the biggest global and Chinese banks. Among the last ones, there was the Bank of Development of the grouping BRICS[13] created in the second half of 2014, which is an organization considered as a synonym of new economic development in the world, within which, apart from the strongest economies in the world, more and more voice begin to have countries representing emerging markets. BRICS, so Brazil, Russia, India, China, and South Africa, gathers the most dynamic ones. This bank has an initial capital of $200 billion and is meant to challenge the USA dominated system Bretton Woods. In other words, it is from Shanghai, not only from Washington that the news about the best investments or which country received how much for development projects are coming.

The project of the central government form March 2009 has consequently been implemented. Overall, there are headquarters of around 300 companies from the renowned list of the Forbes magazine in

[13] Grouping acronym referring to the countries of Brazil, Russia, India, China, and South Africa.

Shanghai now. Around 62 biggest banks in the world have their representatives there. According to the Global Financial Centre Index (GFCI) prepared by London City, Shanghai was on the 35th position in 2009. In 2013, the city was already 24th on the list, gaining 674 points (first on the list was London with 807 points) and in 2014, Shanghai was 20th on the list with 695 points (first on the list was then New York with 786 points). The authorities of the city, however, have a reason to worry, as in the last ranking of GFCI, Shanghai came after Shenzhen (18th), and moreover, is regularly preceded by Hong Kong. The ambitions are, thus, not fully satisfied.

Another big aim in the perspective is new projects and infrastructural solutions. There are "three ports" mentioned in the documents, namely airports, harbours and cyberspace, and "two fast roads," so motorways and fast trains. In addition to that, a new project was added to expand the system of underground rail by four times between 2005–2020. At present, the underground in Shanghai has the longest network in China, longer than the one in Beijing. It is 523 km long and has 14 lines and 330 stations, and it carries c. 2, 5 million passengers per day.

The first communicational undertaking which drew the world's attention to Shanghai as a modern city was finishing, in cooperation with Germany, a part of the magnetic network Maglev on the December 31, 2002. It connected the centre of the city with Pudong airport which was under construction at that time, whereas the old one Hongqiao began to be modernized and enlarged for the expected visitors, mainly Chinese, that were to come for the EXPO. Both big airports, cleverly incorporated in the underground system, are connecting Shanghai with 141 cities in 29 countries.

The changes that happened in China after opening the 40 km part of Maglev (the journey lasts several minutes as the train can reach the speed of 400 km/h) determined the decision to stop building another such part to connect Shanghai with not far Hangzhou. Instead, they quickly started to build fast trains using their own, rather than German, technology. The longest so far (2,298 km), and the most important for China railway connecting Beijing with Shanghai and Guangzhou in the south, was being commissioned in parts between the years 2009–2012. At present, the plan is to extend the railway to Hong Kong. The train can develop a speed of

300 km/h. It could go faster, however, this speed limit was imposed on the train after the first and only catastrophe since its exploitation, in July 2011 in Wenzhou.

Shanghai is, thus, constantly one big construction site. The cost of the infrastructural reforms makes 10% of GDP (out of which 40% goes to the development of the transport system). Despite the move of the present authorities towards the concept of sustainable development, there are no changes in the investment field or rapid urbanization. There is a change, though, in the social security, which transpires through the rising income *per capita*. This goes with another idea of the central government, namely putting emphasis on the national market consumption rather than export. To achieve that, one needs consumer power and middle class, which resembles the creation of *xiaokang shehiu* — the society of moderate prosperity. Within the new course, Shanghai authorities have planned to raise the average income from 45,200 Yuan in 2005 to 157,000 Yuan in 2025. In the years 1990–2005, the income *per capita* was increasing by average 9% in a year, and in 2010 was $11,809. It is expected to grow even faster now. Moreover, they anticipate the process of modernization to gain on speed. The best evidence for that was the new Action Plan for the years 2011–2013, which was about building the so-called Smart City. According to this plan, further development of the city would be based on innovation driven transformation. At the beginning of the process, two aims were outlined, namely, that by 2015 Shanghai would have been connected to Wi-Fi, and all the big buildings would have had access to the fast broadband. Much attention in the document was paid to scientific and technological progress, and innovations in the whole city, not only in specific, technological, or economical spheres.

Even more emphasis on technological and scientific progress was put in the context of the decisions of the central government from August 2013, in the light of which there was to be created a new experimental economical zone — *Shanghai Ziyou Maoyi Shiyangqu*. At first, an area of 29 km² was planned for it; however, it might take up to 1,210 km² and connect to already existing areas of this kind in the Pudong area. The construction started a month after the political decision, so in September 2013. The zone is meant to be an experimental field for new economical and technological solutions. One can conclude, that this time the idea is not only to attract foreign capital but also to welcome new technologies and innovations. With that, Shanghai as the Dragon Head is being subjected to the new strategy of development of the country, which the present authorities of the fifth generation of leaders have been trying to introduce since 2013. According to the strategy, more attention would be paid to the quality of the product and sustainable development rather than quantity and fast growth. The main economical power is expected to come from the domestic consumption and innovative economy rather than from export. The ambitious plans of China's transformation would not be possible without the economical, technological, and architectonical experiments carried out in Shanghai, which has already become a new modern megalopolis on a global scale.

15.7. Conclusions

- In the past three and a half decades, China went through a very important civilization progress. From a developing country plagued by poverty, it developed into the second world economical power, the biggest country disposing large capital and trading on the entire globe. One of the biggest directions of these changes was the process of urbanization, thanks to which China, in 2011, finally, broke from the classic image of the previous civilization, so the domination of peasants in the society.
- In the light of this unprecedented process of fast urbanization after 1992, when China opened its gates to the globalization and foreign markets, Shanghai was elected as the Dragon's Head. From that moment, the city was meant to be the example and proof of new possibilities and growing potential in every aspect.
- Unfortunately, central government in Beijing and the municipal authorities of Shanghai carefully planning the development of the city do not expect any initiatives undertaken by the civil society and their participation in that process. It is still going to be a process centrally planned and directed from above.
- China, and the Dragon's Head which Shanghai represents, are undoubtedly going forward with modern technologies in the urbanization process such as creating more green spots, sustainable development, or building an intelligent city.

- The plans, however, strike with a lack of alternatives for a fast urbanization. There seems to be no fear for the threat to the environment or climate changes, which, according to the latest report of Intergovernmental Panel on Climate Change (IPCC), are largely caused by fast urbanization. The process of movement is still perceived as a positive phenomenon in China, and little thought is being spared for any ecological, or social threats that it might pose. This attitude somehow contradicts the developmental strategy from 2012, on the basis of which a new "green economy" was meant to be implemented. Will this contradiction be ever noticed? There is little mention about this issue in the Chinese literature although the problem of ecological threats is strongly emphasized in the estimation of China by the outside world.
- There is no evidence in the planning documents for further development of Shanghai of any thought about devastating results of fast urbanization for the social structure such as empty estates, high rate of social inequality, and speculation of vast areas for new investments, not to mention destruction of the public sphere.
- There is a plan to improve the standard of living and income for the citizens, but the quality of life plays second role, and the pathology of the urbanization process such as breaking the social bond or reluctance towards foreigners seems to go unnoticed among Chinese and Shanghai authorities.

The history of Shanghai development in the last quarter of a century can be described as a continuous success. This unprecedented and unquestionable urbanization victory calls for more profound reflection, namely, where is the urbanization process leading to? When on July 1, 1997 Hong Kong was being overtaken by the Republic of China, there were fears of its communization. The history of Shanghai in the last years proves a completely opposite process of so-called "hong kong-isation" of still communist China.

What will happen though, when not only the people of Shanghai and Yangtze Delta but of the whole Republic of China, so a population of c. 1.4 billion will fall for the promoted since 2010 Chinese Dream (*Zhongguo Meng*), which is a synonym of the American Dream? It might turn out that if Chinese, and following them Hindu people (population of over 1.3 billion) and representatives of other "rising markets" want to truly live, our planet Earth might be too small for this kind of consumption and innovation. For the fact that Shanghai represents the Dragon's Head, so the fastest developing economic organism on the globe, and wants to be the most modern megalopolis of the contemporary world, it would be worth asking where the civilization is actually going. Are we taking the right path? Is China's approach actually the right one in the face of more questions about the fast climate changes and ecological threats?

Shanghai of the last decades, similarly to China, represents a history of economical success. However, close observation of the phenomenon poses a question if it is only the economical success that is so important. The latest examples undoubtedly show that the attention has been paid to the ecological issues and standard of living of the citizens. Is it enough and not too late though? Although Chinese authorities proudly expose Shanghai as a victory story, a close observer will quickly notice the pros and cons of this fast modernization and urbanization.

References

Acharya, A. (2014). *The End of American World Order.* Oxford: Oxford University Press.

Deng, X. (1993). *Wenxuan* (Selected Works), Vol. III. Beijing: Renmin Chubanshe.

Fact Sheets (2017). "Yangtze River Delta: Fact Sheets": Retrieved from http://2016.export.gov/china/build/groups/public/@bg_cn/documents/webcontent/bg_cn_075985.pdf [access: 21.09.2017].

Hu, A. (2011). *China in 2020: A New Type of Superpower.* Washington: Brookings Institution.

Lardy, N. (2014). *Markets over Mao: The Rise of Private Business in China.* Washington: Peterson Institute for International Economics.

Li, H., G. Yun and S. Qifa (2014). *Chinese Road. Updated Versio.* Beijing: Huang Shan Publishing House.

Li, Keqiang. Speech (2012). Retrieved from http://www.primeeconomics.org/wp-content/uploads/2013/06/Li-Keqiang-China-urbanization-speech.pdf [access: 06.09.2014].

Maddison, A. (1998). *Monitoring the World Economy 1820–1992.* Paris: OECD Publishing.

McKinsey (2009). *Preparing for China's urban billion*. McKinsey Global Institute. March. Retrieved from http://www.mckinsey.com/global-themes/urbanization/preparing-for-chinas-urban-billion [access: 25.03.2017].

Mysak, L. (1990). *Chiński Proces Stulecia*. Warszawa: Alfa Publishing House.

Naughton, B. (1995). *Growing Out of the Plan. Chinese Economic Reform 1978–1993*. Cambridge: Cambridge University Press.

Shanghai (2017). Retrieved from https://www.chinahighlights.com/shanghai/attraction/the-bund.htm [access: 21.09.2017].

Tálas, B. (1991). *Economic Reforms and Political Reform Attempts in China: 1979–1989*. Berlin–New York–Tokyo: Springer-Verlag.

The Economist (2017). "What China can learn from Pearl River delta — Special Report". Retrieved from http://www.economist.com/news/special-report/21720072-pearl-river-delta-chinas-most-dynamic-open-and-innovative-region-says-vijay [access: 21.09.2017].

Vogel, E.F. (2011). *Deng Xiaoping and the Transformation of China*. Cambridge, Massachusetts, London: Harvard University Press.

Wang, Z. (2012). *Never Forget National Humiliation: Historical Memory in Chinese Politics and Foreign Relations*. New York: Columbia University Press.

White, L.T. (1998 and 1999). *Unstately Power, Vol. I: Local Causes of China's Economic Reforms and II: Local Causes of China's Intellectual, Legal and Governmental Reforms*. New York: M.E. Sharpe.

Yan, X. (2011). *Ancient Chinese Thought, Modern Chinese Power*. Princeton: Princeton University Press.

Ye, Z. (2011). *Inside China's Grand Strategy: The Perspective form the People's Republic*. Kentucky: The University of Kentucky Press.

Young, J. (2013). *Hukou System: Markets, Migrants, and Institutional Change*. New York: Palgrave.

16

MEXICO CITY — AN ANTITHESIS OF SUSTAINABLE DEVELOPMENT?

Urszula Żuławska and Elżbieta Żuławska-Sobczyk

16.1. Introduction

Mexico City belongs to the largest agglomerations in the world. The population of the Metropolitan Zone of the Mexican Valley (Spanish: ZMVM),[1] although difficult to estimate, undoubtedly oscillates around 20 million. In 1940s it was growing fast — at the rate of 6.7% per year (Ward, 1998); however, at the turn of the century, the number dropped to 1.8%. Despite the efforts of the public administration to control the process of urbanization, the growth of the agglomeration has usually been a spontaneous process. Due to the historical events, the city was situated in a very specific location, in the mountain basin, 2,000 m above sea level, in a seismic area, surrounded by volcanoes reaching the height of 5,000 m. Therefore, it posed additional difficulties in ensuring the basic municipal services and proper functioning of the city.

A sustained development, which, as a model, occurs when it does not limit the future development possibilities, should be based on three key factors: economic, social, and environmental. One of the aspects which facilitated a boom in the growth of the city in the middle of the 20th century,

[1] *Zona Metropolitana del Valle de Mexico.*

was rapid industrialization, which, directly and indirectly, created jobs for people with and without qualifications; in this case for new migrants from the villages. Notwithstanding, with time both collective and individual cost of functioning of such a large population living in such a disadvantaged location was rising faster than the population itself. The economic factor, thus, made the further growth of the agglomeration difficult although the job opportunities were still very attractive.

Regional and family relationships have always encouraged migration to the city. For villagers, settling down in the city would have been usually impossible without the help of their relatives. Thus, the socio-cultural pillar had a strong, stable position in the megacity system; it not only stimulated the growth of a city but also played an important role in the social relations. However, in the course of time, the sentiments and values brought over from the region of origin gradually faded away being replaced by new, urban ones, not always conclusive. The new paramount socio-cultural elements of proper functioning of an agglomeration were the access to education and, to a slightly smaller extent, to culture and medical care.

Within the scope of socio-cultural damage, apart from the broken relationships and crime, one should include lack of respect towards cultural heritage. Sudden, usually badly or not planned at all, growth of a city may lead to the devastation of historical objects.

The impact of the city growth on the natural environment must be enormous; the question is, however, how much has been done in Mexico City in order to reduce the environmental expense.

In this chapter, we will try to discuss the process of growth of the agglomeration taking into account the three factors of sustained development. Moreover, we will try to present the attempts to control the process by the public administration, the additional issues arising from the historically shaped management system of a metropolitan area, as well as determine and postulate the path for necessary changes.

16.2. The Growth of the Agglomeration

Table 16.1 and Fig. 16.1 present the ratio of population growth of the metropolitan zone of Mexico City. The biggest surge in the population of the agglomeration occurred in the period between the WWII up until the

Table 16.1. The population of the metropolitan zone of Mexico City

Year	Population	Year	Population
1790	104,760	1940	1,802,679
1820	179,830	1950	3,137,599
1857	200,000	1960	5,251,755
1870	225,000	1970	8,799,937
1884	300,000	1980	13,354,271
1895	339,935	1990	15,047,685
1900	344,721	1995	16,387,087
1910	471,066	2000	17,358,715
1921	615,367	2005	18,105,399
1930	1,029,068	2010	20,116,842

Explanations: Up until 1930 estimated data, from 1940 the result of population census.

Source: 1790–2005: Instituto Nacional de Estadística y Geografía (INEGI), Estadisticas Historicas de México 2009, 2010: Consejo Nacional de Población, México enCifras 2010.

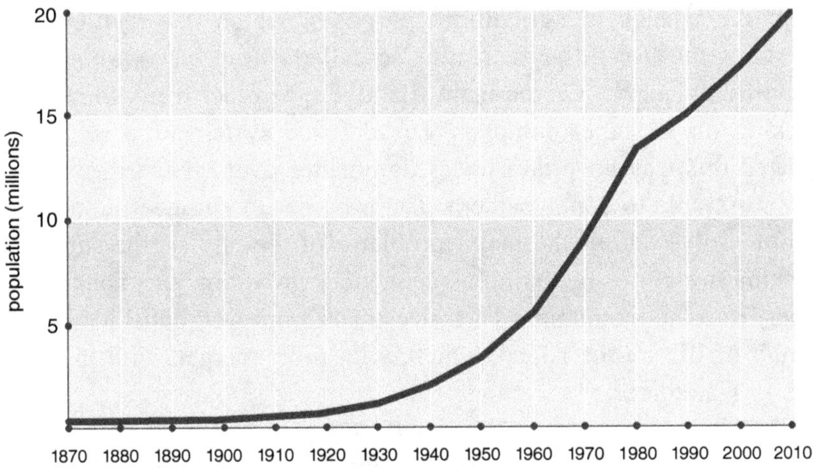

Fig. 16.1. Population of the metropolitan zone of Mexico City

Source: Based on the data presented in Table 16.1.

end of 1980, so in the period of predominant industrialization highly stimulated by the state. The rate of growth has also intensified in the last years. Despite such a fast rate of expansion in population of the metropolitan zone, its input in the general population of all Mexican cities has subsided because the urbanization process has included the smaller cities of the country. The area of constant development of the city in the last 2 centuries has evolved from a Federal District (FD) to the whole basin and so into the neighbouring states. We will discuss the possible implications of this phenomenon for the administration of a metropolitan area further on in the chapter.

16.3. Historical Background of the City

In order to analyze the contemporary problems of Mexico City, we need to go back in history to the pre-Columbian times. The foundation of the city dates back to c. 1325, when, evicted from other regions of the Valle de Mexico, Mexican Indians known as Aztecs settled on two islands on the Texcoco Lake — Tenochtitlan and Tlatelolco. Stronger tribal groups pushed the tribe out of the relatively better regions of the Texcoco Lake; however, the island location of the city was yet to determine the strength of the Aztecs. In order to survive, they needed to adapt the islands to agricultural purposes, which they achieved by extending the area through creating so-called *chinampas* — small plots on artificial islands. On the main island, on the other hand, they began working on a chapel complex. The defence system of a settlement situated this way gave the Aztecs dominance over other tribes and so they were able to conquer them. The progress in engineering allowed them to solve one of the major problems of the city — the supply of drinking water — by building aqueducts providing the island with water from the mountains. This investment improved considerably the quality of life on the island, which, with time, merged with the other one — Tlatelolco.

This "American Venice" greeted Cortes at the beginning of the 16th century. Defeated in numerous battles, he finally managed to take over control of the city by cutting off the water aqueducts. Colonizers built-up the islands, covering the Aztec architecture, and this process, with time, reduced the size of the lake. Due to the lack of the outflow from the Mexican basin, during major rainfalls waters contaminated with various waste would flood the city. Therefore, efforts began to build a sewerage system. At the turn of the 19th and 20th centuries, thus, the main lake and four smaller ones completely disappeared. This enabled a successive merge of smaller cities, formerly built on the shore of the lake like San Angel or Tlalpan, with the main one.

The city was expanding, however not until the industrialization process started, so after gaining the independence (1810–1821) in the second half of the 19th century, it became as dynamic as in the cities of industrial Europe. Streams flowing down the mountains supplied the city with not only water but also energy needed for industry, predominantly textile one. The technology was brought over from Europe, whereas work force and materials were native. Personal relationships of the first industrialists with the government and ruling bodies secured profitable regulations and, in a way, demand for goods.

The first period of this rapid development of the industry was more about territorial rather than demographic expansion. In the years 1858–1910, the population of the urban area increased more than two and a half times, whereas the territory expanded by five times. Although new districts called colonies were being formed, the density of the old regions was not rising. The initiators of the city expansion were land traders, called *fraccionadores*,[2] who were building residential camps along the major transport arteries, which slowly began to shape the public transport.

The utilization of the region can be divided into two types: away from the city centre, surrounded by plenty of green spots and single-family detached buildings, and close or in the centre of the city, an area of compressed buildings, often a few storey tenement houses.

Very specific forms of buildings were the so-called *quarters* with a small road or street in the middle accessible only to the residents of the particular quarter. The original character of some of the residential districts has been preserved up until the second half of the 20th century and some features can still be observed in the contemporary outlook of the city. As for

---

[2] *Fraccionadore* — from Spanish: a sub-divider, a person who sub divides and sells land generally for residential development.

the structure itself, from the beginning of the 1930s, Mexico City retained the characteristics of low-density build-up in the art deco urban style, adjusted to the old natural forms with large green areas. However, from the time of Mexican Revolution in 1910, a considerable increase in the influx of proletariat to the city can be observed, both to the areas formerly occupied primarily by the upper class people and to the new colonies. For the less affluent people, *fraccionadores* were parcelling the land according to the wealth of the migrants. Therefore, the plots sold by them began to get smaller and narrower, which led to formation of so-called *vecindades* — rows of small dwellings surrounding a patio or yard (Vargas, 2009).

In the 20th century, with the rapid urbanization of Mexico, the role of the *fraccionadores* became more prominent and went beyond the land trade. Up until 1920, when the first complex law on the building process was passed (Distrito Federal, 1920), they freely decided on the size of the plot, direction for the construction process, and the building types. In 1927, however, Ley de Planificacion (Planning Law) for Mexico came into force — an early form of development strategy. The biggest influence on the Mexican urbanization process in that period had three architects: Jose Luis Cuevas, Hans Meyer, and Enrique Yanez. The three of them established La Escuela Superior de Planificacion y Urbanismo (Institute of Planning and Urbanism) at the University of Technology in Mexico. Their involvement contributed to the change in the approach towards urbanization problem.

The 1930s brought on a consolidation of the former actions in the urbanization field and further activation in managing the urbanized areas. The outbreak of the WWII speeded up the process of industrialization and migration to the city. Populating the areas of the city was not enough at this stage; therefore, the new districts began to absorb the neighbouring villages. The urban tissue began to expose the social classification, which, in terms of urban planning, could be characterized by smaller plots, downsizing the public space and areas of green spots. The newly created districts usually had an orthogonal street network with predominantly single-family detached houses and multifamily dwellings along the major communicational tracks.

During this period, Mexico was influenced by the thought of a French architect Le Corbusier much appreciated by Mexican architects. Based on Le Corbusier's idea, new multifamily blocks of flats began to emerge together with a new social plan for the residents, green spots, and communication system, giving the opportunity to separate the pedestrians form those using public and private transport. Many of those residential areas were built with the consent of the big national institutions, which were building them for their employees. The flats were available for their staff; however, these were not their property, which very often adversely affected the space and residential buildings (Gortázar, 1994).

One of the architects most impressed and influenced by the ideas of Le Corbusier and his concept on residential flats was Mario Pan, the creator of many residential blocks of flats in the city such as Unidad Presidente Aleman or Tlatelolco, which resemble the council estates like those found for example, in Hackney, NE London. Designed for the middle class in the past, these estates are nowadays a nightmare for the local authorities, for they are mainly inhabited by socially inept people who are often in conflict with law and pose a threat to the other residents.

Technical progress — the result of industrialization — brought on new techniques and building materials. Cement was not only used for the construction of dwellings but also the infrastructure, especially the sewerage system draining water from the former Texcoco lake. Due to the progress in petrochemical industry, they started to use asphalt on a wide range, both for building roads and in construction. Unfortunately, the obsession with creating new arteries badly affected the old part of the city. By opening two new highways — 20 de Noviembre and San Juan de Letran — they destroyed many historical buildings.

The first half of the 20th century did not facilitate the architectonic heritage of the city. Hardly anybody appreciated the value of the old buildings and, as a result, many of them were destroyed to create a space for new, modern ones, usually of little or no architectonic value. Around 3 years later, in 1931, during the International Congress of Modern Architecture (CIAM), the adoption of Athens Charter brought the Law on Conservation of Historical Buildings and Monuments, Residential Areas and Natural Beauty.[3] This law, however, like many subsequent laws on conservation of old buildings, remained dormant for many years.

---

[3] *Ley de Protección y Conservación de Monumentos Arqueológicos e Históricos, Poblaciones Tipicas y Lugares de Belleza Natural.*

In 1950s and 1960s, the flow of migrants to Mexico City gained strength, the city was getting bigger and bigger and the growth became more and more chaotic. The colonies on the outskirts of the city transformed into poor and overpopulated estates. Hence, the rich began to search for a new location, first in the centre of the city, then, with time, in the more remote outskirts formerly considered unsuitable for building. This is how one of the most beautiful estates in Mexico City has been formed — *Jardines de Pedregal de San Angel.* It was designed by Luis Barragana and his associates. The project started in 1948. Jardines (from Spanish: gardens) were created on the terrain rich in volcanic rock, where on each plot they built a single-family high standard house, isolated from the outside world.

The problems of the metropolis began to increase in the following years. They started to evict people from the south and south-west slums in the outskirts to built villas and tall blocks of flats for the middle class. The construction of tower blocks began to be problematic due to the seismic nature of the terrain. At the beginning of 1980s, there were only a few tower blocks in the city. The biggest — 8.1 — earthquake in the history of the city, on September 19, 1985, caused most of the smaller blocks of flats to collapse, leaving only the tallest tower blocks still standing. Many public buildings, mainly hospitals and ministries were destroyed. According to the official data, 9.5 thousand people died as a result of the quake, the unofficial sources (ComunidadInformativa, 2014) talk about as many as 40,000 dead. A total of 412 buildings were completely demolished, 5,728 were damaged. Around 100,000 families lost their homes (De la Madrid, 1986). It has been assessed that some of the reasons of such a severe damage were inappropriate construction techniques (it was mainly the big public buildings that were destroyed), also geological conditions in the city centre, which was originally a lake. After that catastrophe, one might notice a change in the direction of the expansion to the south and west of the city, especially with the formation of office and service buildings. The terrain there was mainly formed on steep slopes formerly utilized in farming or for the purpose of recreation. The eruption of tower buildings took place mainly in the western areas. The location of the new estates caused further problems and rising expense of infrastructure. The other parts of the outskirts were reserved for the poorer part of the society, although the standard of living and social service there were improving. Alas, the metropolitan authorities made more effort to solve the problems of the agglomeration rather than to prevent them.

16.4. Three Pillars of the Sustainable Development

16.4.1. Economy

The region defined as Metropolitan Zone of the Mexico Valley (*Zona Metropolitana de Valle de Mexico*) has a great economical potential. It constitutes about a third of the GDP, more than the GDP of any other Latin American country with the exception of Brazil, Argentina, and Mexico itself. However, in the last two decades the number has slightly dropped by around 2.5 percentage point. One should probably add about 10 percentage points of GDP to this number produced in the informal sector of the agglomeration (Centro de Estudios para la Zona Metropolitana, 2006). Some changes might be observed in the economic structure of the region: from the industrial production to services; from the heavy to light industry; from traditional to modern technology; from concentrating the business in the centre of the city to the metropolitan peripheries; from material consuming production to the use of the latest technologies (Ward, 1998).

When the first factories were built in 19th century — mainly textile ones — it was clear that the best solution is to locate them in the capital for a number of reasons, the geographical conditions (so streams supplying water and energy), job offers for both qualified and unqualified people, easier access to financing and institutional support (Marichal and Cerutti, 1997). Almost two hundred years of industrialization of Mexico City shows a very strong bond with the administration of the country. It would be very difficult to undertake big production projects without personal connections in the governing bodies. On the other hand, the very interventional country created highly sophisticated administrational system, so more job vacancies especially for the middle class people. This created numerous job opportunities in the service sector (house cleaners, chefs, drivers, guardians, gardeners, laundresses, etc.) without demanding qualifications, which was very profitable for the new migrants from the villages. It is important to mention that earnings were rather symbolical;

nevertheless, the employees could get the roof over their heads and food. The big group of the service sector created the need for their own specific demand for goods and service adjusted to their very small profit, and so created other job opportunities (Romer, 2014). This process is practically constant, new generations of immigrants, thanks to the acquired skills and education, improve their material status. They are, however, replaced by new immigrants from the villages. Even though, due to the technological progress, the average number of people employed in the service sector is decreasing, employment in informal trade is increasing. Because of the development of industrial centres along the border with USA, there is no need to keep the heavy industry in the centre of the country anymore. However, the importance of the service grows (INEGI, 2013). The real danger for the economy of the agglomeration is not entirely the disappearance of the industry and economical restructuring — the job market in the metropolis remains the most attractive in the country — but the rising cost of functioning of the mega city. The direct cost of water supply, drainage system, transport negates economic rationale of so densely populated region. It is, thus, important to investigate the balance in the remaining pillars of the sustained development.

16.4.2. Society

The quality of life in the metropolitan region is determined not only by the revenue of a household but also by its material resources and access to the public services. The average income of the household is higher than in other parts of the Mexico, about three times higher than in the poorest regions of the country (Estudio de salarios, 2013). It is also the most variable in the world. Suffice to say, one of the residents of the FD is Carlos Slim, one of the richest people in the world. Access to the communal service is not fast enough comparing to the growth of the megacity, however, in the older districts that already have the infrastructure developed, the only problem would be the irregular water supply. So far, the shortage in water supply happens only at times and can be prevented by collecting water in tanks. The highest expense for those who live in the agglomeration is the cost of local transport. Only the wealthy residents are free from the hassle, for they can fly helicopters. The average time to commute to work in Mexico City is 90 minutes and is constantly increasing. For the poorest people living in the outskirts, apart from the high cost of transport, the main problem is the waste of time (Escobar *et al.*, 2009).

As far as the middle class is concerned, one solution to the situation is to reside near the place of work. Most people, however, do not have the opportunity; they are forced to live in the remote districts where the cost of living is the lowest. The situation on the property market is very bad for people with low income and is steadily getting worse; the index of room per person is dropping (Pantaleón, 2012).

The crucial element determining the attractiveness of the Mexican agglomeration is the job market, although very often informal but enabling stable income. The biggest advantage of living in the agglomeration is the access to public as well as private education at all levels. Education is the fastest way of improving social status, which, in Mexico City, is possible even for those families with very limited income. It would be difficult to name more than one renowned university outside the capital (IMF, 2007).

Mexico City also offers — although only to the formal sector employees and affluent people — access to a medical care of a decent standard, and to some individuals even of the world standard. This is undoubtedly an attractive factor in comparison to other places in Mexico, not mentioning the countryside. One cannot forget, however, that most migrants are not employed in the formal sector, therefore they cannot count on free of charge medical care, it has to be fully paid or delivered by numerous charity organizations.

Access to cultural goods is available for the middle or upper class people, whereas others tend to turn to folklore, which projects the traditional culture from their place of origin. This part of society puts a lot of interest in the green areas, which, due to the lack of their own yards and patios, they use as a place for Sunday family and friends gatherings usually in the company of people coming from the same area of the country. Unfortunately, the amount of green spots in the agglomeration constantly decreases.

In the last several years, one of the main factors bringing people to Mexico City has been a better personal safety than in the smaller towns or villages. It seemingly contradicts the common notion that the crime is constantly increasing in large cities. The plague of the country in the last two decades, however, has been the organized crime successfully controlled and limited in the metropolitan region thanks to the concentration of security forces in the capital (Mayer-Serra, 2012). Security forces are also less connected to the organized crime in the city than in the small provinces. That, however, does not mean it is safe in Mexico City, it is only relatively safer than in other regions of this very dangerous country (Żuławska, 2015). The example here could be the events in the autumn of 2014: while the student manifestation in one province resulted in a massacre and disappearance of 41 manifesting, in the capital it ended in beating of some demonstrators and violation of the autonomy of the university.

16.4.3. Environment

The impact of a developing city on the environment must be enormous; the question is how much has been done in the case of Mexico City to lower the environmental cost of the city growth. Since Cortez's conquer of Mexico City 500 years ago, the traditional unique form of cultivation on artificial islands, *chinampas,* is systematically disappearing. The city also absorbs other agronomic regions including the so-called *ejidos*[4]; the forests are disappearing too. Nevertheless, losing the tillage areas in a huge country such as Mexico does not pose a major issue. Concern that is more important is the loss of recreational areas. The major problems, however, remain the supply of water and air pollution generated predominantly by the car exhaust. Solving these would be much easier if the city was not located in a mountain basin, which keeps the pollution within its boundaries and causes difficulties with water supply.

In the first decade of the 20th century, the water usage in Mexico City was 81.9 m^3 per second. Around 72% of water supply came from the exploitation of the underground resources, 4% from the open water tanks, and the remaining 24% was transported using the Lerma–Cutzaznal system from outside of the metropolitan region (Brena and Brena, 2014).

[4] Areas of communal land used for agriculture, on which community members individually farm designated parcels and collectively maintain communal holdings.

Since 1954, however, the resources of deep water have not been sufficient; its level at present has been dropping by 1 m per year (CONAGUA, 2013). The system of water supply from outside the metropolitan region is extremely costly. It consists of a structure of tanks gathering water, pumping stations (from the height of about 1,600 m above sea level through a pass of 2,700 m above sea level, from a distance of up to 200 km), sewage treatment plants, and tunnels. A new improved system of water supply is, thus, necessary, preferably from the north of the country. Those systems additionally deprive the neighbouring states of water. The water usage increases with the rising standards of life. It is estimated that up to 40% of water is lost in the pipeline system itself. Even nowadays, in certain regions of Mexico, residents experience brief periods of water shortage. In order to ensure the access to water, it is necessary to equip the flats with an individual water gathering system in the form of tanks placed on the roofs usually together with pumps enabling filling up the tanks. This imposes additional cost on the residents. It is believed that by 2025, due to the limited access to groundwater, a crisis in water supply may occur. Another issue is waste drainage from the region of Mexican Valley. The waste there is being pumped out in the north direction, however, many houses in the poorer districts, situated on the slopes above the city, are not connected to the drainage system and that poses a danger of epidemic outburst (CONAGUA, 2013).

Another environmental issue is the air pollution. Despite more liberal than in Europe norms, in the case of ozone in the metropolitan region the norms are exceeded more than half of the days in a year, the dust level is exceeded almost 10% of the days in a year (Ferrer and Escalante, 2014). Half of the pollution is caused by the transport, which, despite huge investments in modern means such as underground, is mainly caused by cars, especially by microbuses. Restrictions which ban driving cars that do not comply with the requirements concerning exhaust emission on certain days in the week are circumvented by purchasing new cars. Industrial pollution is considerably smaller in the southern part of the city, where the administration authorities are located, as compared to the northern part, which is still mostly industrial, and the industrial pollution there makes 32% of all pollution (INEGI, 2014). The natural air treatment is difficult because of the topography of the area. It is estimated that in the agglomeration every day about seven people die of diseases caused by the air pollution (Bicitecas, 2013). Surveillance data suggest a slight improvement in the quality of the air recently. The basic issue is periodical rise in the pollution rate due to the changing weather conditions.

The gradual drop in the quality of the air in the metropolis is also caused by the steady decline of the green spots. In the last half of the century the area of green spots dropped by 6 times (Escobar *et al.*, 2009; Padilla, 2009).

16.5. Management of a Metropolitan Area

Metropolitan area has various roles, connected both with the general functioning of a large urban centre and specific ones connected with its capital character. History proves that a growth of an agglomeration is spontaneous; the authorities tend to solve the issues *post factum* rather than prevent them. It happens in many areas (Rojas, 2005). In accordance with the requirements of the Constitution, local authorities should ensure the citizens have water supply, drainage system, electricity, waste control, trade opportunities, safety, and planning space for various purposes including the recreational one. In order to comply with these requirements, local authorities are allowed to impose local taxes. However, the main difficulty in managing a metropolitan area (7.8 thousands square km, that is 0.5% of the entire country, but on this area line 19% of population) is the administrative structure of the metropolis. The extremely complicated administrative system is a result of historical events and unplanned growth of the city. At present, it causes problems with counteracting the occurrence of various issues or deciding on the solution to them. The metropolitan area (Fig. 16.2) comprises of FD[5] divided into 16 "delegations," 59 municipalities belonging to State of Mexico (please do not confuse the state with the city or country of the same name) and one municipality belonging to the State of Hidalgo.

[5]The reform, which started in January 2016, changed its name to the City of Mexico, and the delegations to the territories managed by mayors. The new unit will have the right to their own constitution, however, limited by the constitution of the state.

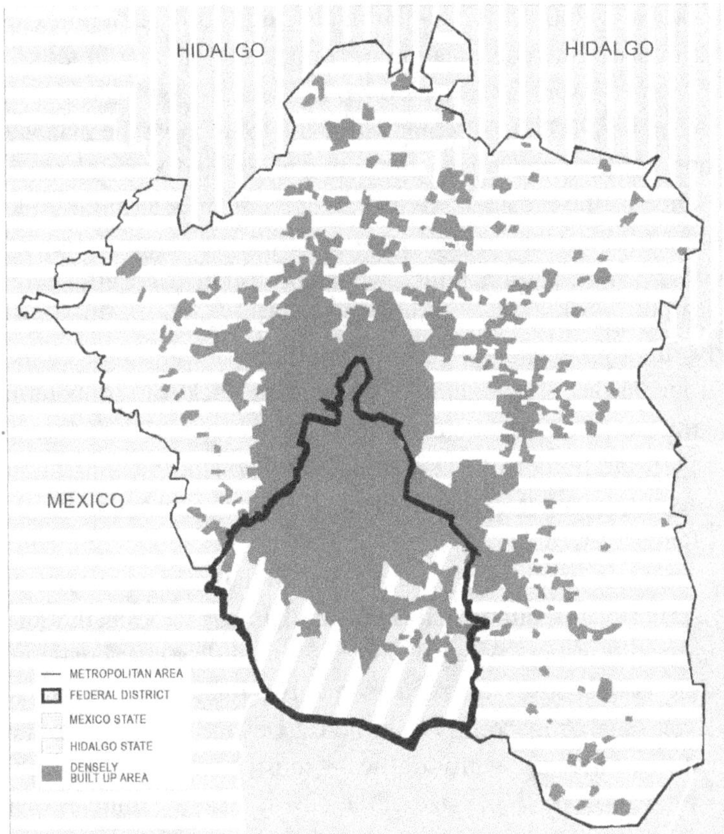

Fig. 16.2. The metropolitan area administration

Nearly half of the population of the agglomeration lives in FD although its area covers less than a third of the entire metropolitan region. Most of the central administrative bodies are situated in FD. From 1824 to 1997 the governors of FD were appointed by the president of the country. That meant they either supported or belonged to the ruling group. From 1997, they have been elected by the people. Rather unfortunately, taking the possibilities to connect the interest of the city and the functions of the capital, the elections are constantly won by the representatives of the opposite left wing Party of Democratic Revolution — PRD (between the years 1934–2000 the party in power was Institutional Revolutionary

Party — PRI, in 2000–2012 — the right wing National Action Party — PAN). It impedes the coordination of actions and gaining funds but also gaining resources such as water from other states.

In December 2005, an attempt was made to improve the management of the metropolitan zone. The authorities of FD and State of Mexico in the presence of the president signed an agreement determining the borders of the Metropolitan Zone of Mexico Valley and appointing special committees whose responsibility would be to solve specific problems such as floods, air pollution, transport, etc. The regions did not function properly mainly because of lack of appropriate legal and administrational foundations. An example of evident lack of cooperation in administration can be the construction of the Hueytlaco viaduct on the motorway at the border of FD and State of Mexico, the construction of which was suspended in 2006 (Grandet, 2014) and finished only 10 years later in January 2016.

Besides water supply and pollution, one of the main responsibilities of the city authorities — although it is not regulated by the Constitution — is ensuring local transport. Mexico City has a well-developed underground system, city trains, buses, microbuses, and two lines of trolley buses. The network of local transport is enormous. Despite this, however, it is estimated that 80% of the city traffic — mostly vehicles stuck in traffic jams — are cars. Due to the size of the city, it takes 90 minutes one way on average to get to work. The transport infrastructure is concentrated in FD although for the residents of the State of Mexico, poorer than their FD neighbours, transport is more important.

16.6. Conclusions

The population boom in the metropolitan zone of Mexico City has recently slowed down slightly in comparison to 1950s and 1960s. That puts the position of the agglomeration further down on the global scale. The life within the cluster is still difficult, however, the attractive job market in Mexico City indicates that without substantial de-centralization process, it will not be possible to slow down the growth of the city, and the cost will be rising. It would seem logical to create other, smaller cities. The authorities took an effort to do so only in the eighties and nineties, when some of the central offices such as Bureau of Statistics or Archives were moved away to the provincial areas. To take the burden away from the city, actions that are more radical, similar to those taken in Brazil or Nigeria, would be necessary. Moving the capital of the country to another city seems impossible and efficiency of this type of actions is rather restricted.

It would undoubtedly be in the interest of the Mexican society to stop the growth of the city as soon as possible. It is the only way to encourage modernization of the city, which would improve the standard of life of the residents, but is being delayed due to increasing problems arising from the size of the metropolis. Another crucial element necessary to manage a metropolitan area is a reform of the administrative system, hardly possible considering the political reasons.

Mexico City is the oldest mega-metropolis within the developing countries. It could serve as an example for the fast developing Asian metropolises. One solid conclusion could be to raise awareness to slow down the process of growth, which was ignored in 1950s and 1960s in Mexico. It would have been logical to concentrate on the development of other urban centres to decelerate the overgrowth of the capital. At present, the population of the Metropolitan Zone has been rising due to the rate of natural increase. Therefore, discussing the functioning of this region in terms of sustainable development theory is very difficult, if not impossible.

References

Bicitecas, (2013). *Mueren 7 personasdiarias por contaminación del aire en el Valle de México.* Retrieved from http://bicitekas.org/cada-dia-mueren-7-personas-por-contaminacion-del-aire-en-la-zona-metropolitana-del-valle-de-mexico/ [access: 02.01.2015].

Brena, P.A.F. and N.J.A. Brena (2014). *Problematica del recursoagua en grandes ciudades: zonametropolitana del valle de Mexico.* Retrieved from http://www.izt.uam.mx/newpage/contactos/anterior/n74ne/aguavalle.pdf [access: 05.12.2014].

Centro de Estudios para la Zona Metropolitana AC (2006). *Unavisión para la Zona Metropolitana del Valle de México,* México: Centro de Estudios para la Zona Metropolitana AC.

ComunidadInformativa, Preventiva y de ApoyosobreTemblores, Sismos y Terremotosen México (2014). *Tembloresen México.* Retrieved from http://www.tembloresenmexico.com/ [access: 05.12.2014].

CONAGUA (2013). *Plan Nacional de Desarrollo, Programa Nacional Hidrico 2013–2018.* México: CONAGUA.

Consejo Nacional de Población (2010). *México en Cifras.* México: CNP.

De la Madrid, M. (1986). *IV InformePresidencial 1.09.1986,* México: Presidencia de la Republica.

Distrito, F. (1920). *Reglamento de Construcciones de la Ciudad de México.* México: DF.

Escobar, D., J. Lorena and J.S. Jiménez Rivera (2009). Urbanismo y sustentabilidad: estado actual deldesarrollo urbano de la ZMVM. *Revista Digital Universitaria* 10(7), 7–XX. Retrieved from http://www.revista.unam.mx/vol.10/num7/art39/int39.htm [access: 11.07.2009].

Estudio de salarios (2013). SG Buzz No. 42. Retrieved from http://sg.com.mx/revista/42/estudio-salarios-sg-2013#.VFo9NzSG9DQ [access: 05.12.2014].

Ferrer, C.J.A. and R.I.S. Escalante (2014). *Contaminación atmosférica y efectossobre la saluden la Zona Metropolitana del Valle de México.* Retrieved from http://www.economia.unam.mx/publicaciones/econinforma/pdfs/360/03escalanteyjimy.pdf [access: 02.01.2015].

Gonzalez Gortázar, F. (ed.) (1994). *"Arquitectura mexicana del siglo XX",* Consejo Nacional para la Cultura y las Artes, México.

Grandet, C. (2014). *Distrito FEderal y Estado de México: la ciudad dividida.* Retrieved from http://imco.org.mx/desarrollo_urbano/distrito-fEd.eral-y-estado-de-mexico-la-ciudad-dividida/ [access: 02.01.2015].

Instituto Nacional de Ecologia (INEGI) (2013). Situaciónambiental de la Zona Metropolitana del Valle de México. Retrieved from http://www2.inecc.gob.mx/publicaciones/libros/268/metro3.html [access: 03.01.2015].

INEGI (2010). *Estadisticas Historicas de México 2009.* México: INEGI.

INEGI (2014). *Cuaderno estatístico y geográfico de la Zona Metropolitan del Valle de Mexico 201.* México: INEGI.

IMF (2007). March of the Cities. *Finance & Development* 44(3), 1–3.

Marichal, C. and M. Cerutti (Ed.) (1997). *Historia de las grandesempresasen Mexico 1850–1930.* México: Fondo de CulturaEconomica.

Mayer-Serra, C.E. (2012). *Con dinero y sin dinero.* México: Debate.

Padilla, G.S. (2009). Temas de sustentabilidad en el urbanismo contemporáneo. Conclusions del SUI. *Revista Digital Universitaria,* 10(7), 7–XX. Retrieved from http://www.revista.unam.mx/vol.10/num7/art39/int39.htm [access: 11.07.2009].

Pantaleón, C.N. (2012). *Segregación residencialen la ZMVM 2000–2010.* México: FLACSO.

Rojas, E. (Ed.). (2005). *Gobernar las metropolis.* Washington DC: Banco-Interamericano de Desarrollo.

Romer, M. (2014). Migrantesindígenas en la ciudad de México. México: INAH.

Vargas, S.R. (Ed.). (2009). *Historia de la arquitectura y el urbanismo Mexicano.* vol. IV, *El siglo XX* tomo I *Arquitectura de la revolucion y revolucion de la arquitectura*, México: UNAM.

Ward, P. (1998). *Mexico City.* Chichester: John Wiley.

Żuławska, U. (2015). Gospodarcze konsekwencje osłabienia państwa — przypadek Meksyku. In E. Mączyńska (Ed.). *Modele ustroju społeczno-gospodarczego. Kontrowersje i dylematy.* Warszawa: PTE.

17

DHAKA — THE PERILS AND PROMISES OF AN ASIAN MEGACITY

Adnan Morshed

There is no single vantage to narrate the urban story of Dhaka. Like other emerging megacities (according to the United Nations Centre for Human Settlements, megacities are "urban agglomerations" with more than 10 million people) of the world, Dhaka has been growing exponentially, particularly since it became the capital of the independent nation of Bangladesh in 1971 (see Fig. 17.1). This urban growth transpired with both promises and perils, introducing contentious debates not only on urbanization, but also on questions of modernity and progress. If modernity is, as Marshall Berman articulated, "a paradoxical unity, a unity of disunity [that] pours us all into a maelstrom of perpetual disintegration and renewal," Dhaka city appears to be a quintessential modernist narrative in which optimism and pessimism, resilience and dysfunction, the spaces of affluence and poverty could not find a more fluid coexistence (Berman, 1982). Marx's observation that in a modern world "all that is solid melts into air" — that is, forces of global capitalism and market leave everything in a perpetual state of transience — presents a prescient portrayal of contemporary Dhaka.

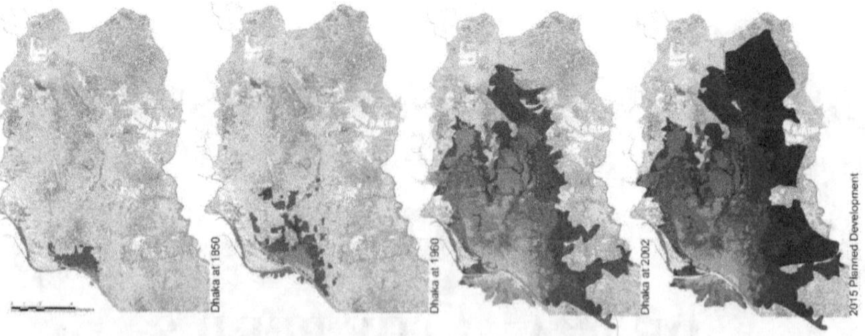

Fig. 17.1. Urban growth of Dhaka

Source: March Thesis, The Catholic University of America.

Thus, Dhaka city is how one wants to see it, even if the city feels like an urban tornado sucking everything into a dizzying vortex of wild land speculation, economic disparities, and environmental challenges. Neither despair nor hope alone can account for the city's exhilarating urbanity. "Howl," the American poet Allen Ginsberg's existential angst over the hyper-modernity of 1950s New York City, could be an apt description of present-day Dhaka. "What sphinx of cement and aluminium hacked open their skulls and ate up their brains and imagination? Robot apartments! Invisible suburbs! Skeleton treasures! Blind capitals! Demonic industries! Spectral nations! Invincible madhouses!" Ginsberg's modern metropolis was hardly a wasteland, but rather an epic battlefield where the social, cultural, and economic forces of modernity engaged in a perpetual struggle. Take a stroll around Farm Gate or Gulisthan and hear Ginzberg's howl! (see Fig. 17.2).

A random mental image inventory of Dhaka would suffice to iterate the city's whirlwind modernity. Enormous shopping arcades all across the city draw in streams of shoppers. City streets are swarmed with pedestrians, rickshaws, cars, tempos, buses, and trucks. Street vendors hawk virtually everything from household goods to the latest garment imports to reprinted *New York Times* bestsellers. The Parliament building premise, Ramna Park, and Hatir Jheel provide an unexpected respite from congestion and noise. Multistoried apartment buildings dominate the city, signalling the rise of an urban bourgeoisie. The impoverished but highly resilient mini-city of the Karail slum in the shadow of the high-end

Fig. 17.2. Farm gate road intersection in Dhaka

(Photos: A. Morshed, private collection).

residential area Gulshan debunks the myth of poverty only occupying the urban periphery. Mannequins at trendy boutique stores gawk at the chaos of everyday life from their lonely perches. Massive billboards rise above squalid shacks advertising mobile phones. There is no single element that dominates Dhaka's urban experience.

Dhaka city presents a jigsaw puzzle of myriad spectacles. It is an urban maze that provokes some observers to dismiss the city as an irredeemable wasteland and some as a resilient urban zone that could be transformed into a livable metropolis by a happy marriage of political goodwill and sustainable planning. There is also somewhat of a "middle path" in the vein of the Dutch architect and urban theorist Rem Koolhaas, who found in the Nigerian city of Lagos "a protean organism that creatively defies constrictive Western ideas of urban order" (Packer, 2006: 64–75). He noted in an unpublished report "Lagos: How It Works" (1997): "What is now fascinating is how, with some level of self-organization, there is a strange combination of extreme underdevelopment and development … what particularly amazes me is how the kinds of infrastructure of modernity in the city trigger off all sorts of unpredictable improvised conditions, so that there is a kind of mutual dependency" (Packer, 2006: 64–75). Although George Packer, an American journalist and author, criticized the Dutch architect's trip to Lagos as "tourism by car," Koolhaas found in the urbanism of developing economies not a predictable western fear of apocalypse, but a realistic image of what to expect in the megacities of the future (Chris, 2016). Koolhaas is perhaps not off base. By 2050, three-quarters of the world's population will live in urban areas and most future megacities will be located in developing countries. Many urban theorists now believe that the great urban experiments that were undertaken in the western metropolises of the 19th and 20th centuries have shifted to the developing world, particularly Asia.

Dhaka's urban growth in the past fifty years or so validates this observation. Bangladesh's urban population was only 7% at independence, meaning that the country was still an agrarian delta punctuated by a few towns, mostly Dhaka and a distant second Chittagong. Dhaka's population grew at more than 6% in the 1970s and at nearly 10% in the early 1980s. By the early 1990s, the capital's population was more than 6 million. In 2017, Dhaka's population, topping 18 million according to some estimates, competes with those of other megacities of the world such as New York, Mexico City, San Paulo, Karachi, and Mumbai. A primate city, Dhaka's contribution to national GDP was 36% (Chittagong was second at 11%), according to the Bangladesh Bureau of Statistics in 2009 (see Fig. 17.3). The migration of impoverished rural population to the city in search of a better life has been the mainstay of this population boom. A varied combination of push and pull factors brings over half a million people from the villages to Dhaka city every year. This population surge results in a liquid-like filling of all "available" spaces in the city. The impoverished rural migrants often find a refuge in what the journalist Doug Saunders called "arrival city," the urban fringe, driven by the everyday entrepreneurship of the underclass (Saunders, 2012). There have been other crucial factors for the city's growth. Territorial expansion, natural growth, concentration of key educational institutions and health care facilities, both formal and informal sector job opportunities, industrialization, and manufacturing, particularly readymade garments, has made Dhaka into a primate city, disproportionately larger than other

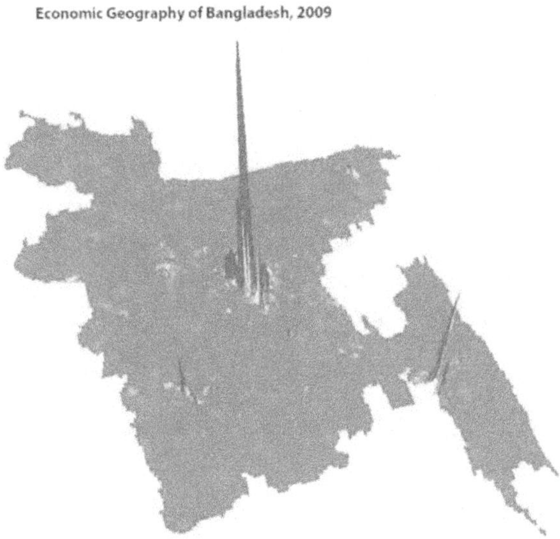

Fig. 17.3. Economic growth of Bangladesh

Source: The World Bank; based on data from the Bangladesh Bureau of Statistics (2009).

cities in the country. Besides, in the popular perception the capital is where one needs to be to pursue big dreams. Dhaka is what London was to England in the 19th century or New York to America in the early 20th century (see Fig. 17.4).

The urbanistic implications of Dhaka's population growth have been manifold. The first and foremost effect has been an unsustainable demand on urban land, leading to a staggering population density and sending urban land value to an economic stratosphere. The pressure on land rapidly altered the city's traditional urban fabric, particularly low-rise residential areas. Consider Dhanmondi, a gridiron patterned low-density residential neighbourhood planned during the East Pakistan era. Back then, generously sized and serviced plots contained mostly 2 or 3 storied buildings. They occupied about 50% of the plot and left the remaining area as green front and backyard. The overall impression was that of an urban pastoral. Even until the early 1980s, Dhanmondi was a quiet, self-sufficient residential neighbourhood with independent homes, a few corner shops catering to the locals, and a lake that wrapped the area with a feeling of ecological

Fig. 17.4. Dhaka's urban sprawl
(Photos: A. Morshed, private collection).

bliss. But from the late 1980s, the pressure of urbanization catalyzed the replacement of Dhanmondi's low-rise single-family houses with rent-worthy multistoried apartment buildings and profitable commercial structures. The formerly exclusive residential neighbourhood's gross population density rose to 26,440 persons per km^2 in 2001. The area's urban character changed from residential to semi-commercial.

Today, the stream of morning walkers along the Dhanmondi Lake and their health consciousness manifested by the proliferation of temporary kiosks offering quick diabetes tests, wall graffitis advertising language coaching in German, Italian, Spanish, Chinese, and Korean for prospective job-seekers abroad, and movements of school children offer images of an urban neighbourhood constantly shifting its character (see Fig. 17.5). The transformation of the Dhanmondi Lake in the 1990s from a local urban element into a larger city attraction typified the *ad hoc* urban interventions with which the political regime sought to improve the life of the city. The debate as to whether the lake should have been designed as a neighbourhood ecological land-waterscape or as an entertainment and

Fig. 17.5. Transformation of Dhanmondi residential area of Dhaka
(Photos: A. Morshed, private collection).

health-themed park for the city provoked Dhaka's urbanites to think about urban planning issues that have an effect on their daily lives.

Dhanmondi presents a microcosm of Dhaka's hyper-urbanization. Gated developer-built apartment buildings, schools, hospitals, clinics, fast food joints, art galleries, restaurants, banks, boutique stores, tailor shops, lakeside promenades, open-air theatres, and other commercial establishments transformed the residential neighbourhood into an urban hodgepodge. Dhanmondi echoes Koolhaas' analysis of Lagos' provisional urban character and, if one is a bit optimistic, Jane Jacobs' celebration of vibrant mixed-used urbanism that laid the foundation for what became known in the West as New Urbanism. Yet, to some urban observers, Dhanmondi signified, like other parts of Dhaka, a failure in land-use regulation and planning.

The demand on urban land also gave rise to a senseless culture of land-grabbing, wetland-filling, and river encroachment that increased Dhaka's ecological risks manifold. The land–water geography that in the early 17th century inspired Islam Khan Chishti (the grandson of Emperor Akbar's spiritual mentor Sheikh Selim Chishti) to shift the provincial Mughal capital of Bengal from Rajmahal to Dhaka has all but disappeared. For the Mughals, Dhaka's hydrographical geography promised both a strategic stronghold to protect the south-eastern frontier of the empire and many commercial advantages by virtue of the city's easy accessibility. In modern times, Dhaka needed to retain its land–water geography for its ecological survival. But a soaring land price made legal and illegal occupation of wetlands, river banks, or government *khas* lands a profitable business. Many political honchos and people with economic muscle occupy lands with a sense of entitlement and impunity (see Fig. 17.6).

Although a civil society-initiated culture of environmental activism began to take shape from the early 1990s, Dhaka continues to face a steep environmental battle. Frenzied gentrification, exacerbated by the epidemic of land-grabbing, frequently drowns out the cry for the preservation of the city's ecological DNA. One of the most remarkable episodes of the 1990s was when real-estate developers became crucial actors in the

Fig. 17.6. Dhaka's eastern edge — a fragile land–water geography under the threat of gentrification

(Photos: A. Morshed, private collection).

politics of the city's growth and future. In 1991, the Real Estate and Housing Association of Bangladesh (REHAB) was formed with 11 members to organize the real estate sector. According to one estimate, in 2015 more than 1,500 real-estate companies operated in Bangladesh. While they provided various housing options to city dwellers, the real-estate companies sometimes played a draconian role in transforming the capital into a cartography of lucrative housing developments.

The governmental agencies responsible for the sustainable growth of the capital often either misunderstood or ignored the environmental cost of rampant urbanization. Consider the case of Khilkhet, an area on the north-eastern edge of the capital, a site of intense housing development on reclaimed lands or low-lying agricultural fields. Khilkhet's crown jewel is the massive housing estate called Lake City Concord — a Third World reincarnation of the iconic mid-20th century public housing project called Pruitt-Igoe in St. Louis, Missouri, USA. Pruitt-Igoe was demolished in 1972 for its alleged dehumanizing design and extreme frugality of space that, according to some observers, provoked antisocial behaviour and delinquency among the project's poor inhabitants. The housing project that architectural theorist Charles Jencks identified with the so-called failure of modern architecture to provide humane, site-specific buildings mushrooms in Khilkhet, Mohammadpur, and other parts of Dhaka. Often presented to the public with exotic names, these projects invoke ecological utopias of lush green, blue water, and unlimited familial happiness, while the reality sometimes is a stark opposite. Billboards promoting these types of utopias have become part of Dhaka's urban iconography. Beyond Lake City Concord in Khilkhet, a vast prairie of *kash bon*, low-lying agricultural lands, swamps, and rivulets had become a postmodern geography of housing-estate signposts, sometimes rising from the water, or from plots filled in for American-style suburbs. A casual stroll in this area convinces one that the coming "war" in Bangladesh is going to be land–water war, between people and corporations, and between corporations and corporations, and between corporations and the state.

Dhaka city's public places are organic and improvised, rather than designed. They are the city's crowded streets and their intersections: the TSC intersection, Shahbag, Farm Gate, Manik Mia Avenue, Shaheed Minar, Gulistan, Babu Bazar, and more. The Mughals introduced many *bags*, meaning gardens, in the city, but these *bags* never developed into public places in the sense of Rome's Piazza Navona or London's Trafalgar Square or even the subcontinent's *maidan*. The south plaza of Louis Kahn's Parliament building, completed in 1983, in many ways became the city's symbol of democratic public space, attracting people of all walks of life. For them, it offered no less an urban oasis in the midst of chaos, congestion, corruption, and urban neurosis. When the plaza was declared off limits to the public sometime after 2001 due to security concerns, it was a sign of how the ruling elite and city administration remained oblivious that a healthy, democratic city needs a network of public places where people can gather, stroll, and breathe fresh air. The recently completed urban project, Hatir Jheel, sought to restore the water footprint of the historic Begunbari canal. Even though it is somewhat driven by a bureaucratic vision of automobile-centric planning ideologies of the yore, the project stimulated the public imagination of the outdoors.

Generally, in the popular reckoning of Dhaka's middle class, going outside the familiar domain — the home and the workplace — has become synonymous with encountering a host of urban pathologies. Lack of security on the street, political agitation, traffic congestion, and environmental pollution create the impression that public places are a dreaded realm that ought to be avoided. The result of this sorry perception has been two-fold. First, people will not venture out of the familiar domain, creating an atmosphere of urban estrangement. Second, city dwellers have developed an apathetic view of the city. The city does not provide them orientation, nor does it reinforce their civic identity. As a result, the city has become a conglomeration of self-alienating private spaces of various sizes and scales. Architecture is invariably about interior space within the bounded plot, removed from any reasoned consideration of the building's relationship to the broader urban context. Great efforts are made to interiorize the individual, a business establishment, or an economic class. The natural inclination of the middle class or the nouveau riche has been to create bubbles of privacy in the public space. That private bubble has been the car, the perceived refuge of the middle class or to-be-middle class, for it provides double dividends: a comforting sense of safety and social class. According to a Bangladesh Road Transport

Authority report, on average 52 newly registered cars entered the streets of Dhaka every day in 2012!

The culture of apartment living reflects the estranged nature of Dhaka's urban life. The general attitude prevalent in apartment buildings has been one of creating for a few families a "safe" private haven — a refuge from a dreadful exterior. In the process, not only does the individual's estrangement from the outside become spatially inscribed and socially enforced within the secure and policed boundaries of apartment complexes, but also, more important, public spheres lose relevance in the vision for the city. The upper-crust residential areas of Bananai, Gulshan, and Baridhara — planned as low density urban enclaves in the 1960s — reflect the city's plot-based growth pattern and the resulting symptoms of alienation from urban life. While there is a busy, mixed-use street life marked by shops, offices, banks, and restaurants, these expensive neighbourhoods embody what could be called an "Antilla effect," the isolation of stand-out and stand-alone buildings. This new urban phenomenon is best represented by India's richest man Mukesh Ambani's 27-storied Mumbai residence Antilla (Ramesh, 2007). This Mumbai "landmark," named after a mythical island, increasingly reflects the pattern of isolationist spaces that the moneyed class seeks to carve out from the boisterous metropolises of the Third World. Dhaka is no exception. Architects here found a niche market and delivered scores of mini-Antillas, seldom considering the environmental well-being of the city. In the absence of a sustainable and ecological vision for the city's future — not just what the city *will be* but what it *should be* — the narrow focus on the plot takes precedence over the broader urban environment.

Dhaka city presents an interesting history in "master planning," a snazzy western concept denoting a long-term supra-planning document that establishes a road map for the future growth of a city or region within a projected timeframe. Master planning typified the modus operandi of planning communities, development professionals, and city administrations in various forms, shades and degrees throughout the 20th century. The concept lost its appeal in the west in the past three decades or so due to revisionist perceptions that the task of master planning was propelled by a bureaucratic and top-down attitude towards growth. And, master planning allegedly occurred at the expense of sustained public participation in the planning process and a bottom-up understanding of the sociocultural context of the city in contention. Dhaka's first comprehensive master plan, proposed in 1959 at the behest of the Dacca Improvement Trust (DIT, later renamed as RAJUK), in many ways exemplified the pros and cons of master planning. The 1959 plan was prepared by the British planning firm of Anthony Minoprio, Hugh Spencely, and P.W. McFarlane, planners who were influenced by the post-World War II British planning ideology steeped in the Garden City movement (Larkham, 1997). Earlier in 1951, the firm prepared a master plan for Kuwait that emphasized zoning, self-sufficient neighbourhoods, and a spacious road network. The Kuwait plan was viewed as a watershed in the Middle-Eastern country's modernization and infrastructure development. But it was also criticized for what was called "mindless westernization," expressed in a layout that was "rigid, geometrical, harsh, and inhumane" and an automobile-driven planning vision (Hewins, 1963). A significant part of Dhaka's urban foot print — particularly along the two major highways, one going north towards Mymensingh via Tongi–Joydebpur and the other northwest towards Aricha via Savar — was created as a result of Minoprio, Spencely, and McFarlane's 1959 plan, projected for a 20-year planning horizon. One of the key goals of Minoprio *et al.* was to tap into the Madhupur terrace as a flood-free land for future expansion of the city. They also argued that when demand grows "it may well be possible to reclaim selected areas of low-lying land nearer to Dhaka with which to augment the present limited supply of building land." They visualized the expansion of Old Dhaka on the south side of Buriganga, in Keraniganj and Postogola. While the firm advocated the de-centralization of new industries to other regions and creation of self-sufficient areas like Tongi, the 1959 master plan was in essence expansionist without the kind of advocacy for environmental stewardship that would preserve the city's character of land-water geography. During the plan's projected period, however, Dhaka witnessed various developments that in many ways shaped the city's urban identity. Some projects were not anticipated and some were foreshadowed in the 1959 plan. For instance, the development of Sher-e-Bangla Nagar as a federal capital centre for the so-called Second Capital under the military regime of Ayub Khan was the result of the era's political expediency. The shifting of Dhaka's international airport from Tejgaon to Kurmitola in the

1970s was necessitated by the demand of expanded aerial connectivity. North of the new airport, Uttara Model Town was proposed in the master plan and developed by DIT since 1965.

There were other mega-plans, most of the time proposed by foreign firms. While such engagements were justified by the lack of local experts and offices, the practice of commissioning foreign firms was burdened with a protracted colonial-era mindset, mainly that only western professionals could bring the right solution. Led by the UK-based Shankland Cox Partnership with the aid of the Asian Development Bank, the 1981 Dhaka Metropolitan Area Integrated Urban Development Project focused on finding solutions to Dhaka's flooding problems. In 1995, the international development consultancy firm Mott Macdonald, in association with Culpin Planning Ltd. and others, proposed the Dhaka Metropolitan Development Plan, a "structure plan" that embodied an expansionist vision, bolstered by the proposed Flood Action Plan and its promise to supply new buildable lands. A lingering misunderstanding of the city's unique ecology, as well as the nature of a society in transition, compromised the long-term sustainability of these plans.

The grandiosity typically associated with a master plan tends to ignore the *genius loci* of a place and its sociopolitical issues. This legacy of master planning more or less defined Dhaka's urban development. Furthermore, the bureaucratization and "*ad hoc*-ism" of the implementation process raised serious questions on the ethics of timely intervention in the affairs of the city. Flyovers, river protection schemes, and the Begunbari canal recovery project, among others, have been the result of rearguard action rather than proactive imagination of the city's future. The Mumbai planner Rahul Mehrotra identified similar problems in the case of Mumbai. The timing of urban interventions becomes an effect of bureaucratic politicking:

> Over the last three decades in Mumbai, planning has been largely concerned with rearguard actions versus the *avant-garde* approaches that traditionally led planning. Thus today most infrastructure follows city growth rather than facilitating and opening up new growth centers within and outside the city's core. In contemporary Mumbai, planning happens systematically "posterior," as a recuperating and securing action.

> Thus, the profession is chiefly engaged in recuperative action, intervening post-facto to clean up the mess! It is therefore no coincidence that in Mumbai there is an increased celebration of projects involving "cleaning up" — whether that is the restoration of historic buildings, precincts or districts, waterfronts and pavements, or the relocation of slums to make way for infrastructure.[1]

Mehrotra's lament of Mumbai's rearguard planning culture could also be viewed as an advocacy for opening up spaces for proactive policy interventions which then could be the basis of what is currently touted as "ecological urbanism." The discourse of planning has lost its innocence of exuberant faith in the doctrines of development and growth. Attitudes on how to plan and grow began to undergo sea changes in the West with various environmental movements in the 1960s and the Oil Crisis in the 1970s. This new awareness compelled America and other industrialized nations to seek renewable sources of energy and articulate new policies of balancing development and the environment. The Club of Rome's 1972 report painted a haunting picture: "If the present growth trends in world population, industrialization, pollution, food, production, and resource depletion continue unchanged, the limits to growth on this planet will be reached sometime in the next one hundreds" (Meadows *et al.,* 1972). The word "environment" increasingly called for ethical human responsibilities and behavioural changes in consumption. In the built environment and its planning, energy efficiency, recycling, reduction of carbon footprint, ecological protection, etc., became policy priorities. The discourse of sustainable development began to favour demand mitigation over unregulated consumption.

Despite a growing culture of environmental activism in the country, Bangladeshi policy wonks continue to focus linearly on a much-mythologized narrative, "growth rate," all too often at the expense of rivers, wetlands, agricultural lands, forests, and air. The official attitude towards urbanization remains entrenched in bureaucratic and technical solutions, divorced from nuanced understandings of the effects of industrialization and urbanization on a land-scarce country like Bangladesh. For instance, the

[1] Rahul Mehrotra quoted in Homi (2010: 80–81).

air-polluting brickfields that contribute to over 1% of Bangladesh's GDP are left to a laissez-faire policy grey zone because brickfields are viewed as a great protagonist in the vaunted growth-rate storyline. Besides, peddling political influence and resorting to hefty bribes, brickfield owners easily bypass environmental regulations. Brickfields that surround Dhaka today meet the building industry's incessant demand of bricks, but they also pollute the air of the metropolis and deplete the agricultural productivity of the land they occupy, legally or illegally. While this paradoxical effect of modernity will not go away, there will be *choice* available to the people. The choice, fortunately, does not have to be entrapped into an "either-or" situation. The choice could embrace an environmentally sensitive vision of urbanization, while ensuring the economic progress of the populace with least disruptive carbon footprints.

References

Berman, M. (1982). *All That is Solid Melts into Air: The Experience of Modernity*. New York: Penguin Books.

Chris, M. (2016). "'Lagos shows how a city can recover from a deep, deep pit': Rem Koolhaas talks to Kunlé Adeyemi," *The Guardian* (Feb. 26, 2016).

Hewins, R. (1963). *A Golden Dream: The Miracle of Kuwait*. London: W.H. Allen, 255.

Homi, K.B. (2010). Mumbai on My Mind: Some Thoughts on Sustainability. In M. Mostafavi (Ed.). *Ecological Urbanism*. Harvard University Graduate School of Design: Lars Muller Publishers.

Larkham, P.J. (1997). Remaking cities: Images, control, and postwar replanning in the United Kingdom. *Environment and Planning*, 25(5).

Meadows, D.H., *et al.* (1972). *The Limits to Growth*. New York: Unverse Books.

Packer, G. (2006). "The Megacity: Decoding the Chaos of Lagos," *The New Yorker*, 64–75.

Ramesh, R. (2007). "£500m Mumbai palace for family of six and 600 staff high-rise era attacked as dawn of new vulgarity," *The Guardian* (June 1, 2007).

Saunders, D. (2012). *Arrival City: How the Largest Migration in History is Reshaping Our World*. New York: Vintage Books.

18

LAGOS — DIRECTIONS OF DEVELOPMENT OF NIGERIAN METROPOLIS IN THE FIRST DECADES OF THE 21ST CENTURY

Malwina Bakalarska

18.1. Introduction

The author presents the analysis of the developmental opportunities and threats faced by the Nigerian metropolis of Lagos in the early decades of the 20th century, offering evidence proving, that this is an example of an urban centre expanding spontaneously and chaotically. The author shows that despite efforts being made by the authorities of the city in attempt to get the construction chaos under control, beautify the city, and create a new business centre, a series of obstacles still have to be overcome if the megacity is to achieve sustainable development. These include lack of security, corruption, and the absence of tourism, which assist developmental processes in other countries in this region of Africa.

The purpose of the chapter is to focus on the largest city in sub-Saharan Africa, which is the Nigerian city of Lagos. It aims to explain the context of its spatial and socio-economic structure for better understanding of the local reality. This chapter can be treated as a short guide to Lagos' threats and opportunities for those who are interested in investing, working, or conducting research in this area. The analysis in the chapter is based on material collected during fieldwork carried out by the author in 2008, 2011, and 2015 as a period to show rapid evolution of this megacity including tangible results achieved by the Governor Babatunde Fashola during his double term from 2007 to 2015.

18.2. Historical Context

In Nigeria, it was primarily the Muslim north where urban centres developed. The coastal south, where economic activities of the colonizers were located, underwent urbanization to a lesser extent. In the north, both climate (calmer in comparison to the south) and traditions of locating Muslim administrative centres facilitated the creation of populated settlements. It was the northern city of Sokoto, seat of the Emir, which oversized any other present-day Nigerian city until the end of the 19th century in terms of population. It was the abolishment of the slave trade, confirmed in 1916, which brought a radical change (Eberechukwu, 2006). It initiated a wave of migrations from the middle of the country towards present-day Lagos.

18.3. Social, Economic, and Cultural Determinants of the Expansion of Lagos

In the colonial times, despite unfavourable natural conditions (wet and sandy grounds, lagoons, and islands), the British launched the construction of a complex of industrial facilities located in direct proximity to the coast. Employment opportunities attracted subsequent groups of migrants, who initiated expansion of the urban area towards the inland. The process lasted uninterruptedly up to the 1990s, when it was channelled in the direction of the lagoon terrains located next to the metropolis.

After Nigeria obtained independence, development of Lagos speeded up. Being the capital of the state (until 1991), and subsequently the location of government, institutions and local industry contributed to the city's growth. Despite the fact that Abuja has become Nigeria's new capital, Lagos had maintained its status of the country's main financial, economic, and industrial hub. The city has been the locus for the headquarters of corporations with Nigerian or international capital and for the main Nigerian banks. There are eight universities and eight technical universities and therefore, internal migrations are — apart from movements in search for employment — mainly caused by influx of students. Lagos is the prime cultural centre of the modern Nigeria. Apart from the underfunded state institutions such as the National Museum or National Theatre, the city is haven of vibrant music clubs, galleries, and entertainment centres. The metropolis is also a home to Nigerian film industry (Nollywood), which produces approximately 1,000 full-length movies yearly — one of the highest rates in the world. Castings organized by film producers attract people from all over the country and region (Barrot, 2005).

18.4. Administrative Factor

Nigeria is divided into 36 states, and the Federal State of Abuja. Federal system created frames for local governments with governors as their heads, and local budgets at disposal, to complement the central government in Abuja. Lagos State is divided into 20 Local Government Areas (LGA). Only 16 of them belong to Lagos metropolis. These are: Agege, Ajeromi-Ifelodun, Alimosho, Amuwo-Odofin, Apapa, Eti-Osa (Victoria Island and Ikoyi), Ifake-Ijaiye, Ikeja, Kosofe, Lagos Island, Lagos Mainland (Yaba), Mushin, Ojo, Oshodi-Isolo, Shomolu, and Surulere. Thanks to such administrative arrangements, Lagos metropolis is the central point for the entire Lagos State, until recently led by Babatunde Fashola (two consecutive terms in 2007–2015). He became one of the most active governors,[1] who earned much respect in the country after success in lifting Lagos from the organizational chaos. Due to its regional independence, Lagos, compared to the rest of Nigeria, is characterized by higher living standards and higher number of job opportunities, which contribute to continued growth of the population of the metropolis.

[1] It is worth to note that each district has its local administrator, *chief*. Analogically in other various cities, these are mayors of districts/counties. In this scheme, mayor of particular city might be equivalent to Lagos governor.

18.5. Lagos as a Metropolis

The population of Lagos is approximately 17 million, which constitutes 5% of Nigeria's estimated population.[2] According to the official information of the Federal Republic of Nigeria, the population of Lagos metropolis grows 10 times faster than the one of New York (Lagos is indeed named the "African New York"). In 1995, when Lagos' population reached 10 million, it was listed as one of the megacities. Migrations into Lagos are very dynamic, which causes overcrowding. Infrastructure designed by the British colonizers is inconsistent with the size of the population.

18.5.1. Zoning

The characteristics of Lagos metropolis go in line with the *zoning* scheme, which enlists districts to serve specific roles to fulfil citizens' needs and to serve economic, political, and cultural functions. In literature, three main types of cities' spatial composition models are defined:

- Type I — concentric built over a scheme of a circle,
- Type II — sector model,
- Type III — *multiple nuclei*, where city grows around several independent points (Harris and Ullman, 1945).

The scheme of the modern Lagos represents Type III of the internal structure of the city. The multi-nuclei spatial model developed as a result of the geographical conditions, which — in this case — relates to the coastal location, access to the sea, and migration processes. Cities built on circular model have one, clearly defined centre. In Lagos there are numerous places which, according to the sociological definition, play such a role. "Centre means power, political, economic, and ideological authority. It is focal point of accumulation of goods and information, place for exchange, manifestation of strength and wealth" (Jałowiecki and Szczepański, 2000). In this Nigerian metropolis, one can point out four central cells of different roles. First is the Lagos Island, a nutshell for the

[2] Data available at http://www.lagosstate.gov.ng/ [access: 12.04.2014].

modern city, where main bus stations are located, as well as city's government headquarters with symbolic objects (monuments, museum, squares) referring to the indigenous Yoruba culture. The Yaba district is often defined as the city's second "central" area. It is a hub for education, culture, and an area where NGOs (non-governmental organizations) and medium businesses are placed. Victoria Island, the third locality important for commerce and hosting government institutions, is located on the coast. The fourth area serving "central" functions, and "transforming into a centre for management and luxury consumption" (Jałowiecki and Szczepański, 2000) is Lekki, located in the south-east part of Lagos.

It is worth noting that industrial centre of Lagos was formed as a result of connecting different industrial districts, originally located near one another. In the contemporary literature on city development, such a process is described as "formation of metropolis by connecting two or more agglomerations and other cities located within a small distance, which form city clusters" (Jałowiecki and Szczepański, 2000). Those terrains in between were populated by immigrating factory workers, accommodated in temporary hotels.

18.5.2. International transportation hub

Lagos has the biggest international airport in Nigeria. It is also a prime communication hub for other West African countries. Lagos has flights connections with European and Asian capitals, as well as with strategic American cities. Connections by airlines from United Arab Emirates and Turkey offer better transfers between continents. It is also a factor contributing to the risk of epidemic outhursts. In 2014, the first case of Ebola outside of Liberia, Sierra Leone, and Guinea, was registered at Lagos airport.

18.5.3. Multi-ethnic and multinational structure of the city's inhabitants

Lagos is currently the most populous city of the sub-Saharan Africa. Located in the south-west part of Nigeria, it grew from a small fishing village into a giant metropolis. It is characterized by (typical for metropolis in the developing world) multi-ethnic nature, melting pot of religions and traditions, big social and economic contrast, dynamic growth, expansion towards neighbouring areas, and complex migratory processes. The zone structure of Lagos' districts developed through the locally dominating Yoruba tradition. In 1970s, when oil was discovered, members of all Nigerian ethnic groups began migrating to Lagos.

Presently, considerable number of headquarters of international corporations incite migrant workers from Europe, USA, Middle East, and Asia. Among non-African groups, Chinese and Lebanese dominate. There are also significant temporary migrations of qualified expats into Lagos — the British, Irish, Germans, and Canadians treat Lagos as a place for investing. They often remain in the city for a few years, contracted in oil industry and in the industrial freight, as experts and managers (in 1960s and 1970s many Polish lecturers and doctors, contributed to the development of Nigerian towns). Foreign workers make up for a multi-ethnic mixture of citizens and residents of the metropolis. It is a factor supporting dynamic exchange of goods and services, transplanting new models of global business management, which helps to elevate local economy's operational standards. On the other hand, concentration of people in a limited space produces numerous social tensions and inequalities on the local job market.

18.5.4. Economic and professional stratification

Migrants are differentiated by economic potential and adopted strategies of professional development. The picture of metropolis is also shaped by consolidation of areas of structural poverty and exclusion, which blocks parallel social and economic development.

Those African migrants with enterprising skills, who arrive to Lagos with a capital, set up mini-stalls with goods for sale per units (instead of stuffed in original packages; which is a widespread practice in developing world), open street canteens, or look for employment as night guards in more prosperous districts of the metropolis. Also migration of the poorer sections of the Nigerian society (and from other west African states) into the former capital is increasing. The attitude of many of them is passive. Groups of such migrants become city-nomads, who settle under bridges together with their cattle, goats, and hens, seeking survival in the big city as they cannot earn a living in their home villages anymore — this is a new phenomenon in sub-Saharan Africa. Lagos is a city where economic stratification is highly visible in the public domain. Internal migrations within the metropolis pushed the state authorities to build new roads and bridges, linking rich neighbourhoods and slums, separated by bays. New, illegal settlement of the homeless has begun popping up along new bridges and busy streets. They have no access to running water or electricity, but they become shelters for the poorest and for migrants from neighbouring countries such as Niger, Benin, and Togo. Inhabitants of those "unfinished settlements" form permanent structures, which contribute to further growth of the city itself. Federal government and non-governmental organizations try to respond to the phenomenon. The former has established an official body, Lagos Megacity Development Authority (LMDA), to fight with slums, and the World Bank has conducted field research. In the result of its estimations, nine major slum-areas have been identified and World Bank has dedicated $200 million in loans to support them (Obono, 2007). Despite those pro-development interventions, social stratification generates high rates of criminal activities, which result in the perception of Lagos as one of the most dangerous cities in the world.

18.5.5. Lagos metropolis' character as an indicator of lifestyle

A big and diverse population keeps the city awake 24 h/day. Many services are offered non-stop, due to constant demand. In many interviews I have conducted with Nigerians who have chosen to settle in Lagos for different reasons (most often for job opportunities and education), respondents have stressed that "Lagos is fun." This phrase was used by mature members of the metropolis' elite, by students, as well as average inhabitants, regardless of their age, sex, and education.

18.5.6. Strategic vision for development — A citizen-friendly city

The industrial facade of the city has contributed to its rapid development, but has also envisaged lack of its harmonized image. Since 2007,

(a) (b)

Fig. 18.1. (a) View on a square within the busy part of Yaba district, in 2008 inhabited illegally by immigrants. (b) View on the same square in 2011 — fenced and transformed into a municipal greenery
(Photos: M. Bakalarska, Lagos, Nigeria, private collection).

Lagos state governor has invested in developing green areas and construction of new networks of public transport. The ban on smoking in public places has been introduced, and programs to increase safety and public health care have been introduced. One of the evident aims of the state's authorities, related to increase in the quality of life in Lagos metropolis, is improving the city's aesthetics. To illustrate the process, the Fig. 18.1 presents the same place in 2008 and in 2011.

18.6. Achievements in Management and Realization of the Strategic Goals

18.6.1. Creation of public sphere and improvements in transportation

Babatunde Fashola, whose term as the Lagos State governor expired in 2015, initiated plans of construction of seven lines of the suburban trains, as well as a cableway, to reduce the car traffic.[3] It was a part of the urban project called Strategic Transport Master Plan (STMP), designed for 30 years. This vision could attract foreign investors, engineers, and intermediate service providers. However, it would be crucial to see how Fashola's successors would follow up on his legacy.

[3] Available at: http://www.lamata-ng.com/cable_car.php [access: 15.01.2014].

Besides, Governor Fashola's term has brought introduction of innovative (in Nigerian terms) regulations for the road safety. They include obligation to wear helmets imposed on motorcyclists, ban on carrying oversized items or extra passengers on motorcycles, sitting on the side of the motorcycle. The city still does not have underground or tram networks, but introduction of the public buses in 2007, as well as establishing ferry connections between islands and the mainland have given impetus for development of the public transport.

18.6.2. Activities for containing chaos in constructions

Several districts have been selected for construction of luxury villas for elites and the growing middle class: northern Ikeja, south-west Lekki, and south-east Ikoyi. Governor Fashola has initiated the creation of modern apartment — business district Lagos Eko Atlantic City. This "city within the city" is being promoted by its comfort and cleanliness. Apart from being a financial centre, it could be a model for development of the middle-class districts (see Fig. 18.2).

Fig. 18.2. Project of the "city of the future" Lagos Eko Atlantic City, being one of the districts of contemporary metropolis

Source: Available at: http://www.ekoatlantic.com/ [access: 10.04.2014].

18.7. Challenges for Sustainable Development of Lagos

Lagos is a metropolis, where — as in many big metropolises — contradictory paths of development can be observed. On one hand, there is a development deriving from consumer behaviour of its citizens (offers of banks, centres of commerce, and entertainment). On the other hand, one can note high unemployment, homelessness, social conflicts, crime, sanitary problems, and problems with transportation (Martison, 2000).

18.7.1. Ineffective system of distribution of energy

Despite the fact that Nigeria is one of the main exporters of crude oil to the western markets, most of its cities regularly face power shortages. The situation is particularly difficult in Lagos. Distribution of energy to households, institutions, and companies is organized on rotating basis, district after district. Lack of access to energy might even last several weeks. During this period, private persons as well as entrepreneurs and organizations must get access to a generator of energy and kerosene to be able to use light and energy in electrical outlets. As a result, the cost of living is high in the metropolis. Multiple generators produce constraint, disturbing noise.

18.7.2. Shortcomings in waste management, occlusion of sewers

Despite the work of the local Lagos State Waste Management Authority, which attempts to monitor the public space and conducts inspections in private households every last Saturday of the month, the garbage problem affects road safety. It is related to the fact that sewage system is stuck and during raining seasons “rivers” of rainwater flood the roads to the level between 20 cm and 1 m above the ground level. Problem of pollution and communal waste management poses a major issue for Lagos and many other African cities.

18.7.3. Traffic jams

Lagos is famous for one of the biggest traffic jams in Africa, which results both from overpopulation and from location of business districts in the south of the city and settlements for the rich on the opposite angle of the metropolis (due to natural directions of the Lagos expansion: towards the inland). Vertical communication axis (related to the spatial planning of the city) makes it difficult to improve public transportation, which falls under responsibility of the Lagos State Traffic Management Authority. Since 2012 the Traffic Radio Station 96.1 FM operates and informs live on the situation on the roads.

18.7.4. Inconsistence with the tourist movement

Despite its location on the coast of the Atlantic Ocean, and the fact it has seven city beaches, which could serve the seaside entertainment, the metropolis is not popular among tourists. Location of the country's most important centres of cultural life and exclusive hotels does not help much. Expats and local financial elite (bankers, lawyers, businessmen from the oil sector) have at their disposal hotels, galleries, clubs and restaurants, which transform images of subsequent districts. Nevertheless, Lagos, contrary to Kenyan metropolis, does not attract tourists who look for holiday destinations. The main reason behind it lays in the lack of security, proliferation of street crime, which involves organized groups of *Area Boys*, and widespread corruption among the military and police force. As a consequence, tourism sector — important contributor to the GDP of many African cities — is not really expanding.

18.7.5. Lack of security and comfort of life

The city of Lagos is characterized by the highest rate of crime in Nigeria. Gangs are regular parts of the street landscape. Killings related to black magic are widespread. Potential investors are afraid to locate their capitals and economic activities in the city due to the fear for their lives and properties. It is normal to hire private security guards. It generates additional costs, and complicates daily functioning.

Besides, Lagos has a stress-producing environment. Pollution, noise, and overpopulation, together with lack of security make living in the city difficult to bear on the psychological level.

Threat of terrorism is another issue to be mentioned. In relation to widespread attacks conducted by the Islamist terror group Boko Haram, Nigeria became one of the countries most vulnerable to the threat of terrorism. Schools, universities, police posts, and markets became regular targets of bombings in the cities of north-east Nigeria. Since 2011, attacks were noted in the capital, Abuja, where central police station and the offices of the United Nations (UN) were raided.

Distance between the main arena of the terrorist attacks, the city of Maiduguri, and Lagos is substantial — 1,708 km (!). Second factor which makes the city relatively safe from Boko Haram's attacks, is a different cultural tradition, different history shaping the people of the north (Islam dominating there since the 7th century), and those from the south (Christianity dominating from the 17th century). Government's success or failure in addressing Boko Haram crisis, including its root causes, will be of vital importance for Lagos. The occurrence of terror attacks in the city could hamper efforts to attract foreign investments and tourism.

In July 2014, biggest epidemic of Ebola reached Nigeria via the Lagos airport. State authorities showed big efforts to combat the virus. In effect, after 20 cases of Ebola, of which eight were fatal, mostly within Lagos metropolis, in October 2014 WHO was able to announce the end of the epidemics in Nigeria. In Lagos metropolis, the authorities were able to quickly conduct almost 18,000 visits in houses of 898 persons, which had or could have had contact with the first Ebola victim. Hospital of Lagos University, experienced in previous epidemics of polio, adapted to conduct tests providing results within 24 hours. What was crucial to fight against developing epidemics in such a difficult, populous environment as Lagos, was nominating a practitioner to serve as the main medical advisor to the governor, and ability to quickly deploy a professionally trained team (Juma, 2014). Containing Ebola in the Lagos state proved the state government's ability to conduct multidimensional crisis management operation, which is a good prognosis for the future.

18.7.6. Corruption

Apart from threat coming from the organized street gangs, high level of corruption poses another problem. Police and the military routinely stop private cars and buses expecting the drivers and passengers to pay bribes.

18.8. Conclusions

Experience of many state governments in Nigeria poses a potentially dangerous trend — with political wrangling around the post of the governor, long-term projects, large-scale investments, or visions for development attributed to a particular politician or party are often discarded as soon as the new governor takes office. Examples include unfinished "first African monorail" in Port Harcourt (capital of Rivers State) abandoned in 2016 by the incoming governor Nyesom Wike, or Tinapa resort — a business and leisure centre located next to Calabar (Cross River state) initiated by governor Donald Duke, but ceased after he left the post in 2007. The major reforms in approach towards development of Lagos and in setting development priorities, are attributed to the personality of Lagos State governor Babatunde Fashola, whose term came to an end in 2015. It would be paramount, though, that his successors do not treat revitalizing public spaces or designing public transportation simply as Fashola's legacy, which can be replaced by their own "signs of times."

To create new parts of the metropolis, formed from scratch as "perfect cities" or enclaves within a wider city, such as the Eko Atlantic City, Lagos authorities must take into account the failed or over-scaled projects from other parts of the world. Empty ghost-towns in Spain or China, shady prospects of populating the proposed twin town of Cairo, and other examples point to dangers of too tight relations between local/regional authorities and developers, with the latter being able to influence decision-making of the former being focused on winning large contracts rather than answering to proper housing needs of maintaining balanced spatial development.

Despite obvious constraints in possibilities of reducing traffic jams or de-crowding overpopulated metropolis, the city/state authorities should consequently push for internationalization and making temporary or permanent residency an attractive prospect for expats. This goal cannot be achieved without long-term focus on general security and development of seaside infrastructure, which could provide an attractive space for living and entertainment.

References

Barrot, P. (2005). *Nollywood: le phénomènevidéo au Nigeria*. Paris, L'Harmatan.

Eberechukwu, A. (2006). *The Abolition of the Slave Trade in Southeastern Nigeria, 1885–1950*. Rochester: University Rochester Press.

Eko Atlantic. Retrieved from www.ekoatlantic.com/ [access: 10.04.2014].

Harris, Ch. D. and E.L. Ullman (1945). The Nature of Cities. *The Annals of the American Academy of Political and Social Science*, 242(1), 7–17.

Jałowiecki, B. and M. Szczepański (2000). *Miasto i przestrzeń w perspektywie socjologicznej*. Warszawa: Scholar.

Juma, C. (2014). "How Nigeria defeated Ebola." *The Guardian*. 31.10.2014. Retrieved from http://www.theguardian.com/global-development-professionals-network/2014/oct/31/ebola-nigeria-state-public-sector-calestous-juma [access: 01.02.2017].

Lagos Metropolitan Area Transport Authority. Retrieved from http://www.lamata-ng.com/cable_car.php [access: 15.01.2014].

Lagos State Government. Retrieved from http://www.lagosstate.gov.ng/ [access: 12.04.2014].

Martison, B. (2000). *American Dreamscape*. New York: Carroll & Graf Publishers.

Obono, O. (2007). A Lagos thing. Rules and realities in the Nigerian megacity. *Georgetown Journal of International Affairs*, VIII, p. 31–38.

19

NEW YORK — A CITY OF PROGRESS

Bohdan Szklarski and Piotr Szyja

19.1. Introduction

Boston is the city of revolution, Philadelphia the city of Constitution, Washington the city of politics, Detroit the city of motors, Chicago the city of modern architecture, St. Louis the gateway to the West, Houston the city of oil, Los Angeles the city of dreams. One could go on and on. Each major American metropolis has its distinctive feature well entrenched in its history and represented by its people. New York stands out as a city of many faces: culture (Broadway), finance (Wall Street), immigration (Ellis Island), wealth (Fifth Avenue) or the American City represented by the Lady in the Harbour. 9/11 earned it the name of a resilient city or a wounded city (Mollenkopf, 2005: 3). But to call it a city of progress seems like an exercise in social engineering — an attempt to manufacture a new identity which will to gloss over the traditional reference values that shaped its history: greed and conflict. Nonetheless, in the light of the various development reports and prognoses "progress" seems like a perfectly adequate name to describe New York City as it wishes to see itself in the next few decades.

Yes, it is still a vision more than reality, but consecutive mayors, no matter which party they come from, propose a new course of the city development consistent with the word progress. The word embraces innovation, opportunity, movement, growth, creativity, change, and improvement. These are not empty words. Each is backed by a behaviour or a way of thinking that is already present in the city among its elites and ordinary residents. There seems to be a widespread consensus among New Yorkers that their city has a potential which only needs to be unleashed and assisted to (Marwell, 2007: 45). The following text makes an attempt to substantiate the claim that New York City is the city of Progress in all abovementioned dimensions. It can be treated as a report card from a process of urban development.

Let's begin with a brief encyclopaedic note, which will help us understand the state of city's development in 2014. Many of the propositions described in the third part of this report will refer to data included below (NYCUSA quickfacts, 2012).

Inhabitants: 8,244,910 in the city (17.7 million in the metro area); population density 10,756/km^2.

Area: 1,214 km^2, including 425 km^2 of waters (34,490 km^2 metro area).

Structure: centralized; 5 boroughs merged into one city in 1898:
Bronx: 1,392,002;
Brooklyn: 2,532,645;
Manhattan: 1,601,948;
Queens: 2,247,848;
Staten Island: 470,467.

Authorities:
Mayor: currently Bill de Blasio, 4-year term;
City council: 51 members, 4-year term;
Borough authorities: president and Council, advisory role.

Public transportation:
Metro: 22 lines, 468 stations, 1,350 km of tracks, 5.3 million passengers daily;
Buses: 230 lines, 5,900 vehicles, 2.01 million passengers daily;
Taxis: 13,270 vehicles, 42,000 drivers (82% of them born outside the US), 241 million passengers annually (Bureau of Transportation, 2015);
Bicycles: 1,480 km of bike lanes, 200,000 daily riders, 10,000 city bikes for rent;

54% of New Yorkers do not own a car. Every day 3.7 million people commute to work, 56% of them work in Manhattan. People commute by metro (41%), by car (24%), by bus (12%), on foot (10%), by train (2%), by taxi (1%), by bike (0.6%), and on ferries (0.2%).

Security:
35,000 policemen, 11,080 firemen;
Decrease in crime between 2000 and 2014 by 43% (between 1993 and 2014 by 75%):
Murders: 673–333;
Rapes: 2,068–1,352;
Assaults: 25,942–20,207;
Burglaries; 38,352–16,765.

Environment:
Waterworks: directly from intakes in the mountains, 200 km of pipes, no purification stations, throughput 4.5 million m^3 of drinking water a day (1,951 levels);
Waste: 36.2 tonnes a day, most carried to dumping sites located in other states; Greenhouse gas emissions: 7.1 tonne[3] (San Francisco 11.2, US average 24.5), which constitutes 1% of total US emissions (2.7% of total US population);
Energy use: 50% of the San Francisco level, 25% of Dallas, TX level.

Culture:
Art galleries: 500;
Theatres with more than 500 seats: 40;
Broadway shows tickets sales: 12.21 million, worth $1.27 billion;
Movie theatres: 80, over 500 auditoriums;
Cultural and artistic social organizations: 2,000;
Parks: 110 km^2, 23 km of public beaches.

Economy:
Budget: $75 billion;
Jobs: 4.2 million;
GCP (Gross City Product): $647 billion.

19.2. Development of New York Until 2014

It is assumed that New York was founded as a trading post in 1624 by Dutch settlers, who named it New Amsterdam. However, the first report of a European ship reaching this area comes from a hundred years before that. Giovanni da Verrazano claimed this land in the name of the King of France. Subsequent travellers, from Portugal and Spain, arrived a few years later. The latter ones created the first map of the region. Henry Hudson, a British employee of the Dutch East India Company, like his predecessors looking for a route to India, discovered the area of today's New York again in 1609. In 1624, the Dutch permanently settled in the territory of today's Manhattan. The longest bridge in the city, the Verrazano–Narrows Bridge, and the Hudson River dividing the states of New York and New Jersey were both named after those first travellers.

A little over 20 years after that, the town went under control of the British and stayed so until 1776. For over 3 centuries, New York was developing first as a seaport for trade and then as an industrial and financial centre. Thanks to the Erie Canal completed in 1825, New York became connected to the Great Lakes and could become a major market for agricultural and industrial goods from the country's interior. The little Ellis Island became a "gateway to America" for millions of European immigrants. Many of them stayed in the city, creating a network of multiethnic neighbourhoods (Weber, 1969: 108). In the 1920s and 1930s, New York, along with other large northern cities, absorbed a large wave of Afro-Americans migrating from the poor and rural South.

The city itself grew to be seen as a symbol of America not only due to the Statue of Liberty, guarding the entrance to the Harbour since 1876. In 1785, New York became the national capital of the newly created United States and remained so for 5 years, during the last year as a first federal capital under the United States Constitution. Here, on the stairs of the Federal Hall, today right next to the stock exchange on Wall Street, George Washington was sworn in as the first US president. Since 1790, New York is the largest city in the United States and is now visited by over 50 million tourists a year, who spend $38.8 billion. Broadway, Times Square, Harlem, Chinatown, Wall Street, Central Park are all names with global fame and recognition.

The architecture of New York is mostly perceived through the lens of Manhattan, which represents everything characteristic for the city: enormous skyscrapers, elegant "European" streets as well as three-floor townhouses typical for industrial America, most of which were constructed between the Civil War and the Great Depression, a period of the most intensive urbanization and industrialization. Interestingly, many murals from the New Deal period scattered through city borough buildings and libraries offer an artistic representation of these processes where they are synonymous with the main theme of the chapter — progress (Szanto, 2003: 27). In 2011, there were 550 skyscrapers measuring over 100 m high in New York, among them 50 towering 200 m. Many, especially those constructed at the beginning of the 20th century, are truly gems of art deco architecture. Outside Manhattan, where land prices were lower, we see neighbourhoods full of brick buildings, terraced houses, as well as ordinary single-family houses.

New York is a city of great diversity, which can be seen as something positive when it comes to cultures, religions, and ways of life, but not so much when it comes to economic and social inequalities (Mumford, 1970). The Gini index for Manhattan, the richest part of the city where median annual household income stands at almost $110,000, is 0.6 (for the entire city it is 0.5). Only around 54% of New Yorkers own their apartments and houses (average for the entire US is 65%), but they earn better than average Americans. Annual household income in New York is at $58,003 (US avg. 53,045) and personal income at $32,382 (US avg. 28,155). Poverty rate (less than $23,338 per month for a 4-person household) almost perfectly reflects the US average — 15.3% vs. 15.4%.

New York is relatively friendly for minorities. There are more businesses owned by members of minorities than on average in the US women 30.4/28.9%, African–Americans 10.4/7.1%, Latinos 10.4/7.1%, Asians 10.1/5.7% — (NYC/USA quickfacts, 2012). When it comes to demographics, the number of children, young adults, and elderly people is very similar to US averages. There are, however, significant differences in the percentages of African–American and Latino populations. The former one constitute 25.5% of New Yorkers, the latter one 28.6%, with the US average being almost 10% lower at 13.2% and 14.1%, respectively.

New York's multi-ethnic character is even more visible when we look at the number of inhabitants born outside the US — in the city it's 22.1%, in the entire US 12.1%.

The costs of living in New York are very high. The median monthly rent in Manhattan is $3,100, and in Brooklyn $2,800. If it wasn't for many social support programs, living in New York would have been inaccessible for average Americans. Almost 7% of New Yorkers (621,212) live in cheap, city-sponsored housing where monthly rent cannot exceed 30% of household income. Over 1 million apartments, almost half of the entire pool, is included into rent control programs, which lowers the median rent to $1,295 per month. Those and other programs supporting tenants were initiated during the Great Depression and in the 1960s.

Despite that, income and wealth inequalities and still among the most important challenges facing New York. In Manhattan, the symbol of the city, annual average income of the poorest 20% of households is only $9,635 (much below the poverty level), whereas the richest 20% of households make on average $389,007, and the richest 5% as much as $799,699. The richest New Yorkers inhabit apartments with a monthly rent exceeding $10,000 per month. The rent and utilities consume a substantial portion of New Yorker's income, for a third of households it's 25%, and for almost half of them (44%) it's 35% of their monthly earnings. It's not surprising, then, that most visions of the future mention affordable housing among the most important problems (Adler, 2015).

Since 1930s, when city's authorities started to regularly plan it's development, housing prices, public transportation, and infrastructure constitute most important categories of development programs. During the last few decades, they were supplemented with environmental protection. It will be more broadly discussed in the third part of this report, devoted to visions of New York in 2050.

19.3. New York — A Planned City: Urban Planning Traditions in New York

Economic, social, and architectural development of New York reflected the inherent features of American character: spontaneity, openness, and dynamism. Those features, however, brought about a certain level of chaos in the public space. As a result, ethnic ghettos, rich enclaves, and poor neighbourhoods, surrounded by industrial and commercial districts emerged. On the eve of the Great Depression, the city was an extraordinary mix of cultures, classes, and lifestyles existing right next to each other. It was becoming more and more challenging to control this dynamic matter. A modern city was waiting for its manager, who would transform it into a coherent organism.

As city's historians commonly agree it was Robert Moses who became the most active architect of New York. The peak of his planning activity came in the first decade after the Second World War. No library, park, hospital, or waterfront could be constructed without his permission (Glaab and Brown, 1967: 126). His centralized, and practically authoritarian, system of planning and management of the public space won him a number of both supporters and opponents.

The former ones look at almost 40 years of Moses' work in the city and enumerate his accomplishments: 13 bridges, 665 km of parkways, 658 playing grounds, 150,000 apartments. It would be impossible for any New Yorker to imagine the city without tunnels and highways such as Cross-Bronx Expressway, Brooklyn–Queens Expressway, Queens–Midtown Tunnel, Belt Parkway, or Triborough, and Varezzano Bridges. Thanks to Moses and his team's planning East River waterfront was regulated and the United Nations headquarters constructed there, the Lincoln Center became a temple of art it is today, and fans of Mets team can enjoy baseball games at the Shea Stadium.

Moses' critics see him as an authoritarian, pragmatic engineer, who put city's material interests, like infrastructure and public space management, above the well-being and cultural customs of local communities, which were cut into pieces by expressways, overpasses leading to enormous bridges, and massive demolitions creating space for modern apartment buildings (Caro, 1975: 12). This is how New York changed from a multiethnic and multicentre city of ethnic ghettos into megacity-metropolis.

Without a doubt, everyone who thinks about urban in planning New York must realize that his or her intentions, style, content of plans as well as ways in which those plans are prepared and implemented will inevitably be compared to the "age of Moses." Sometimes as a warning against excessive grandeur and sometimes as an encouragement to a more visionary approach. Due to their strong mandates, mayors of New York are always confronted with their citizens' expectations regarding the direction of city's development. New Yorkers want their city to be as great as they think it could potentially be. This potential, however, is perceived to be endless.

Robert Moses is often seen as a benchmark, similarly to how Poles saw Eugeniusz Kwiatkowski in the interwar period or Edward Gierek in the times of the People's Republic of Poland. It's hard to imagine a mayor of New York who would refrain from offering a broad and far-reaching vision of the city's future. Every mayor in the last four decades, Ed Koch, David Dinkins, Rudy Giuliani, and Michael Bloomberg, offered such a vision. Those visions can be very bold because Robert Moses demonstrated to New Yorkers that grand visions are not unrealistic and can indeed come true.

Current mayor, Bill de Blasio, has already issued several development plans in various areas such as environmental protection, public safety, flood prevention, and dissemination of digital technologies. His most recent plan, called *One New York*, reaches as far into the future as 2050, when the city, inhabited by 9 million people (8.4 million today) will have two new metro lines, including one in Manhattan, will decrease its production of waste by 90%, will see 800,000 poor citizens move into the middle class, will have 500,000 new apartments and will facilitate a decrease of the average commuting time to 45 mins. De Blasio's plan, announced on April 22, 2015, can be seen as fulfilment of the requirement for a grand vision (worthy of Robert Moses), but can also be interpreted as a practical attempt to demonstrate that the new mayor, who took office in 2013, understands the most important challenges facing New York: horrendous costs of rents, overcrowded public transportation system, growing inequalities, and ecological tensions exemplified by growing costs of waste management (garbage is more and more commonly carried to dump sites located in other states) and increasing sea level (due to greenhouse effect).

There are many simulations of the progression of New York's hydrological problems over the course of the 21st century, and the projections they offer are both interesting and worrying. If sea level continues to rise at a current rate — and according to environmental studies there are few reasons to dispute that — the majority of coastal areas in the city will be flooded as the water rises by 27–50 cm by 2050 and 45–79 cm by 2090 (Harvey, 2015). Flooded metro tunnels in lower Manhattan, flooded underground passages between New York and New Jersey, tens of thousands of apartments without electricity, all caused by hurricane Sandy in 2005 showed how hopeless the richest city in America is when faced with overwhelming force of nature.

The discussion of Robert Moses and his impact on the dynamics of New York's development in the 20th century testifies to the fact that political leaders have a crucial role to play when it comes to city's future (Caro, 1975). It also demonstrates that New York's past development was planned not just when it comes to management of public space. When comparing the image of New York from before the Great Depression and from the 1960s, we see two very different cities, not only in terms of infrastructure, architecture, public transportation, public services, and public space management. New York after Moses became a coherent urban organism, functioning very efficiently but with a lot of unfulfilled potential.

The leap forward experienced by New York over the course of 50 years shows how multidimensional and ambiguous the very term "development" is. Decisions made by planers and politicians affect, not only in a positive way, citizens, local communities, economic connections, and local and ethnic cultures, but also the way information, ideas, and values flow through the city.

During the three decades after Moses' "planned urbanistic revolution," New York experienced another upheaval. This time, however, it had a bottom-up origin and a much more "civic" character. This second revolution was connected to key social movements from the 1960s, and most important roles were played by hippies, ethnic, racial, and sexual minorities as well as by… policemen and businessmen. The most important effect of this was a revival of local communities, especially in Manhattan and Brooklyn. SoHo was taken over by artists, Greenwich Village by hippies and sexual minorities, and Harlem regained it's African–American character. Outside Manhattan, racial and ethnic minorities revitalized declining Bedford–Stuyvesant and sluggish Williamsburg in Brooklyn, as well as southern Bronx, cut in half by Interstate Highway I-95. It was all possible in part due to reform of immigration laws from 1964 which fuelled local ethnic communities in New York with new and fresh energy.

The growing importance of Wall Street, a symptom of rising financial capitalism, also helped to revitalize parts of Manhattan: Chelsea and Meatpacking District. Economic growth, together with new efforts and techniques of combating and preventing crime, had an enormous effect on the very centre of Manhattan — Times Square — transformed from a den for debauchery and drugs into a popular destination for shopping and family entertainment.

19.4. New York in the Future — General Assumptions

The two revolutions mentioned above — urbanistic and socio-cultural — were interconnected and complementary, and as a result New York at the beginning of the 21st century can be seen a completed city. The tragic events of September 11, 2001 only temporarily made New Yorkers doubt themselves, but did not manage to compromise the balance achieved between various aspects of city's development. Diversity brings energy, infrastructure brings coherence, and leadership role brings self-confidence. Social and cultural forces present in New York reaffirm its citizens' belief that their city is a very well structured urban system. When it comes to the future, even as remote as 2050, their past experiences make New Yorkers believe that their current actions will shape the fate of future generations.

When reading various development forecasts, planners' projections, or academic analyses, we see that they are all connected by certain common assumptions:

(1) In the foreseeable future, there seem to be no phenomena that would be impossible to be dealt with by city's authorities or citizens. Majority of threats can be addressed by actions already being planned today.

(2) Development of New York in the next three decades will mostly depend on the management of tendencies and phenomena already observable today. Authorities need to counter negative trends, mostly economic in character: social inequalities, growing rents, growing costs of public services. On the other hand, authorities must encourage

positive trends such as common awareness of citizens' shared responsibility for the environment they inhabit and the types of resources that flow into the city.

(3) Many challenges the city will face in the future will be social in nature and will touch upon relations between citizens and authorities, as well as between groups in the public space.

(4) One of most prominent challenges facing the city is providing for a better integration of the five boroughs, while at the same time decentralizing development by building up areas that can serve as centres for development of local communities.

(5) New York's authorities understand the unique character of their city, serving as a model for other large urban centres in the US. When it comes to city's development and the future, local patriotism transcends party lines.

(6) Planners and analysts define development primarily in terms of creating solutions enabling the city to use its economic, political, and cultural resources in the most efficient way.

(7) Past experiences show that if certain trends and phenomena related to the future development of the city cannot yet be observed, it does not mean that they cannot be initiated. That, in turn, means that one of the most important challenges for the city is related to innovations and new technologies.

(8) When it comes to the future of New York, uncertainty seems to be related primarily with unexpected natural disasters. Hurricane Sandy from 2005 can be seen a reference point in this respect. It caused $19 billion in damages, left 600,000 people without electricity, flooded metro tunes, and caused closures (lasting over 2 days) of 4 major bridges, 4 tunnels, and 3 major airports.

When asked about the most pressing challenges New York is likely to face in the future, vast majority of planners and analysts think that most problems the city is likely to face are related to ensuring a proper quality of life for citizens. This, however, has little to do with economic issues, such as employment and jobs and is mostly connected to public space management, effective allocation of existing resources, and generating new ones that will make New Yorkers' lives better.

In other words, visions of New York's future are clearly centred on the improvement of the way human, institutional, and economic resources are employed. This, also interpreted as progress, is often understood as an intellectual endeavour aimed at creating new and innovative systemic solutions.

As the analysis of exemplary anticipated problems will demonstrate, citizens, economic structures, and social groups are both subjects and objects (or tools) of this intellectual endeavour. It is city authorities' goal to improve the quality of life for their citizens, but steps suggested to be undertaken in order to achieve that goal involve using resources possessed by the citizens themselves: energy, creativity, ingenuity, which in the case of such a racially and ethnically diverse city like New York might actually be amplified by this multicultural construct (Beveridge and Weber, 2003: 14).

Visions of New York in 2050 focus on de-centralization and personalization of progress. The city and its authorities, structures, and rules play a secondary role. Their task is centred on creating conditions which will allow for citizens and institutional actors to pool and share their resources. No person even vaguely aware of American political traditions and political culture should be surprised by this statement. The idea of American exceptionalism, connected to a conviction that Americans have a very strong sense of their civic rights and duties, both in rural and urban environment (Abrams, 1969: 34), allows urban planners to assume that by 2030 New Yorkers will themselves decide to limit their production of waste by 90% if only proper recycling solutions and opportunities are presented to them and their benefits are adequately explained.

The very same logic is applied to the issue of public transportation: if the city constructs a network of public bike stations and biking routes, and then explains why using bikes is important and beneficial, the citizens will themselves gradually stop using cars when commuting to work. It is now time to look at a practical side of the aforementioned visions.

19.5. New York in 2015 — A More Concrete Vision

Concrete steps towards planning the development of New York to 2050 were taken in 2006 by the administration of city's major Michael Bloomberg, who got 25 employees from various offices and commissions to focus on making a vision of "greener and greater" NYC come true. The plan was called *PlaNYC* and after only 1 year 97% of 127 initiatives were started. In 2011, five new initiatives were added to the plan. In addition, 400 concrete indicators were enumerated and were going to be used to measure progress in plan's implementation over the next 2 years. Authorities approached the task of implementing their far-reaching vision with an impressive attention to detail. In 2013, when Bill de Blasio was elected as the new mayor (2013), he continued his predecessor's efforts, in accordance with city's tradition.

The plan creates a three-dimensional framework for actions: (1) Opening the city for over 1 million new inhabitants (15%) (OpeNYC); (2) Reparation of ageing infrastructure, most importantly bridges, major water pipes, and power grid, improvement of the public transportation system and changes in construction laws (MaintaiNYC); (3) More cautious use of natural resources, with the assumption that greenhouse gases emission will be cut by 30% by 2017 (GreeNYC).

This last date was in 2015 postponed until 2050, when greenhouse gases emission is projected to decrease by 80% in relation to 2005. This ambitious goal will be reached thanks to following the example of London and introducing congestion pricing (taxes for driving through Manhattan during rush hours on weekdays) and increasing New Yorker's use of public transportation. State legislature in Albany has been, so far, preventing such solutions from being introduced in New York, but the new mayor promised to increase efforts aimed at changing that.

Looking at how quickly CO_2 emission has been decreasing in New York the 2050 goal may not be so ambitious after all. Only changes in construction laws resulted in decreasing emission by 16% between 2005 and 2015. Plan for a green New York stresses increasing citizen's awareness regarding environmentally friendly behaviours, sometimes as mundane as thermostat control or waste segregation (Rosenberg, 2016). This educational task is being carried out by leaflets and announcements, but most importantly through social media and the Internet, considered to be high-impact and low-cost methods.

Apart from continuing the three plans introduced by his predecessor, mayor de Blasio proposed a series of solutions in the realm of socio-economic relations that will positively impact the quality of life in the city, especially for its poorest citizens. Those solutions include constructing new housing projects on public lands and renovating existing buildings in order to decrease costs of utilities.

Mayor's *OneNYC* plan also proposes adding a new clause to construction permits for apartment buildings with rent determined by market, which will require that a number of apartments with subsidized rent will also be constructed (inclusionary housing). As a result the number of people living in poverty (800,000 people today) should dramatically decrease.

The following list includes large-scale actions as well as small steps aimed at transforming *PlaNYC* and *OneNYC* — Michael Bloomberg's and Bill de Blasio's visions of New York between 2030 and 2050 — to realities.

19.5.1. Environment

19.5.1.1. *Water*

(1) New buildings must be fitted with water-saving technologies; replacing toilet tanks with lower capacity ones, installation of water meters, promoting water-saving behaviours.
(2) Similarly to what the *Bluebelt* plan for Staten Island from 2005 proposed, rainwater will be more effectively collected from public spaces and directed into city's sewer system and subsequently through purification system in order to make it free from dangerous chemicals. Slowing down the flow of water in various systems will decrease soil erosion in natural waterways and help prevent floods.
(3) The city will purchase lands which have their ecosystems threated by human activity. In addition, various species of animals will be reintroduced into their natural habitats. In a more distant future new natural parks will be established on areas protected by the city.
(4) Streets in newly constructed neighbourhoods will be more narrow and will have plants and trees along them. As the example of Seattle has proven, lowering the average driving speed does not create problems with traffic. Streets in New York will less resemble communication channels but will instead be more integrated with the character of their surroundings.
(5) Non-toxic cleaning supplies will be purchased for city's buildings and their use will be limited by 5%.

19.5.1.2. *Air*

In order to improve the quality of air the city will have to primarily decrease emissions of toxic and other gases contributing to the greenhouse effect. Emissions are planned to be reduced by 80% between 2005 and 2050.

(1) Vehicles operated by the city will be supplied with modern engines: hybrids and low-emissions diesels.
(2) Lightbulbs in traffic lights will be replaced by LED's.
(3) Coal heat boilers in public buildings will be replaced with gas ones.
(4) Assuming that half of the buildings existing in 2050 has not yet been constructed the city will change construction laws and make it mandatory to construct so-called ecological buildings. When it comes to buildings owned by the city, such technologies will reduce the use of energy necessary for heating by 30–70% and for air conditioning by 10–50%. Overall use of energy in New York should decrease by 45–55% by 2050.
(5) The city will plant over 1 million new trees by 2030, a 20% increase in green areas. It will be a public–private partnership, the city will be responsible for 70% of new trees and 30% will be planted by building owners and local organizations.
(6) New technologies will be used to create a citywide system of air pollution monitoring (*NYC Breathe*). Information about pollution levels will be in real time distributed among citizens, primarily with the use of digital technologies.
(7) With global warming increasing the probability of hurricanes and causing rising sea levels the city forecasts that 118,000 buildings inhabited by 809,000 people will by 2050 be located on lands threatened by floods. The area of those lands will increase by 425% in relation to 2005. New York will cooperate with FEMA and create a system for evacuation, disaster prevention, and provision of basic resourced and services in case of a natural disaster (drinking water, transportation, medical care, communication, and energy supply). This operation will cost $50 billion by 2050.

19.5.1.3. *Solid waste*

(1) The city is currently implementing a program of office paper saving and offers a set of incentives for private users, including businesses. The program includes duplex printing, using electronic forms of communication instead of paper-based ones, purchasing paper with 50% recycled content.

(2) Increasing the amount of recycled content in paper used by the city from 30% to 50% will have substantial ecological effects: 8% decrease of the use of energy, 8% decrease in CO_2 emission, 11% decrease in the amount of waste produced, 18% decrease in the amount of dangerous chemicals in water, 29% decrease in demand for wood.

(3) The city will introduce a system of regulations and incentives aimed at reducing the amount of waste carried to dump sites to zero by 2030.

(4) The city will introduce a program for reclaiming lands currently used for dumping sites and creating parks and green areas on those lands.

(5) Expecting further development of waste segregation techniques, the city plans to replace a solution based on segregating waste by citizens with a more modern one, based on collecting a so-called single stream commodity waste material. Decrease in the number of trash bags and bins will greatly decrease the number of garbage trucks and therefore help reduce CO_2 emissions.

(6) Replacement of plastic garbage bags, which cost the city US$10 million annually to reprocess, with more modern ones made of biodegradable materials or paper with recycled content.

(7) The city plans to reduce the production of solid waste by businesses, offices, restaurants, shops, and factories by 90% by 2030. Currently only a third of this waste is being recycled. A very large decrease will be possible thanks to the use of modern technologies, changes in laws and educational programs.

(8) The city will clean off and develop post-industrial and abandoned lots, over 3,000 of which need to be rehabilitated. Those lands will then be managed by boroughs and opened for public use.

(9) The city will create public parks on lands used for now-abandoned overground metro lines. In order to create as little inconvenience for citizens as possible those lines will not be demolished, but included into projects. This innovative solution will create an interesting effect of combining post-industrial modernity with ecology. 2 km of an abandoned metro line turned into a green park and walking space in Manhattan's Chelsea neighbourhood serves as a model for this solution.

(10) In order to increase the area of common public space the city will attempt to develop public spaces, including streets without substantial traffic, into common spaces with parks, benches and playgrounds. Streets with calm traffic will be closed on weekends for the organization of festivities bringing together local communities. Public buildings will be fitted with dayrooms for the youth and the elderly.

19.5.2. Social inequalities

The city aims at decreasing the number of people living in poverty by 800,000 by 2025. This trend will continue afterwards until poverty among New Yorkers is eliminated.

(1) The city will construct new housing projects with subsidized rent, independently or with the use of public–private partnership. $200,000 new apartments will be constructed every decade by 2050.
(2) Minimum wage will be increased to $15 per hour (from current $7.25) by 2020.
(3) The city will take action aimed at decreasing the rate of premature deaths by 25%. New Yorkers will have access to better quality health care at affordable prices.
(4) Establishment of Family Justice Centres focused at combating domestic violence.
(5) Better integration of public services. Better circulation of public information, increased use of social media and digital technologies.
(6) Expanding a network of broadband, affordable Internet access. About 22% of New Yorkers do not have access to such network today. Internet access is crucial for an effective circulation of public information and using online services, including consulting.

(7) Better cooperation between the city and its boroughs, aimed at problem-solving.
(8) The city will invest in human capital by launching a *Career Pathways* program, aimed at supporting young and talented New Yorkers in looking for well-paid jobs. Development of another program — First Look — will help traditionally excluded minorities and communities gain access to better employment opportunities.
(9) In order to help young people who do not attend colleges the city will support vocational training to better prepare them for competing in the 21st century economy. Students will be encouraged to get involved with trade unions to get access to well-paid jobs in unionized industries.
(10) Ethnic minorities and immigrants will gain access to bilingual education (in English and their mother tongue) in order to help them enter the job market.
(11) Changing dietary habits of the less well-off citizens and encouraging them to eat five servings a day, including more fruits and vegetables.
(12) Promoting job market solutions which will lead to a structure of employment related to the proportions of minorities in overall population. The city will create a system for monitoring employment procedures in offices, will conduct employment reviews and will establish a system for selecting most talented high school students (Managing Diversity and Inclusion Leadership Initiative, MDLI).

19.5.3. Public infrastructure

In 2005, hurricane Sandy made New York authorities realize how dangerous environmental threats are, especially those related to rising sea level and natural disasters (Moss, 2005: 97) Global warming increased the likelihood of threatening weather conditions. City's waterfronts in all boroughs are threatened with flooding as sea level will rise even by 75 cm by 2050.

(1) Establishment of emergency forces and services which will help victims of natural disasters. Police force will be equipped with boats

and dinghies. Students, teachers, and other school personnel will be trained in disaster preparedness.

(2) Strengthening New York's position as a centre of regional development. New areas will be covered by metro area regulations. Better integration of the metro area through public transportation.

(3) Abandoned and unused lands, like the Bronx River bed and Hudson and East Rivers waterfronts (where old warehouses and docks are located), will be reclaimed and developed. One of the most important projects involves reclaiming the lad used by old Brooklyn Navy Yard. This area itself is capable of accommodating over 100,000 apartments.

(4) Public transportation network will be extended. Two new metro lines will be constructed, one in Manhattan along the 2nd Avenue and the other one in Brooklyn south of Utica Avenue.

(5) Average commuting time for over 1.8 million New Yorkers should not exceed 45 minutes a day.

(6) In 2040, the number of New Yorkers over 60 years of age will exceed the number of school children in the city. Abandoned property in all boroughs will be renovated and turned into community centres for seniors.

(7) The city will undertake strategic action aimed at attracting investments to all the boroughs. Centres of boroughs and neighbourhoods will be revitalized in order to serve as true centres of social and commercial activity.

(8) By 2050, climate change will increase average temperature in the city by 2–2.3°C, increase rain downfalls by 11% and increase sea and river levels by 27–53 cm. This creates a need for additional flood prevention infrastructure, including dykes protecting especially threatened areas.

(9) The average number of days in a year with temperature exceeding 29°C will double. Apart from driving demand for energy up this will bring new health risks for seniors and children, especially those from less well-off households inhabiting old buildings, where outdated electric and ventilation installations prevent modern energy and money saving technologies from being implemented.

(10) If New York wants to maintain its status of a global innovations capital it needs to support innovative economic enterprises by

providing high-quality office spaces in key business districts, which should be created in all boroughs.

(11) Mixed-use areas will be created in order to balance the character of neighbourhoods, especially by developing commercial infrastructure and supporting class diversity in resident areas.

(12) The city will support cultural diversity by creating and financing local community centres (*Community Arts Development Program*, CADP).

(13) CADP will gain additional support in the form of using public spaces for artistic events. The city wants to encourage citizens to express their identities in interactions with other minorities. Over 200 languages can be heard spoken on the streets of New York.

(14) Central and integrated city information system will be created. New Yorkers will be able to call 311 and get reliable and exact information about public and social services and health care.

(15) Community gardens will be created, enabling citizens to get involved in growing healthy foods. The gardens will also serve as centres for social interaction and education related to health and nutrition.

(16) De-centralization of green energy production from local reusable sources: photovoltaics, geothermal energy, biomass, incineration.

(17) Development of sea and river waterfronts.

19.5.4. Economy

(1) Currently 38.4% of New York's GDP is produced in Manhattan. Economic development of the city needs to be more well-balanced.

(2) The city needs to attract new investors, who will create well-paying jobs for citizens. New trainings centres will be established for people who want to change or increase their qualifications in order to meet the requirements of a modern job market.

(3) The city will support industries that generate large profit margins and employ many people, like the Broadway industry or fashion industry. Those branches will see better conditions for increasing investments in New York, for example, thanks to a more adequate management of public properties and lots. The fashion industry employed 5.5% of

New York's workforce in 2005 (183,000 people), paying $11 billion in wages and $1.3 billion in taxes. Every year over 75 large commercial fashion shows take place in the city. The industry is expected to grow by 15% over the next 25 years.

(4) Entertainment industry grew by 13% over the last 3 years. Broadway theatres generate $11.9 billion in income and employ 87,000 people. Movie and television industries note $7.1 billion in expenses, pay $400,000 in taxes while employing 130,000 people.

(5) Traditional branches of industry in the city, like the meat industry, will also be supported. Authorities will revitalize and modernize places like the Hunts Point Food Distribution Center, one of the largest fresh meat and fish distribution centres in the world. Industry cluster is expected to be created there. The city will construct modern utilization facilities and treatment plants and will reconstruct two nearby highways in order to make Hunts Point easier to reach.

(6) Programs supporting medium (up to 100 employees) and small (up to 20 employees) enterprises will be established. Over the next 5 years the city will spend $27 million on improvements of administrative procedures like registration, issuing licenses, and permissions.

(7) The city will support schools preparing students to work with new information technologies and in the IT industry. *Career and Technical Education* (CTE) programs will be expanded to cover at least 120,000 students.

19.5.5. Public transportation

(1) Improvement of communication connections between three major New York airports.

(2) Construction of new metro lines, especially outside Manhattan, with special attention paid to connecting borough centres.

(3) Establishment of bus lanes with adequate monitoring and surveillance systems.

(4) Local transportation systems within boroughs need to be improved. The city will analyze street's traffic capacity, introduce special bus lanes, and earlier traffic lights.

(5) A strategy for integrating suburban population into the city within the New York metro area (17.7 million inhabitants) will be created.

(6) East and Hudson Rivers will be used for ferry transportation, both along and across them.
(7) There are few possibilities for constructing new highways, but many of the existing ones have been built during the Great Depression or after the World War II and they need to be repaired and modernized.
(8) Traffic control system will be improved in areas heavily used for cargo transportation, like airports and their surroundings. JFK airport will gain a new cargo terminal.
(9) Since 2000 the use of bicycles for communication within the city has increased by 337%. The city plans to add 200 miles of bike lanes annually to the existing 2,000 miles by 2020. Possibilities of crossing bridges on bikes will be improved.

19.5.6. Security

(1) Crime preventions systems need to be more just and citizens must be included into them in order to make sure that the people's sense of safety and social justice is not impaired.
(2) Incarnation should to a certain extent be replaced with community service and other forms of non-custodial sentences.
(3) Police force will be equipped with modern communication tools which will help policemen to better identify potential suspects and improve their relations with local communities.
(4) The city will support the development of *ShotSpotter* technology, a system allowing to identify a gunshot with an accuracy of 25 m.
(5) Attempts will be made to eliminate deaths in traffic accidents (*Vision Zero*). The number of people killed in traffic accidents is systematically decreasing: In 1990 there were 701 victims, in 2000 381 and in 2011 only 249 including 182 pedestrians. The goal is to bring that number to zero in 2020. A series of steps will be undertaken to achieve that, including narrowing streets, traffic and speed limitations, and a broad educational campaign aimed at both drivers and pedestrians.

19.6. New York in 2050: A Summary

Solutions proposed by authorities and planners clearly indicate that there are no major threats to the continuation of already observed development trends. The most important challenge is related to natural disasters, sudden like hurricanes and progressing like global warming. The city, however, establishes programs and institutions in order to manage disasters when they arrive.

In the socio-economic realm New York prepares for the future by improving the way in which resources possessed by authorities and citizens are used and managed. The future seen as a sate which approaches gradually and which can be prepared for, and sometimes even influenced, is the most important feature of the way in which development of the city is imagined.

Influencing the future will be possible only if societal and politico-administrative forces work together. Public–private-citizen partnership is the foundation of long-term visions for New York.

Most of the planned changes are evolutionary in nature. Changes are brought by enhancing already existing and observable tendencies and phenomena.

In the spirit of Robert Moses, citizens undertake both large- and small-scale actions aimed at distant future. However, unlike in the times of this great reformer and constructor, plans and actions are supposed to make changes more down-to-earth in character and more human related. Visions of New York in 2050 are not based on creative destruction. To the contrary, most programs are based on rebuilding, revitalizing, and strengthening institutions and infrastructure.

The most important thing for making New York a city of progress is to reach out to the pool of human capital, which is assumed to exist by almost all the planners. Their plans do not envisage any destruction of communities or social structures which may stay in the way of reforms. It's the people who will be behind changes, they must direct and legitimize them. New York in 2050 is a great city with a human face, created by the people and for the people.

The example of New York proves that negative development trends can be reversed if only effective leadership manages to energize citizens. Moreover, reformers are convinced that city's development during the last three decades has proven, in almost all areas of life, that New York can serve a model for other cities. When compared to California, which is often thought of as being on the *avant-garde* of social and economic transformations, New York definitely prevails in areas such as security, environmental protection, and respect for social diversity.

Because of all that, major challenges facing New York are related primarily to ensuring the proper quality of life for its citizens. Economic issues, like job creation, are not among chief concerns. Important tasks concern management of public space, use of already existing resources and creation of new ones, which will altogether improve the quality of life in the city. In order to achieve all the long-term goals New York plans, projects, examines, asks, checks, talks, tests, verifies, and engages everyone concerned about the city's future in a debate leading to common action. The city is not afraid to think boldly about its future. Every person who takes the time to go through many analyses covering the future of New York, both more realistic and more futuristic ones, is bound to conclude that this complete city is becoming a city of progress in the very way it thinks about itself.

References

Abrams, R. (Ed.) (1969). *The Issues of the Populist and Progressive Eras 1892–1912*. Columbia: University of South Carolina Press.

Adler, B. (2015). Brooklyn's Median Household Income is less than $45,000 so How Can Anyone Afford to Live There, 2014. Retrieved from http://www.slate.com/articles/business/moneybox/2014/01/new_york_city_census_data_manhattan_and_brooklyn_are_much_poorer_than_you.html [access: 01.05.2015].

Beveridge, A. and S. Weber (2003). Race and class in the developing New York and Los Angeles metropolies. In D. Halle (Ed.). *New York & Los Angeles. Politics, Society, and Culture. A Comparative View*. Chicago: University of Chicago Press, pp. 49–78.

Caro, R. (1975). *The Power Broker. Robert Moses and the Fall of New York*. New York: Vintage Books.

Glaab, Ch. and T. Brown (1967). *A History of Urban America*. New York: Macmillan.

GreeNYC. Retrieved from http://huntergatherer.net/project/greenyc/ [access: 26.04.2015].

Harvey, Ch. (2015). "These are the parts of New York City that will flood when sea levels rise," *Business Insider*. Retrieved from http://www.businessinsider.com/new-york-city-flood-map-2020-2050-2015-2#ixzz3YKJPaoWa [access: 02.05.2015].

Marwell, N. (2007). *Bargaining for Brooklyn. Community Organizations in an Entrepreneurial City*. Chicago: University of Chicago Press.

Mollenkopf, J. (Ed.). (2005). *The Contentious City. The Politics of Recovery in New York City.* New York: Russell Sage Foundation.

Moss, M. (2005). The Redevelopment of Lower Manhattan. The Role of the City. In J. Mollenkopf (Ed.). *The Contentious City. The Politics of Recovery in New York City.* New York: Russell Sage Foundation, pp. 95–111.

Mumford, L. (1970). *The Pentagon of Power. The Myth of the Machine.* New York: Hrcourt Brace and Javanovich.

NYCUSA quickfacts (2012). Retrieved from http://quickfacts.census.gov/qfd/states/36000.html [access: 30.05.2015].

OneNYC. *A plan for a strong and just city*, Retrieved from http://www1.nyc.gov/html/onenyc/index.html [access: 16.05.2015].

OpeNYC. Retrieved from http://www.nyc.gov/html/planyc/html/home/home.shtml [access: 29.04.2013].

Rosenberg, Z. (2016). Reducing Greenhouse Gas Emissions. Retrieved from http://ny.curbed.com/2016/8/24/12626522/nyc-greenhouse-gas-emissions-report [access: 28.03.2017].

Szanto, A. (2003). Some Contrasts between the Visual Art Worlds of New York and Los Angeles. In D. Halle (Ed.). *New York & Los Angeles. Politics, Society, and Culture. A Comparative View.* Chicago: University of Chicago Press, pp. 393–421.

Weber, E. (1969). The growth of cities in the nineteenth century. In R. Abrams (Ed.). *The Issues of the Populist and Progressive Eras 1892–1912*. Columbia: University of South Carolina Press, pp. 100–111.

Part IV

Epilogue

20

IN LIEU OF A CONCLUSION: MEGACITIES — BOON OR BANE?

Jerzy Kleer and Katarzyna A. Nawrot

These closing remarks will sum up a few of the many threads that have been discussed in this volume, considering how they contribute to our emerging overall picture of the longer-term impact of megacities on the future world.

It was not until the modern era arrived that the problems related to megacities started to gather momentum. There are a number of reasons for this, at least two of which carry special significance: booming population growth and civilizational transitions. We should devote special attention to the consequences of the population boom, chiefly because of its impact both on the growth of existing and emerging megacities and on the threats they are facing. Nonetheless, the issue of civilizational turning points will be also explored in these remarks. We will first look at the threats generally posed by booming population growth. We then proceed to consider where such surging population numbers are taking us, an issue depicted here as a four-way configuration of interrelated factors (an insufficient food supply, education, urban population growth, and a shortage of jobs). Next, we summarize some of the environmental consequences of the rise of megacities, and look at the challenging shifts underway in the relations between megacity and state.

20.1. Threats Posed by Booming Population Growth

As the starting point for this analysis, we take global population forecasts through 2100 (the median variant). The world's population stood at 7.3 billion in 2015, and it is expected to reach 9.7 billion in 2050 and 11.2 billion in 2100 (UNDESA, 2015). Such a dramatic surge is something unprecedented in the history of mankind, and its economic, social, and perhaps above all political consequences will be difficult to predict. Its impact on development and especially its degree of complexity can only be understood properly when viewed in the context of the heterogeneous distribution of this population growth, not only on a global scale but also between specific regions.

Two different approaches might be taken to such uneven population growth. Firstly, it can be described from a more general standpoint, broken down into areas of the world that are more vs. less developed, and secondly, it might be analyzed according to regional (geographic) divisions, for example, the individual continents. These two approaches often coincide and yet can sometimes cross-cut one another; this applies in particular to Asia, which while being a continent with numerous developing countries also includes a number of developed countries and emerging economies.

And so, here let us first take the former approach. For the world's more developed regions, projected population growth rates for the period between 2015 and 2050 are practically imperceptible. Standing at 1.251 billion in 2015, the population inhabiting such regions is expected to reach 1.286 billion in 2050. An increase of just 35 million spread over 35 years is close to the level of statistical error. What is more, the population of the developed regions is expected to shrink to 1.277 billion by 2100. By contrast, the population of the less developed regions stood at 6.098 billion in 2015, and it is expected to rise to 8.439 billion by 2050, and 9.936 by 2100 (UNDESA, 2015). At the same time, preliminary projections say that there will be around 50 megacities by 2050 and more than 80 by 2100, together comprising a population of around 1 and 2 billion people, respectively, according to modest estimates (Hoornweg and Pope, 2014).

These projections alone illustrate the enormous economic, social, and political challenges that lie ahead. What might be done to resolve the escalating problems, especially in the light of the emergence of a distinctive weapon engendered by the information revolution: The increased visibility of social processes, which makes disparities in the standards of living and income differentials especially strongly felt? One can be hardly surprised by surging migrations, both movements from rural areas to cities and migrations to developed countries, especially in Europe and North America.

If we now look at the phenomenon broken down somewhat differently, following the second approach of looking in terms of the world's geographic regions (continents), we will see that such growth will be especially high in Africa, whose population is expected to rise from 1.186 in 2015 to 2.478 billion in 2050 and 4.387 billion by 2100, followed by Asia, whose population will grow from 4.393 billion in 2015 to 5.267 billion in 2050. It is expected that population in Asia will start to decrease in the latter half of the 21st century, to stand at 4.889 billion by 2100. Europe's population, by contrast, is actually projected to edge back from 738 million in 2015 to 707 million in 2050 and 646 million in 2100 (UNDESA, 2015).

The overall economic and social consequences of this surging world population growth will not be dealt with in more detail here (the reader is encouraged to refer to the more in-depth discussions in other contributions to the present volume); instead, we will focus on listing several consequences of its widely disparate, uneven distribution across the world. To begin with, note that although the whole of the burden associated with population growth will fall on the world's less developed regions, especially Africa, at the same time it also remains the least developed continent in social and economic terms. More importantly, its social and economic institutions are not yet sufficiently prepared for the emerging challenges and threats. The most important consequences of this situation, both in the present and in the future, will include the continued growth of Africa's existing cities and megacities and the emergence of new megacities, ones which as yet cannot be accurately pinpointed. On the other hand, these consequences will also continue to drive a growing exodus of people within the continent and to other continents, especially to Europe (as is already happening to a certain extent). The results of the latter process are partially visible in the attempts of specific countries to avoid taking in growing numbers of refugees and in the rise of various populist, xenophobic, and nationalistic ideologies, which may be seen as the most negative phenomenon from the point of view of not only those immigrants but also of communities within those specific societies.

At this point, it is hard to predict the consequences of those processes for Europe, in particular the EU. We can nonetheless say that the closing off of specific states will continue over the next decade and we will witness a certain, probably temporary erosion of the European Union. At the same time, however, it is impossible to rule out more dramatic consequences in the form of various kinds of tensions, the escalation of terrorism, and various provocations leading to armed conflicts posing dangers characterized by various levels of intensity.

The particular tragedy of the situation, it appears, lies mainly in the fact that the modern elite has no long-term vision for how to resolve this problem and indeed gives such little thought to what consequences putting off its resolution will bring.

20.2. Where is World Population Growth Leading?

The surge in population numbers predicted for the current century is not only historically unprecedented but also, and more importantly, it poses enormous challenges and threats. These stem from the great scale of the related phenomena and from the fact that this growth will be experienced practically entirely by less developed economies. Meeting these challenges will require enormous capital and financial resources, which is, paradoxically, precisely something these particular regions do not have at their disposal. This may seem to be a banal observation to make, but it is nonetheless helpful to begin with a general examination of the major challenges and threats of surging population numbers. While one may argue over the relative hierarchy of importance of the individual challenges, the configuration presented below is intended not to evaluate their significance but to merely highlight the most important ones among them, which could be described as falling into a four-way configuration, determining the survival of both the newly emerging and partially also the previously existing population.

The first and arguably most important component of this configuration is the food supply. We bring this point to the fore here with very good reason: Resolving the problem of famine in less developed regions is a task of priority importance, and this is a well-known and well-documented fact.[1] And yet, to date, the issue has proved not to be solved, despite numerous varied efforts and measures, not only on the part of the less developed countries but also involving assistance (though arguably not sufficiently satisfactory) from developed countries and international organizations. Thus, the provision of sufficient food for the future population should be treated as one of the most important challenges as well as threats. This is because it will affect, in particular, the major urban agglomerations and megacities, which will be inhabited by a significant share of the future population, and many of its members might have no permanent employment. At the same time, it cannot be ruled out that the struggle over food resources might be dramatic.

The second component, directly linked to the first, pertains to the problem of education. There are, as yet, no long-term forecasts for the future share of the world population (aged 15 and older) who will be able to read and write. At the beginning of the present decade, this figure was approx. 74% in developing countries, while reaching 66% among women and around 43% among women in least developed countries (UNDP, 2002). Such statistics are an important gauge reflecting people's ability to judge the surrounding reality properly and to relatively actively participate in the process of development. Reliable forecasts in this regard would, in particular, facilitate better assessments of the threats related to underdevelopment, not so much (and not only) for a specific country as for the future financial and professional situation of the inhabitants themselves.

The importance of education is particularly evident also when we compare the share of university students in the population of developed countries to that of developing countries. The gross enrolment ratio in tertiary education in developing countries stood at 25% in 2008–2014, while in the least developed countries it was at only 8%. The same ratio in countries of very high human development reached 77% (UNDP, 2015). Likewise, we need to view this problem through the prism of ongoing civilizational transitions in the world.

The degradation of the traditional agrarian civilization in the countries characterized by low levels of development and the highest rates of

[1] Refer i.e. to Nawrot (2014: 164–167).

population growth not only speeded up the transition to the industrial stage of civilization but also created conditions for varying capacities to take advantage of benefits from the knowledge-based civilization. However, knowledge-based civilization requires different and much more complex qualifications that may be contributed to a significant degree by a robust system of higher education, especially the research sector. Modern-day development in less-developed countries cannot rely exclusively on imitation, because this model fails to take account of the distinctive characteristics of individual states and economies. Hence, the importance of forms of education that do take local characteristics into account stem from specific countries or regions.

The third component of this configuration is the development of cities and rapid urban population growth. City dwellers accounted for 54% of the world's population in 2015, and this share is expected to rise to 66.4% in 2050 (UNDESA, 2014). Two-thirds of the world's population will then be living in cities, creating a highly volatile, potentially explosive mixture. Cities will be nexuses where wealth will come face-to-face with and clash with poverty, and where conflicts will arise against the backdrop of multiculturalism. Urban population growth will be especially fast in less-developed regions. The share of the urban population in those regions stood at 49% in 2015 and is expected to rise to 63.4% in 2050. In developed regions, in turn, the share of the urban population will rise from 78.3% to 85.4% (UNDESA, 2014).

What does this growth in urban population numbers entail in practice? While again leaving more detailed analysis of this issue to various other contributions to this volume, here we should point out several important consequences of the modern type of urbanization. To begin with, we can assume that urban development in most of the big cities, especially megacities, will be chaotic and largely uncontrolled: this is already largely the case, and this trend will only grow in the future, chiefly as a result of the fast-growing urban population combined with a lack of adequate city governance. The consequences will include (or strictly speaking already include) a shortage of housing, their low standard, homelessness, the emergence of vast areas of poverty, mediocre standards of living, criminogenic behaviour, and above all the general devastation of the public sphere, both in cities that have long traditions and ones that were established in the modern era. Such a phenomenon is typical of urban agglomerations in both less developed and well developed regions of the world. The differences pertain only to the scope and form of devastation. All this results in a growing lack of security in the broad sense, in most spheres of urban life in connection with increasing instability.

The fourth component of this four-way configuration is the growing shortage of jobs. It results on the one hand from the massive influx of people from rural areas as well as from other countries or regions, and on the other hand from the fact that the number of new jobs is growing at a much slower pace than in the past, especially when compared against growth in labour supply, which has increased many times over as a result of booming demographic growth. This is also because significant shifts are underway in the very nature of labour itself, effected by technological advancements in traditional aspects of economic and social activity as well as in the new areas linked to the information revolution. In the latter field, the issue of relevant education in the broad sense is turning into an increasingly important factor. In turn, growing unemployment, which occurs especially in less developed countries, may and probably will entail long-term socio-political consequences. Above all, we might witness what could be described as an increasing state of people feeling socially excluded or superfluous: A precarious psychological and economic condition experienced by those unable to earn enough money to support themselves, their families, or their loved ones. The effects will include various conflicts, ranging from individual conflicts of different degrees of criminogenic behaviour to the emergence of organized crime groups as well as intergroup conflicts, especially in the socio-political sphere. This is where diverse forms of populism can and will emerge, as will other ideologies that might push people towards armed conflicts. The latter often have other sources, resulting from processes of de-colonization, which occurred when the same ethnic groups were present in various countries and different religious conflicts arose.

Although such conflicts do not always occur in cities, such hostility, or such hostile ideologies, have their roots in particular in urban centres, especially big cities and megacities.

20.3. Consequences for the Environment

Booming population growth also has a very distinctive impact on the natural environment, above all leading to its degradation. The rapid development of urban areas plays a special role in this process, with megacities being an especially destructive factor in this regard. We will once again not present a detailed analysis of this phenomenon here, but will nevertheless point out some of its main manifestations.

The first and most probably most important of these is the negative contribution of both big and small cities to global warming. This is especially due to two factors: heating and transport. The system of heating prevalent in densely populated areas continues to rely heavily on coal and wood as primary sources of energy; the negative effects include in particular carbon dioxide emissions in the atmosphere. The many international agreements attempting to combat this phenomenon have yet to bring the expected results. In practice, many countries ignore those commitments due to the attendant costs and the interests of certain groups that derive benefits from preserving the existing model. The system of urban transportation links, in turn, has developed on a large scale, at least over the past several decades, in connection with the automotive sector, with cars becoming a commonly used means of transport; the consequences for global warming are similar to those of traditional heating.

Another important manifestation of the degradation of the natural environment comes with the territorial expansion and urban sprawl, which often takes on certain predatory characteristics, causing the degradation of ever-larger areas of land. Unfortunately, today's expansion of cities is largely not based on calculations of the rationality of their size, but is rather spontaneous and barely under any control. In theory, however, one could image it being planned in a way that factors in not only purely economic calculations but also, and perhaps even more importantly, the accompanying social costs. There is, as yet, no approach that manages to satisfy these requirements, at least in an overwhelming majority of less developed countries, which are characterized by the highest rate of urban growth and will be inhabited by the largest share of the population in the coming decades. The aptness of this conclusion is demonstrated by simple calculations based on existing urban population projections: according to the figures cited above, megacities will be inhabited by nearly one-tenth of the world's population around 2050.

20.4. Relations between Megacities and the State: Present and Future

Relations between megacities and the state represent a multifaceted and extremely complex problem that is only just beginning to be addressed, both in practice and in the theoretical literature. On the one hand, the reflections presented here are based on an analysis of the current situation, but on the other hand, they also attempt to anticipate the future development of the relations between the central authorities and those of megacities.

First, here we should stress that in the existing model of the state, which was developed in the course of the industrial revolution and evolved towards a closed territory with the centre of government being located in the capital, any specific relations maintained by the state and the directions of those relations, especially internal ones, must have the express approval of the central authorities. Admittedly, in the course of the development of the democratic model, certain powers have been devolved to lower levels of administration in various countries and to different degrees. This situation has now changed fundamentally with the arrival of globalization and the information revolution, which have forced the sovereign nation states to open their borders to the movement of goods, capital, services, and people.

Multinational corporations have emerged in the field of business activity, the role of the financial markets has changed, and the structure of the Gross Domestic Product (GDP) has shifted, with services accounting for an ever growing share of the GDP and becoming increasingly centred in urban areas, in particular in major cities. As a result, a large share of capital and many skilled workers are now focused around new forms of business activity. Big-city populations are growing faster and faster as a result of migrations from areas characterized by the collapse of industry, already overpopulated villages, and booming demographic growth.

From the economic perspective, big cities are growing in strength in view of their role as the decision-making centres of multinational corporations and international banks, explosive growth in higher education establishments and modern research and scientific centres, the presence of the creative intelligentsia, and the large supply of advanced services and skilled workers. This process has been extremely fast-paced, having taken place over the past several decades. It began in the late 1970s and early 1980s, a period that witnessed the erosion of socialism (which would fully collapse a decade later) and the formal end of the great process of de-colonization. Major migration processes started, especially from former colonies, but also from former socialist countries.

The world is nowadays a very different place, and yet the traditional model of the state as a product of the industrial revolution has not changed to a considerable degree. Within this model, the central authorities and power in the centralized state have experienced the emergence of a new competitive force in the form of major cities, which have if not political clout than at least economic power and numerous strong interconnectivities at their disposal. Note that the long-term interests of big cities (sometimes megacities) do not always converge with their home state's ongoing political or economic interests. This holds true for both capital cities (London's example in the 2016 Brexit referendum) and for other urban hubs like New York (as was the case with the 2016 presidential elections in the United States).

Nevertheless, the problem is even broader and more complex. Profound changes taking place as a result of civilizational transitions are increasingly necessitating a new division of powers between the central and the local authorities. More often than not, the latter are economically more powerful yet remain formally limited by the central authorities. Qualitative changes are therefore needed here, especially the devolution of much broader powers so as to prevent the possible formal or informal secession of major urban areas, especially the expanding megacities.

*

In lieu of an overall conclusion, therefore, we can close by reiterating what might be seen as the central underlying question addressed by the various contributions to this volume: Are megacities a blessing for the world, now and in the foreseeable future, or do are they more of a threat? In short, will they be a bane or a boon to tomorrow's world?

As it turns out and as we have seen, there is, as yet, no satisfactory answer to this question. This fact can only encourage us to continue to pose it, again and again — be it in the capacity of scientific researchers, as citizens of the world, as global citizens or as urban residents.

References

Hoornweg, D. and K. Pope (2014). Socioeconomic Pathways and Regional Distribution of the World's 101 Largest Cities. *Global Cities Institute Working Paper No. 04*. Toronto.

Nawrot, K.A. (2014). *Kraje rozwijające się we współczesnej gospodarce światowej. Przyczynek do ekonomii rozwoju*. Warszawa: Wydawnictwo Naukowe Scholar.

UNDESA (2014). United Nations, Department of Economic and Social Affairs, Population Division. *World Urbanization Prospects: The 2014 Revision*, CD-ROM Edition. New York.

UNDESA (2015). United Nations, Department of Economic and Social Affairs, Population Division. *World Population Prospects: The 2015 Revision,* Data Booklet. New York.

UNDP (2002). *Human Development Report 2002: Deepening Democracy in the Fragmented World.* United Nations Development Programme (UNDP). New York & Oxford: Oxford University Press.

UNDP (2015). *Human Development Report 2015: Work for Human Development.* New York: United Nations Development Programme.

INDEX

C

F

H

J

K

L

Q

R

S

V

W

www.ingramcontent.com/pod-product-compliance
Lightning Source LLC
LaVergne TN
LVHW011657200926
848484LV00004B/971